2nd Edition

The Employee Performance Handbook

Smart Strategies for Coaching Employees

Margie Mader-Clark and Lisa Guerin, J.D.

NOLO
LAW for ALL

SECOND EDITION

Book Design	SUSAN PUTNEY
Editor	SACHI BARREIRO
Proofreading	ROBERT WELLS
Index	VICTORIA BAKER
Printing	BANG PRINTING

For information on bulk purchases or corporate premium sales, please contact the Special Sales Department. For academic sales or textbook adoptions, ask for Academic Sales. Call 800-955-4775 or write to Nolo, 950 Parker Street, Berkeley, CA 94710.

Acknowledgments

Thank you for the opportunity to put together an important book that recognizes that employees with performance issues are fundamentally worth saving, and that it's not as hard as it may seem!

As always, huge thanks to my cowriter, Lisa Guerin, who makes the complex simple, and to my beloved family, Austin and Calvin, I adore you guys.

—Margie Mader-Clark

About the Advisory Board

Booker McClain

Booker McClain serves as the human resources director for the Continuing Education of the Bar (CEB), University of California, the largest continuing legal education provider in the state. In his 30+ years in human resources, Mr. McClain has held of variety of leadership roles in human resources at the University of California, Los Angeles, and at the UC's Office of the President.

Sigrid Metson

Sigrid Metson has held senior management positions at several leading publishers including Nolo, West, Bancroft-Whitney (the Thomson Corporation), CareThere, and Reference Software. Ms. Metson also played leadership roles in the acquisition and integrations of Legal Solutions, The Rutter Group, Barclay's, and West Publishing. In addition, she has edited several titles herself, including *Secrets of Successful Writing* (RSI).

Mollie Sullivan

Mollie Sullivan is a licensed Marriage and Family Therapist working as a social research specialist in the School of Social Work at the University of North Carolina at Chapel Hill. Ms. Sullivan holds an M.S. in Clinical Psychology from San Francisco State University and a B.A. in Psychology from the University of Michigan, Ann Arbor.

Mary Walti

Mary Walti is currently a Senior Human Resources Business Partner at Athenahealth. She has previously held various senior human resources positions at Kodak Easyshare Gallery (a wholly owned subsidiary of Eastman Kodak Company), PGP Corporation, and Lithium Technologies. She received her undergraduate degree from the University of California, Santa Barbara, in Political Science, and completed the Executive/Professional M.B.A. program at the University of San Francisco.

About the Authors

Margie Mader-Clark

For more than 20 years, Margie Mader-Clark has worked in the fields of human resources and effectiveness consulting, primarily in the fast-paced world of the Silicon Valley. She has experienced first-hand the power of good management—and sadly, the devastating impact of poor management. She practices a simple, commonsense approach to her work, and this book takes the same philosophy. While working through disciplinary issues is difficult, mastering these skills builds a quality workforce, minimizes expensive replacement costs, and breeds long-term success. Mader-Clark has implemented and taught these basic principles in companies like Netscape, Hyperion Solutions, and a number of Internet start-ups. She is the author of *The Job Description Handbook* and has contributed to other Nolo publications, including *The Manager's Legal Handbook*, *The Performance Appraisal Handbook*, and Nolo's online library.

Lisa Guerin

Lisa is the author or coauthor of several Nolo books, including *The Manager's Legal Handbook, Dealing With Problem Employees, The Essential Guide to Federal Employment Laws, The Essential Guide to Workplace Investigations*, and *Create Your Own Employee Handbook*. Lisa has practiced employment law in government, public interest, and private practice, where she represented clients at all levels of state and federal courts and in agency proceedings. She is a graduate of Boalt Hall School of Law at the University of California at Berkeley.

Table of Contents

PART I
An Overview of Employee Discipline

PART II
Is It Time for Discipline?

PART III
Smart Performance Management Skills

PART V
If Discipline Fails

Appendixes

BONUS
Minimizing Legal Risk When Firing an Employee

Introduction

If you're like most managers, you don't look forward to telling employees that they aren't meeting the company's expectations. Nobody wants to be "the bad guy," and most of us are averse to the confrontation inherent in correcting behavior and performance. You might avoid the conversation, hoping that your wayward employee will improve without your intervention. When you do sit down with the employee, you might feel unsure about what to say and how to say it, anxious about how the employee will react, or uncertain of how you should document the meeting and follow up afterward. You might even be worried about lawsuits and other legal problems.

Unfortunately, even though managing performance and conduct is a very important part of a manager's job, many managers receive precious little guidance on handling such issues. While many companies have a progressive discipline system or policy in place, they don't always take the time to train their managers in the nuts and bolts of *how* to implement the policy in a way that gets results. And even when companies do provide some guidelines, managers are left alone to face the stress, uncertainty, and difficult emotions that accompany most discipline situations.

That's where this book comes in: It provides all of the information you need to handle performance and conduct issues confidently, fairly, and effectively. In the chapters that follow, you'll learn how to decide when coaching is necessary; how to plan for a disciplinary meeting; what to say to the employee; how to deal with a difficult reaction from an employee; how to document the meeting; how to follow up to make sure that the employee is improving; how to handle terminations; and much more. The tools, techniques, and strategies we provide in this book will help you identify and correct performance, attendance, and conduct problems, through a collaborative, respectful process that will work within any company's disciplinary system. Using this process will protect you and your company from legal trouble—and you can rest assured that you've handled performance or conduct issues fairly, consistently, and constructively.

What Is Progressive Discipline?

You're probably already familiar with the concept of progressive discipline as a way of improving performance. At the most basic level, progressive discipline is any employee discipline system that provides a graduated range of responses to employee performance or conduct problems. These disciplinary measures range from mild to severe, depending on the nature and frequency of the issue. For example, an informal coaching session or verbal warning might be appropriate for an employee who violates a minor work rule, while a more serious intervention—even termination—might be called for if an employee commits serious misconduct (such as sexual harassment) or does not improve a performance or conduct problem after receiving several opportunities to do so.

Most large companies use some form of progressive discipline, although they don't necessarily call it by that name. Whether they are called positive discipline programs, performance improvement plans, corrective action procedures, or something else, these systems are similar at their core, although they can vary in the details. However, all progressive discipline systems are based on the same principle: that the company's disciplinary response should be appropriate and proportionate to the employee's conduct.

The Benefits of Employee Discipline

If you are familiar with the benefits a good coach can confer on a team or individual team members, you will instantly understand how a discipline process can help you turn an uneven performer into a star player. It can help you get employees back on track and thereby avoid the consequences of continued poor performance, misconduct, or expensive replacement costs. Done right, coaching and progressive discipline can:

- allow managers to intervene and correct employee behavior at the first sign of trouble
- enhance communication between managers and employees
- help managers achieve higher performance and productivity from their employees
- improve employee morale and engagement by demonstrating that there are rewards for good performance and consequences for poor performance
- avoid expensive replacement costs
- ensure consistency and fairness in dealing with employee problems, and
- lay the groundwork for a fair, legally defensible termination for employees who cannot or will not improve.

If those benefits aren't enough to convince you that coaching and discipline are tremendously important parts of your job, consider what could happen if you didn't step in to correct an employee's problems. Unless you intervene, the employee may not know that his or her behavior or actions are unacceptable. Your company will suffer the direct consequences of the employee's actions: reduced productivity; quality control problems; dollars, opportunities, or customers lost; or worse. There may also be indirect consequences, such as low employee morale, lack of confidence in your management skills, and high turnover. If you multiply these effects by the number of managers in your company, you can see the true cost of failing to manage performance and conduct problems effectively.

Getting Results by Improving Performance

While company policy or practice often dictates the level of discipline to be imposed for particular problems or infractions, there's a lot more to the success of the discipline process. A discipline policy with escalating responses provides a basic framework for handling employee problems fairly and consistently, but a policy is only a start: To get the best results, you can't just move mechanically from one step in the discipline process to the next, until it's time to fire the employee. Instead, you must involve the employee in the process. The employee's engagement in improving his or her performance, behavior, or attitude will ultimately determine whether your efforts are successful.

This book will teach you a variety of techniques and strategies for working collaboratively with your employees to find solutions to performance and conduct problems. You'll learn how to:

- communicate your expectations clearly
- help your employees understand why improvement is necessary and important to the company's success
- work together to develop solutions
- provide the resources necessary for employees to succeed, and
- monitor the employee's progress toward his or her goals.

By collaborating with the employee to resolve disciplinary problems, you will enhance the employee's sense of commitment to the solution and to the company's overall success.

Avoiding Legal Trouble

Mishandled employee discipline can lead to serious legal problems, including discrimination lawsuits, claims of wrongful termination, retaliation charges, and more. And it's not only your company that's at risk: In some situations, employees can also sue individual managers for damages. This can have devastating consequences for you, your reputation, your career, and even your personal finances.

Fortunately, it's not difficult to avoid making the mistakes that lead to lawsuits. In each chapter, we call your attention to any important legal principles and consequences you should consider as you prepare for, dispense, document, and follow up on employee discipline. We also devote an entire chapter (Chapter 3) to legal issues that may arise when disciplining employees. Armed with this information, you will know that you're on safe legal ground when managing performance and behavior problems.

As you read through the chapters that follow, you'll also learn the many ways that regular and documented discipline can actually protect your company from legal trouble. The techniques we advocate will help you let employees know what you expect; be fair, consistent, and objective when managing employees; include employees in the process of improvement; and document your actions and decisions properly. If you follow these strategies, employees who are unable or unwilling to improve won't have the legal ammunition necessary to fuel a lawsuit. And, if you consistently use the respectful, collaborative process we advocate, very few employees will be motivated to sue.

Who Should Read This Book

Anyone who supervises employees can use this book to improve performance, enhance communication and teamwork, minimize behavior and conduct problems, and avoid legal trouble. It can be used by:

- supervisors and line managers
- senior managers and executives
- business owners, and
- human resource professionals.

This book is primarily for managers and supervisors who work for private sector companies. If you work for the federal, state, or local government, you may have to follow a long list of required procedures when disciplining employees, and those procedures may differ from what we describe here. However, you will still find much of this book useful, particularly in helping you communicate with your employees.

If your workplace is unionized, you may have to use a disciplinary process that differs significantly from the one presented in this book. In a union workplace, the collective bargaining agreement (CBA)—the contract that defines the rights and obligations of the union and the company—usually dictates how and when managers may discipline employees. The CBA may state when discipline is appropriate, which types of discipline apply to which types of offenses, and what rights the employee has throughout the disciplinary process. Typically, CBAs also give employees the right to file a grievance over disciplinary issues, which will ultimately be decided in arbitration if the company and union can't reach an agreement. Because of these complications, you should talk to a lawyer to find out exactly what's allowed (and what isn't). This book provides plenty of techniques and strategies that you can put to use within the disciplinary options available to you, but it cannot help you interpret your company's collective bargaining agreement.

How to Use This Book

To help you understand each stage of the discipline process, we have divided this book into parts. Here's what you'll find in each:

- **Part I: An Overview of Employee Discipline** describes what an effective discipline policy looks like, how it works, and how to stay out of legal trouble when implementing it.
- **Part II: Is It Time for Discipline?** explains how to decide whether discipline is necessary, including how to identify problems, evaluate their severity, and choose an appropriate response.
- **Part III: Smart Performance Management Skills** teaches you the techniques you need to effectively communicate with employees, handle typical reactions, document discussions and decisions, and involve others in the company.

- **Part IV: The Disciplinary Steps** explains how and when to use each of the measures available in typical progressive discipline systems, from informal coaching sessions to written warnings.
- **Part V: If Discipline Fails** describes how to terminate employment when necessary, and how to help your company and team move on after an employee's departure.

This book is intended as a companion to your company's discipline procedures. By following the strategies and tools we describe, you can coach your employees in a more effective, collaborative, and results-oriented way, all while staying out of legal trouble.

To illustrate the concepts we describe, this book uses a model discipline system, with steps ranging from informal coaching to termination of employment. We've chosen this system—and offered forms and samples for use with it—because it includes all of the steps you are likely to find in your company's own discipline policy. If you do not already have a discipline system in place, you can use our model to develop one. However, if your company does have a system and it differs from the one we describe, or if your company requires you to use particular forms or terminology, you should adhere to your company's requirements. If, after reading this book, you believe that your company's system could create some legal exposure or simply could stand some improvement, raise the issue with your manager, human resources department, or legal counsel.

Get Forms, Updates and More on Nolo.com

All of the forms, checklists, and policies used throughout this book are available for download at this book's online companion page at:

www.nolo.com/back-of-book/SDHB.html

You'll find other useful information there, too, including legal updates, podcasts, and blog posts. See Appendix D for details.

PART

I

An Overview of Employee Discipline

Discipline Basics

A smart discipline policy gives managers a flexible structure for handling any employee problem, from poor performance to spotty attendance to misconduct. That's why so many companies use some form of discipline to manage employees who are not meeting expectations. Because these systems vary in details, however, it can be tough to get a handle on exactly what effective discipline looks like and how it works.

Although they may go by different names, all discipline systems have a few things in common:

- They offer a range of disciplinary measures to respond appropriately to employee problems.
- They are systems of proportional response, in which the severity of the discipline depends on the severity of the problem.
- They give employees a meaningful opportunity to improve when problems arise, unless the employee's behavior is so extreme that immediate termination is required.

This chapter explains what a good discipline policy should look like and how to effectively implement it. For those whose companies have already adopted a policy, we also provide some tips on using this book to stay safe and legal in conjunction with that policy.

What a Smart Discipline Policy Should Look Like

Before you can begin to use discipline to maximize employee performance, you need to know what a good policy should include. This information will help you understand the basic tools available to you. If your company doesn't have a written discipline policy, you can use this information, and the sample policy in Appendix A, to create one. (An electronic copy is available to download at this book's online companion page; see Appendix D for the link.)

> **CAUTION**
>
> **Follow your company's policy.** We can't say it enough times: If your company already has a discipline policy that differs from the model policy we use in this book, you must adhere to your company's policy. If you believe, after reading this book, that your company's policy could create legal exposure, we encourage you to

raise that issue with the appropriate people, such as your manager, human resources department, and/or legal counsel.

Effective discipline systems offer the best of both worlds: They give managers the structure they need to treat employees consistently, with the flexibility to take unique situations and problems into account.

The following disciplinary measures are typically available in most companies' policies (although they might go by different names):

- coaching
- verbal warning
- written warning, and
- termination.

Coaching

In today's workplace, most managers know that creating successful employees isn't always about directing and controlling, it's often about encouraging and developing. This process is often referred to as coaching. In this context, coaching is a manner of relating to and managing your employees to help them maximize their performance and build their skills and competencies. As such, coaching is not simply—or even primarily—a disciplinary measure, but is instead a management approach that emphasizes communication, collaboration, goal setting, mentoring, and assistance to help your employees realize their full potential.

In this book, however, we use the term "coaching" in a more limited sense, to refer to the first step of a formal discipline system. Although you might be coaching your employees in the broader sense all the time, you are coaching under our definition only when you are using your collaborative and communication skills to correct a performance or behavior problem. While it requires the same set of skills, coaching in this context ensures specified goals are reached and gives you options to escalate discipline if they aren't.

Considered the least harsh measure, coaching can be used at the first sign of relatively minor trouble. The purpose of coaching is to work through and correct an action or behavior before it becomes a larger problem. Coaching is typically handled in a face-to-face meeting. Done well, coaching can nip potential problems in the bud while conveying to the employee that his or her performance and conduct matter to you and the company. You'll find strategies and step-by-step instructions for coaching employees in Chapter 11.

> **CAUTION**
>
> **Keep track of your coaching sessions.** In many companies, managers coach employees as many times as they wish, even on the same disciplinary issue, before they decide that the employee should formally enter the company's discipline system with an official verbal warning. The problem with this practice is that it allows for inconsistent treatment among employees, with all of the possible legal problems that this can create, including claims of discrimination (see Chapter 3 for more information on the dangers of inconsistency). That's one reason to treat coaching as a distinct step in the disciplinary process and to document it. Although you don't have to tell the employee that your coaching conversation constitutes a form of discipline, you should make some notes on the conversation and escalate to a verbal warning if the situation doesn't improve. (You'll find information on documentation in Chapter 9.)

Verbal Warning

If a problem continues despite your coaching efforts, a formal verbal warning is often the next step. Typically, a manager delivers a verbal warning in a formal meeting, where the employee is told that the behavior or action is unacceptable. The term "warning" is used to communicate that there is a real problem, one which must be resolved if the employee is to get back on track. Verbal warnings differ from coaching because they are more formal. The employee is notified that he or she is being disciplined, and the incident is usually documented in the employee's personnel file. Verbal warnings are covered in Chapter 12.

Written Warning

You have coached your employee and given a formal verbal warning that he or she must improve, but the problem continues. Or, an employee's behavior is serious enough to warrant an immediate, forceful response, but not so extreme as to require termination. Providing a written warning conveys that the employee's job is at risk unless the problem is solved. Often, company polices require the manager to involve higher management or the human resources department when giving a written warning. We cover how to prepare for, give, and document a written warning in Chapter 13.

Termination

Nothing has worked. All attempts to correct the employee's performance or behavior have failed. The employee's unacceptable actions, despite numerous warnings, continue. Or, the employee has done something so egregious that immediate termination is appropriate (for example, stealing from the company or coworkers, or committing violence).

Termination of employment isn't really a disciplinary measure: It represents the failure of the disciplinary process. If discipline doesn't work despite your best efforts to help the employee improve, you know that there's nothing more you can do. We discuss terminations in more detail in Chapter 14.

Why Disciplinary Policies Should Be in Writing

Some employers tell us that they don't want to adopt a written progressive discipline policy and distribute it to their employees. Usually, companies go this route because they fear lawsuits by employees claiming that they are entitled to every step in a written policy and can't be fired unless they have received the full process.

However, refusing to write down a progressive discipline policy won't protect a company from this type of claim. If a company uses a progressive discipline system—even if it never puts its policy in writing—the employee could argue that the employer's practices created an *implied contract*. (For more on implied contracts, see Chapter 3.) In this situation, the employee could use the employer's actions to argue that, because the employer always applied particular disciplinary measures to particular offenses, the employee was contractually entitled to the same treatment.

A properly written disciplinary policy will guard against this type of lawsuit by reiterating that the company is an at-will employer and by reserving the right to discipline as it sees fit. The sample policy we provide in Appendix A demonstrates how to both convey the company's intent to provide progressive discipline and reserve the company's right to terminate employment at will.

How Discipline Works

Many companies either have a discipline policy in place or follow one in practice. And it's not hard to see why: Used properly, these policies give managers the tools they need to make fair, consistent, and legally defensible disciplinary decisions. Because it is based on communication and collaboration, a truly effective discipline policy also helps employees improve—the ultimate goal of any disciplinary system.

"That's all well and good," you might be thinking, "but how do I do it?" How do you decide what type of action is appropriate in any given situation? And how do you deliver the difficult message in a way that produces actual improvement?

When you confront a situation that might call for discipline, follow these steps:

1. **Gather information.** Before you act, make sure you know what happened, and that you've heard all sides of the story.
2. **Assess the severity.** Consider how the problem is affecting the employee, the team, and the company.
3. **Decide how to respond.** Choose the appropriate disciplinary measure, based on the severity and frequency of the problem and how your company has addressed similar issues in the past.
4. **Prepare to talk to the employee.** Plan your disciplinary meeting, including what you will say and how you will say it.
5. **Meet with the employee.** Talk about what has happened and collaborate with the employee to create a plan for improvement.
6. **Document.** Make a written record of the discipline imposed and the plan for improvement.
7. **Follow up.** Check back in to make sure the employee is meeting his or her commitments.

Gather Information

Before you jump in to take action, you have to understand what is really going on. Some situations are relatively clear cut—for example, an employee has been showing up late to work, missed a deadline, or failed to follow required safety procedures. You might not know all of the reasons for the employee's actions until you talk to him or her, but you do know that a rule was violated or a performance standard wasn't met, and that the employee is responsible. Taking the time to find out why a behavior or issue occurred is critical to determining the right response. In most cases, start by asking the employee why the rule was violated or the standard wasn't met. Then, you can move on to assessing the severity of the problem.

Other situations are trickier to untangle, especially if more than one employee is involved. If, for example, your team is not meeting its performance goals, you might not know exactly who or what caused the problem. Or, if one employee accuses another of misconduct (like harassment or threats of violence), you may need to gather more information before deciding what to do. If you can't figure out who is responsible for a problem, you might need to investigate before you take action. (For detailed information and step-by-step instructions on how to conduct an investigation, see *The Essential Guide to Workplace Investigations*, by Lisa Guerin (Nolo).)

TIP

Don't just react to problems—prevent them. The best managers know that they can't get the most out of their teams just by stepping in when disaster strikes. Instead, they continuously manage employee performance by communicating frequently with their teams, giving regular feedback, and providing the resources necessary for success. You'll find tips and techniques for this type of performance management in Chapter 4.

Assess the Severity

Before you decide whether or what type of response is in order, you need to know how the problem is affecting you, your employees, and your company. There are several important reasons for doing this:

- The corrective measure you impose should depend, in large part, on how serious the problem is. If the employee's behavior is having or could have a direct and significant impact on the company's ability to get out its products or serve its customers, a higher level of discipline may be in order.

- It will be easier to leave your emotions at the door and make objective, fair disciplinary decisions if you focus on the effect of the employee's behavior—and not on your own anger or disappointment. It's easy to let negative feelings enter into your decisions, especially if the employee's actions have undermined your authority or caused you to miss your own performance goals.

- Knowing how the problem is affecting the team and the company—and having a few examples ready when you meet with the employee—communicates the importance of the issue and gives the employee the proper context to understand the problem. It demonstrates that the employee is a crucial member of the team and that his or her performance plays an important role in the company's success. And it will help both of you troubleshoot solutions, to make sure that they address both the employee's concerns and the needs of the company.

EXAMPLE: You sit your accounts payable clerk down and say, "Your lack of attention to detail is causing us to have to double-check your work, and causing our customers to suspect the integrity of their invoices. This is costing the company money and time, and we need to figure out a way to fix it." His first response is to ask for more information: What lack of detail? Who has had to go over the work, in which accounts? Which customers are upset?

Because you took the time to consider the impact of the clerk's problem, you are armed with a few examples, such as, "The Jones Company has found errors in their invoices twice. This means that the sales rep, Tom, has had to spend time on the phone assuring them that we will correct the invoice and are not charging them for products they didn't order. This embarrasses our company and hurts our reputation, and it also hurts our future business. Because Tom's time with them is limited, this means we're using it to correct a problem instead of giving Tom the opportunity to sell them more products. Long-term, persistent errors like this make the company look as though it doesn't take its billing or its invoicing seriously—sending the signal that clients shouldn't take payment of our invoices seriously, either."

Once the clerk understands that his performance actually endangered the company's relationship with a customer and squandered a chance for the company to make more money, he can see how important it is for him to do his job right—and will better understand why you feel the need to intervene. Now, you can begin to collaboratively find a solution.

When the measure you take is based on how an employee's problems are affecting the company, and you focus your corrective efforts on changing that situation, you and your employee will be on the same page: Working to improve the situation, rather than arguing about what happened and whether it's really a problem. The employee will see that you are acting fairly and will be less likely to respond negatively. You'll find specific strategies for assessing the impact of an employee's performance or behavior problems in Chapter 5.

Decide How to Respond

The key to effective discipline is a proportionate response: In other words, the corrective measure you choose should reflect how serious the problem is. If, for example, your employee has been late to the office one time, a written warning is probably too harsh. A simple coaching session—even a brief chat at the employee's desk—will probably do the trick.

When trying to figure out how serious a particular problem is—and therefore, what type of disciplinary measure to impose—there are several factors to consider:

- **The effect of the behavior.** Understanding how an employee's problem affects the work of other employees, customers, and business opportunities is fundamental to deciding how to respond.
- **The frequency of the behavior.** When one employee misses a single deadline after years of on-time delivery, it is less worrisome than when another is routinely late with assignments. A repeat problem can mean that the employee doesn't understand your expectations, doesn't know how to meet them, doesn't have the resources to meet them, or simply has entrenched behaviors—like procrastination—that must be improved.
- **Disciplinary history.** If you've already met with the employee about the issue and come up with a reasonable action plan that hasn't been executed, a tougher response will be necessary.
- **The legality of the behavior.** If the employee has done something illegal, such as harassed or threatened another employee, misrepresented the company's financials to shareholders, or used company computer equipment to download pirated software, a very serious response is in

order. In these situations, how the company responds could determine its liability to a third party.

> **EXAMPLE:** Steve asks Claudia out several times, but she turns him down. When Steve asks her to be his date at a company party, Claudia says, "Look, I've tried to be polite about this, but I just don't want to go out with you. Please stop asking me; I'm not going to change my mind." Steve then begins leaving romantic notes on the windshield of Claudia's car in the company parking lot, and on her desk. Claudia tells him to stop and reports his behavior to John, the human resources manager.
>
> John gives Steve a verbal warning and tells him to stop bothering Claudia. Steve stops leaving notes for Claudia but begins going out of his way to see her. He times his arrival and departure from the office to coincide with hers, he hangs out in the hallway outside of her office and stares at her, and he "just happens" to cross her path during her twice weekly lunchtime walks on a nearby bike path. Claudia again complains to John, who gives Steve another verbal warning.

What's wrong with this picture? The response is disproportionate to the problem. Steve is stalking Claudia and is receiving nothing more than a slap on the wrist. The company hasn't let Steve know that his actions are inappropriate and will not be tolerated. Claudia will be able to argue that the company should be legally responsible for any harm she suffers as a result of Steve's actions, including her emotional distress.

Prepare to Talk to the Employee

Even if you will just be engaging in simple coaching, spend a little time preparing your approach. Planning will give you some important breathing space, so you won't respond emotionally. It will also help you get all your ducks in a row prior to taking action, so you can explain the problem and its effects to the employee.

The keys to good preparation are:

- **Get the facts.** When you meet with the employee, it's very important to be specific. Be prepared to offer concrete examples of the issue you want to correct and how this behavior falls short of your expectations. You should also be prepared to explain clearly what the employee needs to improve and why—you might find it helpful to bring a copy of particular company policies, the employee's job description, performance appraisals, or other documents where these expectations are expressly stated. The more general you are, the more likely the employee will be to respond by challenging you or being defensive, rather than understanding the problem. If the employee doesn't see exactly what needs to improve and why, you won't be able to craft a solution together.

- **Run your plan by others, if necessary.** Some companies require managers to get permission—from their manager or the human resources department, for example—before imposing a verbal or written warning. Of course, you should do this if your company requires it. But there are good reasons to seek out feedback, even if you don't have to. You can get ideas on what to say, how to say it, and what solutions might work. You can also find out how similar situations have been handled in the past—a critical factor in making sure that your disciplinary decisions can withstand legal scrutiny.

- **Think about what you will say.** No matter what type of action you decide to take, you'll have to sit down with the employee and talk about it. Script your first few sentences—what are the most important points you want to make? Because the meeting should be a collaborative exchange between you and the employee, you shouldn't write out everything you plan to say; just consider how you'll open the conversation and make a list of key issues to cover.

- **Prepare for possible responses.** Will this employee take responsibility and immediately move on to solving the problem? Or will you be met with resistance? If you're uncomfortable about emotional confrontations, plan how you will respond if the employee reacts with anger or tears. (You can find much more about preparing for an employee's reaction in Chapter 8.)

Meet With the Employee

Now you are ready to address the issue face to face with your employee. This is where your preparation will pay off in an honest, respectful session that paves the way for improvement. In a typical meeting, you will progress through these steps:

- **State the issue.** At the outset, you should tell the employee exactly what you are there to discuss. If you start the conversation with anything other than the actual performance or conduct issue, you risk sending a mixed message to the employee. Being clear from the start will help you set the stage for an honest conversation and avoid catching the employee off guard. Follow up with a sentence or two explaining the impact on others or the company.

  > EXAMPLE: "Karen, I wanted to meet with you today to talk about your attendance. You were at least half an hour late twice last week, on Tuesday and Wednesday. On both days, Mark tried to cover your phone, but he wasn't able to take all of your calls along with his own. This means customers had to wait longer to talk to a representative, which doesn't reflect well on us."

- **Review previous discussions, if any.** If you and the employee have already talked about this issue—whether in a disciplinary meeting or a casual conversation—briefly summarize those discussions. This will remind the employee that he or she knew about the problem and agreed to improve. It helps justify your continued attention to the problem and focus the employee on what needs to change.

  > EXAMPLE: "You and I discussed tardiness several months ago, after you were late for the first time. As you'll recall, I reminded you that one of your job requirements is to be at work promptly at 9:00 a.m., every morning. You agreed that you would arrive on time from then on."

- **Get the employee's buy-in.** Before you move on, try to get the employee to agree about what happened. If you're wrong about the facts, you should find out right away, before you try to begin solving a problem you might not have. And, if the employee reacts defensively or with anger, you'll want to make sure that you can at least agree about what happened, even if you disagree about why.

  > EXAMPLE: Karen responds to the statement above by saying, "I don't think I was that late. Besides, I had to drop my daughter off at her grandmother's house those days."
  >
  > Rather than arguing, simply restate the facts and ask the employee to agree to them. "Karen, the time clock shows that you punched in at 9:40 on

Tuesday and 9:45 on Wednesday. As you know, you are scheduled to start work—and that means be at your desk, ready to answer phones—at 9:00. So before we start talking about why you were late, I want to make sure you agree that you were late on those days."

- **Hear the employee out.** Once you and the employee agree on the facts, the employee will probably want to offer reasons (or excuses) for his or her behavior. Listen carefully to what the employee says—you may learn things you didn't know about the situation, or about how your employees get along or understand their work assignments. Show that you're listening by repeating back what you hear.

  > EXAMPLE: Karen says, "I didn't realize I was that late; I'm sorry. I had to take my daughter to her grandmother's house because she was sick and couldn't go to school. It's so far out of my way, and I got caught in traffic."
  > You respond, "So you were late because you hit traffic and had to drive farther than usual, in order to take your daughter to her grandmother's house?"

- **Start working together on solutions.** During this process, you'll want to help the employee come up with ways to solve the problem and offer any resources or help you can. It's also a good idea to get the employee's input on how to fix the problem; this leads to higher engagement and investment on the part of the employee.

  > EXAMPLE: You move the conversation to problem solving by saying, "Karen, I think I understand why you were late last week. But we need you here on time, every day, so our customers get the service we promise them. What can you do to make sure you get here on time?"

- **Decide on a plan.** Sometimes, you and the employee will come up with several ideas; other times—particularly if you are dealing with misconduct—the only solution is for the employee to stop the problem behavior. Either way, once you determine the best course of action, restate it so you both understand what will happen next.

  > EXAMPLE: Karen says, "Well, I'm hoping this won't be an issue, but I suppose my daughter could get sick again. I guess I could leave earlier, now that I know how long it takes to get here from her grandmother's house.

Or, if I'm running late, I could ask my husband to drop her off on his way to work; after all, it's his mother!"

You respond, "Those sound like good ideas. So next time your daughter has to go to her grandmother's, you'll either leave earlier so you can get here on time or have your husband take her."

- **Decide what will happen next.** If you're managing a performance problem, state what you want to see change and by when. Also plan to check in with the employee in the interim, to make sure things are moving forward as planned.

    EXAMPLE: In Karen's case, very little follow up will be required, although you might want to ask her to check in with you the next time her daughter is sick, to make sure that her ideas for arriving on time worked.

You'll find detailed information on how to hold coaching sessions and give verbal and written warnings in Chapters 11 through 13, and strategies for communicating effectively with employees in Chapter 7.

Document

It is vitally important to document disciplinary matters. Of course, you'll want written proof that the employee was aware of the problem and was given a fair chance to improve, should the issue ever end up in court. But there are many other reasons to put your disciplinary decisions and actions in writing:

- It helps you make sure that you and the employee agree on what happened, what is expected, how the employee will improve, and by when.
- It creates a record for you or the employee's future managers to use if discipline becomes necessary again.
- It can help you identify patterns on your team. For example, if several of your reports have trouble meeting deadlines, you might want to examine your own scheduling practices. Are you giving people enough time? Does your team know why these deadlines are important? Does the team have enough resources to get the job done? Do you need to create a calendaring system, send out email reminders, or come up with another way to keep everyone on track?

You'll find detailed instructions on how to document, including a sample form you can use, in Chapter 9.

Follow Up

The ultimate goal of workplace discipline is to fix the problem and improve the employee's performance. The only way to do this is to adhere strictly to your agreements, stay on top of the employee's performance going forward, check in often on the status of the action plan, and work closely with your employee to ensure a positive outcome. Discipline is a process, not a single meeting or document. To get the most out of the process, you need to stay involved until the problem is truly resolved.

Using This Book With Your Company's Policy

The techniques described above are universal: You can use them to assess and deal with any performance or conduct problem. If your company already has a discipline policy, you can apply these strategies within your company's rules to make the system—and your management skills—more effective.

This doesn't mean you can ignore your company's requirements, however. Your company's policies dictate its relationship with its employees: They reflect how the company wants and expects you to deal with workers. Deviating from established company policies can create legal risks for the company—and obviously, can get you into trouble at work, as well.

Here are some tips to get the most out of this book while complying with your company's rules:

- **When in doubt, follow company policy.** If the terms, forms, or advice we use are different from your company's policy, follow the policy. If you have questions about what you should do or whether the policy is fair or legal, talk to your manager or human resources department.
- **Pay close attention to terminology.** For example, your company might have a disciplinary measure it calls an "oral reprimand," which is in all ways identical to what we refer to as a "verbal warning." If it's clear that we're all talking about the same thing, you can follow the advice we provide on verbal warnings to give an oral reprimand. If you aren't certain, follow your company's policy.

- **Focus on strategy.** Even if your company's policy is different from our model, you can apply the planning, communication, collaboration, documentation, and follow up techniques we provide here. Your company's policy provides the structure for discipline (the disciplinary measures available and when they should be used); we provide strategies to make your discipline most effective no matter what form of discipline your company requires.

SMART SUMMARY:
Progressive Discipline Basics

- If your company has a discipline policy, you should follow it. The techniques in this book, including planning, communication, collaboration, documentation, and follow up, can be used in conjunction with that policy. When in doubt about what to do, what your company policy requires, or whether the policy creates legal risks for the company, you should talk to your manager, human resources department, or legal counsel.

- A carefully written discipline policy notifies employees that they'll be disciplined for violating company policy, gives managers guidance about how to apply company policy, tells employees that they'll have a fair opportunity to improve, and reserves the right to deviate from the policy when appropriate and to terminate employment at will.

- When faced with a performance or behavior problem, you'll have to gather information, assess the severity, decide how to respond, meet with the employee, document, and follow up.

- Discipline should be proportionate to the seriousness of the problem, considering things like the effect of the behavior, the frequency of the behavior, the employee's disciplinary history, and the legality of the employee's conduct.

Principles of Effective Discipline

Today, most large companies use some form of progressive discipline to manage performance and other problems. But it hasn't always been so: Fifty or sixty years ago, workers were routinely fired, without warning or discussion, for slow production, absenteeism, insubordination, or just rubbing the boss the wrong way. Workers served primarily as cogs in a manufacturing assembly line—if a cog was "broken," it made more sense to replace it than to spend time and energy trying to fix it. Managers also played a different role: Rather than offering direction, coaching, and support, bosses issued demands and directions—and imposed punishment if orders weren't followed.

A lot has changed since then. Along with the advent of civil rights, the maturing of human resources as a profession, and the accumulation of labor laws and other worker protections, significant technological innovations have transformed the way we work. The late Peter Drucker, a well-known management guru, coined the term "knowledge workers" in the late 1960s to refer to people who do their jobs primarily with their brains (as opposed to manual labor). As technology has developed, so has the number of knowledge workers, and with this change has come a shift in the skills, abilities, and expectations of the average worker.

Knowledge workers expect to be treated as individuals who have unique and valuable contributions to make. Because their work product is so often intangible—there's rarely a cog produced anymore—knowledge workers understand their roles when they see how their performance affects the overall product and the company as a whole. Gone are the days of making life decisions for your employees, tightly controlling their activities, and rigidly maintaining their hours. Flexibility in working with individual employees is critical in today's workplace.

As a result, the job of a manager has shifted from a purely supervisory role—watching, monitoring, and punishing—to more of a mentoring or coaching role—identifying goals collaboratively, providing the resources necessary to accomplish them, and removing roadblocks along the way. This "management edge" can make or break a company. How well you as a leader respond to the challenges of managing your team of knowledge workers will define your success (and your company's as well). As Jack Welch, General Electric's legendary former CEO, explains, "[I]f you pick the right people and give them the opportunity to spread their wings and put compensation as a carrier behind it you almost don't have to manage them." This enlightened management style helped to take General Electric from a sleepy "Old Economy" company with a market capitalization of $4 billion to a dynamic new one worth nearly half a trillion dollars.

Progressive discipline has developed and changed in response to these kind of shifts. Although the term "progressive discipline" has been around for a while, particularly in unionized settings, it used to refer to a rigid system in which particular punitive measures were required for particular types of misconduct. In contrast, today's progressive discipline embraces the "manager as coach" model of the modern workplace.

This chapter explains the principles on which modern progressive discipline is based. Understanding these fundamentals will help you stay on track and keep the big picture in mind as you manage performance and conduct in the workplace.

Principle 1: Your Goal Is Retention—Not Termination

Many people mistakenly believe that the purpose of discipline is to build a case to fire employees down the road. Of course, handling disciplinary issues properly, as described in this book, will help you preserve your right to end the employment relationship legally, if an employee can't improve. But that's just one of the benefits of the system, not its purpose.

As a manager, your goal when dealing with employees who've gotten off track isn't to fire them, but to help them improve their performance and develop a renewed dedication to the job. In other words, your goal is to truly engage them in the success of the company. Termination is seldom the best outcome for the business. The potential downsides of firing an employee rather than helping the employee improve include:

- real dollars and time: the cost of hiring and training a new employee
- morale and productivity: a feeling among your remaining team members that they may be "next," resulting in lower productivity, increased anxiety, and unwanted transfers or resignations
- competition for talent: difficulty replacing the employee quickly in today's competitive hiring landscape

- opportunity cost: increased expenses and lost revenues associated with having an open position for a period of time, and
- legal expenses and problems: legal exposure for both you and the company, if the employee challenges the termination.

Let's do a quick estimation of the replacement cost of an employee with an annual salary of $75,000.

Cost to Replace an Employee		
Item of Loss	**Metric**	**Cost**
Cost to hire new employee (includes recruitment fees, advertising costs, employee referral fees, relocation expenses, and so on)	30% of the base salary	$22,500
Reduced productivity of having an empty position	3 months of base salary	$18,750
Management time to interview and hire new employee	20 hours at $60 per hour (based on a $125,000 annual salary)	$1,200
Interview time for other members of interview team	12 hours at $36 per hour (based on a $75,000 annual salary)	$432
	Total cost:	$42,882 (or 57% of the base salary)

As you can see, the cost of losing an employee can be significant. And, this figure doesn't even account for lost productivity over the interview process or the ramp up time for the new employee. This could add another 20% to 25% of the base salary to the equation.

Principle 2: Discipline Should Be Proportionate

If you truly want to improve performance, you will need to respond to an employee's behavior with a disciplinary measure of corresponding seriousness. Responding to a relatively minor issue with an informal coaching session lets an employee know that you've identified a problem and that you want to give him or her every chance to improve. By contrast, giving a written warning to an employee who has engaged in serious misconduct indicates that the behavior is unacceptable and must stop immediately. In either case, the employee you discipline is not the only audience for your action: Other employees will also see (or hear about) how you handle these issues and will get a better understanding of what you and the company expect.

As you'll learn in Chapter 5, there are many ways to measure how serious a problem is. One important consideration, both in deciding how to deal with the problem and in communicating with the employee, is how it affects coworkers, your team, and the rest of the company. Figuring out the impact an employee's problem is having on the company will help you be certain that you're not overreacting to—or downplaying—the employee's behavior. It will also allow your employees to see the direct effects of their behaviors or actions, which not only conveys that they are important to the company, but also explains why continued problems cannot be tolerated. Communicating how the employee has affected the company will also help you maintain your focus on the business, which will help you avoid personalizing the issue and reacting emotionally.

Principle 3: Have the Facts at Your Fingertips

Before you meet with your employee to discuss a problem, you'll need to be ready to explain why correction is necessary. Employees need to understand the scope of the problem and to be included in the decision-making process. This means you can't just hand over a written warning; instead, you have to be prepared to explain the problem clearly, with pertinent examples and potential solutions.

Principle 4: Listen to Your Employees

Your ability to listen to your employees as you discuss performance or conduct issues will make or break the discipline process. If you monopolize the conversation or ignore your employee's effort to explain his or her side of the story, your relationship with the employee might be damaged beyond repair—and you may not solve an otherwise solvable problem. Steven Covey, author of the enormously successful *Seven Habits of Highly Effective People*, says, "When another person is speaking, we usually 'listen' at one of four levels: ignoring, pretending, selective listening, or attentive listening. We should be using the fifth, highest form of listening—empathic listening …. Empathic listening is listening with intent to understand the other person's frame of reference and feelings. You must listen with your ears, your eyes and your heart."

Empathic listening allows you to understand the root of the problem and gives you and the employee common ground for coming up with a solution. It will also help you make sure that you've chosen the right corrective response. Moreover, an employee who feels heard and understood is often more willing to engage in the corrective process and move forward with a positive attitude. An employee who feels ignored, on the other hand, is more likely to feel resentful, angry, and antagonistic toward you and the company.

Principle 5: Collaboration Is the Key to Success

After you have explained how the employee's behavior is affecting the company and listened to the employee's side of the story, it's time to work together to develop an action plan for improvement. This collaboration allows the employee to feel some ownership of the resolution and take responsibility for making it happen. If you come into a disciplinary meeting with all the answers, your employee won't have to actively participate—and is more likely to disengage emotionally.

Remember, you hired your employees for their smarts and skills. If you ignore those qualities so you can dictate a specific remedy for the problem at hand, you could lose not only the employee's emotional dedication to the job, but also his or her willingness to share ideas about the problem and possible solutions. An employee who has a voice in the process is more engaged and feels more responsible for a successful outcome. This principle holds true no matter what position the employee holds or how pervasive the problem is.

Principle 6: Be Flexible Within a Consistent Framework

Progressive discipline systems are fair because they require consistency. These systems require managers to treat similar problems alike and to differentiate between less serious and more serious issues. This framework gives you a solid basis for making disciplinary decisions and deciding how to handle all of the particular and unique issues that might come up on your team.

However, because progressive discipline is rooted in collaboration, you must be flexible in handling disciplinary discussions, coming up with potential solutions, and working with employees to help them improve. Although the particular action you take will typically be dictated by the employee's behavior, the way you apply the techniques and tactics described in this book will depend on the employee and the situation.

> **EXAMPLE:** Lauren supervises a team of technicians who service the company's technology needs. They handle problems with the company's computers, servers, telephone system, website, and so on. Lauren has received similar complaints about two of her reports: Yasmin and Stefan. In each case, the technician was slow to respond to an employee's request for help with a computer problem. Because neither Yasmin nor Stefan has had any problems before, and because the complaints don't seem overly serious, Lauren decides to coach each of them.
>
> Lauren sits down with Yasmin and says, "I need your help with a problem. Phil in Sales told me that he asked you for help when he couldn't get his spreadsheet software to work properly, and you didn't help him until late the next afternoon. This caused lots of problems for him because he was trying to generate a price quote for a client, who had to wait until the following week to get the information. What happened?" Yasmin responds, "I was so busy with a server problem that I didn't have any time for Phil. I told him he could ask someone else for help, but I guess he didn't do that." Lauren says, "Yasmin, it's our responsibility to provide help when employees ask for it. If there's a problem that you can't handle on the day someone asks you for help, I expect you to let me know. That way, I can decide how important the problem is and juggle workloads to free up someone to work on it, if necessary." Yasmin says, "Wow, I didn't know that. I'll be happy to do that from now on—it will really help me manage my workload."

Next, Lauren sits down with Stefan. She says, "Stefan, I need to talk to you about something. Dayna told me that she had to wait two days for you to help her with a website problem. She needed to change the content on several pages, and she couldn't do it without your help. This set her whole team back on their schedule for the website transition. Why did this happen?" Stefan says, "Geez, I didn't know it was such a big rush—and now she's talking about me behind my back?" Lauren responds, "Stefan, our team has a reputation for providing fast, excellent service to the rest of the company. Dayna was counting on that when she had the website problem, and she didn't get it. She's entitled to talk to me about it—in fact, I want all of the company managers to let me know how we're doing. The problem isn't Dayna: It's the slow response time. What happened here? Why was there a delay?" After a few more exchanges, Stefan finally admits that he's not really up to speed on the company's website content program, and he had to take some time to read up on it before he could help Dayna. Lauren says, "Because we all have to pitch in when problems come up, the whole team has to understand the basics of every program the company uses. I know that website software is complicated, and I'd be happy to send you to a training program on it." Stefan agrees that this would help solve the problem.

Principle 7: Some Employment Relationships Don't Work Out

Although the goal of progressive discipline is to help employees improve, some employment relationships were just not meant to be. If an employee really can't or won't take the necessary steps to solve a problem, you've laid the proper foundation for a fair and legal termination process.

Many managers say that terminating employees is their least favorite part of the job, but it can be easier if you have used progressive discipline. As Jack Welch of General Electric described, "[M]y main job was developing talent. I was a gardener providing water and other nourishment to our top 750 people. Of course, I had to pull out some weeds, too." An employee who has not improved after being given opportunities to understand the impact of his or her behavior; to participate in coming up with a solution; and to get the time, resources, and coaching necessary to improve, has basically self-selected out of the company. Because you've done all you can, you can now terminate employment and replace the employee with a clear conscience.

You will also have plenty of legal protection. Because progressive discipline requires you to be consistent and proportionate, fired employees will have a tough time arguing that they were treated unfairly, discriminated against, or wrongfully terminated. You will have all of the documentation you need to prove that you had legitimate, job-based reasons for your actions. And chances are good that you won't ever see the inside of a courtroom: Employees who have had the benefit of progressive discipline generally feel fairly treated (and, therefore, don't feel motivated to sue), even if the job doesn't work out.

SMART SUMMARY:
Principles of Effective Discipline

- The number one goal of discipline is retention—not termination. That means working collaboratively with your employees to solve problems, not mechanically going through the discipline steps until you terminate employment.

- Taking proportionate actions communicates to the employee how serious the problem is; it also tells other employees what the company expects.

- Listening to your employees is fundamental. If you do all the talking, you won't understand the basis of the employee's thoughts or actions, and you'll have a hard time addressing the problem with a relevant solution.

- Today's workers expect to be treated as individuals with unique and valuable contributions to make. That's why it's important to enlist the employee's help in crafting a solution.

- Progressive discipline gives you the flexibility to develop solutions relevant to individual employees and their working styles. However, at the same time, it's important to administer discipline consistently—to respond similarly to similar problems.

Avoiding Legal Trouble

One of the reasons managers find discipline stressful is that mishandling a performance or misconduct problem could lead to a lawsuit. But if you're tempted to alleviate this stress by avoiding discipline altogether, think again. Failing to step in when necessary can lead to legal exposure, too. It also allows workplace problems to grow unchecked. The only way to successfully lead and manage the employees who report to you is by setting reasonable expectations and encouraging employees to meet them, through recognition, rewards, mentoring, and—when necessary—discipline.

The good news is, once you understand the basic legal principles explained in this chapter, you can manage and correct employees without the constant worry that you'll have to explain yourself in court. By following the strategies explained in this book, you'll help protect your company—and yourself—from legal liability. To use discipline effectively, you must have legitimate, objective reasons for your actions; be fair and consistent; consider the employee's situation carefully; communicate your expectations clearly; and document your discussions and decisions thoroughly.

What's more, employees who are treated fairly and respectfully through a smart discipline policy are unlikely to sue. Even employees who eventually have to be fired because they couldn't (or wouldn't) get back on track will at least feel that they were given a fair shake, and they will be less motivated to seek revenge in the courtroom.

However, there are no guarantees. Even though employment lawsuits are relatively uncommon, and even though our techniques will help you limit your company's exposure, there is always the chance that a problem employee will decide to sue. For the unlucky managers who find themselves in this situation, how they handled disciplinary issues takes center stage in the courtroom. The judge and jury will consider questions like these:

- Did the manager apply the company's policies and rules fairly and consistently, or was the employee singled out?
- Was the employee given a real opportunity to improve, or did the manager set the employee up for failure?
- Did the manager have legitimate, business-related reasons for disciplining and firing the employee, or was the termination retaliatory or motivated by prejudice?
- Did the manager document the employee's problems as they happened, or was the employee taken by surprise by the termination?

(Or worse, does it look like the company fabricated evidence, after the fact, to try to justify the termination?)

Mishandled discipline—especially if the employee is eventually terminated —is a major source of employment litigation. Typically, the employee uses disciplinary actions as evidence that the company singled out the employee for poor treatment for an illegal reason (for example, because of the employee's race, gender, or disability; because the employee recently complained of sexual harassment or illegal activity; or because the employee took leave to serve in the military or to care for an ailing family member). In essence, the employee claims that he or she was fired, not because of poor performance or misconduct, but because of illegal discriminatory or retaliatory reasons.

> **CAUTION**
>
> **You could be targeted in a lawsuit.** Some employment laws including the Family and Medical Leave Act (FMLA) and some state antidiscrimination laws allow employees to sue individual managers for damages. Employees can also name managers in certain other types of lawsuits (defamation is a common example). Although the company is almost always the main target because it has "deeper pockets," the supervisor or line manager—who represents the company in day-to-day dealings with the employee— is the more likely object of the employee's anger or hurt feelings over being fired.

This chapter provides ten valuable strategies that will help you avoid legal traps—and fulfill your legal obligations—when managing employee performance and behavior. It also covers some common mistakes managers make and how to avoid them. And, if you eventually have to fire a problem employee, the information in this chapter will help you make sure that you've followed the rules and can prove it in court, if it comes to that.

Strategy 1: Don't Compromise At-Will Employment

Most managers and human resource specialists are familiar with the term "employment at will." If you need a quick refresher, it means that workers who are employed at will can quit at any time, for any reason, and they can be fired at any time, for any reason *that isn't illegal.* An illegal reason is one that violates certain employee rights. For example, you may not fire employees because of their race or ethnicity, because they were called to serve on a jury, or because they have raised concerns about workplace safety.

However, you don't need good cause—such as poor performance or serious misconduct—to fire at-will employees. Of course, most savvy companies don't fire employees for frivolous reasons, even if they have the right to do so. It doesn't make good business sense to fire without a good reason, as it leads to poor morale and expensive replacement costs. And any employment lawyer will tell you that firing for no apparent reason can also lead to lawsuits, simply because workers who feel they were treated unfairly are more motivated to sue. They may suspect that the company had a hidden, illegitimate reason for firing them. Even when employees lose these lawsuits, they are expensive, time consuming, and stressful for the company.

Nonetheless, the right to fire at will is very important, even if your company wisely chooses not to exercise it. If your company is sued by an at-will employee, you don't have to prove that you had good cause to fire; you only have to prove that your reasons were not illegal. You won't have to argue over whether the employee's performance, conduct, or attitude was *really* bad enough to justify termination. In fact, chances are good that this type of case will never see the inside of a courtroom; few lawyers are willing to represent an at-will employee who doesn't have some proof that he or she was wrongfully fired.

EXAMPLE: Jackie manages a team that develops national advertising and branding campaigns for their clients' products and services. Brian, one of her reports, just doesn't seem to have the creativity necessary for the job. The rest of the team isn't excited by his ideas, and the few concepts he's presented to clients have fallen flat. Jackie has coached him on developing new ideas, partnered with him on a project, and addressed the problem through the company's discipline system, but Brian hasn't improved. Although Brian is very skilled at graphic design, turns in all of his projects on time, and is well-liked in the company, Jackie wants to replace him with someone who can come up with interesting, fresh ways to bring in new customers for their clients. So she fires him. Brian is angry and decides to sue the company.

If Brian was not an at-will employee, but instead had an employment contract, the company would have to prove that it had good cause to fire him. The company would have to show that Brian's creativity measurably lagged behind the rest of the team and that this gap was significant enough to justify firing him. To prove this, the company might have to ask Brian's coworkers—or worse, the company's clients—to testify on its behalf. And what if Brian can show that other team members missed deadlines, had trouble with the technical aspects of graphic design, or occasionally came up with a concept that missed the mark? As you can see, it can be hard to win an argument over whether conduct or performance was "bad enough" to justify firing.

Now assume that Brian was an at-will employee. The lawyer he talks to will try to find out whether the company had an illegal reason for firing him. If there is no evidence of discrimination, retaliation, or another improper motive, the lawyer will most likely send Brian on his way after advising him that he won't win a lawsuit. And, even if Brian finds a lawyer willing to take the gamble, the case will probably be thrown out before it ever gets to trial.

Contracts and At-Will Employment

Most employees work at will unless they have a contract that limits the company's right to fire. For example, many companies lure top executives with an employment contract that promises employment for a set term (for example, one or two years) as long as the employee doesn't commit specified types of misconduct. The purpose of these contracts is to attract and retain employees who are vital to the company's success—and who would probably be hot commodities on the open market. The contract binds the employee to the company and vice versa. During the contract's term, these employees can be fired only for the reasons described in the contract.

Not every contract is in writing. For example, an employee might have an oral contract, based on statements made during the hiring process. An oral agreement is every bit as binding as a written agreement, although it can be much harder to prove. If there's a later dispute over an oral contract, it will be the employee's word against the company's. Just like written contracts, oral contracts can limit a company's right to fire. For example, imagine that the company president said this to a candidate for the position of department manager: "If you'll make a one-year commitment to the company, we'll give you that long to turn this department around." The company is bound to the agreement, just as if it were written down and signed. The company would be on shaky legal ground if it fired the manager during that first year.

The trickiest type of contract, from a legal point of view, is an implied contract. An implied contract is neither written down nor explicitly stated aloud. Instead, it is implied from the words and actions of the parties. If you or other company managers give employees the impression that they have job security, you can create an implied contract. This is something you want to avoid, because it ties your hands in future dealings with your employees.

How Discipline Can Erode At-Will Employment

There are two ways discipline can undermine the at-will relationship: through company policies and through the actions of individual managers. If a company's discipline policy appears to require particular responses to particular actions, that could create an implied contract that the employee will not be fired unless and until he or she has had the benefit of every step in the company's disciplinary system. Similarly, if the policy reserves termination only for a list of serious offenses, that might give an employee the right not to be fired unless he or she commits one of the specified acts. Most larger companies have disciplinary policies that have been carefully vetted by lawyers to avoid these traps, but if yours does not—or if you'd like to troubleshoot your company's policy—compare it to the sample policy at this book's online companion page (see Appendix D for the link).

Even if your company's policy doesn't create any legal problems, your own actions might. If you say, do, or write anything that appears to promise continued employment, you could be undermining the at-will relationship. Typically, this comes up when managers are discussing the consequences of continued poor performance or misconduct, or the rewards of improving. Employees might argue that your comments gave them a contractual right either to be fired only for certain reasons or to receive the rewards you promised for improvement.

Of course, the ultimate goal of coaching and discipline is to improve employee performance. To improve performance while maintaining accountability, you must set measurable goals, with deadlines for meeting them. However, some managers make the mistake of adding on a threat or a promise, to make sure the employee understands why the goals must be met. This is where managers run the risk of undermining the company's at-will rights. Some examples are shown below.

Statement: "Tom, I can't promise you a future here unless you can bring your sales numbers up."

But What If: Tom improves his numbers, but does so by inappropriately pressuring an important client to order more than it needs, which strains the relationship.

Problem: Tom might claim he was promised a future with the company if he brought his numbers up and that he can't be fired because he did bring them up.

Instead Say: "Tom, the company requires its sales representatives to bring in $10,000 in business per month, and you are currently falling short of that mark. You must bring up your numbers to meet this job requirement."

Statement: "Mary, the company would like to promote you to my position when I retire, but you'll have to improve your communication skills."

But What If: Mary improves her communication skills, but a more qualified external candidate is hired for the job.

Problem: Mary can argue that she did what she was told she needed to in order to get the job and is therefore entitled to the position

Instead Say: "Mary, your position as marketing manager requires that you have excellent communication skills, so that you can market our products to potential purchasers. The feedback we've received from customers so far is that it's very difficult to talk to you because you don't seem to be paying attention when others are speaking, and you cut people off abruptly. This behavior needs to improve. "

Statement: "David, you are on a one-year probation period. If I receive one more complaint from a customer about your attitude, I'll have no choice but to let you go."

But What If: David receives no more customer complaints in the next year, but coworkers complain about how David treats them.

Problem: David can contend that he is a "permanent" employee and can't be fired because he did what he was told was necessary to finish probation.

Instead Say: "David, I have received three complaints from customers that you were rude and raised your voice during a call. That behavior isn't acceptable. For the next month, I will randomly monitor five of your calls per week. You will also repeat the customer service training for new telephone representatives."

Statement: "Bob's records show that he scans and delivers an average of 30 packages a day, while his coworkers average 50 packages. I've told him that if he can't improve his productivity, I'll have to put him on written warning."

But What If: Bob's productivity dips even lower, and he starts delivering 10 packages a day.

Problem: The company might have to give Bob a written warning before it can terminate his employment.

Instead Say: "Bob's records show that he scans and delivers an average of 30 packages a day, while his coworkers average 50 packages. I have told him that he must scan an average of 50 packages a day, starting February 1. In the interim, Claire will work with him every Monday morning to make sure he understands proper scanning procedures."

All these statements could lock the company into one course of action, rather than allowing it the flexibility provided by at-will employment. As you can see, it's all too easy to inadvertently make promises that undermine the at-will relationship. Happily, the solution is just as easy: Don't make any promises about what the future will bring, for better or for worse. Explain the goal you want the employee to reach, not what you or the company plan to do if that goal is or is not met.

Strategy 2: Be Consistent

Done properly, smart employee discipline offers a lot of flexibility: You and the employee work together to come up with ways to solve whatever problem the employee is having. This allows you to craft a plan that takes into account the employee's unique situation and perspective, as well as the needs of the company.

But with flexibility comes the responsibility to be consistent. You must adhere to the basic disciplinary steps, and your company's discipline policy, whenever you have to deal with an employee whose performance or conduct is unacceptable. You can still work with your employees to come up with customized, flexible solutions for improving performance, but the measures you use—whether it's an informal coaching session or a written warning—should be the same for similar problems.

If you are seen as playing favorites, you'll quickly lose the benefits of collaborative discipline. Employees won't feel fairly treated or respected, and they won't understand the consequences of poor performance or behavior. Instead, they'll believe the system is rigged in favor of some employees and against others. They'll believe that punishments and rewards flow from being on your good side, not from doing what the company needs them to do.

The biggest danger of inconsistency, from a legal point of view, is that it can lead to discrimination lawsuits. Employees who are treated differently quickly start to wonder why. And if employees have any reason to believe that your inconsistent treatment is based on a protected characteristic—one that federal or state law dictates may not be the basis of employment decisions—you could be facing major legal trouble.

Federal law prohibits discrimination based on race, color, national origin, gender (including pregnancy), religion, disability, age (if the employee is at least 40 years old), and genetic information. Typically, federal antidiscrimination laws apply to all but very small employers; see "Which Federal Antidiscrimination Laws Apply to Your Company?" below, for more information.

Virtually every state also has an antidiscrimination law. Some of these laws apply to smaller employers, and some prohibit additional types of discrimination, such as discrimination based on marital status, sexual orientation, or gender identity. (For more information on state antidiscrimination laws, see "State Laws Prohibiting Discrimination in Employment," in Appendix C.)

If you treat employees inconsistently, and there appears to be a link between the employees' race, gender, or other protected characteristic and the degree or type of discipline you impose, you could be accused of discrimination.

EXAMPLE: Tanya manages a large group of warehouse workers. Some of the workers have been at the company for years and don't always follow safety rules to the letter. Because they're good at their jobs and haven't had any accidents, Tanya lets it go.

One day, Tanya notices a newer employee using the forklift incorrectly, and she's worried that he might damage the property he's moving. She realizes that she needs to enforce the safety rules because the more senior workers are passing their bad habits down to new employees. She schedules a meeting with the employee who misused the forklift. At the meeting, the employee complains that other workers haven't been disciplined for ignoring safety rules. Even though Tanya has a valid reason for discipline, she could face problems if, for example, she and the more senior workers are white and the newer worker is Latino. The employee might wonder whether his race played a role in Tanya's decision, and other workers might start to question her impartiality. This suspicion could lead to a lawsuit, and Tanya's decision to impose discipline would be scrutinized.

It can be tough to balance the need to be flexible in dealing with employee concerns with the need to be consistent. The best course of action is to be consistent in applying discipline—that is, impose the same discipline for the same infractions or problems—and be flexible in working with your employees to come up with ways to help them meet the company's expectations.

Which Federal Antidiscrimination Laws Apply to Your Company?

Not every antidiscrimination law applies to every employer. Federal anti-discrimination laws apply only to employers with more than a minimum number of employees—and this minimum number is different for each law.

Name of Law:	Discrimination Prohibited on the Basis of:	Applies to:
Title VII	Race, color, national origin, religion, sex	Employers with 15 or more employees
Age Discrimination in Employment Act	Age (40 and over only)	Employers with 20 or more employees
Americans with Disabilities Act	Physical or mental disability	Employers with 15 or more employees
Equal Pay Act	Sex (applies only to wage discrimination)	All employers
Civil Rights Act of 1866	Race, ethnicity	All employers
Immigration Reform and Control Act	Citizenship status, national origin	Employers with 4 or more employees
Genetic Information Nondiscrimination Act	Genetic information	Employers with at least 15 employees

Strategy 3: Be Objective

To manage performance and behavior issues effectively, you must be objective. This means you have to stay above the fray, figure out what happened and why, then decide on the appropriate response based on the facts. Your response should not be based on your feelings or frustrations, or on what you privately think of the employees involved. This can be harder than it sounds, though. It's human nature to develop personal opinions of the people we work with, to like some and dislike others. It's also quite natural to be at least a little upset when you have to confront an employee who has failed to meet your expectations, acted inappropriately, or even affected your ability to meet your own performance goals. But allowing these feelings to enter into employment decisions can lead to all sorts of problems, from accusations of favoritism to charges of discrimination.

Making objective, business-based employment decisions has two important legal benefits. First, it eliminates potential discrimination claims. Employees won't be able to claim that you had illegitimate motives for your decisions if you can point to sound, objective reasons for your actions. Second, if you ever have to prove that you had good cause for discipline, it's much easier to prove objective facts than subjective opinions. (See "Strategy 10: Document Everything," below, and Chapter 9 for tips on documenting factual reasons for discipline.)

Making decisions based on the company's business needs is also a core element of smart discipline. As explained in Chapter 5, you must consider—and explain to the employee—how the employee's actions have affected the company. This will help you focus on the objective, measurable reasons for your response and avoid acting on your emotions.

> **EXAMPLE:** Maureen is 65 years old and has worked in the accounts receivable department for many years. She frequently challenges her supervisor, Alan, who is 35 years old. Maureen tells Alan that she should have been supervisor of the department and that he should not tell her how to do her job. Alan's department runs into major trouble when Maureen doesn't meet an important deadline for entering customer information into a new software program. Maureen tells him that she thinks the company should keep using the old software and that she is in no rush to convert to the new program. Alan decides it's time to step in.

Here's a portion of what Alan planned to write in Maureen's written warning: "Maureen has a bad attitude and is insubordinate. I know she is unhappy about having to report to a younger supervisor, but that's no excuse. She thinks she knows everything, but in fact she is unable to keep up with new technology and the changing needs of our customers. She insists on doing things the same way she's been doing them for the last 30 years. If she can't handle changes in the field, she should consider retirement."

You can probably see why Alan thought about writing this. Hopefully, you can also see why he shouldn't. First of all, this document would be Exhibit A in Maureen's age discrimination case against the company: It sounds like Alan is saying that this old dog is unwilling to learn a new trick. Second, Alan has used subjective terms like "bad attitude" and "insubordinate" without explaining what he means. He won't be able to prove that he had good reason for disciplining Maureen if he has to rely on this warning.

Once Alan's had some time to cool off, he writes this instead: "Maureen missed her March 15 deadline to enter customer information into the department's new *BillItNow* software program. As a result, all of our invoices for the month went out two weeks late, and we were unable to meet our deadline for the company's quarterly report. At our team meetings in January and February, I talked about the importance of making this deadline and urged anyone who was having trouble learning the new program to talk to me. Maureen never informed me that she would have any trouble with the deadline. When I asked Maureen what happened, she told me that she did not agree with the decision to purchase new software and did not feel that it was important to meet the deadline."

This is much better. Instead of characterizing Maureen's behavior, Alan simply reports it factually. He explains what he said and did, what Maureen said and did, and the consequences of her actions. This is also a more effective way to get his point across: He doesn't have to come right out and say that Maureen is insubordinate, because the last sentence of his documentation makes that painfully obvious.

Strategy 4: Don't Retaliate

Many employment laws prohibit retaliation against employees who exercise their rights under those laws. Typically, employers are prohibited from retaliating against an employee who takes advantage of a benefit provided by the law (for example, an employee who takes protected family medical leave) and against an employee who complains that the employer violated the law (for example, an employee who files a sexual harassment complaint). Most employment laws prohibit retaliation for a very simple reason: If they didn't, there would be no way for employees to enforce their rights under the law, and the rights would be meaningless. If an employer was free to fire any employee who complained of harassment, for example, employees would quickly learn that they had to put up with harassment if they wanted to keep their jobs.

 TIP

You may not make employment decisions based on an employee's litigiousness. Some managers believe that they are perfectly within their rights to turn the cold shoulder to an employee who has sued, or threatened to sue, the company. After all, the employee has mistreated the company, so the company can return the favor. Right? Wrong. It is retaliation to treat an employee less favorably (for example, to discipline, refuse to promote, or route unpopular assignments to the employee) because he or she has filed or talked about filing a lawsuit. This is true even if you believe that the lawsuit is groundless, and even if the lawsuit is against a previous employer.

Here are some of the most frequently invoked retaliation protections:

- **Antidiscrimination laws.** Employers may not retaliate against an employee who complains of harassment or discrimination, whether the employee makes that complaint within the company (to the human resources department, for example) or to a court or government agency.
- **Leave laws.** Virtually all laws that allow employees to take time off for certain reasons also prohibit employers from disciplining or firing an employee who requests or takes leave for those reasons. (For more information on leave laws, see "Strategy 6: Be Careful When Disciplining for Absences," below).
- **Health and safety laws.** The Occupational Safety and Health Act and similar state laws prohibit employers from retaliating against employees who complain of unsafe working conditions.
- **Whistleblower prohibitions.** Whistleblower laws prohibit employers from punishing employees who come forward, either to company managers or to government enforcement agencies, with complaints that the company has done something illegal or unethical. The

whistleblower law that's gotten the most press in recent years is the Sarbanes-Oxley Act of 2002, which prohibits publicly traded companies from retaliating against employees who raise good faith complaints about shareholder fraud. And many state courts have found that employees who are fired for raising legitimate concerns about other company illegalities can sue for wrongful termination.

- **Labor law violations.** The National Labor Relations Act (NLRA) prohibits employers from retaliating against employees who engage in protected concerted activities. Protected concerted activity is defined broadly to include any conversations or actions, involving more than one employee, that are aimed at improving working conditions or the terms of employment. This prohibition applies whether a workplace is unionized or not. In recent years, the law has been interpreted to protect employees from being disciplined for their work-related social media posts. (See "Social Media Posts and Discipline," below.

Even if you have perfectly legitimate reasons for disciplining an employee, the timing of the discipline can create problems. If you crack down after an employee has exercised a legal right or made a complaint, the employee may claim that you imposed discipline to punish him or her (in other words, that your actions were retaliatory). Of course, nothing prevents you from disciplining an employee—even an employee who has just filed a lawsuit— for violating workplace rules or poor performance. But you must be able to prove that you would have taken the same action if the employee hadn't complained or exercised legal rights, ideally through documents showing that the employee's problems predated his or her protected activity.

Proceed with caution—and preferably, only after getting the green light from your legal counsel—if you want to discipline or terminate an employee in any of these circumstances:

- The employee recently requested to take protected leave (for example, to give birth, care for a seriously ill family member, or serve in the military).
- The employee recently requested a reasonable accommodation for a disability (see "Strategy 5: Make Reasonable Accommodations for Employees With Disabilities," below, for more information).

Social Media Posts and Discipline

In the last few years, the National Labor Relations Board (NLRB), the federal government agency that interprets and enforces the NLRA and other labor laws, has paid particular attention to employer policies and practices regarding social media. The NLRB's concern is that these policies inhibit employees' rights to talk freely among themselves about their working conditions and to act together to try to change those conditions.

If, for example, you discipline an employee for posting a comment on Facebook criticizing the company, you may be violating the NLRA. Whether it's legal to discipline an employee for a social media comment depends on these three things:

- Was the employee engaged in concerted activity? In other words, did the employee seek input from coworkers? Did other employees respond to the post with their own comments? Was the employee's post part of a conversation or an effort to rally coworkers to take action? Or was the comment simply solo grumbling (which is not protected)?
- Was the employee complaining about working terms and conditions (safety problems, wages, overtime, or even a manager who is difficult to work with)? Or was the employee simply saying that the company or a particular manager "sucks"?
- Did the employee cross the line into malicious or reckless statements? If so, the employee's statement is not protected and can subject the employee to discipline. An employee who posts that she is frustrated with a particular manager for assigning heavy workloads and asks coworkers how they feel about it is likely protected. However, an employee who calls the manager bad names and threatens to harm him may not be protected.

As you can see, this newly developing area of law is a bit confusing. To make sure you don't inadvertently run afoul of this protection, talk to a lawyer before disciplining an employee based on online posts or comments.

- The employee recently revealed that he or she is in a protected class (for example, of a certain race, ethnicity, or religion).
- The employee recently filed a workers' compensation claim.
- The employee recently made a complaint, within the company or to an outside agency, of harassment, discrimination, health and safety violations, wage and hour violations, or other allegedly illegal conduct.
- The employee recently helped another employee make a complaint, or testified, acted as a witness, or otherwise participated in an investigation into workplace violations.
- The employee recently filed a lawsuit against the company.
- The employee recently criticized, or discussed trying to change, working conditions or job terms (like compensation) with other employees, whether online or off.

> **TIP**
>
> **Retaliation claims are a clear and present danger.** Employers have a very real reason to be concerned about retaliation claims. Juries seem to be particularly suspicious when employers take action against employees who are trying to serve the public good. An employee who wins a retaliation claim could be awarded significant damages, especially if the employee claims to have been fired for complaining of illegal conduct. And these cases can be tough for employers to win: Even if the employer can prove that the underlying complaint—of sexual harassment or unsafe working conditions, for example—isn't valid, it can still lose the retaliation case.

Strategy 5: Make Reasonable Accommodations for Employees With Disabilities

If an employee's performance or conduct problems are the result of a disability, you have special obligations. You cannot simply ignore the employee's disability and proceed with your corrective actions. Instead, you must consult with the employee to figure out whether some accommodation would help him or her do the job successfully. On the other hand, you are not required to lower your standards or avoid disciplining employees who cannot meet the company's expectations. This section explains the rules for accommodating employees with disabilities.

Your Legal Obligations to Employees With Disabilities

The Americans with Disabilities Act (ADA) prohibits private employers with at least 15 employees from discriminating against a person with a disability. (42 U.S.C. §§ 12101–12213.) However, the ADA doesn't require companies to hire or retain workers whose disabilities make them unable to do their jobs. Only qualified workers with disabilities—those who can perform the essential functions of the job, with or without a reasonable accommodation—are protected from discrimination. And an employer does not need to make a reasonable accommodation if it would cause an undue hardship.

The ADA can be a difficult law to understand, partly because of how it defines basic terms. You may think you know what a disability or an accommodation is, for example, but the ADA uses its own very specific definitions. Here is a quick introduction to some common ADA terms:

- **Person with a disability.** Under the ADA, there are three ways someone might qualify as a person with a disability:
    - The person has a long-term physical or mental impairment that substantially limits a major life activity (such as the ability to walk, talk, see, hear, breathe, reason, work, or take care of oneself) or a major bodily function (such as cell growth and the proper functioning of the neurological, digestive, reproductive, or respiratory system).
    - The person has a history of disability (for example, he or she suffered from depression or cancer in the past).
    - The person is regarded as having a disability. This sometimes comes up when a worker has an obvious impairment, such as a limp, that is not disabling but appears so to the employer.
- **Qualified worker.** A worker is qualified if he or she has the necessary experience, skills, training, licenses, and so on to do the job and can perform its essential functions with or without a reasonable accommodation.
- **Essential functions.** Essential job functions are the fundamental duties of the position, those things that the person holding the position absolutely must be able to do (as opposed to occasional or tangential duties).
- **Reasonable accommodation.** Reasonable accommodations include assistance or changes to the job or workplace that will enable an employee with a disability to do the job. Examples include a lowered desktop or accessible washroom for an employee who uses

a wheelchair; voice recognition software for an employee who has carpal tunnel syndrome, severe learning disabilities, or limited vision; or a temporary part-time schedule for a worker who is getting chemotherapy or radiation treatment for cancer.

- **Undue hardship.** An accommodation creates an undue hardship if it would involve significant difficulty or expense for the employer or if it would fundamentally alter the nature or operation of the business. Whether an accommodation creates an undue hardship depends on a number of factors, including:
  - the cost of the accommodation
  - the size and financial resources of the business
  - the structure of the business, and
  - the effect the accommodation would have on the business.

TIP

ADA coverage is broad. In 2008, Congress amended the ADA in response to a series of U.S. Supreme Court and lower court rulings against employees with disabilities. In the ADA Amendments Act, Congress expanded some of the definitions in the ADA to make its coverage broader. As a result, employees are more likely to qualify as employees with disabilities who are entitled to the protections of the law. Given these changes, the best strategy when faced with an employee with a limiting health or medical condition is to assume that the ADA will apply and start considering possible accommodations (or consult with a lawyer).

Disabilities and Discipline

Many managers are understandably confused by the interaction of two of the ADA's basic principles. On the one hand, the ADA protects workers only if they can do the job's essential functions; you are not legally required to lower production or performance standards for workers with disabilities. On the other hand, you may have a legal obligation to accommodate a worker's disability, if it doesn't create an undue hardship. When an employee's performance or conduct is falling short because of his or her disability, it can be tough to figure out whether the employee is capable of doing the job's essential functions and whether a reasonable accommodation would make a difference.

Your job is easiest at the extremes: if a simple accommodation would allow the employee to meet your expectations, or if there's simply no way to help the employee do the job.

EXAMPLE 1: Leroy, a retail merchandiser, uses a wheelchair. His numbers are missing the mark. When his supervisor, Loretta, talks to him about it, she learns that it's very time-consuming for him to load product samples each morning because there's no accessible parking near the warehouse, and he can only carry one or two boxes of samples at a time. Loretta creates a parking space for him by the loading bay door and arranges for a warehouse worker to meet him there at a set time each morning to load the samples in his van. This saves Leroy time, making it possible for him to make more sales calls. His numbers go up immediately. Problem solved.

EXAMPLE 2: Now assume that Leroy doesn't have any trouble loading samples but still isn't making his numbers for a different reason. Leroy's company sells camping gear to outdoor supply companies. Part of his job is to demonstrate how easy it is to set up the company's tents. The problem is that it's fairly difficult and time-consuming for Leroy to set up the tents. And Leroy can't demonstrate the tents' cool interior features, because his wheelchair won't fit inside. Leroy's stores aren't buying because Leroy's disability makes it almost impossible for him to effectively present this product, and it's hard to come up with a reasonable accommodation that wouldn't pose an undue burden. This job is probably just a bad fit for Leroy.

As long as you've met your obligation to provide a reasonable accommodation (if one is available), it is perfectly acceptable to discipline an employee with a disability for failing to meet performance or conduct standards. In some cases, though, it might be a reasonable accommodation to change a workplace rule, if doing so is feasible and does not pose an undue hardship to the company. For example, an employee might be groggy in the morning after taking antidepressant medication. You might allow this employee to come in a couple of hours late (and stay a couple of hours late) as a reasonable accommodation, if it doesn't really matter when he or she works. On the other hand, if the employee is a dispatcher for your delivery team and must be at work by 8 a.m. to get the trucks on the road, it would probably be an undue hardship to let him or her come in late.

In coming up with a possible accommodation, you may want to start by asking the employee what would help him or her do the job. However, you are not required to provide the specific accommodation requested by the employee, if there is an alternate accommodation that would be effective.

Disabilities That Are Not Obvious

If your employee is blind or uses a wheelchair, you know that he or she has a disability. Other disabilities are not so obvious, however. In fact, you might learn of an employee's disability only after you decide to impose discipline.

If an employee tells you that his or her performance or misconduct problems are related to a disability, you have an obligation to explore the possibility of providing a reasonable accommodation moving forward. However, you don't have to rescind discipline you've already imposed. The duty to accommodate exists only after you know of the employee's disability.

 RELATED TOPIC

More information on the ADA and reasonable accommodation.
The ADA is enforced by the federal Equal Employment Opportunity Commission (EEOC). You can find lots of free information on the ADA at the EEOC's website, www.eeoc.gov. Click "Disability" for some basic information and a list of links to EEOC factsheets and enforcement guides. For a wealth of information on possible accommodations, including specific suggestions for accommodating various disabilities in the workplace, check out the website of the Job Accommodation Network, www.askjan.org.

Strategy 6: Be Careful When Disciplining for Absences

Attendance is a very basic requirement of many jobs: If the employee doesn't show up to work regularly, the work won't get done. Recognizing this, many companies have adopted attendance policies. Typically, these policies provide that employees who exceed a certain number of absences, regardless of the reason, will be subject to discipline, up to and including termination. Even companies that don't have a written attendance policy typically follow one in practice.

There are several traps lurking here for the unwary manager. First, if you discipline employees for taking leave to which they are legally entitled, you have broken the law and could face an enforcement action by a government agency, or even a lawsuit. Second, even though it's very easy to bend the attendance rules when employees seem to have an urgent need for leave, granting exceptions means treating employees differently, which could lead to discrimination claims. And third, it's important to initiate corrective measures at the first sign of trouble, not after an employee has racked up piles of unexcused absences.

Legally Protected Absences

Many types of absences are legally protected. State and federal laws give employees the right to take time off for a variety of reasons, from attending school conferences or National Guard training to giving birth or healing from a workplace injury. If you penalize employees for taking a protected absence—even if the protected absence follows a long string of unexcused and unprotected days off—you have violated the law.

Here are some of the most common types of protected absences:

- **Family medical leave.** Under the federal Family and Medical Leave Act (FMLA), eligible employees are entitled to take up to 12 weeks of unpaid leave each year (1) for the birth, adoption, or placement of a child; (2) to care for a family member with a serious health condition; (3) to recover from the employee's own serious health condition; or (4) to handle certain practical issues arising from a family member's military deployment. The FMLA also gives employees the right to take up to 26 weeks off in a single 12-month period to care for a family member who has suffered a serious injury while on active military duty. Employers may not discipline or fire employees for taking FMLA-protected leave and must reinstate returning employees to the positions they held prior to taking leave. Although the FMLA applies only to employers that have at least 50 employees, some states have similar laws that cover smaller companies and/or provide more generous leave benefits. A handful of states also allow employees to take protected leave for specified reasons, such as to donate bone marrow or take a child or elderly relative to the doctor or dentist.

- **Military leave.** The federal Uniformed Services Employment and Reemployment Rights Act (USERRA) prohibits discrimination against members of the armed services and requires employers to reinstate employees who take up to five years of leave for military service. Many states have similar laws that protect those who serve in the state guard or militia. Employers may not discipline or fire employees for taking protected leave under these statutes.

- **Jury duty.** Almost every state prohibits employers from disciplining or firing an employee who takes time off to respond to a jury summons or to serve on a jury. Typically, the employee must meet certain requirements, such as providing advanced notice of the need for leave. Some states require employers to pay for all or some of this time; others do not.

- **Voting.** Many states require employers to allow employees to take at least a couple of hours off to vote, if the employee otherwise would not be able to get to the polls in time. An employer may not fire or otherwise discipline an employee for taking this time off, as long as the employee meets any requirements imposed by the law (for example, the employee may have to give notice in advance or provide proof, upon returning to work, that he or she actually voted).

- **School events.** Some states prohibit employers from disciplining or firing employees who take time off for a child's school activities, such as attending parent-teacher conferences, volunteering in the classroom, or responding to a child's emergency at school. The amount of protected time off varies from state to state, as do the reasons for taking leave.

- **Domestic violence.** Some states require employers to allow employees to take time off to deal with issues relating to domestic violence, such as medical appointments, counseling, attending legal proceedings, or relocating to a safe environment. Employees may not be disciplined or fired for taking leave for these purposes. In some states, an employee may take leave to assist a family member who is the victim of domestic violence.

- **Disabilities.** As explained above, the Americans with Disabilities Act (ADA) requires certain employers to provide reasonable accommodations to employees with disabilities. Time off from work might be such an accommodation if the employee needs the time for required medical treatment or recuperation from a disability-related illness, for example. An employer may not discipline or fire an employee for requesting or taking leave as a reasonable accommodation. And the employer may not otherwise penalize the employee by, for example, refusing to take the leave into account when calculating the employee's annual productivity numbers.

- **Work-related injuries and illnesses.** Most companies are required to carry workers' compensation insurance, which reimburses employees for medical expenses incurred and wages lost due to on-the-job injuries and illnesses. Virtually all states prohibit companies from discriminating or retaliating against an employee for filing a workers' comp claim, and some states interpret this prohibition to include disciplining or firing a worker because he or she is on leave due to an injury covered by workers' compensation.

- **Paid sick leave.** A handful of states and numerous cities and local governments require employers to provide paid sick leave. These laws generally require employers to provide employees with a certain number of paid sick days to use for their own illnesses or to care for a family member who is ill. Details vary from state to state and city to city, including which employees are eligible, how leave accrues, how much leave an employee may take, and how much leave an employee may carry over into a new year. If an employee is entitled to paid sick leave and uses it for an allowable purpose under the law, you may not discipline the employee for that absence.

> **TIP**
>
> **Get help untangling leave requirements for injured, ill, or disabled employees.** There is plenty of overlap among the ADA, FMLA, paid sick leave laws, and workers' compensation laws. Although these laws have different purposes and requirements, they regulate some of the same issues, which can lead to confusing—and sometimes conflicting—obligations for employers. If you're faced with a difficult question regarding an injured, ill, or disabled employee and you're not absolutely clear on your obligations, talk to an employment lawyer.

Making Exceptions

Consistency can also be a problem when disciplining for absences. As a manager, you know that you must be consistent in imposing discipline. As a human being, however, you will undoubtedly have more sympathy for an employee who misses work because his friend was in a serious car accident than one who misses work to go to the ball game.

Although you have to apply company policies consistently, this doesn't mean that you have to turn a blind eye to significant events in an employee's life, even if they don't come with a legally protected right to take time off. It's certainly acceptable to allow an employee to take time off beyond what would ordinarily be allowed under your company policies for a reason that's compelling but not legally protected. If you do, however, remember that you'll have to be ready to grant that same privilege to other employees who need leave for legitimate reasons, or risk being accused of playing favorites or, much worse, discriminating.

> **EXAMPLE:** Rob's ex-wife, with whom he shares custody of their young daughter, must move to another state immediately to care for her dying father. Rob calls in Monday morning and asks for permission to take the week off so he can spend time with his daughter and take care of her while his ex-wife prepares to move. Although Rob didn't follow company policies that require written notice before taking leave for personal reasons, John, Rob's manager, decides to grant the request. Rob is generally reliable and seems to have a good reason for taking time off.
>
> Carla, another employee who reports to John, is upset when she finds out about Rob's leave. John gave Carla a verbal warning when she failed to give written notice to take personal leave when her teenage son was chosen at the last minute to compete in a regional spelling bee out of state. Now John could be in trouble: Although Rob's request seems more urgent than Carla's, John has bent the rules for a father and enforced them against a mother. If this starts to look like a pattern of disciplining women and not men for leave violations, the company could be looking at a discrimination claim—not to mention some angry female employees.

Here's another very good reason to be careful when granting exceptions to your usual leave rules: Courts will consider your company's past practices when deciding whether an employee is entitled to leave as a reasonable accommodation. You will have a harder time arguing that it would be an undue hardship to give an employee four months off to recover from surgery related to a disability if you gave another employee the same amount of leave to go on a trek in the Himalayas.

Don't Let Absences Slide

Some managers don't pay much attention to employee absences until they start creating real trouble in the workplace. For example, let's say you have a report who routinely extends his vacations by taking a few "sick" days and tends to fall ill on the day after a long weekend. Clearly, you have reason to believe this employee is abusing the company's sick leave policy, but it might not cause you any real grief until the team starts missing deadlines or failing to meet production quotas. If you initiate corrective action only after a handful of unexcused absences, you've done your company a real disservice, for several reasons:

- Coworkers have noticed the free ride this employee got, and they are undoubtedly resentful at having to pick up the extra work he left undone on his "sick" days. Some of them have probably also decided that they could use an extra day or two off themselves, especially when they see that there are no consequences for abusing sick leave.

- If you decide to be more vigilant about employee absences from now on, you will have a consistency problem, and therefore a potential discrimination problem. Employees who face discipline after their first unexcused absence will have a legitimate gripe that they were treated less favorably than the employee who got away with all those extra sick days.

- You still can't impose discipline for legally protected absences, which can be very frustrating if an employee has already taken a lot of time off for other reasons. For example, let's say your employee racked up several weeks' worth of unexcused absences before you decided it was time for a verbal warning. The employee then informs you that he plans to take two more months off after his wife has a baby. You might think, "Enough is enough! This guy has some nerve, responding to my warning with a request for more time off!" But if the leave is protected, you can't discipline him for it. On the other hand, if you had stepped in right away after the first unexcused absence, he would either have shown up for work on the days he missed or be looking for another job after you terminated employment.

Strategy 7: Deal With Dangerous Situations Right Away

If an employee is endangering coworkers or company property, you must step in immediately. There are, of course, many practical reasons for doing so, from maintaining morale to keeping workers safe. But there is also a very important legal reason to take action: Any harm a dangerous worker causes after the company becomes aware of the problem may be legally attributable to the company.

Here are some types of misconduct that should result in immediate action by the company:

- harassment or discrimination
- health or safety violations that could cause significant harm to workers or company property
- illegal conduct that could affect the company's customers, clients, or shareholders
- theft of the company's intellectual or other property
- threats to harm someone, stalking, fights, bringing weapons to work or threatening to use a weapon, and other types of violence
- vandalism or sabotage of company property
- use of company property for an illicit purpose
- stealing from the company's customers or clients, or
- substance abuse that affects an employee's ability to work safely and efficiently.

Your Company's Liability for Illegal Conduct

If an employee does something illegal, how you respond could have very serious ramifications. Your response must clearly communicate that the employee's actions are unacceptable and that the company will not condone illegal behavior. If you decide not to fire the employee—for example, because the employee violated the law inadvertently or otherwise didn't understand the situation—you must make very sure that your response stops the problem.

The reason for this is simple: Your company might be held liable for harm caused by the employee's actions. There are several ways this might happen:

- Under a legal theory called "respondeat superior," the employer is generally liable for harm its employees cause to third parties when acting within the course and scope of employment.

- Some states allow third parties to sue an employer for negligent hiring, retention, or supervision of an employee, if the employer knew or should have known that the employee posed a danger to others, yet failed to take action. The U.S. Supreme Court has held that employers are legally liable for certain types of harassment if they fail to take reasonable steps to discover, investigate, and end the harassment.

CAUTION

Workers' compensation is typically the only remedy for an injured employee. The workers' compensation system allows employees to claim benefits for most injuries suffered on the job, no matter who caused the injury. However, it also imposes a limitation on employer liability for these injuries: Employees may not sue their employers for workplace injuries, except in a few circumstances (for example, if the employer intentionally caused the harm). Although this rule does not prevent employees from suing for harassment or discrimination, it does effectively prevent most personal injury claims by employees against their employers.

If You Don't Know All the Facts

If you learn of potentially dangerous behavior, you must intervene right away to keep other employees, third parties, and company property safe. However, you may not have enough information to discipline or fire the allegedly dangerous employee. The best course of action in these circumstances is to suspend the employee immediately, with pay. That will give you time to investigate and figure out exactly what happened and what you should do about it. For detailed information on conducting a thorough and legal investigation, see *The Essential Guide to Workplace Investigations,* by Lisa Guerin.

CAUTION

Don't suspend employees without pay while you investigate. No matter what an employee is accused of doing, it's always a bad idea to suspend employees without pay pending an investigation. An unpaid suspension signals that you believe the employee is probably guilty, which can cause bad feelings and potential legal problems. Suspending exempt employees (those who are not entitled to earn overtime) without pay can also lead to wage and hour problems. In the long run, it's a better idea to simply pay the employee for a few days off while you figure out what happened.

Handling Safety Rule Violations

An employee who violates a workplace safety rule could be endangering himself or herself and others. This is reason enough to impose discipline, but there's another important reason to discipline for safety violations: It could protect your company in an enforcement action by the federal Occupational Safety and Health Administration (OSHA).

OSHA enforces the Occupational Safety and Health Act, a federal law that requires employers to provide a safe workplace and to take certain actions to protect workers. OSHA creates and administers health and safety rules, in part by investigating workplace accidents or incidents in which employees are seriously injured or killed. When it investigates, OSHA looks to see whether the employer established and enforced proper workplace safety rules. If the employee was injured despite the employer's best efforts, the employer might not receive a citation. If, however, the employer didn't adopt safety rules—or didn't take its safety rules seriously—it could face penalties, fines, and even criminal sanctions.

In determining whether an employer is responsible for a workplace injury, OSHA and the courts will consider whether the employer enforced its safety rules effectively. If an employer can show evidence that it consistently enforced its safety rules by training employees and disciplining those who broke the rules, it will have a better chance of not being held liable. If you regularly discipline for safety violations, imposing more serious measures for repeat offenses or for particularly dangerous behavior, and you document your actions carefully, your company will be well-positioned to fight an OSHA citation.

SEE AN EXPERT

Get expert help for serious misconduct issues. Before suspending an employee accused of engaging in serious misconduct, you may want to consult with an employment lawyer. A lawyer can help you investigate the allegations or advise you on what action to take once you've completed your own investigation. If you're worried about potential violence, a workplace violence consultant can help you think through the issues and come up with a plan.

Strategy 8: Keep It Confidential

It's never a good idea to discuss specific instances of employee discipline with anyone who doesn't have a need to know. First and foremost, it shows disrespect for the employee you had to discipline, who certainly doesn't want his or her failures broadcast throughout the workplace. Second, it can breach the trust you've established through the collaborative process. Once you start talking about an employee's performance problems or misconduct, you can be sure that the rest of your team will too. This can lead to plenty of gossip, potential bad feelings, and unproductive work time.

An employee who believes that you have spread false, damaging information about him or her might have more than just hurt feelings: That employee might also have a valid legal claim for defamation. When you discipline an employee, you are communicating that the employee has done something wrong or failed to meet company expectations in some way. If you are wrong about the employee's performance or conduct, or if you make the discipline public in a way that falsely maligns the employee, you might be vulnerable to a defamation claim.

Another danger of talking unnecessarily about discipline is that it compromises employee privacy. Often, personal problems spill into the workplace to create performance problems. So when you meet with an employee to talk about performance or conduct issues, you shouldn't be surprised if you end up hearing more about his or her private life than about the job.

But this doesn't give you carte blanche to repeat that information to others in the company. This is not only disrespectful and very hurtful to the employee who confided in you, but it could also lead to legal claims of invasion of privacy. Even though you (hopefully) didn't pry this information out of the employee, you could face a lawsuit if you reveal it to others who have no legitimate need to know about it.

The best practice is to reveal information an employee tells you in confidence only if you must. For example, if you have a coaching session with an employee whose performance is slipping, and she tells you that she's having trouble concentrating at work because a coworker is sexually harassing her, you cannot keep that information confidential. You have a duty to the company and the employee to escalate the complaint appropriately and make sure it's investigated. If, however, the employee tells you that her performance is suffering because her husband is having an affair, that would be something to keep to yourself.

> **EXAMPLE:** Roger has a coaching session with Sherry for poor performance. When Roger asks Sherry why her productivity is down, Sherry confides she is preoccupied by her son's recent arrest for drug possession. Roger and Sherry brainstorm together to come up with some short-term solutions, such as allowing Sherry to leave a bit early for the next two weeks and make up the time on the weekend, so she can make sure her son comes straight home from school.
>
> Afterwards, Roger considers what to do with this information. He can't think of any reason why others in the company would need to know about Sherry's son, and he knows that Sherry is deeply embarrassed by the whole situation. He decides that he won't reveal her son's problems. If anyone in the company asks him why Sherry is leaving early, he will simply say, "We've adjusted Sherry's schedule for the time being; she'll make up the time later."

Strategy 9: Remember: You Represent the Company

Sometimes, you may be called upon to deliver discipline that you don't entirely agree with. This can be especially hard if you have to fire an employee. Maybe you think the company's rules are too harsh or the employee deserves another chance. Maybe you just like the employee and don't want to see him or her go. It's a tough situation to be in, but it's also part of being a manager. Although you might have made a different decision if you were in charge, letting the employee know that can lead to problems.

> **EXAMPLE:** Rich is Eddie's manager and friend. Recently, Eddie has had trouble meeting the company's new productivity standards. These standards are strict, and the company has instructed managers to initiate discipline proceedings immediately with employees who are unable to meet them. After Rich arranged for Eddie to be retrained in the new system, Eddie's numbers improved, but they're still falling short. The company decides to terminate Eddie's employment. There's nothing illegal about this decision, but Rich doesn't like it.
>
> At the termination meeting, Rich tells Eddie the bad news. He also says, "If it were up to me, you'd still have a job here. These new quotas are pretty tough

on long-term employees who are used to the old system. Your performance has always been great, and I wish the company had taken that into account." Based on Rich's comments, Eddie might start wondering if the quotas were fair, and if his firing was legally justified.

As a manager, you represent the company. What you say is legally attributable to the company and can be used against it, even if you intended only to express your personal opinion. If you don't agree with the company's disciplinary decision, raise the issue with higher management, the human resources department, or legal counsel *before* you talk to the employee.

If you have a problem with discipline you've been asked to impose, keep it brief when you meet with the employee, and stick to the facts. There's nothing wrong with expressing sympathy for the employee's situation or sadness to see the employee go, as long as you don't cross the line into blaming the company for what happened. There's a difference between "I'm sorry to see you go" and "You never should have been fired."

Strategy 10: Document Everything

As a manager, you're probably already aware of the importance of documentation. It's especially important when you discipline an employee, because discipline (especially termination) can lead to lawsuits. Keeping a written record of the reasons you intervened, the employee's response, and the plan of action you and the employee decided on will help you prove that you acted fairly and legally.

Documentation can also help you troubleshoot your disciplinary decisions and managerial skills. For example, do you always impose the same discipline for the same offense? Are you consistent in the way you treat your reports? Do your reports seem to have similar problems, which could indicate that they need some training or other help? Could any of these problems be the result of the way you manage?

Here are some of the additional benefits of documentation:

- It will help jog your memory, if you later have to explain (or testify about) why you imposed discipline.
- It will help dispel claims that you had an improper motive, such as discrimination or retaliation.

- It will help show that you gave the employee notice and a chance to improve. Most jurors are employees rather than employers, and they are very interested in whether you gave the employee a fair shake.
- It will help show that the employee was part of the process, which will take the wind out of an argument that he or she was treated unfairly or taken by surprise.

Chapter 9 explains how to document disciplinary decisions and provides a sample form you can use in preparing your own documentation.

SMART SUMMARY:
Avoiding Legal Trouble

- You can terminate the employment of an at-will employee at any time, for any reason that isn't illegal. Don't undermine at-will employment or lock your company into a specific course of action by making threats or promises of what will happen if the employee does or doesn't improve.

- When you discipline, find out how others in the company have handled similar issues in the past. This helps you apply discipline consistently and objectively.

- If you grant leave to employees when it's not required by law, you must do it consistently among all employees to avoid looking like you're playing favorites, or worse, discriminating.

- Dangerous situations can create serious liability for the company, especially if not handled immediately. When an employee does something dangerous, act quickly to put a stop to it.

- Don't promise employees confidentiality, but maintain it when possible. Show your employees you respect their privacy and avoid defamation claims.

- Documenting your discipline decisions serves many purposes. It creates a written record of why you imposed discipline, the employee's response, and the plan of action you and the employee decide on. This may be very important if you ever have to justify your actions in a lawsuit.

Build Your Skills: An Overview of Employee Discipline

Questions

1. A smart discipline policy requires you to follow these steps: coaching, verbal warning, written warning, and finally, termination. ☐ True ☐ False

2. What is the main purpose of employee discipline?

   _____

   _____

   _____

   _____

3. When disciplining an employee, you should listen to his or her side of the story, and then explain how to solve the problem. ☐ True ☐ False

4. Caroline catches one of her employees, Norma, violating a company dress code. Which of these factors should she consider when deciding what level of discipline is appropriate?

   a. Norma works in the food service industry and wears open-toed shoes and shorts to work, which violates health codes.

   b. Norma has never been disciplined for her attire before.

   c. Both A and B.

   d. Neither A nor B.

5. Melissa and Alejandra are caught reading magazines and chatting on the job. Melissa has been disciplined for making personal phone calls during work time; Alejandra has no previous disciplinary history. Should their boss, Ida, impose the same discipline on each of them?

   a. Yes, because they were doing the same thing.

   b. Yes, because it isn't fair to take Melissa's previous disciplinary record into account, since it was for something different.

   c. No, because Melissa has a previous disciplinary history for a similar incident, but Alejandra doesn't.

   d. No, but only if Alejandra apologizes.

6. An at-will employee can be fired at any time, for any reason.

   ☐ True   ☐ False

7. You can create a legal contract without ever writing down an agreement or making a verbal promise.   ☐ True   ☐ False

8. To motivate an employee with a performance problem, it's a good idea to tell the employee what disciplinary measure you'll impose next if the problem doesn't improve.   ☐ True   ☐ False

9. What is a reasonable accommodation?

10. Dalton calls you on Monday morning to ask if he can take the morning off to wait for a contractor; his roof started leaking during a major storm over the weekend, and he needs to have it repaired right away. Although you don't have to allow him the extra time, you understand his situation and tell him that's fine. If Michael calls you to ask for the morning off because his car has broken down and he needs to get it to a mechanic, which of these reasons justify treating Michael differently?

    a. Dalton has worked for you for a long time, and you trust him, whereas Michael is a new employee.

    b. Michael just took 12 weeks off under the FMLA, and you want him to start catching up on the work that piled up while he was out.

    c. Michael had plenty of time to take his car to the mechanic while he was on FMLA leave.

    d. None of the above.

Answers

1. False. Although coaching, verbal warning, written warning, and termination are the typical steps in a progressive discipline policy, whether you follow this pattern will depend on different factors, including your company's policy and the seriousness of the problem. For example, if an employee steals $10,000 from the company, company policy and common sense should tell you to terminate employment, even if the employee has never been disciplined before.

2. The main purpose of discipline is employee retention, engagement, and improvement. That means you're constantly working to help your employee meet the job's requirements, not pushing that employee toward termination.

3. False. It's true that you should make sure you know all the facts and listen to the employee's side of the story. However, once you have done so, you should work *with* the employee to collaboratively find solutions together, not tell the employee how to solve the problem.

4. C. You should determine the seriousness of a problem—and thus what level of discipline is appropriate—by considering the problem's effect, the severity of the behavior, the employee's disciplinary history, and the legality of the behavior. Here, Norma's behavior violates health codes, a legal factor Caroline will definitely want to take into account. However, she'll also want to consider the fact that Norma's never been disciplined for this behavior before. Maybe Norma doesn't know the rule, or maybe correcting it now can prevent it from occurring again.

5. C. While it is important to administer consistent discipline for similar problems, you should also take into account the employee's unique situation and disciplinary history. Here, Melissa has already been disciplined for making personal phone calls during work time, which means she's already been caught chatting on the job. In this case, it's fair to take that into account and to impose different discipline on the two women as a result.

6. False. An at-will employee can be fired at any time, for any reason *that isn't illegal*. For example, it is illegal to fire an at-will employee because he or she is a certain race, has complained to a government agency about illegal behavior, or has taken a legally protected leave of absence.

7. True. Sometimes, contracts can be *implied* by statements or actions. For example, a statement like "If you complete the improvement plan, you'll become a permanent employee" could be interpreted to mean that you are promising continued employment as long as the improvement plan is carried out. This could limit your right to fire the employee if he or she has other performance problems not addressed in the improvement plan, for example.

8. False. Telling the employee what the next step is could obligate you to provide that step, even if you later decide that a more serious action is warranted. To maximize flexibility, focus on the immediate problem and solution, not on what might happen down the line.

9. Reasonable accommodation includes assistance or changes to the job or workplace that will enable an employee with a disability to do the job. If you know an employee has a disability, your company has a legal duty to provide that employee with a reasonable accommodation, as long as it won't create an undue hardship for the business (for instance, because it's so expensive that it would make it difficult for the company to keep operating).

10. D. While it's perfectly acceptable to offer extra time off when it's not legally required, you have to be prepared to offer it on an issue-by-issue basis, not an employee-by-employee basis. Here, if you're going to allow Dalton to take time off to take care of an urgent personal matter, you should allow Michael the same. And you can't penalize Michael for taking legally protected FMLA leave.

PART

II

Is It Time for Discipline?

Identifying Potential Problems

Y ou may have been in this situation before: You're dealing with a time-consuming discipline challenge, and suddenly you realize that there were early indications of trouble brewing, which you ignored, failed to take seriously, or weren't even aware of. While some employee problems truly do blindside us, there are often warning signs that hint at bigger problems to come. By paying closer attention, we can intervene sooner, thereby solving the problem before it causes any real harm or requires a disciplinary solution.

If you're able to identify potential problems early on, you can prevent them from becoming more serious, saving you time and avoiding stress. In this chapter, we'll explain three types of common employee problems, so you'll know what to look for. Then we'll discuss methods to identify, and ideally prevent, these problems, including:

- setting clear expectations
- communicating openly with your employees, and
- looking for specific signs of trouble.

Knowing What to Look For:
The Three Types of Employee Problems

No two employees are alike, and neither are any two employee problems. Each issue you face will involve slightly different facts. However, virtually all employee problems fit into these three categories:

- poor performance
- attendance problems (absenteeism and tardiness), or
- misconduct.

Some employees have a problem in only one of these areas. For example, an employee who is often late might do excellent work and behave appropriately once he finally shows up. Similarly, an employee might have a perfect attendance record and follow every workplace rule but have difficulty completing work on time. Identifying the type of problem the employee is having will help you keep your conversation focused and come up with an effective solution for that specific issue. It will also allow you to emphasize what the employee is doing well, which should help you encourage the employee to improve his or her problem area.

EXAMPLE: Reed is an editor for a weekly news magazine. His manager, Bernadette, needs to coach him about an attendance problem. Because Reed is an otherwise excellent editor, Bernadette starts the conversation like this: "Reed, I need to talk to you about a problem I've noticed. A couple of times a week, you return late from lunch by ten or fifteen minutes. Your editing is excellent, you get your work done quickly, and you're always willing to help other editors with their stories. These are all great qualities, but the long lunches are causing some resentment among your coworkers and holding us back. When you're late, we have to either start the afternoon story meeting without you or wait for you to return. As a result, we either don't get your input on the stories—which is too bad, because I really value your opinion—or we have to kill time waiting for you to show up."

Unfortunately, some employees have a problem in one area that causes problems in others. For example, an employee who spends a lot of work time sending personal emails to friends and surfing the Internet (misconduct) might also have trouble getting his or her job done (poor performance) as a result. In these situations, your disciplinary efforts will be effective only if you can identify and deal with the underlying issue. In the Internet example, the employee's performance isn't going to improve until you get him or her offline. You should certainly point out that the employee's performance is not to company standards and that the employee must improve. But you won't be able to come up with an action plan that will really turn things around until you identify the underlying issue.

EXAMPLE: Let's use the example of the employee who spends too much time online, discussed above. Kristen is an administrative assistant in an accounting firm; Roger is her manager. When Roger meets with Kristen, he might start by saying, "Kristen, I've noticed that when I walk by your workstation, you're often using your private email account, checking Facebook, or visiting websites that don't seem to be work-related. Two other partners have mentioned this to me, as well. And since we set up Internet access for you, you have missed two important deadlines and fallen behind in some of your basic responsibilities, like filing and returning telephone calls. As you know, company policy and good business practice restrict personal use of the Internet, except during breaks and other nonworking hours. Your Internet use is affecting your performance, and we need to deal with this right away."

Here are the three basic types of employee problems, with some examples that will help you quickly identify the particular issue you're facing.

What About Personal Problems?

As we all know, it can be tough to do a good job at work when you're worried about trouble at home. A failing relationship, trouble with one's kids, money problems, a seriously ill friend or relative, and other personal problems can make it hard to concentrate on the job and lead to performance issues.

So what can a manager do when an employee is having a personal problem that is affecting his or her performance? First of all, listen. Hear the employee out and express your sympathy. If your company has an employee assistance program (EAP) that might be able to help, offer the employee a referral. If the employee needs to spend some time away from work (for example, to attend therapy sessions) or make a temporary change to his or her schedule (to take a friend to chemotherapy, perhaps), consider whether you can accommodate that need without causing disruption to your operations. Also, explain any leave to which the employee may be entitled, such as a personal leave of absence, bereavement leave, or family and medical leave.

As you try to help the employee deal with his or her immediate situation, however, remember that the company's work still needs to get done with a minimally acceptable level of performance. When you talk to the employee, make it clear that the employee needs to figure out a way to do his or her job, even though personal issues are making that difficult. If the employee is unable to improve after you have discussed the issue and made whatever changes you can, it may be time to move into the disciplinary system.

Poor Performance

When an employee fails to perform to set expectations, meet his or her goals, or fulfill his or her job responsibilities, you have a performance problem. Typical performance problems include:

- missing deadlines (failing to complete assignments or hand in work on time)
- missing productivity targets or other numerical goals (such as failing to make a required number of calls per day or failing to meet sales quotas)

- poor work quality (such as handing in written assignments that are missing important information or contain errors, creating faulty products, or providing poor service to customers and clients)
- failure to follow through (for example, not returning phone calls or responding to emails in a timely manner, or not completing the proper paperwork), and
- communication problems (such as failing to touch base with other team members working on a project, having difficulty interacting with clients or customers, or failing to keep you informed of important developments—any of these issues might rise to the level of misconduct if the employee is rude or insubordinate).

What constitutes poor performance depends on the job's requirements. For example, a bookkeeper whose job consists entirely of paying bills and tracking company expenses needs good math skills, but might not need exceptional writing or customer service skills. On the other hand, a bookkeeper who also handles collection activities needs to be able to communicate well with customers, on the phone and in writing, to succeed at the job.

Attendance Problems

Attendance problems occur when an employee is absent or tardy in violation of company policy. Absenteeism problems arise when employees either exceed their allotment of days off or don't follow required procedures for taking time off. For example, it might violate company policy for an employee to take several sick days without providing a doctor's note, or to take a vacation day without getting permission in advance from a manager. Missed work days result in lower productivity and deadlines not being met.

Some employees don't take entire days off but persist in showing up late, taking long breaks, returning late from lunch, or leaving early. If your employee is required (by the nature of his or her position, or company policy) to work particular hours or accomplish a minimum number of tasks, and he or she does not meet those requirements, then it will no doubt affect the job. For instance, a receptionist who is supposed to be the face of the company and greet every visitor cannot be repeatedly late for his or her job. This would leave the post unstaffed and visitors ungreeted.

Misconduct

An employee commits misconduct when he or she violates a workplace rule; treats coworkers, customers, clients, or managers with disrespect; acts dishonestly; or otherwise behaves inappropriately in the workplace. Unlike poor performance, which involves an employee's failure to meet your expectations for the job, misconduct often involves the employee's failure to meet company policies or standards of polite and professional behavior, in his or her dealings with other people or with the company itself.

Common types of misconduct include:

- violation of safety rules
- failing to meet dress code, uniform, or grooming requirements
- horseplay
- fighting
- insubordination
- misuse of company property
- harassment
- discrimination
- theft
- excessive personal use of company email, Internet, phones, vehicles, and so on
- sleeping on the job
- use of alcohol or illegal drugs at work
- dishonesty, and
- illegal activities.

How to Spot Employee Problems

While many problems will be obvious once they're full-scale disasters, you might not know how to spot problems in the early stages, when they're more manageable. Once you know what to look for, you can use these techniques to detect employee problems early on.

Set Clear Expectations

One way to identify and prevent problems is to set very clear expectations for your employees. This serves several purposes: It establishes the minimum requirements for doing a good job, lets employees understand what is expected of them, and helps you recognize problems by giving you an objective standard by which to measure performance and conduct.

Human resource experts tell us that when employees fail to meet their employer's expectations, it's not because they're lazy, incompetent, or spiteful. Rather, the number one reason employees don't meet expectations is because they don't know what those expectations are. This means that you can reap great benefits by being very clear about what you and the company expect, right from the start. It also means that you must jump in and course correct at the first sign of trouble, so your employees understand what you want and have a fair opportunity to meet your expectations.

Define Expectations

Many discipline problems start out as simple misunderstandings between manager and employee about what should be done and when. Setting clear expectations avoids these mishaps, but it requires deliberate effort on your part. Before you begin communicating your expectations to your team, you need to spend some time clearly defining what your expectations are.

Performance Expectations

Performance management begins with setting goals for your employees. As part of your performance appraisal process or new hire orientation, you should sit down with employees to review job requirements (what you expect anyone holding that job to accomplish) and set performance goals (developmental goals designed to nurture the employee's strengths, work on weaknesses, and build skills).

If you have a job description that lays out the essential functions of the position, that will give you a place to start. Before you meet with the employee, you should review the job description and make a list of the job's requirements.

EXAMPLE: Corey just accepted a position as a customer service representative at a call center for a software company. His manager, Judy, meets with him to discuss her performance expectations. Based on the job description for the position, Judy tells Corey that the job requirements are:

- to answer phone calls from customers with questions or concerns about the company's products

- to deal with customers in a courteous, cheerful manner

- to answer an average of at least 20 calls per day

- to complete required paperwork on customer complaints

- to process refunds on a same-day basis

- to pass customers on to Judy if the representative does not know how to handle the customer's issue, and

- to be at work and available to answer phones from 6 a.m. to 2:30 p.m., Monday through Friday.

TIP

Don't forget to provide context. When you tell employees exactly what the job requires, also let them know the purpose of these requirements. Employees are more likely to meet your expectations—and excel in their jobs—if they know why their efforts are important to the company. In the example above, Judy could tell Corey, "Our company distinguishes itself, in part, by its excellent customer service. By answering every call right away and handling complaints and refunds on a same-day basis, we let our customers know that we really value their business."

When you meet with the employee, you should collaborate to come up with some specific performance goals as well. Unlike job requirements, which must be met by everyone who holds that position, performance goals are tailored to each employee individually, to reflect things he or she would like to improve or capitalize on.

EXAMPLE: Judy also wants to develop some performance goals for Corey. She knows, from interviewing Corey and reading his résumé, that he is interested in polishing up his Spanish language skills. Because a good portion of the company's customers speak Spanish as a first language, Judy tells Corey that she would like for him to take a Spanish class, with an emphasis on learning technical terms, so he can handle some calls in Spanish. Corey agrees to this goal, which they write as follows:

"Within the next month, Corey will enroll in a Spanish class that includes computer terminology. The company will pay the cost of the class and for the time Corey spends taking the class. Within three months, Corey will handle an average of one call in Spanish per workday."

The acronym SMART can help you define good performance goals:

- **S**pecific: Each goal needs to focus on a very precise task.
- **M**easurable: Each goal must provide an objective means to measure success, such as a completion date, hourly rate, productivity number, or dollar figure.
- **A**chievable: If you set unrealistic goals, not only will the employee not achieve them, he or she might be too discouraged to even try.
- **R**elevant: Each goal should relate to the job's duties and the employee's skills, giving the employee the opportunity to develop professionally.
- **T**ime sensitive: Goals should have deadlines, or they might get lost in the shuffle.

Once you have specified the job requirements and agreed upon performance goals, write them down and give a copy to the employee. This will give both of you a way to measure whether the employee is meeting your expectations. You can use the document to evaluate the employee throughout the year, so you will know right away if the employee's performance starts to slip. You can also use it to create the employee's performance appraisal for the current year and as a starting point to develop goals for the next year.

RELATED TOPIC

Get help setting goals and measuring performance. For help drafting job descriptions and using them as a tool to develop performance expectations, see *The Job Description Handbook,* by Margie Mader-Clark (Nolo). For detailed information on setting and documenting performance objectives, evaluating employee performance, and giving performance feedback throughout the year, see *The Performance Appraisal Handbook,* by Amy DelPo (Nolo).

Behavioral Expectations

Typically, behavioral standards are prescribed by company policy or codes of conduct. For example, your company's employee handbook probably includes rules about professional conduct, harassment, use of safety equipment, dealing with customers, dress codes, and more.

However, if you have expectations of your team that go beyond these basic rules, you must communicate them. Many times, managers have unwritten or unspoken expectations. Sometimes, these expectations may seem so obvious to you that you don't explain them to your team. When thinking about what you expect, consider:

- **How you want your team to work together.** Some managers encourage employees to use each other as resources (to answer questions, provide alternate perspectives, or verify intended courses of action), even when they're not working together on a project. Others prefer that an employee facing a challenge take it right to management for guidance or direction.

- **Time frame for responses.** If you want phone calls returned or emails answered within a certain time frame, communicate that to your employees. If it varies based on audience—whether the communication is to you, coworkers, clients, or others—you must explain that expectation as well.

- **Desired work hours.** If you need or want to see your employees at their desks at a particular time, let them know.

- **Resolving differences.** If you want your employees to work to solve problems among themselves before coming to you, you need to tell them. Likewise, let them know when you expect to be involved right away.

- **Staying in touch with you.** Are you an email person, do you prefer voicemail, or do you like to mainly discuss things in person? Tell your employees how you like to be contacted.

Likewise, as you think about what you expect of your employees, remember to be consistent in how you treat each of them. It is difficult for employees to understand appropriate behavior when you set double standards. For example, if you're friendly with one employee and exchange jokes or personal stories, but you try to limit that kind of behavior among other employees, frustration and confusion will often result.

TIP

Lead by example. It's not fair to hold employees to minimum professional standards that you don't meet yourself. If you expect punctuality, you must be punctual. If professional dress is important to you, you must dress professionally. "Do as I say, not as I do" is never an effective leadership strategy.

Sometimes, there are important reasons to maintain different behavioral standards for different employees. For example, you may expect employees who have direct contact with the public, such as receptionists or salespeople, to dress in business attire or put clients at ease with light banter or joking. On the other hand, you may expect employees who work in a warehouse setting to follow safety regulations that don't apply to others, such as wearing hard hats and limiting joking and horseplay.

While having these different standards is acceptable, make sure they are based on the needs of the job and not on your relationships with the employees. Moreover, you need to communicate to your team why the rules are different. While the reasons may be obvious to you, don't assume the same is true for your employees.

Communicate Expectations to Your Team

Once you have set expectations for performance and behavior, you'll need to communicate them to your team. While you will discuss the details with each employee, particularly for specific performance goals, you can perform a group exercise that will help you get started. The exercise below will help you understand what your employees currently believe your expectations are and how you have communicated those expectations. It will give you an opportunity to learn about the messages you're sending, consciously or unconsciously, and to correct and clarify misconceptions.

After you have had the opportunity to do this group activity, follow it up with individual sessions with each of your employees. At that time, discuss the specific expectations you have for each individual. When communicating expectations, the clearer you are the better. For example, telling an employee "I expect you to finish this project on a reasonable timeline" doesn't give the employee any real idea of when the project needs to be done. "Reasonable" to you could be the next day, and if the employee doesn't complete the project by then, he or she will have let you down without knowing it. However, giving the employee an objective deadline, such as "I expect you to complete the project by next Friday" makes it possible for the employee to meet your goal (or, at least, to let you know if he or she might have trouble doing so).

Follow up each conversation with a written confirmation of those expectations, even in an informal format like email, so that you can make sure you and the employee are on the same page. Be sure that the employee knows he or she needs to inform you if the expectations are unclear or can't be met. Continue to reevaluate and communicate your expectations, accounting for the changing needs of the organization, developing skills of the employee, and shifts in team goals.

When you set clear expectations and communicate them to your employees, problems will stick out like a sore thumb. After all, if everyone in your organization knows what is expected, it will be obvious when an employee is not pulling his or her weight. And, because you've already told the employee what you expect, you can discipline quickly and confidently, knowing that the employee won't be surprised to learn that he or she is falling short.

Communicate With Your Employees

One of the best ways to learn about problems is to hear about them directly from your employees. After all, employees who are struggling often want the help or intervention of management, even if they don't always know how to ask for it. Moreover, if your team understands that you want to be informed about potential problems, they'll know to flag them for you when they come up. You can help them do this by:

- establishing regular one-on-one communication
- fostering open communication, and
- building a culture of ownership.

Establish Regular One-on-One Communication

"One-on-ones"—regular meetings in which you check in individually with each of your direct reports—keep you up to speed on what employees are doing, how they are doing, and whether any issues require your attention or intervention. For example, an employee can notify you if he or she isn't going to meet a deadline, is struggling with a project, or is having trouble with a coworker.

Ideally, you should meet regularly (perhaps once a week) with each employee that reports to you. Treating these sessions as an ongoing commitment, not a one-time aberration, will not only give you valuable and regular information about the state of your business, but it will also let your team know that you are invested in them and committed to their success. They will be accustomed to sharing the status of their work, the challenges they face, and how the team is doing as a whole.

Skills Enhancement 1: Setting Expectations

Allow 90 minutes to two hours for this exercise. Gather your team in a room with a large writing area (whiteboard or paper posted on the walls). Designate someone who will transcribe everything the team comes up with (you may choose to use an outside facilitator for that task). Tell your team that you are leaving the room for 30 minutes, and during that time, they should write down every question that they can think of relating to you as a manager, such as:

- How do you prefer to communicate with your employees?
- What is your management style?
- When will we know if we did a good job?
- When will we know if we did a bad job?
- And so on.

You may also choose to open up these questions to things your employees may want to know about you as a person—such as your favorite foods or colors or what you like to do with your free time.

After 30 minutes, reenter the room. For the next hour or so, answer each of the questions posed by the group. If there are other important details that you want to communicate about your expectations, take the opportunity to build on the discussion and share that information.

If you're not already meeting with your employees this way, sitting down the first time might feel awkward, for both you and the employee. After all, employees who aren't used to dealing with the boss may think they're in trouble if they get called in. To prevent this from happening—and gossip from spreading—let each report know that you plan to do regular check-ins. Make sure you know something about each employee's projects, so you can ask questions about the progress on those projects. As the process becomes more familiar, employees will be ready to fill you in on how things are going before you even ask.

You'll quickly be attuned to warning signs of potential problems during these sessions, too. You will notice if there are changes in an employee's behavior. For example, perhaps a formerly forthcoming employee will be reluctant to talk about workload, or a normally positive employee will become sullen, despondent, or angry. Likewise, if you meet with employees regularly and know their schedules, you'll know when deadlines are in danger of being missed and when deliverables are slipping.

Of course, not every employee is the same; one may finish projects far ahead of deadline, while another finishes only at the last minute. As long as the work gets done well and on time without impacting others, neither approach calls for discipline. Spending time with each of your employees allows you to get to know their various work styles. Once you have a baseline, you'll be able to notice changes to their usual style and performance, which will clue you in to trouble that may be brewing.

> **EXAMPLE:** Stephen manages a small regional office for a large national mortgage broker. He has four brokers reporting to him, as well as a client group for whom he works directly. Stephen has structured half-hour meetings every week with each of his direct reports. Here is the typical agenda for these meetings:
>
> Ten minutes: Business update—number and amount of loans, potential close dates.
>
> Ten minutes: Forecasting—monthly and annually.
>
> Five minutes: Prospecting—potential new business.
>
> Five minutes: Resources and problems—anything the employee needs to do a better job, or barriers the employee is facing that Stephen can help remove.
>
> At the conclusion of each 30-minute meeting, Stephen understands what is going on with each employee on his team.

Foster Open Communication

Have you ever heard senior managers whispering to each other in the break room? Do you wonder what is going on when your boss shuts his or her office door? Do you sometimes learn about new policies, developments, or company directions from gossip rather than through official channels? If the answer to any of these questions is "yes," you probably know how debilitating closed, secretive communication can be to the work environment.

Of course, there are perfectly valid reasons to communicate privately, and not every employee can be privy to every decision and conversation. But too much secrecy sends a message that says, "I am keeping things from you," or "You are not important enough for me to speak with directly." If you send your reports implicit messages like these, you can be certain that you'll get the same in return. That means even if your employees are aware of problems, they won't share that information with you, and you'll lose out on valuable opportunities to nip problems in the bud.

On the other hand, if you communicate directly with the people who report to you, they'll recognize that you see their insights and participation as valuable and fundamental to the team's success. That means they'll keep you informed about what's going on.

There are several ways you can foster open communication with your employees. These include:

- **Meet regularly with your entire team.** This will send the message that you all work together and solve problems together. It will help everyone keep abreast of the status of each others' workloads and provide a platform to discuss departmental and company-wide goals or problems.
- **Keep the closed door to a minimum.** If you are having a private meeting, keep the door shut. However, if you are working and can be interrupted, stay accessible by keeping the door open and encouraging your employees to talk to you as needed.
- **Treat all team members professionally.** It's natural that you might feel more comfortable with some team members than others. However, be aware that developing those relationships can create a perception that you're "playing favorites." Be particularly careful about talking to your employees about each other, even in a strictly professional context.
- **Keep your employees informed about what you're doing.** Avoid resentment by keeping your team informed about what you're up to. They'll appreciate that it's a two-way street.

Build a Culture of Ownership

Another way to keep the lines of communication open with your employees is to create a "culture of ownership": An environment where each employee is invested in the company's success and takes personal responsibility for both accomplishments and failures. Creating this type of culture gives employees an incentive to share their concerns, because their own success will depend on the success of the company.

	Hierarchy	Shared Ownership
Setting Goals	Manager delegates tasks to be completed within a certain time frame.	Team looks at shared goals and determines roles and timelines together.
Briefing Upper Management	Manager creates a PowerPoint slide show on team accomplishments and presents it to senior management.	Each team member creates slides showcasing his or her areas of responsibility, and the team presents the slide show to senior management together.
Hiring	The manager tells the team that a new employee has been hired just before—or even after—that person starts work.	The team participates in creating the job description and the interview process and has input on the hiring decision.
Budgeting	Each quarter, employees are told how much money they can spend and what they can spend it on during the next three months.	Each quarter, each employee submits budget requests for proposed projects that include a cost/benefit analysis explaining why the project should be considered.

If your company offers employees real ownership, through benefits like stock options and profit-sharing plans, that will certainly help. But there are many other ways to create a culture of shared ownership. The best way to start is by making sure that each of your employees understands how he or she fits into the big picture. In other words, how the employee doing his or her job well helps the company succeed. Aligning individual goals with the company's goals, rewarding performance that supports the company's success, and engaging your employees in coming up with business solutions are all ways to create shared ownership.

Use the chart above to identify some specific opportunities to create shared ownership in your own company:

When you give employees a sense of ownership, you are much more likely to find out about problems and opportunities early. Employees who feel a sense of ownership care about the success of the team as a whole, so they're going to tell you when they think something will inhibit the team. This gives you the opportunity to look into problems that you otherwise might not even have known about.

> **CAUTION**
>
> **Encourage teamwork, not backstabbing.** Some employees view an information-sharing environment as an invitation to monitor and criticize their coworkers, particularly if each employee's performance will be judged, in part, by how well the team does as a whole. Fostering shared ownership does not mean building a culture where employees try to throw each other under the bus at the first sign of trouble. Make clear to your team that they must work together to accomplish their collective goals and that each team member has a unique contribution to make.

Look for Signs of Trouble

Sometimes, the hardest part of identifying employee problems or potential problems is seeing the warning signs that precede them. While communicating with your employees gives you an opportunity to identify problems, you also need to know what specific conduct might signify that trouble is brewing.

Signs of trouble often fit into three categories:
- declining performance
- changed behavior, or
- tension in your team.

Essentially, you should be looking for changes in the way your employees conduct themselves. This means you have to understand how your employees act and behave under normal circumstances, so you can recognize changes when they occur.

Declining Performance
When an employee has a drastic drop in output or suddenly misses every deadline, it's easy to see that there's a problem. Much more difficult to

recognize are problems that begin with subtle changes in the performance of a normally good employee. It is easy to ignore declining performance if it is not typical for an employee. You may even be tempted to rationalize away the decline because you don't want to come down too hard on someone who usually does a good job.

> **EXAMPLE:** Justin has been with ABC Mills for four years. His performance reviews show he is one of the highest performers in the company. As a result, his boss, Mary, has made him one of her "go-to" guys. She gives him a large number of complex projects and knows that she can rely on him to get them done.
>
> Justin is fast approaching a project milestone. He needs to have a complete analysis of the milling process ready by Friday, so Mary's team can begin the next phase of the project: looking for ways to streamline and improve the process. Mary meets with Justin on Friday, confident that she will be seeing the process analysis. Justin tells Mary that the analysis is not quite finished and asks for a few more days. She gives him another week.
>
> Mary has complete confidence in Justin, so much so that she neglects to ask him a very important question: Why is he having trouble getting the project milestone done? Her confidence in him is preventing her from considering that he may need help with the project or that there may be other forces that are causing him to miss deadlines.

When an employee's performance declines, make sure you understand why. Talk to the employee about it as soon as you recognize it. If the employee is overworked or overwhelmed, you may need to decrease his or her workload, get additional help, or provide more training. On the other hand, if there are no good reasons for the changes, you may need to begin the discipline process.

Changes in Behavior

After you've worked with your employees for a while, you'll get to know quite a bit about their work styles and personalities. One employee may be naturally extroverted, talking to you and other employees about every aspect of the job. Another may be quiet or shy, reluctant to disturb anyone unnecessarily.

But when an employee's behavior begins to change, you should immediately ask why. There can be many different reasons: It may signal that the employee is unhappy with the work environment, coworkers, or the workload. In other instances, it may be related to issues at home. The behavior changes that you need to address are those that either are inappropriate for the workplace or have the potential to negatively affect the employee's performance.

Behavioral changes that are warning signs of potential problems include:

- **Withdrawal.** An employee's participation in group meetings, one-on-ones, or other team gatherings decreases.
- **Quick to anger or frustration.** An employee seems to be set off by the smallest things or is easily frustrated.
- **Excessive absenteeism or tardiness.** An employee is out of the office more than normal or shows up later than usual.
- **Discomfort or tension.** An employee who normally seems comfortable interacting with you seems ill at ease around you, and maybe even avoids you.

These are just a few of the changes in behavior that may signal more serious problems. As mentioned, any unexplained negative change in behavior can be cause for concern. Whenever you observe a negative behavior change your first step is simple: Talk to the employee. Explain what you see and give examples. Find out if the employee realizes that his or her behavior has changed. Sometimes, an employee isn't aware of how his or her behavior is coming off. Other times, the employee may need to discuss the problems or get additional help. He or she may even appreciate that you noticed the change.

TIP

Avoid making it personal. When you approach an employee about a behavioral change, stick to objective facts and focus on the impact that the behavior is having on the employee's work. For example, instead of saying "You seem upset and sad a lot," say "You have not been contributing at meetings lately" and then ask what is going on.

Tension in the Team

Sometimes, potential problems will manifest themselves not in individual performance or behavior, but in team performance or behavior. At times, your team may operate like a well-oiled machine, everyone knowing the importance of his or her individual role and the role of the team as a whole. At other times, friction may cause parts of the machine to grind together. Employees may treat each other differently, or team objectives may not be met.

When you see this friction, find its source. It may be the pressure of a heavy workload or something more insidious, such as one team member who is working against the others. To figure this out, you may have to ask different team members for their perspectives, until you get a full picture.

> **EXAMPLE:** Jerry manages a team of carpenters who are building a custom home on a tight deadline. At the end of each day, the team has a ten-minute status meeting to monitor overall progress. Because steps in the process must be completed in a very specific order—for example, the roof must be laid before the floor is—these meetings keep the team communicating and ensures that they stay on the project timeline.
>
> During a status meeting one day, Jerry notices that the normal joking and teasing amongst the team is not occurring and that everyone seems sullen or uncomfortable. After the meeting is over, Jerry asks Mike, one of the natural leaders on the team, to stay behind. "What's going on, Mike?" Jerry asks. "It seemed like folks weren't themselves today." Mike is quiet a moment, then replies, "You probably want to ask Leslie that question." Jerry digs deeper and discovers that Leslie has showed up late for three straight days and asked the team not to tell Jerry. Because this could delay the overall project, the team had grown increasingly uncomfortable about having to cover for Leslie.

As this example illustrates, team tension may signal not only problems for the team as a cohesive unit, but problems for individual employees as well. Although the whole team was delayed, the problem here was really Leslie's, and Jerry might not have discovered the problem if he hadn't taken the time to follow up on the changed behavior of other team members.

If your employees seem to have trouble working together, and interact in a way that is unfamiliar or uncomfortable, be sure to find out why. You'd rather know before the problem gets serious, and you're fortunate to have easy access to the very people—your employees—who know this information.

SMART SUMMARY:
Identifying Potential Problems

- There are three broad categories of employee problems: performance problems, attendance problems, and misconduct. Sometimes, an employee will have trouble in one of these areas, and it will affect another. In those instances, make sure your discipline addresses the root of the problem.

- If your employees don't know what your expectations are, they're likely to disappoint you. Take the time to define your expectations of performance and behavior, giving your employees full opportunity to grow and succeed.

- Communicating regularly and openly with your employees keeps you up to speed on how they're doing and gives you advance warning of possible problems. At the same time, it gives employees a sense of ownership and investment in their jobs, motivating them to succeed.

- To help spot employee problems, look for signs of trouble like declining performance, changed behavior, and tension among team members.

Deciding What Action to Take

Once an employee issue comes to your attention, you must decide whether and how to intervene. In some instances, discipline might not be the right response; you might decide instead to make a note to yourself to monitor the situation or even reconsider the wisdom of a particular rule or policy. Even if you know you'll have to take action (for example, because an employee has made a serious mistake, engaged in obvious misconduct, or been counseled about the same problem already), you'll have to decide what type of corrective measure to use.

In many cases, the appropriate corrective measure is immediately obvious. For extreme misconduct, such as blatant harassment, theft, or violence, termination of employment is often appropriate. For first-time performance issues or minor misconduct, you will typically want to follow each disciplinary measure in your company's policy in sequence, starting with the least serious (coaching, in our model policy). However, there are plenty of employee problems that fall somewhere between these two extremes. And sometimes, you're faced with one employee who exhibits a number of failings, all of which add up to one big problem.

In this chapter, we'll explain how to decide whether discipline is in order, gauge the effect and seriousness of the problem you're facing, and use that information to come up with the right disciplinary response.

Is Discipline Appropriate?

Before you think about what type of corrective measure might be appropriate, you have to decide whether to discipline at all. In some situations, it might not be fair—or legally defensible—to hold an employee responsible for a workplace problem.

To make this decision, you must be able to answer three questions:

1. Did the employee know of the performance, conduct, or other standard that was violated?
2. Did the employee actually violate that standard?
3. Did the employee have a legal right to do so?

In many cases, the answers to these questions will be obvious. For example, let's say you tell an employee to complete an assignment by the end of the month. The employee misses the deadline by a few days and tells you that she's late because she didn't realize how long the assignment would take. Your performance expectations were clear, the employee didn't meet them, and nothing in her explanation demonstrates that she had a legally protected right to blow the deadline. This is probably all you need to know before moving on to consider the severity of the problem and decide how to intervene.

In some situations, however, you'll need more information to decide whether discipline is appropriate. What you learn may convince you that there isn't a problem after all, or that the problem really lies with you, the company, or another employee, not with the employee who you originally thought was at fault.

Did the Employee Know the Rule?

Start by taking a close look at the policy, rule, or standard that appears to have been violated. Did the employee know what you, or the company, expected? As long as the employee was aware of the rule that applied here, it's fair to impose discipline for violating it. On the other hand, if the rule was not obvious, not communicated, not achievable, not consistently applied, or not clear, discipline is probably not a fair response.

Here are some guidelines to determine whether the employee knew—or should have known—that his or her behavior could result in discipline:

- **Written company policies.** Did the employee's conduct violate company policy, as expressed in the employee handbook or other documents distributed to employees?
- **Company practices and procedures.** Did the employee violate a rule or custom known in the workplace, even if not written down?
- **Your instructions.** Did you tell the employee what you required (for example, deadlines for a project, numerical goals or quotas, quality standards, or dress code requirements)?
- **Job requirements.** Did the employee understand what to do based on, for example, the job description or orientation process?
- **Performance goals.** Did the employee's performance appraisals or discussions with you about performance state the company's expectations?

- **The law.** Are the employee's actions illegal? For example, did the employee commit unlawful harassment, steal from the company or its customers, or threaten to harm someone?
- **Common sense.** Was the employee's behavior obviously inappropriate or dangerous, even if it isn't illegal or explicitly prohibited by company policies?

EXAMPLE: Sam is upset with Scott, the warehouse manager, who recently gave him a lukewarm performance appraisal. Sam decides to get back at Scott by playing a prank. He comes in on the weekend, moves all of the furniture and decorations out of Scott's office, and recreates the office on the warehouse floor. Sam's joke disrupts an entire shift of work and creates a hazard for the other warehouse employees; it's also very disrespectful of Scott's authority and personal space. Although this probably isn't illegal, and most companies don't expressly prohibit relocating someone else's workspace, Sam should be disciplined.

If you conclude that the employee had fair notice of the possible consequences of his or her behavior, you can move on to the next step. If not, however, you might have to plan some training, communicate your expectations better, or enforce the rules more consistently. This will lay the groundwork for discipline if the rule is violated in the future. It may even help prevent problems in the first place because your employees will better understand your expectations and the consequences of failing to meet them.

EXAMPLE: Jeanette is heading to a meeting and is waiting impatiently for the agenda to show up on the department's printer. Jeanette has to wait through someone else's print job, a scholarly article on the Amazon rainforest. Because the company produces database software, Jeanette knows the article is not work related.

Sarah, one of Jeanette's reports, shows up to get the article. When Jeanette asks what it's for, Sarah says that her husband, an anthropology student, asked her to print it out for him. Jeanette says, "Sarah, you know that our employee handbook says you can't use company property for personal reasons."

Sarah is flustered, and replies, "Oh, I didn't know that applied to the printer. It seems like everyone uses the printer to print party invitations, directions, and other personal stuff, so I figured it was okay to print this."

Thinking about it, Jeanette realizes Sarah is right. She also realizes she has used the printer and copier for personal items herself. Jeanette decides not to discipline

Sarah. In fact, she realizes it wasn't really fair to reprimand her, given the confusion over what the company's policy means. She stops by Sarah's office and says, "You know, Sarah, you're right. The company is sending mixed signals about printer use and it's leading to confusion. I was especially concerned today because I was waiting for an important document and it was delayed because of personal use. I'll talk to human resources so we can figure out what the policy is for everyone." Jeanette then consults with the human resources department to clarify what the policy requires. Once the policy is clarified, Jeanette explains it to her reports and enforces that interpretation consistently.

Did the Employee Violate the Rule?

Once you've determined that the employee knew of your—or the company's —expectations, you must consider whether a particular employee's performance or conduct actually fell short of the mark. To answer this question, you might have to investigate the situation to make sure that you know exactly what happened: that wrongdoing actually occurred and that the employee you plan to discipline is actually responsible for it.

Whenever you are uncertain about key facts, you should investigate. This comes up most often when there is employee misconduct, particularly if anonymous wrongdoing occurs (for example, racist graffiti shows up in the company washroom or an unpopular manager's car is keyed in the parking lot) or if one employee accuses another of harassment, intimidation, or other interpersonal misconduct. In these situations, you'll need to talk to the employees involved, examine any related documents or other evidence, and reach a conclusion as to what actually happened.

RELATED TOPIC

Need information on how to investigate? Pick up a copy of *The Essential Guide to Workplace Investigations*, by Lisa Guerin (Nolo). It includes step-by-step instructions on investigating misconduct and other problems, with special emphasis on harassment, discrimination, theft, violence, and substance abuse. The book also includes detailed information on how to conduct interviews, gather evidence, decide what to do, and document your findings.

On rare occasions, however, you might have to investigate a performance or attendance issue, too. Again, these occasions typically involve more than one employee. For example, if two employees are known not to get along, and one accuses the other of taking frequent and long breaks, you might want to investigate (by keeping an eye on the employee accused of loafing or by talking to both employees) before you step in. Similarly, if you assigned a project to a team of employees, they might blame each other for missing important deadlines. You might have to sit down with each team member to get to the bottom of things.

Did the Employee Have a Legal Right to Break the Rule?

You may not discipline an employee who violates a workplace rule or standard if he or she was exercising a legal right. For example, an employee has the legal right to take time off for jury duty. If all of your employees are required to go to an important training session on a particular day, and an employee is unable to attend because of jury duty, you may not discipline that employee for failing to show up.

Here are a few situations when an employee might have a legal right to violate a workplace rule or requirement:

- **The employee takes time off for a legally protected reason.** As explained above, you may not discipline an employee for taking legally protected leave, even if the employee is absent longer than your policies ordinarily allow or misses important events as a result. See Chapter 3 for more information on legally protected time off.
- **The employee refuses to work because of unsafe conditions.** Employees have a legal right, pursuant to the Occupational Safety and Health Act (OSH Act), to refuse to work if they believe that they are in imminent danger of serious harm or death due to unsafe workplace conditions or procedures. However, employees may exercise this right only if the employer refuses to correct the condition and the hazard is so urgent that there's no time to address the condition by making a complaint to the Occupational Safety and Health Administration (OSHA).
- **The employee refuses to participate in illegal conduct.** Many states allow employees to sue their current or former employers if they are

disciplined or fired for refusing to do something illegal. For example, if an employee is disciplined or fired for refusing to make false statements to the government or misstate the company's income on shareholder documents, that employee probably has a pretty good legal claim against the company.

- **The employee is entitled to a reasonable accommodation.** As explained in Chapter 3, an employee with a disability may be entitled to a reasonable accommodation, which might include bending the usual workplace rules. For example, an employee who is taking antidepressants that make him groggy in the morning might ask to come in to work a couple of hours later. Even if your company requires everyone to report to work at 9:00 a.m., it might be reasonable to allow one person to come in a bit later.

You can find more information on these legal protections in Chapter 3.

How Serious Is the Problem?

Now you know what type of problem you're facing, and you've decided that corrective action is appropriate. Your next step is to figure out how serious the problem is so that you can choose an appropriate disciplinary response: One that communicates the importance of the problem and demonstrates the company's concern with getting it resolved.

Even if you know what disciplinary measure you will use—because it's dictated by company policy, for example—you should still review this section and consider each of the factors listed below. Your meeting with the employee will be more productive if you've organized your thoughts and can explain how the employee's behavior is causing problems for the company. This information will help the employee take responsibility for his or her actions and help both of you come up with an effective solution.

Here are some factors to consider when analyzing how serious a problem is (each is explained in detail below):

- the effect of the behavior
- the frequency of the behavior
- the employee's disciplinary history, and
- the legality of the behavior.

Effect

How has the employee's misconduct, poor performance, or attendance problem affected the company? Because effective discipline requires a proportionate response, a problem that has caused major damage should be met with a more serious disciplinary measure than a problem that has had very little impact on anyone.

Here are some things to consider when analyzing how a problem has affected the company:

- **Cost.** How much money has been spent—or how much money has the business missed out on—because of the employee's behavior? Putting a price on the employee's behavior will really help the employee see why things need to change.
- **Time.** How much time have you and other employees had to spend dealing with the employee's problem? For example, have coworkers had to put their work aside to cover for a tardy employee or finish a project the employee failed to complete?
- **Lost opportunities.** Sometimes, an employee's behavior botches a future sale, partnership, or other business opportunity.
- **Damage to relationships.** Has the employee's behavior caused tension on your team or soured interactions with a customer or client? Has morale on your team suffered?
- **Damage to reputation.** If the employee's problems caused you or your team to miss an important deadline, do poor-quality work, fail to hit your numbers, or otherwise not pull your weight within the company, this makes your team look bad (and hurts your reputation as a manager). Even worse, if the problem affects your relationships with customers or clients, the company's reputation could suffer.
- **Legal exposure.** If the employee breached a contract, violated the legal rights of coworkers or customers, or otherwise broke the law, the company might be liable to third parties for damages.
- **Future problems.** Don't limit yourself to considering the immediate effect of the problem. To really get through to the employee, you should also think about what could happen if the problem continues or gets worse: The consequences can become even more serious, and the long-term costs even higher.

EXAMPLE: Ed manages a small group of in-house recruiting professionals, who are responsible for finding and landing candidates for open positions in a large multinational company. Each recruiter has a monthly target number of hires. Ed also uses some qualitative standards to measure each recruiter's performance.

- Sharon reports to Ed and has consistently maintained excellent recruiting numbers; in fact, she exceeds her monthly targets regularly. However, Ed has heard from another manager, June, that Sharon pushed her very hard to take on a candidate that June didn't feel was fully qualified. This is a red flag for Ed, who knows that when it comes to hiring, it's about quality first and quantity second. Ed talks to the other managers with whom Sharon has placed candidates in the last few months and hears the same criticism from another manager, Sam. The others seem happy with Sharon's work.

- Ed considers the effect of Sharon's behavior. If her hires succeed, this demonstrates that Sharon doesn't have a problem with her recruiting skills, but instead with her ability to convey to the managers exactly how a particular candidate will be able to meet their needs. Because Sharon has strained her relationship with June and Sam, Ed could coach her on how to repair her relationships—and communicate more clearly—with the company's managers.

- Now assume that one or both of the hires does not work out. This exposes an entirely different—and more significant—problem, with a far greater impact on the company. The company will have to spend time and money trying to help these hires improve. If they cannot improve, the company might have to fire them and find replacements, which will cost the company tens of thousands of dollars. On top of that, Sharon's pressure tactics and poor judgment in choosing candidates could sour the other managers on the recruiters' ability to do their jobs and harm the recruiting team's reputation in the company. In this scenario, Ed might justifiably decide to skip the coaching and move right to a verbal or written warning, to make very clear to Sharon that her behavior is causing the company harm and must stop immediately.

Assessing the impact of an employee's problem will help you come up with a proportionate disciplinary response. While it might seem time-consuming to think this through every time you have to discipline an employee, you'll soon get the hang of it. Once you start thinking about how a problem is affecting the company, you'll find yourself weighing these factors automatically, without having to sit down and consider every item on the list.

Frequency

How many times has the employee exhibited this particular problem? Often, a recurring problem merits a stronger response, particularly if you've already had to discipline the employee for the same behavior. (See "Disciplinary History," below, for more on this issue.) If the employee simply isn't taking your coaching seriously, or is trying to "get away with" troubling behavior, you need to demonstrate that you will enforce the company's rules through escalating discipline.

However, repeat offenders aren't always asking for stronger discipline. Sometimes, recurring problems are a sign that the employee either doesn't understand what you expect or doesn't understand why. In this situation, your job is to explain exactly what the rules are and why it's important for the employee to follow them.

> **EXAMPLE:** Marissa works for an event planning company. The company puts on parties, conventions, training programs, and other gatherings for corporate clients. The team plans events from start to finish, coordinating food, entertainment, media presentations, and so on; supervising outside vendors and contractors; booking the space and making arrangements for those who attend; and working the floor during the event.
>
> When Marissa was hired, she was told that she was to prepare a brief weekly report covering each event's progress for her supervisor, Carrie. During the first few months of her employment, Marissa dutifully handed in her reports every week. However, Marissa's last few reports have been late and haven't included sufficient detail.
>
> Carrie meets with Marissa to discuss the situation. Because this has become a recurring problem, Carrie is thinking of issuing a verbal warning. But when she asks Marissa what's going on, Marissa says, "I didn't know those reports were important. I used to do them right away, and I spent an hour or more on them, but you never said anything about what I wrote. I guess I figured it was just a paperwork requirement. We're so busy right now, and I assumed you'd want me to prioritize the TechnoSoft event and get to the reports later."
>
> Carrie realizes that Marissa doesn't understand why the reports are important, in part, because Carrie hasn't done a good job of making that clear. Carrie tells her, "I'm sorry that I didn't talk to you about the reports you've already done. I should have explained to you what I use them for and why they're so important. As you

know, we have a long list of preferred vendors, contractors, and venues, and one of my job responsibilities is to constantly update that list and stay on top of those relationships. If someone on our list is coming in over budget, showing up late, or otherwise not satisfying the client, I need to know right away so I can get involved. I also want to know someone on our list is doing a great job. If they are already on the list, I'll try to throw more work their way. If not, I'll consider adding them."

When Marissa hears this, she understands the purpose of the reports, what she should include in them, and why it's important to hand them in on time. She tells Carrie, "I'm really sorry I didn't run this by you first. I guess I just assumed that this wasn't a priority."

Carrie responds, "It sounds like we had a misunderstanding, and I'm also sorry I wasn't clear about this. I do need for you to prioritize these reports; will you do that for me?" Marissa agrees to get the reports done on time, every week, and the meeting is over. Because Carrie is partially responsible for the situation, she decides to call it a coaching session rather than issue a verbal warning.

Disciplinary History

Of course, you should also consider whether the employee has already been disciplined—by you or a previous manager—when deciding whether and what type of discipline is appropriate. The weight you give to prior discipline should depend on whether the discipline was for the same problem or for something else entirely.

Prior Discipline for the Same Problem

If the employee has already been disciplined for the same behavior, it's time to escalate your response. Before you proceed, though, take a hard look at the solutions you came up with last time around, to make sure that the employee had all of the resources and support necessary to succeed. Assuming that you didn't give the employee impossible goals or impose unrealistic requirements, you should take the employee's continued problems as a sign that stronger discipline is necessary.

Before you make your final decision, however, you should also consider how long it's been since the problem last occurred. Part of helping employees improve is reinforcing the message that problems can be overcome. If you consider problems from the distant past when dealing with an immediate issue, that message can be contradicted. For example, an employee who had an attendance problem several years ago, but has since turned things around, may be entitled to a clean slate if the issue reoccurs. On the other hand, an employee who persists in taking unauthorized days off month after month should face a more serious disciplinary measure.

To deal with this issue, some companies give disciplinary measures a "shelf life." For example, a verbal or written warning might be removed from the employee's file—and not used in future disciplinary decisions—after a year without any further problems. If your company has a policy like this, you shouldn't consider any disciplinary actions taken before the cutoff date.

Prior Discipline for Other Problems

Employees who exhibit a variety of problems on the job can be very tough to manage. On the one hand, every new problem is a new opportunity to coach and correct. The employee might not understand what you expect or might need some help or training to get the job done right. This is why some human resource experts advise managers to treat each new problem as a separate issue and allow the employee to advance through the disciplinary process for each one.

On the other hand, an employee who exhibits multiple problems can cause a lot of disruption and take up a lot of your time. It can be very frustrating for a manager to have to restart the process every time an employee misbehaves. And sometimes, these multiple offenders are really demonstrating one big problem: a lack of respect for your company's rules and/or for you as a manager. In this situation, you're really dealing with insubordination, a serious form of misconduct that must be met with strong discipline.

> **EXAMPLE:** You supervise Ted, an employee who has an attendance problem. After Ted failed to call in on two occasions to explain he wasn't going to be in, as required, you had a coaching session. You issued a verbal warning when Ted continued to violate the company's attendance policy. Now, Ted has failed to complete his portion of a project your team has been working on for a month. Should you escalate to a written warning for Ted's overall failure to meet the job's requirements, or plan a coaching session to focus on the performance problem as a separate issue?

The answer depends on the facts. If Ted is showing improvement in other ways, or if the current problem is the result of the earlier (now solved) problem, you might want to start again with coaching. Let's say, for instance, that Ted seems to have turned things around with his attendance. He was having trouble arranging care for his ailing mother and had to take days off unexpectedly. Now, his caretaking situation is worked out, and he's been showing up diligently every day. If his earlier absences led him to miss the deadline for the team project, you might want to have a coaching session. Because he seems to have solved his attendance problem, you could simply point out that missing deadlines is one consequence of unexcused absences, and that you expect things to change now that he's back at work regularly.

Now, consider how you'd respond if the facts were different. Ted's attendance problem is continuing, and he isn't responding to your efforts to help him improve. During your verbal warning session, Ted said, "You know, I need a day off sometimes for personal reasons. If that violates your rules, then I'm sorry."

When he misses the deadline for the team project, Ted reacts angrily to your questions about it, saying, "That deadline was arbitrary anyway. I know you have until Friday to finalize that project. You gave me the hardest part of the work, and you're just going to have to wait until I have time to finish it."

Responding to this with coaching would be irresponsible and ineffective. Ted is blatantly disregarding the company's rules and your authority, and he will continue to do so until he faces serious consequences. Allowing him to continue to behave this way will also do serious damage to your team's morale and your reputation as a manager. It will also cause Ted to believe that such behavior is acceptable. In this case, a written warning is needed.

Legality

If an employee does something illegal, your response must clearly communicate that the employee's actions are unacceptable and that the company will not condone illegal behavior. After all, as discussed in Chapter 3, your company might be held liable to others for harm caused by the employee's actions.

If you decide not to fire an employee who violates a law—for example, because the employee violated the law inadvertently or otherwise didn't understand the situation—you must make very sure that your response stops the problem. You also need to make sure that you've documented very thoroughly, just in case you have to justify your actions in the future.

EXAMPLE: Ralph works at a large property management company. He supervises a group of employees who find tenants for the apartment buildings the company manages in Los Angeles. Ralph's employees screen and select tenants, inspect the apartments, give approval for repairs and improvements, and so on.

Cyrus is one of Ralph's new employees. The company is upgrading the heating and cooling systems in some of its older buildings, so Ralph asks Cyrus to inspect the systems at a building he will be responsible for. Later that day, Ralph receives a phone call from an angry tenant, who complains that Cyrus just entered her apartment without giving any advance notice. Ralph immediately calls Cyrus and tells him to return to the office.

Ralph asks Cyrus to come into his office, and says, "I just got a call from a very distressed tenant, who says that you entered her apartment without any notice or warning. I'm sure you know that this is against the law unless there's an emergency. The company could get in big trouble for this." Cyrus looks panicked and says, "At my last job, our secretary handled all of the appointments with tenants. When you asked me to inspect the building, I guess I just assumed that someone had given the required notices. Oh man, I really screwed this up. I'm so sorry."

Because Cyrus didn't violate the law on purpose, and because he seems to have a plausible explanation for his error, Ralph decides not to fire him. On the other hand, Cyrus's actions could cause problems for the company, and Ralph doesn't want to invite legal trouble. Ralph gives Cyrus a written warning and explains in detail the company's procedures for entering apartments.

Choosing the Right Response

By this point, you've already done a lot of work. You've identified the problem, determined that discipline is appropriate, and decided how serious the problem is. Now, it's time to use all of this information to choose the right disciplinary response.

If you haven't already disciplined the employee for the same problem, you should consider whether it's appropriate to begin with the first step in the disciplinary process: coaching, in our model system. After all, one of the primary purposes of a discipline system is to give the employee notice of the problem and an opportunity to improve. The best way to do that is to begin with the least severe disciplinary measure and escalate your disciplinary response only if the employee fails to improve.

As you've no doubt learned from the previous sections, however, there are times when it would be irresponsible not to skip to a more serious disciplinary measure. If an employee has harmed someone, cost the company an important client, or damaged company property, for example, coaching the employee would send the message that the company doesn't take this behavior seriously. It could put people and property at risk, damage the company's reputation, bring down employee morale, and expose the company to legal liability. The trick is to figure out when coaching is the right response and when more serious discipline is in order.

Discipline for Poor Performance

Performance problems can often be resolved at the coaching level. In fact, many performance issues can be handled through simple requests or reminders ("I need those records returned to the central file at the end of each day, Bob, so they can be properly logged. Please make sure you don't leave any on your desk when you leave for the evening.") Particularly if a performance problem appears to stem from a misunderstanding about your expectations, coaching is often quite effective at turning things around.

So when should you consider skipping to a verbal or written warning? Here are some situations when moving to a more serious response might be appropriate:

- You (or another manager) already coached the employee on the same issue (for example, an employee transfers from another department where he or she was coached for problems with accuracy or speed, and continues to have the same problems in your department).
- The employee's performance problem has caused significant harm to the company (for example, the employee's failure to back up certain computer files resulted in important data being lost).
- The employee's poor performance has created legal liability for the company (for example, the employee threw confidential customer information into the garbage rather than shredding or otherwise destroying it).

Discipline for Attendance Problems

Like performance problems, first-time attendance or tardiness problems are typically handled through coaching. If the problem continues, you should escalate to a verbal warning and proceed through the other disciplinary measures provided by your company's policy.

In rare instances, however, you might want to skip straight to a verbal warning or a stronger disciplinary measure. Here are some circumstances when you should consider a more serious response:

- You (or another manager) already coached the employee on the same issue.
- The employee has essentially gone AWOL: that is, the employee has taken unauthorized leave and has not checked in with the company or responded to your efforts to reach him or her for more than a day or two. (Some companies deem that an employee has abandoned the job after several days of unexcused absences; in that case, the employee does not need to be disciplined because the employment relationship has ended, though it should be documented.) Unless the employee has a medical emergency or some other very good excuse, this type of behavior warrants a stronger response.
- The employee's absence or tardiness has caused significant damage (for example, the employee shows up an hour late for an important pitch meeting with a potential client, and the client decides to go with another company as a result).

Discipline for Misconduct

Unlike performance and attendance problems, which should almost always be met with coaching for a first offense, first-time misconduct can call for a more serious disciplinary response, depending on the problem. And termination of employment is the only appropriate way to handle certain types of extreme misconduct.

To decide on an appropriate disciplinary measure, you'll have to weigh the factors covered in "How Serious Is the Problem?," above. Typically, you'll want to consider a stronger response in the following cases:

- The employee endangered, or actually damaged, people or property.
- The employee disregarded important safety rules.

- The employee was insubordinate.
- The employee's misconduct involved dishonesty (for example, falsifying records).
- The employee's actions were illegal.

When to Consider Immediate Termination

There are some types of misconduct that justify termination of employment, even for a first-time offense. If an employee appears to have engaged in dangerous, illegal, or deceptive actions, you should investigate immediately. If your investigation reveals that the employee is to blame, you should seriously consider terminating employment.

Any of the following types of misconduct might justify immediate termination, without any second chances:

- **Violence.** This includes fighting with coworkers; pushing and shoving; throwing books, furniture, or office items; vandalizing company property; or any other physical acts taken with the intent to harm people or damage property.
- **Threats of violence.** Statements by a worker that he or she will harm, "get," or kill anyone (including himself or herself) or will bring a weapon to work merit immediate attention.
- **Stalking.** This comes up most often in cases of sexual harassment or workplace romance gone awry but can also arise out of pure hostility. For example, an employee may stalk a supervisor or manager in order to intimidate that person.
- **Possession of an unauthorized weapon.** Your workplace policies should clearly spell out that weapons are not allowed in the workplace unless authorized and necessary to perform work duties.
- **Theft or criminal behavior directed toward the company.** This includes embezzling, defrauding the company, or illegally using the company's intellectual property.
- **Dishonesty about important business issues.** The occasional fudge about progress on a project or reasons for taking time off is probably not a firing offense, but an employee who lies about whether orders have been filled, customers have been served, or important business goals have been met must be dealt with.

- **Use of illegal drugs or alcohol at work.** Using drugs or alcohol at work (other than drinking at company events where alcohol is served, such as office parties or happy hours), or showing up at work obviously impaired, is cause for concern. (See "Dealing with Drug and Alcohol Problems," below, for more information.)
- **Harassing or discriminatory conduct.** If an employee is accused of serious harassment—such as touching another employee sexually or insisting on sexual favors—you must look into it immediately. The same is true of discriminatory conduct (for example, using homophobic slurs, making sexist comments, or refusing to use vendors or contractors of a particular race).
- **Endangering health and safety in the workplace.** An employee who fails to follow important safety rules, uses machinery in a dangerous way, or exposes coworkers to injury—whether intentionally or through lack of care—could be a huge liability.
- **Assisting a competing business.** Revealing your company's trade secrets to a competitor or using its intellectual property to work for or start a competing company is extremely serious misconduct.

Dealing With Drug and Alcohol Problems

Employees who abuse alcohol and drugs (including illegal drugs, prescription drugs, and over-the-counter drugs) can pose significant and wide-ranging problems for their employers and their managers. These employees often have poor performance or productivity and high rates of absenteeism and tardiness. They can also make a workplace more volatile and more dangerous, and they can expose your company to increased legal liability.

Alcohol Use at Work

Your company's policies should clearly state that drinking on the job is not allowed. (If current policies don't speak to this, raise the issue with your manager, human resources, or legal counsel.) If you catch an employee actually consuming alcohol at work, you should impose discipline. The disciplinary measure you use should depend on the circumstances, including whether the employee has to deal with customers or clients, whether the employee has a safety-sensitive position, and how impaired the employee gets.

EXAMPLE: Cynthia manages the bookkeeping department for a chain of department stores. One day, she sees six of the department's secretaries having a party in a conference room, near closing time. When she enters, she sees that they are sharing cake and a bottle of champagne to celebrate a coworker's fiftieth birthday. Although this is against company rules, the secretaries are almost done with their work day, don't deal with customers, and don't have to operate heavy machinery or otherwise carry out potentially dangerous tasks. None of them is drunk. Cynthia decides that a verbal warning is appropriate.

Now, let's say Cynthia supervises the loading dock for the same department store chain. She is at a meeting for company managers all morning. When she returns to the loading dock after lunch, she hears lots of loud noise. She learns that, while she was out, some of the workers picked up a keg of beer, and they are drinking while listening to a World Cup soccer game. They have also invited some of the delivery drivers to join them. These workers drive, operate forklifts and other heavy equipment, and load and unload very heavy items. While none of them seems completely bombed, Cynthia places all of the workers who have been drinking on immediate suspension and calls cabs to take all of them home. After investigating the incident, she decides to terminate the employment of the two ringleaders and give written warnings to the others.

Use of Legal Drugs

Many employees properly use prescribed or over-the-counter drugs, such as sleeping aids, cold medication, or painkillers. Sometimes, however, an employee's use of legal drugs can affect his or her ability to do the job safely and well. For example, a medication that causes drowsiness might make it dangerous for a worker to do a job that requires driving.

In this situation, federal and state laws that prohibit disability discrimination might limit your options. As explained in Chapter 3, a company has a legal duty to provide a reasonable accommodation to an employee with a disability, and this duty extends to accommodating the employee's use of legal drugs that are necessary to treat the disability. If you discover that an employee's on-the-job impairment is caused by drugs used to treat a disability, you should discuss the matter with your employee and try to come up with a reasonable accommodation. (You can find lots of helpful information on various types of accommodations at the website of the Job Accommodation Network, www.askjan.org.)

Often, you will find that an employee who is impaired by an over-the-counter or legally prescribed drug is taking the drug for the first time and didn't know how it would affect him or her. In this situation, it's best to send the employee home (after arranging for safe transportation) and discuss the matter later. As long as this is a one-time occurrence, a coaching session is probably appropriate.

Choosing the Right Response		
Type of Problem:	**You Should:**	**Consider Stronger Discipline If:**
Poor performance	Coach	• Employee has already been coached for the same problem • Employee's problem caused significant harm to the company • Employee's problem created legal liability for the company
Poor attendance/ tardiness	Coach	• Employee has already been coached for the same problem • Employee has gone AWOL • Employee's absence has caused significant harm to the company
Misconduct	Determine how serious the problem is	• Employee endangered or actually damaged people or property • Employee disregarded important safety rules • Employee was insubordinate • Employee's misconduct involved dishonesty (for example, falsifying records) • Employee's actions were illegal
Problems relating to drugs and alcohol	Determine how serious the problem is	• Employee deals with customers or clients • Employee holds a safety-sensitive position • Employee endangered or actually harmed other people or property • Employee's actions were illegal

Use and Possession of Illegal Drugs

If an employee is under the influence of illegal drugs at work, disability rights laws do not limit your options. If the employee has not created a safety threat and does not hold a highly sensitive position, a written warning might be appropriate. However, if the employee endangers the physical safety of others, something more drastic is called for. If the employee has a drug abuse problem, one option is to suspend the employee until he or she successfully completes a treatment program. Some employers, however, opt for a zero-tolerance policy.

Because using or selling illegal drugs is a crime, most employers immediately terminate employment when employees engage in this type of behavior at work.

SMART SUMMARY:
Deciding What Action to Take

- Before deciding to discipline, make sure the employee knew the rule that was violated, actually violated the rule without good reason, and isn't protected by law from complying with the rule.

- When deciding what level of discipline is appropriate, remember that the discipline should be proportionate to the problem. Consider the effect of the problem, the frequency of the problem, the employee's disciplinary history, and the legality of the behavior.

- In most instances, when an employee first exhibits poor performance, you can begin the discipline process at the very beginning: by coaching the employee.

- Some behavior is so serious that immediate termination of employment should be considered. Typically, this is true when an employee engages in seriously inappropriate misconduct, such as violence, stalking, dishonesty, use of illegal drugs at work, or harassment.

Build Your Skills: Is It Time for Discipline?

Questions

1. What are the three types of employee problems?

   _____

   _____

   _____

   _____

2. When an employee has a problem in one area that causes problems in another area, you must discipline that employee twice.　☐ True　☐ False

3. Which of these will help you define your expectations of employee performance?

   a. The job description.

   b. Individual performance goals.

   c. Both A and B.

   d. Neither A nor B.

4. Esther tells Fred that she needs a report "on her desk" by Friday. On Friday at 6:30 p.m., Fred puts the report in her "in" basket. Esther is already gone for the day, and she's flying to a regional office on Monday morning. She needs the report for that trip. Since Fred didn't bring it to her until Friday evening, and he didn't email it to her, she wants to discipline him. Is discipline justified?

   a. Yes, because Fred should have known that "by Friday" meant by the close of business—5 p.m.—on Friday.

   b. Yes, because Fred should have emailed her the report.

   c. No, but only if Esther's usual practice was to receive hard copies instead of email.

   d. No, because Esther never specified that the report needed to be handed in by 5 p.m. or emailed to her.

5. When an employee's behavior changes in a negative way, it could mean that a discipline problem is developing.　☐ True　☐ False

6. It isn't fair to discipline an employee for an inappropriate action or behavior if company policy didn't prohibit it; after all, the employee had no way of knowing the behavior wasn't allowed. ☐ True ☐ False

7. In which of these situations is it probably appropriate to first coach an employee, before moving to a more serious form of discipline?

   a. The employee makes some small calculation errors on a department efficiency analysis report, which goes to the department manager, the employee's boss.

   b. The employee fails to show up to work or call in sick for two days in a row.

   c. The employee plays a practical joke on a coworker, yanking the chair out from under her when she's about to sit down for a meeting. The coworker falls to the ground, injuring herself.

   d. None of the above.

8. You should always give employees a second chance before terminating employment. ☐ True ☐ False

9. You should terminate the employment of anyone using drugs or alcohol at work. ☐ True ☐ False

10. If an employee repeats the same mistake over and over, progressive discipline requires you to escalate your response. ☐ True ☐ False

Answers

1. The three types of employee problems are performance problems, attendance problems, and misconduct.

2. False. Whether an employee needs to be disciplined for one or both problems depends on the facts of the specific situation. Usually, if you identify and fix the underlying problem, both problems will be solved. In the example in Chapter 4, Kristen spent too much time on the Internet in violation of company policy (misconduct), which meant she had a hard time getting her job done (poor performance). However, it's possible that just by disciplining her for using the Internet, her manager also solved her performance problem, because she'll now have more time to do her work.

3. C. A job's objective requirements, and individual performance goals, will help you define performance expectations. The job requirements will tell you what any person holding the position is expected to accomplish. Performance goals are just as important: They tell you what specific goals will nurture the employee's strengths, work on weaknesses, and build skills.

4. D. Managers commonly believe that some expectations are so obvious that they don't need to be verbalized. Then, they're disappointed when employees don't meet those expectations. Here, Esther expected Fred to get her the report by the close of business Friday or to email it to her. Unless she told Fred either of these things, though, it isn't really fair to discipline him. After all, he did get the report to her by Friday; he even stayed late to do it. Esther needs to be clearer about her expectations, so Fred will have the opportunity to meet them.

5. True. When an employee exhibits a negative behavioral change, you'll want to check in. It could mean that the employee is having a work-related problem that requires your intervention, or it could mean that the employee is having personal problems unrelated to his or her work or performance. Either way, getting involved shows the employee you care and gives you the opportunity to identify and perhaps prevent a workplace problem.

6. False. Although company policies give employees guidelines for acceptable behavior, they're not the only source. Some behavior that isn't specifically prohibited by company guidelines also justifies discipline (for example, if an employee violates the law or doesn't follow explicit instructions you've given).

7. A. Many employee performance problems can be overcome with coaching. Often coaching provides the opportunity to further educate an employee or identify additional resources to help the employee get the job done. In this case, the employee's errors didn't cause too much trouble because her boss caught them. The boss can use this opportunity to coach the employee and figure out whether additional resources are needed.

8. False. Some behavior is so egregious that it justifies immediate termination. If an employee's acts endanger or damage others or the employee's misconduct involves dishonesty, for example, termination is appropriate.

9. False. Although you can prohibit employees from drinking alcohol or using illegal drugs at work and can discipline employees for violating those rules, you must be careful when dealing with legal drugs. Your duty to provide reasonable accommodation to an employee with a disability may include accommodating the employee's use of drugs to treat or manage the disability.

10. False. Sometimes, employees repeat the same behavior because they don't understand what you expect or why. Before escalating discipline, consider whether the rule, and its rationale, were clearly laid out for the employee.

PART

III

Smart Performance Management Skills

Why Discipline Is Hard

Managing performance and conduct issues is not easy. More than most of your other responsibilities, it is fraught with complex emotions. After all, you're dealing with people who may be angry, hurt, or critical of you. And it's not only the employee's emotions that affect the process. You will probably struggle with some of your own emotions: the fear of confrontation, the need to be liked, and apprehension about what people might be saying about you.

Because these emotions can be so overwhelming, anticipating and understanding them before you enter the discipline process will help you avoid being stymied by them and allow you to focus on finding a solution to the problem at hand.

Understanding Your Emotions

Even though you probably don't spend too much of your work time actually disciplining employees, it is an essential part of your job as a manager. After all, your core responsibility is making sure that your team succeeds on all fronts. In order to maximize performance and efficiency, you have to hire the right people, set clear expectations, provide incentives for doing good work. And, on occasion, you must deal with employees who are not meeting your (or the company's) standards.

Recognizing that discipline is a necessary part of your job as a manager should help alleviate some of the stress that you may be feeling. However, you may still feel uncomfortable about imposing discipline. After all, it involves confrontation and criticism, and it can give rise to complicated emotions, both in you and in the employees you correct. Often, what you want on a personal level—for example, to be friendly, be liked, or avoid confrontation—will conflict with your managerial duty.

The best way to deal with these emotions is to anticipate and plan for them. This chapter is designed to help you deal with the stress of the discipline and help you deal with these realities:

- **Confrontation is awkward.** Having to confront someone about a problem can be difficult. It's easy to make excuses to avoid it.
- **It's tempting to be liked.** Who doesn't want to be popular? And giving people bad news, no matter how well deserved, can make you feel like the "bad guy."

- **You want to be fair.** Every situation is a little bit different, and it can be tough to be fair when dealing with performance and conduct issues.
- **The unknown is scary.** It is impossible to accurately predict how someone will react to bad news. Sometimes, when we don't know what to expect, the anticipation can be even more intimidating than the experience itself. What if others second-guess your decision, or the employee becomes so upset that he or she decides to talk to a lawyer?

This chapter will help you acknowledge these concerns and prepare yourself to deal with them, so you can enter the discipline process confidently.

Confrontation Is Awkward

Webster defines awkward as "Hard to deal with; especially causing pain or embarrassment." If ever a situation fit that definition, the discipline process is it. Nearly every step in the process has the potential to cause pain or embarrassment, often on both sides. You may feel uncomfortable criticizing an employee, especially if it's someone with whom you've always had a good relationship and genuinely like, or if you're discussing a mistake you've also made at some point in your career. And the employee probably feels awkward about being confronted with a shortcoming, especially if he or she is already aware of—and insecure about—the problem.

Here are a few dos and don'ts that will help you overcome this awkwardness and confront these matters head on.

Do:

- **Accept that you may feel uncomfortable.** Don't waste precious time trying to convince yourself that you should feel perfectly at ease or getting down on yourself for finding the situation awkward. It is a natural reaction, and it would be even more awkward to try to ignore it. Put your energy toward preparing to make the meeting as productive as possible.
- **Know that the employee may also feel awkward.** You may not want to point this out, but you should adapt your communication style to your employee's reaction. If the employee appears to be uncomfortable or embarrassed, you might want to provide an opportunity for him or her to get over that reaction. For example, you could say, "Why don't

we take a minute before we continue" or you could acknowledge that the situation is a bit uncomfortable.

- **Keep the conversation focused.** Even though you both may be uncomfortable, you are there to discipline, and that's what you'll have to do. Using a prefacing sentence can sometimes help to diffuse feelings of awkwardness, such as "I understand that this is uncomfortable, but I want to clearly communicate my concerns."

- **Allow enough time.** Don't rush the process. Despite your other pressing demands, allow enough time for you and your employee to work through the problem at hand. Both of you will feel more comfortable if you know that you'll have the opportunity to fully discuss your concerns and ideas.

Don't:

- **Lose the opportunity to collaborate.** Sometimes it's tempting to do anything you can to get out of an awkward situation as quickly as possible, but rushing through the conversation could cost you an otherwise productive dialogue. Listen closely to what your employee has to say. Stay in the moment and let the emotions run their course. You can still draw your employee into a constructive conversation, even if both of you feel a bit uncomfortable.

- **Be afraid of silence or emotions.** Give your employee time to process what you are saying as he or she sees fit (as long as it's appropriate for a work environment), even if that means you have to sit through some awkward silence. Accept that the employee may not say anything while processing, may respond with strong emotions, or might put you on the spot with questions like "Why didn't you tell me this before?" or "What did I do wrong?"

You Like to Be Liked

You've heard it before: "Carol is such a nice girl. She didn't deserve to be fired. I can't believe Chuck let her go. He is such a hard manager." Or, "Can you believe the nerve of that woman? She didn't even give Stan a chance before she wrote him up." When you discipline an employee, others who don't have the full story will probably speculate about what happened and they might blame you. Particularly if the employee is popular or especially vocal, you can expect to be perceived as the bad guy.

It's natural: We all liked to be liked. If you feel that you're being criticized unfairly, you may lose confidence and even start to second-guess your decisions. This "bad guy syndrome" is also frustrating because you usually don't get the chance to justify your actions or defend yourself.

Even if the gossip doesn't lead to criticism and blame, you may still feel excluded and ostracized as your employees talk to each other about what's going on in the workplace. You've probably participated in these "water cooler" discussions yourself—either earlier in your career, when you gossiped with coworkers, or now, when you have these discussions with other managers. Your employees do the same thing. They spend time catching up on each others' lives, dissecting last night's hit TV show, and speculating on management decisions that they know little about. These discussions—even when critical of management—are a natural occurrence and a necessary outlet. Your employees can and will talk about everything you do, how you do it, and whether you should have done it differently.

As a manager, you have to learn to rise above the chatter. If you are dealing with employee problems fairly and judiciously, and you are communicating constructively with the employee who is being disciplined, you have to trust your own decisions and overcome the need to be liked. Your job is not to manage the conversation flow out there, nor is it to defend yourself against what you may be hearing. And, as explained in Chapter 10, you could even get in trouble if you reveal too many details about a particular disciplinary situation to employees who don't have a need to know.

So what can you do to ease the pain? Here are some dos and don'ts to help you overcome your need to be liked when managing employees:

Do:

- **Keep your employees focused.** When discipline issues get employees sidetracked, you need to get your employees focused on their own ongoing responsibilities and performance. Often, it's necessary to remind your team what you expect and what success looks like. Although this won't entirely stop the gossip, it will keep employees busy and provide something more constructive to talk about.

- **Set clear expectations.** When all team members understand your expectations, they will also understand that discipline is the logical consequence of failing to meet them. The chatter and blame will subside when your employees see that the rules are clear and everyone gets a fair shot.
- **Know the facts.** Get all of the information you need to make the right decision. If you've worked to thoroughly understand the problem, you can take action confidently, without having to worry that one of your armchair quarterbacks will come up with something you missed.
- **Engage the employee.** If you've taken the time to get the employee's perspective, then you'll know you've also given the employee a fair shot. An employee who knows that you were listening respectfully may even be your best advocate when others second-guess your actions.

Don't:

- **Get defensive.** You do not need to explain your actions to your team, except to the person involved. Even then, you only need to demonstrate that discipline is the expected and justifiable response to the problem. Trying to justify your actions to other members of your team will only make you look weak and defensive, perhaps even unsure of the actions you have taken. Moreover, this is a confidential matter between the employee and the company; revealing too much to other employees will only lead to distrust and potential legal trouble.
- **Dwell on short-term popularity.** You are doing what you have to do as a manager—improving each employee's performance and the overall performance of your team—which is your ultimate goal and responsibility to the company. Remember that objective when you start to worry about whether you are liked or not, and talk to a higher-up, like your boss, when you need reassurance. Don't expect that affirmation from your team members, who don't know all the facts or share your responsibility for the group's performance.

You Want to Be Fair

We all want to be fair, and you probably feel that you need to treat employees the same in similar situations. For the most part, you're probably right: There are many good reasons, as we've discussed, to take consistent corrective actions.

However, you may have found that treating employees exactly the same isn't always fair. Sometimes, you should treat employees differently. For example, one employee may have a history of performance problems that another does not, or one employee's actions might be justified while another's are not. In these situations, treating employees differently *is* fair because the situations really are different.

But when you make the decision to treat employees differently, you'll face extra challenges. You have to be able to explain to the employee why he or she is being treated differently. And you'll have to accept that the situation might not look fair to an outsider who doesn't have all the facts.

In addition to treating employees consistently, as we talked about in Chapter 2, part of effective discipline is imposing a corrective measure that sufficiently addresses the recognized problem without being too harsh. Nothing will cause others to second-guess the fairness of your actions like apparent over- or under-reactions to employee problems. If an employee has really surprised you or let you down, you might react with high emotion, making rash discipline decisions. If you fear the employee's reaction, on the other hand, you might not impose sufficiently stringent discipline. If you respond proportionately, you can be confident that you're doing the right thing.

Given how emotionally charged the discipline process is, it's hard to know whether you're being fair. Follow these steps to maintain fairness.

Do:

- **Make decisions based on fact.** Discover and rely on actual facts when making disciplinary decisions. Do not factor in how you feel about a particular employee.
- **Research how it's been done in the past.** Consider how you, and others in the company, have handled the same or similar issues. If you are acting consistently, you are much more likely to be fair.
- **Consult a trusted adviser.** Second opinions can provide a clarity that you wouldn't get otherwise. Talk to your boss, human resources department, or legal counsel to get another perspective on the situation, especially if you have strong feelings or emotions. These feelings can cloud your judgment, without you even realizing it.

Don't:

- **Ignore your gut.** If you feel uncomfortable about treating two employees differently or choosing an appropriate response based on the facts in front of you, figure out the source of your discomfort. It may just be that the disciplinary process is inherently uncomfortable, but it may be that the corrective measure you're considering isn't consistent or proportionate.
- **Assume that you are naturally fair.** Be your own worst critic, and explore the fairness of each discipline decision you make, before you make it. Imagine how you would feel if you were the employee: Would you be surprised? Would you feel you were treated fairly? Ask your boss or human resources department for an alternate perspective to see whether your behavior seems objectively fair, based on the facts.

You Fear the Unknown

Perhaps the hardest thing about discipline is that you simply don't know how the employee will react to it. This can leave you dreading the encounter, wondering if the employee will lash out or withdraw, or even wondering whether there might be lasting repercussions that reflect poorly on you. You may also worry that you'll be so overwhelmed or surprised by the employee's response that you won't know what to do next.

It's not at all unusual for an employee to lash out and try to damage the manager who is imposing discipline. While it's important to acknowledge that this could happen, it's even more important not to let your fear prevent you from using the process fairly and consistently. As long as you follow the strategies we explain in this book, even the most disgruntled employee will have very little ammunition to use against you. Stay the course, apply smart management techniques, and lasting negative repercussions become a moot point.

Of course, knowing you're doing the right thing won't help you overcome the feelings of dread you might have when it's actually time to do it. Fortunately, you can anticipate the range of potential reactions and prepare yourself to handle any of them. (We address difficult employee reactions in Chapter 8.) While this won't alleviate your fears entirely, it can help you plan for your meeting and prevent you from feeling totally blindsided when an employee's reaction isn't what you expect.

EXAMPLE 1: Grace had been the receptionist at a music distribution company for many years. She has become the "face of the company," knows everyone by name, and is known for her sunny personality and kind demeanor. Grace is responsible for answering the phone, maintaining customer records, and managing office logistics.

One of Grace's responsibilities is to keep accurate and up-to-date customer records, which the sales team uses to make customer calls and track sales. Over several months, many salespeople discover that as they make their sales calls, the phone numbers are wrong and some of the customer names are incorrect. Reluctantly, they report the issue to Grace's supervisor, Jeremy.

Jeremy looks into the issue, finds it to be true, and decides to coach Grace. He's always had a good working relationship with her, so he's confident that she'll understand the problem and respond well. Jeremy calls Grace into his office and explains the problem. Grace responds quickly, with a raised voice, "It wasn't me." Jeremy is taken aback. Grace is the only one with read and write access to the customer database, and the only one tasked with this job. "What do you mean it wasn't you? Of course it was you!" Jeremy blurts out before he can think. Grace crosses her arms, sits back in her chair, and repeats, "It wasn't me." Jeremy sits silently, without knowing what to say.

Now Grace and Jeremy are at a standstill. Jeremy is caught by surprise at Grace's anger and denial, and he hasn't planned what to do next. He isn't able to coach Grace as originally planned. Even though Jeremy expected and hoped that Grace would react positively to discipline, he shouldn't have taken for granted that her response would be as he desired. If Jeremy had anticipated that Grace might react defensively, he would have been in a better position to deliver the discipline. Now let's look at the same scenario, but this time, Jeremy is prepared to be met with some resistance.

EXAMPLE 2: Grace tells Jeremy that she is not responsible for the errors in the records. "Grace, aren't you the only one who has access to the customer records?" Jeremy asks. "Yes," she agrees reluctantly. Jeremy continues, "And doesn't the customer records database track who makes changes or updates, and when they're made?" "Yes," she replies again. "Did someone else have access to your password?" Jeremy asks. "No," Grace replies.

"Well, I checked the records the sales team reported had errors. All the records were entered or updated by you in the last three months. Can we at least agree that you were the one who made these entries?"

Because Jeremy has prepared ahead of time and has solid facts to relay, he's able to move beyond Grace's reaction. Even if she still isn't willing to acknowledge her responsibility, Jeremy knows his actions are justified, and he hasn't allowed Grace's resistance to convince him otherwise.

To overcome your fear of the unknown, follow these dos and don'ts.

Do:

- **Prepare.** Do your investigation and research. If you know your facts, you can impose fair discipline even when faced with an employee's emotional reaction. Preparing carefully will also help you avoid having your own emotions take over: You don't have to feel defensive or uncertain, because you know that you're doing the right thing.
- **Stay even keeled.** Keep on point, focus on the problem and the facts behind it, and keep your personal reactions in check. Use a level, calm voice throughout the session.
- **Stick to the facts.** Don't get sidetracked by emotions. You're there to discuss a problem, and that's what you should do.

Don't:

- **Be a friend.** While you may be tempted to offer comfort to a sad employee or a sympathetic ear to an angry one, you can send a mixed message when you act like a friend, instead of a manager. By all means, offer a tissue or a moment for the employee to regain composure, but don't forget your purpose and role in the meeting.
- **Expect to have all the answers.** You will probably be surprised by a reaction at some point and may not know what to do. Don't let this deter you: If you need a break, take one and come back later.

Accept the Challenge

Even if you apply all these principles, you will probably still find the discipline process a challenge. It's never going to be fun to tell employees that they need to improve performance or behavior. Remember, though, that you are ultimately responsible for the success of your individual employees and your team. Both will grow only if challenged to overcome obstacles. You'll do your employees no favors if you ignore problems, instead, you'll see problems grow and watch employee morale dip.

On the other hand, if you work through discipline problems even when you dread them, you'll achieve results. Not only will you overcome the immediate problem, but you will also improve relations with your team generally. Employees will understand what they need to do to meet your expectations, and they'll be motivated to do so without worrying that you might blindside them with discipline. The result will be a team of high performers who trust you to deal openly and fairly with them and who know that discipline will be imposed only when expectations aren't met.

SMART SUMMARY:
Why Discipline Is Hard

- Accept that discipline might feel awkward, for both you and the employee. Plan to acknowledge and deal with this discomfort.

- Your job isn't to be liked by all your employees. Your job is to ensure your team members' success, which may mean you have to impose consistent and fair discipline at times. Don't allow your desire or need to be liked to affect your management decisions.

- Know that employees who don't know the whole story may think you're not being fair when you decide to discipline someone. If you have all the facts, evaluate the problem thoroughly, and respond consistently, you know you're being fair, even if your employees don't.

- The only way to know with certainty how an employee will react is to actually discipline and experience the reaction. Prepare yourself for different possibilities, but don't delay discipline because you're dreading the reaction.

- Even though it's often uncomfortable to discipline, doing so sets expectations for your team. This will motivate employees to try and meet your expectations and help limit future problems.

How to Discuss a Discipline Problem With an Employee

Successful discipline depends on your ability to work with your employee to identify the problem, understand its impact, develop solutions collaboratively, and continue to work together until the issue is fully resolved. Typically, the whole process requires a number of conversations that can be hard to initiate and even more challenging to navigate. How you choose to talk to someone, what you decide to say, and how well you listen to responses are all vital to successfully overcoming a performance or conduct problem. The more thought and preparation you put into a discussion, and the more active listening you do during the discussion, the more likely you are to engage your employee in actually fixing the problem.

This chapter explains how to get your message across and enlist your employee in finding solutions to the problem at hand. The strategies covered here will help you communicate effectively, no matter what type of problem you're facing or which disciplinary measure you're imposing. Those strategies are:

- **Prepare.** Create a rough outline of the points you want to get across, and think about how your points may be received.
- **Guide.** Set appropriate boundaries for the conversation by choosing the right tone at the outset.
- **Demonstrate.** Show an employee what the problem is by giving clear, legitimate examples.
- **Wait.** Allow the employee time to process what you are saying; don't talk just to fill silence, and don't move on until you know the employee understands what is being discussed.
- **Listen.** Listen empathically and actively and communicate to the employee that you hear his or her concerns.
- **Adapt.** Be prepared to deal with new findings. Even though you have prepared for this meeting and anticipated its potential outcomes, you may learn new information that could affect your decision or the way you proceed.
- **Act.** End each session with an action plan, crafted by you and the employee.

Prepare Your Opening Statement

Sometimes, the hardest part of a discipline conversation is getting started. A little forethought will help you figure out how to raise the issue and get the conversation off on the right foot. By jotting down a couple of sentences and thinking about how you will begin the conversation, you can make your most important points while you have your employee's full attention.

As the conversation continues, your employee may be processing what you're saying, struggling to understand why you're disciplining at all, internally preparing responses, or reacting emotionally to what you've said. That's why what you say in the first few sentences is so important; it may be the only time in the conversation that you'll have the employee's full attention. Don't waste this valuable opportunity by fumbling your opening line or not knowing where to start. If you begin with small talk or unscripted language, you may confuse your employee, shifting focus away from the real reason for the discussion.

To make the most of your opening lines, write down what you consider your most important points. Craft a sentence or two that captures those points and sets the right tone for the conversation (we'll discuss appropriate tone below). You don't necessarily need to have these notes in front of you as you begin the conversation, but they should be in the forefront of your mind. You might even want to practice out loud, just to overcome any awkwardness or ambiguity that you can't see on paper.

Set the Tone

To have a productive conversation about a performance or conduct problem, you need to guide the direction of the conversation. The best way to do this is to set the appropriate tone at the outset. Your tone tells the employee how serious the problem is, as well as how committed you are to solving it.

Webster's defines tone two different ways: "the quality of a person's voice" and "the general atmosphere of a place or situation and the effect that it has on people." When considering the appropriate tone, it is critical to think of both of these things.

Skills Enhancement 2: Opening Discussions

Let's take a moment to put together a few sample openings based on a couple of different scenarios. After reading each example, take a moment to jot down how you would open the disciplinary meeting.

EXAMPLE 1: Terry needs to talk to Jill about continued errors in her reports. As the office administrative assistant, Jill is responsible for delivering accurate reports. Lately she has been forwarding reports without verifying that the sales numbers are accurate. How would you, as Terry, open the discussion with Jill?

In the this example, Terry really needs to know the whole story. He can open the discussion in several ways. While Terry certainly knows the outcome—others in the company don't feel they can rely on the team's sales numbers—he does not know *why* Jill is making the mistakes. And while the reason for Jill's flawed reports won't change the company's need for accurate information, it may change the direction of Terry's discipline.

Based on the need to garner more information, here are a couple of potential opening lines Terry could use:

- Jill, I'd like to talk to you about inaccuracies we've been finding in the sales reports. Can you help me understand why this has been happening?
- Jill, when we don't provide accurate sales figures, others in the company feel that they can't rely on us. You've had inaccurate numbers on the reports a few times, and I'm concerned about the negative effect this is having on our team. Can you tell me how we might be able to address this together?

EXAMPLE 2: Damon sends out a joke over the office intranet. While some people find the joke funny, it leaves others uneasy, as its central figures are Catholic priests. Tricia manages Damon and wants to talk to him about the boundaries of appropriate humor in the workplace. If you were Tricia, how would you open the conversation with Damon?

In this scenario, Tricia has a difficult task. She must communicate to Damon that his joke wasn't appropriate. At the same time, she doesn't want Damon to think that a sense of humor is unappreciated. Here, the goal is not to understand what Damon was thinking, but to let him know that others might find it offensive. A couple of opening lines might be:

Skills Enhancement 2:
Opening Discussions, continued

- Damon, I wanted to talk to you about the joke you sent out on the office intranet. The joke wasn't appropriate for the workplace, and some people expressed that it made them uncomfortable. When you think about the joke, do you see how that could have happened?
- Damon, I appreciate your good sense of humor, but the joke you sent wasn't appropriate. A joke that stereotypes different religious groups could really anger or offend some of your coworkers. That's one of the reasons company policy restricts use of the intranet to work-related communications—it's really not a tool to use for personal reasons. Do you understand?

Tone of Voice

Your tone can convey many things, including nervousness, confidence, anger, determination, concern, caring, and so on. Different tones are appropriate for different conversations. You'll want to choose a tone that is appropriate for your discipline discussion ahead of time, so that you can maintain consistency throughout the session. If your tone of voice doesn't match your point, you'll send mixed messages.

Choose an Appropriate Environment

The location of your meetings also sends a message to the employee. You should pick a location that illustrates the seriousness of the situation and avoids any distractions that might derail the discussion. There is a reason the police interview suspects in windowless rooms with folding chairs and plain tables. This atmosphere says universally, "You are in serious trouble, and you will be provided no distractions as we discuss it." You need to be similarly conscious about how the physical surroundings affect the tone of your meeting.

Skills Enhancement 3:
Choosing Tone of Voice

Consider the following examples and jot down the tone of voice that you would adopt if you were dealing with each issue:

EXAMPLE 1: Rick manages the receptionist in his law firm, who has done an exemplary job of being the "face of the firm." However, instead of being her normal welcoming self, she has recently seemed sad and uninterested in her work. Rick decides to discuss the issue with her.

EXAMPLE 2: Carrie is the CFO of a major corporation. One day she is in the restroom and sees a woman curled in the corner of the bathroom, disheveled, sobbing, and with bruises on her wrists. With some careful coaxing, Carrie learns that the woman has been physically assaulted by a coworker after she told him she would not date him any longer. Carrie comforts the woman, gets her medical help, enlists the aid of the legal and human resources departments in investigating the situation quickly and thoroughly, and is ready to sit down with the coworker in question.

EXAMPLE 3: Rosanne has worked with Maggie for nearly ten years. They worked together at several companies and socialize outside of work. Lately, Maggie has been finishing projects late—an issue Rosanne has addressed with Maggie before. Maggie always replies, "Oh, you know me! I'm worth the wait!" Rosanne decides to meet with Maggie to talk about the problem.

How would you handle these situations? While there is no "right" answer, the most important thing is to match your tone to the gravity of the situation. If Rick took a cold, authoritarian tone instead of a questioning tone, the receptionist might immediately feel defensive and clam up. Likewise, if Carrie were to sit down with the woman's alleged abuser and use a concerned or friendly tone instead of a stern one, it would send the message that the company does not crack down on violence in the workplace.

The example of Rosanne and Maggie is the trickiest. The women have a friendship that extends outside the office and a history of working together. Maggie is letting those lines blur as she gets coached by Rosanne and, thus, is not taking the problem seriously. It is up to Rosanne to assert her leadership position and convey to Maggie that the problem must be dealt with, despite their friendship. Her tone should be firm and professional to get this message across.

There are a few basics that always apply:

- You need to be able to hear each other speak.
- You should be facing the employee so you can make eye contact.
- You should not be distracted by other things.
- You should have space to take notes.

Think about what you'll be doing in the meeting. Do you need a desk between you to convey authority? If you need white space to design solutions to issues, go to a conference room with a whiteboard. You may also want to choose your location based on the type of corrective action you are taking, selecting progressively more formal environments as the discipline gets more serious. We'll discuss this in greater detail in Chapters 11 to 14.

Engage in Active Listening

If a disciplinary conversation is about egregious behavior that the employee simply needs to stop, it may be fine for you to do most of the talking. However, in most cases, you and the employee should be working toward a collaborative solution. If you're too busy talking, you may not be doing any listening. Even when you do give the employee the chance to speak, you may be so busy trying to figure out what to say next that you don't hear what the employee is saying.

Failing to listen attentively has a dramatic effect on the disciplinary conversation. While the employee may get the message that he or she is doing something wrong, you won't show the employee that you want to hear his or her side or work to create a solution. In essence, you might as well have just sent the employee a letter. This makes the most important part of collaborative discipline—finding a solution together—nearly impossible.

To listen well, you must:

- **Set the scene for a distraction-free conversation.** Eliminate things that will keep you from focusing on the employee and issue at hand.
- **Play back what you are hearing.** When you respond, begin with statements reflecting that you have heard your employee's viewpoint.
- **Listen empathically.** Imagine you are the person speaking. Don't just think about what that person is saying; think about what he or she is feeling.

Set the Scene for a Distraction-Free Conversation

Although it sounds intuitive, paying attention is one of the most difficult skills to master. And unfortunately, it's easy for others to notice if you aren't doing it well. You've probably seen it many times in others: When a person's mind is full and racing along, especially while someone else is talking, there's an obvious vacancy in the person's eyes.

Of course, that's not the only way lack of attention manifests itself. You might answer the wrong question. You might pick up only pieces of what is being said, losing potentially important information along the way. As a result, the conversation will be fragmented and incomplete, and the employee may feel you don't value his or her perspective.

You need to recognize that your attention may wander and set the scene to prevent that from happening. These tips help create an environment as free from distractions as possible:

- Turn off your phone.
- Turn your computer screen away from you and turn off the sound.
- Lower the blinds or close the curtains if the view is distracting.
- Shut your door or grab a private room.
- Make it clear to everyone else that you're not to be disturbed, perhaps by posting a sign on the door.
- Sit directly across from the person you are talking to so you can maintain eye contact.
- Clear your mind prior to walking into the meeting; physically and mentally set aside other things you are working on.

Play Back What You Are Hearing

Another way to make sure you are listening attentively is to repeat what the employee has just said. At a natural break in the conversation, say something like:

- "Let me see if I understand what you are saying …"
- "Tell me if I am following you …"
- "What I think you are saying is …"

Follow those openings with a paraphrased version of what you just heard. This tells the employee that you are listening and understanding what is being said. And, if you didn't get the employee's point, he or she can correct you right away.

> **EXAMPLE:** Samantha is the company controller and Del is her boss, the CFO. Del is having a conversation with Samantha about her continuing errors in general ledger accounting. Del has prepared well and explained the problem and the impact it is having on the company. He prefaces this portion of the conversation by telling Samantha that he would like to understand what she believes the problem to be. Samantha replies, "You are asking me to do way too much work in too short of a time frame. Not only do I have to do general ledger accounting, but I am also handling receivables, payables, budgeting, and forecasting. With that much to do, mistakes will get made."
>
> Del responds, "If I understand what you are saying correctly, your workload is too heavy, causing you to make mistakes on the general ledger, is that right?"
>
> Samantha adds a previously unspoken, but implied, "My workload would cause *anyone* to make mistakes."

By playing back what he heard, Del conveyed to Samantha that he was listening attentively. In turn, Samantha felt comfortable sharing more about her state of mind, giving Del an opportunity to understand her perspective and see a more complete picture.

When you reiterate what the employee says, play it back straight, without any editorializing or judgment from you. Avoid statements that interpret the employee's motives, thoughts, or feelings. For example, if an employee misses a deadline because he or she forgot about it, don't reply with "You missed the deadline because you didn't bother to write it down" or "You blew the deadline because you can't handle more than one project at a time." In both these cases, the statements communicate that you're judging rather than listening. The moment you add anything that smacks of judgment or opinion about what you are hearing, the employee may feel defensive, attacked, or misunderstood.

Listen Empathically

Another key element to a disciplinary meeting is listening empathically. Empathic listening, also called active listening or reflective listening, is about trying to experience the feelings of another person. As you listen to your employee, put yourself in his or her shoes, and work to understand what it's like to *be* the speaker in that moment. This will help you understand why the problem is occurring and what an effective solution might look like.

So how do you listen empathically?

1. **Temporarily set aside your other priorities.** Clear your calendar and your mind to make room for what you are about to hear.

2. **Focus solely and nonjudgmentally on your employee.** Be prepared to hear and understand the issue from the employee's perspective.

3. **From time to time, tell the employee what you are hearing.** Use a few of your own words (don't parrot the employee) to explain what you understand the employee is communicating, without incorporating your own agenda or opinions.

While you want to interject your perceptions throughout the discussion, you don't want to interrupt. Think of a butter knife under a stream of water. If the blade is vertical, the water continues by with barely a ripple: This is interjecting. If the butter knife is horizontal, causing the water to change directions and spill over the sides, that is interrupting. When interjecting with feedback about what the employee is feeling, you are signaling that you are listening closely, and working hard to understand and empathize. A few phrases that indicate you are interjecting are:

- "So *you* think that ..."
- "What *you* need now is ..."
- "So *you're* anxious about ..."
- "Seems *you're* unsure of ..."
- "Sounds like *you're* really feeling ..."

You can see by these phrases that you are not agreeing with your employee about the facts or even validating the employee's thoughts, feelings, or beliefs; you are simply summarizing what he or she has said. Each of these phrases indicates that you hear, understand, and empathize, without excusing the behavior.

Why is empathic listening so important?

- Your employee is more likely to keep explaining instead of defending, blaming, shutting down, or withdrawing.
- You will minimize misunderstandings as you signal that you are really hearing what the employee is saying.

- You may help your employee clarify emotions, ideas, and needs by sharing your periodic nonjudgmental summaries.
- When the employee feels heard and understood, he or she will feel invested in solving the problem.

Be Flexible

Even if you've done your homework and investigated an issue before you talk to the employee, your discussion may very well bring new information to light. In that case, you'll have to be open to changing your plans to account for the new data.

New information you might get could include:
- new facts about what happened
- insight into what motivated the employee or how the employee perceives the situation
- new details about how your team operates
- the role other people might play in creating or exacerbating the problem
- insight into how the employee is understanding and interpreting the signals you send
- an understanding of your employee's commitment to the company and his or her ongoing success, and
- a different perspective on what next steps might effectively solve the problem.

If new facts make you reconsider whether the action you've decided to take will be effective, don't be afraid to walk away and reevaluate. After all, you can always come back to the discussion later. And thinking about how the new facts affect the situation make it possible for you craft more effective solutions.

> ⚠ CAUTION
>
> **Don't be bullied.** There's a big difference between staying open to new facts and allowing an employee to push you around. Some employees will make excuses for their behavior or call your disciplinary decisions into question. Unless the employee raises new information that you should consider, however, you shouldn't let the employee's response change your mind. If you've followed the smart discipline

strategies in this book, you've prepared carefully and chosen the appropriate response. Even if the employee has more seniority or experience than you, only you—the manager—can decide when corrective action is in order.

Agree on an Action Plan

If you walk out of a discipline meeting without getting a commitment from your employee for future action, it wasn't a successful meeting. Remember that the purpose of discipline is to improve the employee's behavior or performance. If you don't have an action plan, that means there is no concrete way to measure improvement.

So how do you go about building an action plan? Here are a few steps to get you started:

1. Agree on the facts and the impact of the problem.
2. Define your role and make sure the employee understands that he or she ultimately owns the problem.
3. Brainstorm and negotiate a plan of action.
4. Follow up to ensure that the action plan is working.

This doesn't have to be a lengthy exercise. Indeed, in some cases, the plan may be very quick and obvious. In the case of unwanted actions that don't seem to have a systemic root, the action plan may just be, "Don't do that anymore." Things like tardiness, absenteeism, and misconduct can often be dealt with this way. More detailed action plans may be necessary for dealing with more complicated issues, however.

Agree on the Facts and the Impact

During the difficult conversation you are having, you must make sure not only that you understand the employee's point of view, but also that the employee understands the issue and his or her responsibility for dealing with it.

EXAMPLE: Chris is a line supervisor for an auto parts manufacturer. His team is responsible for delivering 2,500 carburetors per month. This goal is based on past performance, so the whole team knows that it is achievable, though challenging. Manuel, an employee with more than ten years of experience, is responsible for packaging the carburetors in boxes and sending them to the distribution department. Lately, he has not been completing this task on time, and it is reducing the number of carburetors that go out each day.

Chris sits Manuel down in a conference room to discuss the issue. He explains how Manuel's performance is affecting the whole team and underlines it by saying that they are in danger of not meeting their 2,500 carburetor commitment. Chris listens carefully to Manuel's response, interjecting to signal his understanding and empathy for Manuel's position.

Chris moves on to planning the course of action going forward. He asks Manuel for his ideas. Manuel replies, "I just told you the solution. We need to lower the number of carburetors that we deliver. We cannot continue to work at this pace. Everyone is feeling the pressure."

Chris realizes he has not adequately outlined the importance of meeting the departmental commitment, the genesis of the measurement, or Manuel's direct and singular role in it. He starts over again, this time working to put ownership of Manuel's performance problem where it belongs: with Manuel.

In the beginning of this example, it seemed like Chris was doing everything right. He went to great lengths to understand Manuel's point of view and engage him in developing a solution. But as you may have seen in poor performers who report to you, Manuel is not taking responsibility for the problem. Instead, he suggests that the whole team has a problem. Chris needs to get back on course with a difficult message: "No, Manuel. This is not a team issue, nor an issue of capacity. This is you not performing up to the standards of the rest of the team. That is what we have to focus on." Manuel also does not understand that the output requirement is not negotiable. It is a business imperative that is put at risk by poor performance. Chris must make these points more clearly.

Once an employee understands his or her personal responsibility in an identified problem, you can focus on fixing it through productive action planning. But don't be surprised if you have to come back to the issue more than once. You may even go so far as to ask outright, "Do you believe that this is your issue to solve?" Keep talking through it until the employee acknowledges his or her personal responsibility; this is the only way to make sure that the employee is truly committed to improvement.

Define Your Role

In the process of acknowledging ownership and working to craft a solution, the employee needs to understand what your role is. You are a coach. You provide methods, game plans, resources, and ideas. You decide who plays when, and you set the direction for the entire team. You monitor performance along the way, looking at agreed-upon metrics, and you make adjustments if necessary. Ultimately, however, your employee has to put the ball over the goal line.

If the employee seems unclear on your role, state it directly. For example: "John, I am here to support you in improving your efficiency in this area. I can be a sounding board, brainstorm ideas with you, and let you know how you are doing, but the responsibility for improvement lies with you." For the rest of the meeting with John, you must be careful not to take any action that might blur the lines of ownership of the problem and your role as a coach. Your job is then to monitor John's progress and coach him along the way. Making your role clear to your employee provides a solid boundary about who is there to offer support and facilitate improvement (you) and who has to improve (the employee).

Brainstorm and Negotiate a Solution

Imagine guiding your employee into building a step-by-step plan that not only addresses the problem, but also ensures improved future performance. You will be spared the difficult (and expensive) process of hiring and training a replacement, and you will have a motivated employee committed to successful job performance.

To accomplish this task, you must give the employee the opportunity to evaluate different solutions to the problem. The easiest way to do this is to begin a brainstorming session.

Skills Enhancement 4:
Brainstorming an Action Plan

Use this exercise to brainstorm a plan of action with your employee.

Step 1: With the employee, write down the problem in objective terms.

Step 2: Write down how the problem is affecting others involved, such as the company, the team, and you, the manager.

Step 3: Spend five minutes talking with your employee about what an ideal solution would look like. Write down everything this ideal solution would have to accomplish. Try to open it up to all possibilities, even if they seem to go beyond your resources or budget.

Step 4: Take ten minutes to talk about what is necessary to go from where your employee is right now to the great solution outlined above. This may include attitude changes, skill enhancements, more time, help with prioritizing, and so on. Everything is fair game; you'll negotiate what is really possible later.

Step 5: Capture this list on paper. You'll need it to determine the agreed-upon plan.

While the potential solutions may turn out to be unreasonable or undoable, the basis of good collaboration is a willingness to consider anything. Now that you have worked with the employee to talk about possibilities, think about whether any of the potential solutions are practical for both the business and the employee. Consider these questions:

- Can your business afford the time and money necessary to make the plan work?
- Is the employee capable of achieving the plan?
- Are the results worth both the time and energy it will take?
- Does this really solve the problem to the satisfaction of those directly involved?

Once you have the answers to these questions, your list of realistic potential solutions will likely be much shorter. From this shorter list, you and the employee can decide which solutions work best. Be practical, and modify options if they can be made better or workable. You do not want to sponsor a plan that just won't or can't happen.

Sample Action Steps	
Issues	**Potential Action Steps**
Tardiness	For the next 30 days, check in with me when you arrive.
	Provide 24 hours' notice if you are going to be late.
	Arrive to meetings five minutes early.
Lack of Attention to Detail	Review each document at least three times. Make sure you take at least an hour break between checks. Mark the document each time you review it.
	Store each deliverable overnight and reappraise it in the morning with fresh eyes.
	Create checklists of each step required to get something done. Attach the checklist to the item and physically check off each step as you complete it.
Bad Attitude	Take half a day to evaluate and chart the pros and cons of working here. Meet tomorrow to discuss those pros and cons.
	Examine how you would characterize your attitude, whether and how you think it needs to change, and what you think would help you bring about that change. Meet the day after tomorrow to talk about your findings.
	When something about your job frustrates you, write it down. Then consider what you can do to change the situation. At the end of the week, meet with me to discuss what caused your frustrations and what we can do about it.
Missed Deadlines	Make a list of things you think contribute to missing your deadlines. Do you have too much to do? Do you lack the skills necessary to do the work? Are there too many things on your plate? Meet over coffee this afternoon to go over the list.
	Take a class to learn how to negotiate realistic deadlines.
	When you have an assignment, create a formal project schedule and give yourself a deadline a day or two before it is due. Allow the last day(s) for contending with unforeseen problems and error proofing.
Anger Management	Attend a course on managing your emotions in the workplace.
	When you feel yourself getting angry, take a 15-minute break to walk around the building and regain control.

Sample Action Steps, continued	
Issues	**Potential Action Steps**
Missed Sales Numbers	Build your cold-calling skills by targeting potential new clients; do so until you've acquired at least one new customer per month. Reevaluate in three months.
	Analyze your performance against the sales cycle to determine where your weaknesses are. Draft potential solutions to these problems and meet again next week to discuss.
	Write up account development plans for existing accounts. Include new sales targets and what steps you will take to achieve the targets.

Follow Up on the Action Plan

At the end of any good action plan is a brief section on how you intend to review ongoing progress, as well as a time frame for "getting well." This doesn't have to be complicated. You could agree to meet every week for 15 minutes to go over each step of the plan. Or you could agree to a set of measures that would indicate that the employee is back on track.

Whatever methodology you choose, make sure you follow through. Seeing the plan through to its conclusion will send the right message to the employee. Your continued commitment tells the employee that you are in it for the long haul. Moreover, the employee can feel proud and empowered when he or she meets the goals of the plan.

You also need to create a reasonable time frame for the plan. This gives the employee the opportunity to succeed and a renewed confidence in his or her ability to set performance goals and achieve them. Giving an employee too many tasks to accomplish in a short time, on the other hand, will discourage the employee and will likely result in failure.

If you follow these strategies when discussing a performance or conduct problem with an employee, you'll walk away from the conversation having given the employee the motivation and opportunity to succeed. And with dedication, your action plan will lead to sustainable improved performance.

SMART SUMMARY:
Smart Talk

- Before you meet with your employee, prepare for the discussion. Examine the issue from all perspectives, jot down your opening sentences, and don't assume you know the whole story. Be ready for a variety of emotional responses.

- Remember that you're there to improve the employee's workplace performance or behavior. Set the tone for the meeting by choosing an appropriate environment and using a tone of voice that conveys the gravity of the situation.

- When it's time to hear the employee's perspective, make sure you're not distracted, and focus on what the employee says and feels. Give your employee time to process, too, even if it means awkward silences.

- Give the employee the opportunity to share new, relevant information, but don't doubt what you know. Don't allow the employee to blame others if the blame is misplaced.

- Don't walk away from a discipline discussion without an action plan. And remember, while you can provide encouragement, resources, and support, it's ultimately your employee's responsibility to solve the problem.

Smart Ways to Deal With Difficult Employee Reactions

The confrontation and criticism inherent in discipline can lead to unexpected—and often powerful—emotional responses from your employees. In fact, some managers avoid these conversations altogether so they won't have to face these reactions. "Oh, Henry will get so mad, and his performance isn't *that* bad" or "Janice takes criticism so badly, there's no point talking to her about her tardiness." There is no doubt that wading into these emotional waters requires courage on your part. But with a few of the smart strategies outlined in this chapter, you can learn how to handle the most common negative reactions with confidence.

In an ideal disciplinary meeting, you point out the problem, the employee sees it as an opportunity to improve and succeed in the organization, and you both walk away from the meeting with a handshake, an action plan, and a renewed optimism about the future. Unfortunately, that's not always what happens. Instead, some employees respond strongly—and negatively—to discipline. Negative responses typically fall into one of two categories: emotional responses and masking responses. An emotional response is a quick, often uncontrolled reaction based on the employee's immediate thoughts or feelings; a masking response is intended to deflect or protect the person's real emotions about an issue.

The most common emotional reactions to discipline include:

- **Anger.** "You have no right to say that."
- **Grief.** "I never dreamed you felt that way about me. I am crushed."
- **Anxiety.** "Oh my God, my career is ruined!"
- **Violence or threats.** "You'll be sorry you ever brought this up!"

The most common masking reactions are:

- **Denial.** "I didn't do that."
- **Silence.** "If I don't say anything, you won't be able to pin this on me."
- **Blame.** "You've got it all wrong. It was someone else."
- **Dispassion.** "Fine, whatever."

Both types of responses can be challenging for a manager. Emotional responses involve very deep-rooted (and often extreme) feelings, while masking reactions typically signal that the employee is having a hard time processing the situation or, in the worst cases, is unwilling to accept responsibility.

These reactions can occur at any step in the process, from a coaching session to the middle of what you thought was a successful improvement plan all the way to a termination meeting. Moreover, the employee may exhibit different emotions at different stages in the process, or may express more than one of these reactions at once.

That's why it's best to go in knowing what you might encounter. While these emotions can be challenging, if you know some strategies for dealing with them in the moment, you can usually work through them toward solutions.

Emotional Reactions

Sometimes, employees react very emotionally, allowing what they feel to control what they say or do. Many of these emotions, and their manifestations, feel out of place in the work environment. However, as we know deep down, the work self is intimately intertwined with the whole person. Employees who are emotionally invested in what they do are usually more passionate and dedicated to their jobs.

This means there are benefits to having an employee respond with strong emotions. It usually means the employee cares about the job, which means he or she can likely be motivated to improve. In those situations, you can often work together to direct the employee's energy into creating a solution to the problem.

Anger

Anger can be an alarming reaction. It may build gradually and explode very suddenly, often without much apparent connection to what is actually happening in the moment. If an employee has been frustrated about a situation for a long time and is suddenly confronted with his or her responsibility for it, dormant anger can be released unexpectedly. More alarming, anger can be expressed many ways, most of which are very uncomfortable if you are on the receiving end. It may manifest itself in a raised voice, a pounded fist, angry words, or a verbal attack. At its worst, anger can become violent, which we'll discuss separately below.

But anger isn't necessarily all bad; it communicates that the employee really cares and has something significant to communicate to you. It also signals that the employee is willing to lose a little control to make sure you understand.

While anger may be a potentially constructive reaction, that doesn't mean it's an acceptable one. If anger manifests itself in personal attacks or inappropriate behavior like yelling or name calling, you must immediately put an end to it. While you want to hear the employee's point of view, you must show that mutual respect and professionalism are mandatory in the work environment.

Let's look at a few smart strategies for working through a disciplinary session that is fraught with anger:

1. Slow the meeting down. Instead of plowing forward to the next point you want to make, explain to the employee that he or she needs to calm down before you can proceed. Take a moment or two to allow for this.

2. If the employee does calm down, acknowledge that you understand that he or she has something important to say, but saying it in anger is not an acceptable way to deliver the message.

3. If the employee is incapable of controlling his or her anger, or your fear grows, tell the employee that you are going to end the conversation for now. Institute a cooldown period, most likely away from the office. Pick a time to reengage. If the employee denies that such a meeting will be productive, commit to revisiting the issue later. Anger may be preventing the employee from seeing the situation rationally now, but that may change with time.

4. Don't compromise your safety or the safety of your team. If you're afraid that the employee's anger will erupt into violence, immediately seek help.

EXAMPLE: Pedro, a restaurant manager, decides to give Luis a verbal warning because he is not bussing the tables at his station quickly enough, even though Pedro has previously coached him on the issue. Pedro calls Luis into his office and tells him that he is still working too slowly and doesn't seem to have implemented the ideas they came up with together in their coaching session. Luis, normally even tempered, clenches his fists and turns red. "I cannot believe you are picking on me again! I am working so hard to get these tables bussed and nothing is good enough for you!"

Which of the following is an appropriate response?

- Luis, I know this is upsetting, and I want to figure out a way we can improve this situation. Take a minute to calm down, and then let's resume the conversation."

- "Luis, anger won't help you at all here. If you don't get focused on solving this issue right away, you can bet there will be repercussions."

Here, the first response is the appropriate one. Pedro gives Luis time to calm down and an opportunity to reengage in the discussion later, instead of making threats. Hopefully, the two will be able to have a productive conversation.

Grief

As a manager, it can be very uncomfortable when an employee is saddened or wounded by discipline. After all, your intent isn't to hurt the employee's feelings, but to help him or her succeed in the organization. But there is a positive side to grief: It shows that the employee is really invested in his or her performance and reputation. More than any other negative reaction, true grief can usually be worked out, and the employee focused on improving performance.

If your employee expresses grief—for example, by crying—it might mean one of two things: The employee is genuinely upset about having done poorly, or the employee is trying to manipulate the situation. The latter typically happens when an employee knows how to push your buttons. When an employee's grief is sincere, though, it is usually accompanied by an immediate and overwhelming reaction and continues to crop up throughout the discussion.

Either way, it is important to go into these sessions knowing how you are likely to respond to expressions of grief. If you know that tears or sadness pluck at your heartstrings and you tend to try to comfort those who are feeling sad, you may lose sight of your original purpose: to deal openly and honestly with a performance or conduct problem to help the employee succeed in the organization. If you are embarrassed by tears, practice talking through the grief, even if it's just to get to the point in the discussion where you'll arrange to reschedule the meeting. You need to focus not on how the grief makes you feel, but on how to solve the problem at hand.

If an employee cries or exhibits sadness, offer a tissue if necessary, but not a shoulder to cry on. It may be tempting to make comforting statements like "It will be okay" or "Don't worry about it, things are going to be fine." However, statements like this send the wrong message: that there isn't really a problem, that the employee is not responsible for it, or that the employee's job is secure no matter what happens.

If your employee can't get past grief and into a productive discussion, try these strategies:

1. **Acknowledge the response.** Say something like "I can see how this is affecting you." Allow enough time for the employee to recover, silent time in which the employee can begin to gather his or her thoughts again. Be practical about the time allowed. If it looks like the employee is going have a hard time regaining composure, end the session and schedule a follow-up meeting.

2. **Stay focused.** Don't let the conversation shift from the problem to the employee's reaction. Focus your employee by bringing him or her back to the topic at hand and letting the employee know that you need to work through this as soon as he or she is able.

3. **Continue to maintain professionalism.** If you do, the employee may find it easier to get his or her emotions in check.

4. **Accept that the grief might not disappear entirely.** Even if the employee has a hard time hiding all feelings of grief, the conversation can still be productive.

EXAMPLE: Using the example of Pedro and Luis above, imagine Luis instead responded to Pedro by saying, "Oh man, I really let you down. I can't believe how badly I screwed up. I just can't believe this happened." He lowers his head into his hands and covers his eyes.

How should Pedro respond?

- "Luis, I can see how badly you feel. That let's me know how important this job is to you. When you are ready, let's talk about how we can fix this problem once and for all."

- "Luis, man, please don't get upset. I didn't mean to make you feel bad. Forget it, it isn't worth getting worked up about."

Both answers have the effect of calming Luis, but only the first will actually get Luis focused on the problem at hand.

Anxiety

For some employees, the discipline process brings up feelings of inadequacy or rejection from the past. The employee may feel like a failure, or that termination of employment is inevitable. All of this can hit quickly and cause anxiety or, in the worst cases, panic. When panic or anxiety strikes, it is hard to get the employee to concentrate on the problem that necessitated the conversation in the first place.

Add to the conundrum that anxiety is catching. If you aren't nervous already, the employee's anxiety may cause you to feel a bit uneasy yourself. When that happens, employ the following strategies to get your employee (and yourself) comfortable and focused on improvement.

If your employee spirals into anxiety or panic:

1. **Slow down the meeting.** Refocus the employee on the problem at hand, not the fears in his or her head. Reiterate exactly what you are talking about, and provide adequate examples.

2. **Put the problem in the context of the overall discipline process.** If the employee thinks that he or she is about to be fired when that's not the case, he or she may not be prepared to think about solutions, but instead may just be anxiously waiting for the ax to fall. So be sure to tell the employee where you are in the discipline continuum (but remember not to make any promises about the future; see Chapter 3).

3. **Check in frequently with your employee during the meeting.** Does he or she clearly understand the scope of what is being discussed, or has he or she blown it out of proportion? Ask simple questions like "Am I being clear?" or "Is there anything you don't understand?" or "Does this make sense to you?"

4. **Reinforce that solutions are possible.** If the employee is panicked, he or she may have a hard time thinking of ways to solve the problem.

TIP

When dealing with terminations, keep it brief. If your discussion is a termination discussion, the employee (and you!) might be filled with anxiety, but you shouldn't refocus that energy on improving the problem. The situation is already beyond repair, and you don't want to get into an involved discussion that won't be fruitful. Instead, focus on closing the meeting by wrapping up logistical, and very practical, issues, such as the final paycheck, continued health coverage, and packing up.

EXAMPLE: Let's go back to the example of Pedro and Luis. To open the conversation, Pedro makes his short introductory statement about the nature of the meeting. As he is talking, he sees Luis begin to drum his fingers on the tabletop. Luis's knee begins bouncing and he begins to sweat. Pedro can tell that Luis is feeling anxious.

Pulling Luis out of his anxiety and back into a productive meeting is not easy. Which way improves Pedro's chances of doing so?

"Luis, it's good to see that you know this is important. If this doesn't improve, it could cost you your job. Now pay attention and let's try to solve this."

"Luis, I can see that this makes you anxious. The problem worries me, too, but the good news is that you have a chance to fix this before it gets worse. Do you feel like you can talk about how we can improve your bussing times, or do you need a minute?"

In the second response, Pedro acknowledges the problem but focuses on the benefit of improving. He also gives Luis the opportunity to step away, if he needs to. This is much better than the slightly threatening first response, which could just make Luis more anxious.

Violence

It's unfortunate but true: Sometimes, employees react violently to workplace stress. This reaction to discipline is unacceptable and, unlike other reactions, it usually cannot be overcome. A violent employee puts you and your team members at serious physical risk and leaves your company exposed to legal liability, too. If the company doesn't take action to terminate a violent employee, and that employee later harms a coworker or client, the company could be held responsible.

If an employee reacts violently or you believe violence is likely because of threatening statements, gestures, or other behaviors, try these steps:

1. **Prepare for the possibility.** If you think it's possible that an employee may be violent, let others know. Sit nearest the door so that you can get out if you need to.

2. **Have security personnel available and prepared to assist.** If your company is not big enough for a security force, make sure that you have adequate help standing by, ready to intervene if you need it.

3. **Meet with a potentially violent employee at a time when fewer coworkers will be present,** such as late in the day or at the end of the workweek.

4. **Stay calm.** If the employee has not acted violently but you think he or she might, continue to listen to what he or she is saying and maintain eye contact. The employee will feel heard, which may calm him or her down, or it may allow you to discreetly seek assistance without being noticed.

5. **Get help.** If the employee has already acted violently, signal or call for help immediately and loudly. However, if the employee hasn't yet become physical, such a call for help might agitate him or her further. If possible, motion or call for help quietly, perhaps by stepping out to signal to a coworker or security personnel.

6. **Keep the situation contained.** Leave the room with the door shut until help arrives, or move the employee off the premises as quickly as possible.

7. **Report the incident.** Document it thoroughly; discuss it with your supervisor as well as your human resources department or legal counsel.

8. **Don't compromise the safety of your employees going forward.** Take extra precautionary steps to maintain safety in the workplace. You may need to notify law enforcement or your security team or to tell your employees about the situation and give them instructions on what to do if this person returns to the workplace.

Masking Reactions

Instead of acting out emotionally, some employees use defense mechanisms to mask their emotions. Noted psychotherapist Mollie Sullivan says, "People have these reactions because at some point in time, it served them really well. They have 'worked' in some way and protected this person from unpleasant situations." Of course, that can make it very hard to break through a masking response, especially if you want to turn a defensive reaction into a productive discussion.

Denial

Denial usually occurs early in the discipline process, when you first confront an employee with a problem. Instead of acknowledging the problem and focusing on the solution, the employee rejects either the existence of the problem or his or her responsibility for it. He or she may say things like "You're wrong" or "It wasn't me" or "I have no idea what you're talking about."

When someone denies ownership of the problem like this, your natural response is to try harder to make the person understand his or her responsibility. But working too hard at this can undermine your message, giving the employee control of the conversation as you try in vain to come up with the "right answer" that will get the employee to acknowledge the problem. Instead of working together to find a solution, you'll spend your time trying to convince the employee that there is a problem in the first place.

Remember: By following the smart discipline process, you'll have entered this conversation with discreet examples of the problem behavior. If the employee still isn't acknowledging responsibility after hearing what you have to say, try these steps:

1. **Go through the examples one by one.** Ask the employee, "Do you remember this happening?" or "Do you understand your role in what occurred?" Find out whether the employee sees his or her responsibility for at least part of the problem.

2. **Remember to acknowledge what the employee is saying.** Even if you disagree with what the employee is saying, be sure to indicate that you hear his or her perspective.

3. **Be willing to revisit the issue.** If you are given new facts and need to investigate further, say so.

4. **Change the way you say it.** Sometimes, all the employee needs to understand the problem is a few different words or phrases. Consider whether you can express the same concept another way.

5. **Frankly acknowledge the employee's denial;** it may be something he or she isn't consciously aware of. Say something like "It seems you're having a hard time acknowledging your responsibility for this problem. Why don't you take some time to think about your involvement, and what we should do going forward?" Set up a follow up date and time.

Of course, it's important that the employee acknowledge the existence of the problem. After all, how can you fix a problem that the employee doesn't believe exists or believes is someone else's fault? If you follow the steps above and are still not successful, you'll have to address this with the employee. You may have to craft an improvement strategy on your own, but the employee should know that the likelihood of success is much diminished without his or her commitment to acknowledging and fixing the problem.

> **EXAMPLE:** Martha is the night shift supervisor in the children's department of a department store. Venetia is the top salesperson in her department and often works in the evenings. About once a week, the register has come up about $100 short. Martha notices that it happens only on the nights that Venetia is working. Martha monitors the situation for two additional weeks, and while she does not see Venetia take the money, she realizes that no one else has access to the register during the time the money is disappearing.
>
> Martha approaches Venetia and explains the situation. Venetia is caught completely off guard and says, "It wasn't me! There is no way I'd do anything to put my job at risk. It had to be Mike over in Men's Suits; when I take my break, he keeps an eye on the department."
>
> Martha responds, "But Venetia, even when he's watching the floor, he doesn't have access to the register. How do you explain that?"
>
> Venetia simply repeats, "It wasn't me."
>
> Martha now needs to decide what to do to proceed. Which would be the most effective way to deal with Venetia's denial?
>
> "Venetia, it sounds to me like you think Mike accessed the cash drawer while you were on your break. Is that right?"
>
> "So Venetia, what you are saying is: This isn't your problem?"
>
> Here, Martha recognizes that she needs to gather more information. The first option shows Venetia that Martha is really listening, and it helps Martha understand whether Venetia feels she is responsible for the problem or not. This is more effective than the second response, which just allows Venetia to deny involvement, without requiring her to explain why she's not responsible or how Mike could be involved.

Silence

Sometimes, an employee won't respond at all but will sit silently. There are many reasons for silence. Often, the employee is trying to process new or unanticipated information. The employee may feel overwhelmed, humiliated, or saddened and not know what to say. Additionally, the employee may be using silence as a "holding pattern": a time to put together a defense and respond. These reasons for silence are acceptable in the disciplinary conversation, to a point. That point is determined by the length of time spent sitting quietly. If it truly looks like the employee is internally processing what you have said, give the employee enough time to do so. If the silence drags on beyond what makes sense, or it's clear that the employee is trying to avoid talking altogether, end the session with a promise to address the issue later.

In the discipline process, the least effective way to deal with silence is to fill it. If you do, you might say things that let the employee off the hook, share more information than is necessary, or suggest to the employee that you need to justify your actions. Another problem with filling the silence is that the employee doesn't have time to think about what you are saying. If the employee is just busy trying to keep up with you, he or she won't be thinking about the important points you made at the beginning of the discussion.

Dealing With Abject Silence

There is one form of silence that will require extra effort and must be specifically targeted: abject silence. You will probably recognize it when you see it. In fact, it may already sound familiar. This silence often looks like petulance and can't be broken after a reasonable time. The employee may sit with crossed arms or tightly closed lips, responding only when directly addressed and with the briefest of answers.

Abject silence is typically a form of denial. By refusing to communicate with you, the employee is refusing to acknowledge the problem and move forward to a solution. When an employee's tone, mannerisms, or body language indicate that he or she is closed to discussion, you'll have to take extra steps to overcome the silence. Begin by asking "yes or no" questions, such as "Do you remember that incident?" If the employee still won't respond, ask progressively more complicated questions like "In your eyes, what could you have done differently in that incident?" If that doesn't engage the employee, end the meeting with a promise to resume soon. Make it clear that ongoing abject silence is insubordination and cause for a more serious response.

If an employee gives you the silent treatment, try these steps:

1. **Wait patiently.** The employee may feel shocked, embarrassed, or saddened. Allow the employee a moment to overcome that reaction.

2. **Respect the employee's feelings.** Tell the employee that you want to hear his or her thoughts and feelings. Don't mow over the silence; it is part of the process for the employee, and you should respect it. Remember, however, that your job is to deal with the underlying problem; the silence can't be permitted to go on forever.

3. **Meet again.** If the first meeting is unproductive, meet again. Explain to the employee that you can't get to the solution until you both acknowledge there is a problem and work together to fix it.

4. **Be firm.** While you may permit silence now, tell the employee explicitly and definitively that you expect to discuss the problem at a specific future date and time.

Silence that takes the form of self-defense can often be broken if you're willing to deal with the employee's immediate needs, instead of focusing only on the results you need to get out of the meeting. It is okay to stray a bit from your agenda if doing so may help engage the employee in the discussion and develop a solution. Be practical about how far you are willing to stray; you still have a very real issue to deal with. By expressing your commitment to the employee's success, and acknowledging that this is a hard message to hear, you may be able to break through the silence and proceed with a rich discussion.

> **EXAMPLE:** Think back to example of Martha and Venetia. What if Venetia responded with stony silence? How should Martha proceed?
>
> "Venetia, do you have anything to say? No? You leave me no choice but to terminate your employment."
>
> "Venetia, given how serious this matter is, I'm going to give you a chance to collect your thoughts. If you choose not to reply, I am going to have to move forward without your input."
>
> Actually, Martha wouldn't be completely wrong in either of these situations. But the second option recognizes that Venetia may be dealing with difficult emotions that can be overcome. If Venetia is able to process what's happening, she may eventually choose to engage in a discussion with Martha about it.

Blame

Some employees are simply unwilling to accept responsibility for a performance or conduct problem. This often manifests itself in blame; the employee may accuse another person, or even you, for his or her failure. At its root, blame is a defense mechanism. When it happens, you can easily be pulled off track and sucked into a discussion you aren't prepared for. You may even begin to doubt yourself. When this happens, the employee, takes control of the meeting.

When an employee lays blame on someone else, take a moment to verify what is being said. Ask a few probing questions to find out how the employee has come to this conclusion. Do the answers sound like a plausible story? Does it bear looking into further? Or does it differ too much from what you already know? After hearing the employee out, explain what you plan to do with the information.

If the employee continues to blame other people or things, try these steps:

1. **State the facts.** Ask the employee to confirm that your understanding is accurate. Use questions like "Did you see it that way?" or "Do you agree that this happened?" or "Did you say that to her?"

2. **If you need to investigate further, step away.** If the employee's accusations have merit, end the session and don't deliver discipline until you know the whole story.

3. **Explain what research you've done and what conclusions you've come to.** This is where the discipline will begin, whether or not the employee is willing to participate.

4. **Don't discuss the responsibilities of others.** Even if other people are also responsible and will be disciplined, the employee needs to focus on his or her behavior, not that of others.

Dispassion

You often come to a discipline meeting only after thinking through the issues, worrying about whether you've done the right thing, and committing to helping your employee improve. That's why it's frustrating when an employee responds dispassionately or refuses to engage, perhaps by acting like he or she just doesn't care or isn't interested.

You always hope that your employees care enough to want to be successful, and true dispassion is typically a sign that an employee doesn't want to work hard. However, what initially appears to be dispassion may in fact be born of other emotions. An employee who is hurt or embarrassed when confronted with problems may want to give you the impression that he or she "just doesn't care" or that's it's not a big deal.

In rare cases, though, the employee really *doesn't* care enough to work to improve the problem. You'll know because as the conversation progresses, the employee will continue to be nonresponsive. Employees who are hurt or embarrassed will likely become uncomfortable when directly confronted with the issues, perhaps avoiding eye contact, mumbling, or physically withdrawing with head bowed or shoulders slumped. A dispassionate employee, on the other hand, will affect complete comfort with the situation, perhaps even meeting your eye, slouching comfortably in the chair, or allowing his or her attention to wander.

If an employee stays dispassionate and doesn't engage in the discussion, take these steps:

1. **Explain the problem.** Be very clear and have your facts in order. Ask frequent validating questions such as "Do you understand what I'm saying?" Yes or no answers are often the start of a deeper conversation.

2. **Deepen the discussion.** Start with easy questions such as "You were there that day, right?" Wait patiently for the answer, and then move on to a slightly more involved question, like "Do you remember talking to Paul about that?" Continue to ask more probing questions to get more relevant information.

3. **Stick to your agenda.** Describe what you would like to accomplish. If you are receiving no response, ask the employee how he or she would like to work toward a mutually agreeable outcome. Let the employee know that the disengagement can't continue much longer.

4. **Warn the employee of the consequences.** If the employee isn't willing to address the problem with you, whether now or in the near future, explain that you'll have no choice but to take a more serious action.

It takes a lot of energy to maintain disinterest in something that affects you a lot, which is why dispassion can usually be overcome. As we've described, it is usually a protective reaction that the employee adopts when he or she perceives something as an attack. Once the employee understands that the point of the discussion is to improve and succeed, he or she may overcome the dispassionate response.

> **EXAMPLE:** What if, early in the discipline process, Martha had said to Venetia, "As you know, I add the register's totals each night. I have noticed that four times in the last two weeks, the register has been short $100. I've looked into this and I've discovered it is happening only on nights you work. Can you explain why?" Venetia doesn't say anything. Instead, she looks down at her lap, appearing not to notice or care about the discussion.
>
> Of the two following replies, which would most likely solicit a response?
>
> "Venetia, I need you to reply. In fact, if you don't respond right away, I'm going to assume that you took the money."
>
> "Venetia, do you understand what I am asking?"
>
> While the first response may solicit a reaction from Venetia, that reaction could be an angry one. On the other hand, if Martha begins by asking Venetia whether she understands the question, Venetia has little choice but to respond with a "yes" or "no." Martha can continue to ask small, closed questions until she gets Venetia engaged in the discussion.

Dealing with employees' emotions can be a tough and confusing process. Once you've done so, however, you can focus on other issues, like setting goals and improving performance. Although you might not feel like it at the time, employees will appreciate it. Showing that you are committed to fixing problems, even when employees react emotionally, will communicate to your team that their success is important.

SMART SUMMARY:
Smart Ways to Deal With Employee Responses

- When an employee responds with anger, be prepared to slow the conversation down and walk away temporarily if needed. However, make sure that the employee understands that mutual respect is required. If the employee acts violently or you fear violence, get help right away.

- A grieving employee is usually very invested in his or her job. With time, that grief can often be overcome. Don't allow yourself to be manipulated by it, though; that won't help you solve your problem.

- An anxious employee often simply can't hear what's being said: He or she is too concerned about what it means for the future. Do your best to focus the employee on the here and now, especially if the problem can be corrected.

- When an employee exhibits a masking reaction, there is usually a lot more going on internally. See if you can draw the employee out, but keep the discussion focused on the underlying problem, not the employee's response.

Smart Documentation

f you're like most managers, you have plenty of paperwork to do. Sometimes, it might even seem like you spend more time dotting "i"s and crossing "t"s than you do dealing with the employees you supervise. But paperwork serves a very important purpose: It creates a written record of important decisions and conversations. Documenting disciplinary actions helps you prove that your actions are justified, whether to the employee, your human resources department, or a judge or jury. And of course, your written records will help you stay on top of employee problems, managing your team more successfully.

Just because documenting discipline is important doesn't mean it should take up a lot of your time, however. This chapter gives you the information you need to document employee discipline, efficiently and effectively. First, we explain the benefits of documenting your decisions. Next, we give you guidelines for creating written records that give employees the information they need to improve performance, while protecting your company legally. Finally, we'll provide a step-by-step process, including a sample form, for documenting formal disciplinary meetings, as well as some tips on documenting less formal coaching sessions and follow-up meetings.

The Benefits of Documenting Discipline

Keeping written records of your disciplinary decisions can help you do a better job of managing your employees. Documentation serves a variety of purposes: It can help you communicate with your employees, remember past disciplinary actions and decisions, and justify your decisions to others in the company.

Of course, documentation will be absolutely crucial if your decision is ever challenged in court: It's the best proof of why discipline was necessary and what type of discipline you imposed. But documenting disciplinary issues can also help you:

- **Ensure that you and the employee are on the same page.** As you'll see below, we recommend that you share formal disciplinary documentation with the employee and secure the employee's signature of acknowledgment. While the employee may not agree that discipline was necessary, you should be able to at least agree on the facts—such as what happened, when, and who was involved—and collaboratively develop a plan of action.

- **Track the employee's disciplinary history.** If you supervise a lot of employees or you are faced with an employee with a recurring disciplinary issue, your records will help you remember what's already happened as you decide how to handle a current issue or how to follow up with an employee.

- **Record the employee's disciplinary history for company use.** Very few employees and managers stay in the same job at the same company forever. If you or the employee take a different position, or if you leave the company altogether, your documentation gives the company a complete record of discipline for that employee. This will give the employee's next manager the information he or she needs to handle any future problems appropriately.

- **Treat employees consistently.** To avoid the accusation that you're playing favorites—or worse, discriminating against particular employees—you must apply discipline consistently. If you have to decide what level of discipline is appropriate, documentation allows you to review how you've handled similar problems with other employees in the past. You can make sure that you're not overreacting to or downplaying a problem by checking your track record. You can also assure yourself that your response is justified, if you have to escalate discipline when an employee doesn't improve.

- **Track problems on your team.** Disciplinary documentation lets you know what types of problems your employees have. It may also help you see larger patterns developing. Do you have several employees who seem to be unclear on their responsibilities? Frequent safety violations? A sexual harassment problem? Your disciplinary records will help you see the larger picture, so you can provide training, give better guidance, communicate your expectations more clearly, or take any other actions necessary to help your team improve.

- **Prove what you did and why.** When you keep good records, you'll be able to justify your discipline decisions to anyone. And sometimes, good documentation will help convince an employee (or more often, his or her lawyer) not to sue. But if you can't avoid a lawsuit, documentation will at least help you prove your side of the story. It will give you written evidence of the actions you took and the reasons behind them. It will also show the judge or jury that you tried to help the employee improve and that the employee had notice of his or her problems.

Guidelines for Effective Documentation

Before you dive into the details of what you should include in your records, there are some basic rules you should keep in mind. No matter what type of disciplinary problem you're facing, following these rules will help you draft effective, thorough documentation that will protect your company from legal trouble without taking up too much of your time.

Document Immediately

The best written records are contemporaneous: They are created at the time of the incidents and discussions they describe. As a practical matter, you probably won't be in a position to record conversations and events as they're happening. If you wait too long to document, however, it's all too easy to forget a few of the details, especially if you're juggling a lot of different issues or responsibilities at one time. The best way to make sure your recollections are accurate and complete is to document immediately after things happen.

Another important reason to create an immediate written record is to avoid suspicion that you're trying to create trumped-up charges against the employee. Even if you have perfectly innocent reasons for delaying your documentation, the employee could be suspicious of written records created after the fact, particularly if you wait until you know that you might have to fire the employee. From the employee's perspective, it might look like you are trying to justify an unfair termination.

> **TIP**
>
> **Adopt a same-day practice.** The best practice is to document events and discussions on the day they happen, if possible, but certainly within the same week. If a situation appears to be worsening rapidly, you must be especially careful to document everything immediately. Otherwise, you might need to have another disciplinary meeting before you can document what occurred and was agreed upon in the previous meeting. You'll want to be able to show that the employee had notice of the problem and of your expectations for improvement before you disciplined a second time.

Be Objective

Everything you write should be factual and objective. Personnel records are not the place for speculation, unfounded conclusions, or personal opinions. Instead, stick to what you saw, heard, or said. If you find yourself writing about what you think might have happened rather than what did happen, you've gotten off track.

This mistake is easier to make than you might think. For example, if an employee cried or yelled in a meeting, you might be tempted to write that the employee was "sad" or "angry." Instead, your documentation should indicate what the employee did or said, not what you thought it meant about his or her feelings or state of mind.

> **EXAMPLE:** Chad missed a deadline for an important assignment. He seems unhappy lately, and he's spending a lot of time on the phone rather than doing his work. Because Chad's mistake caused big problems for the company, and because he didn't give you any warning that he might miss the deadline, you decide to give him a written warning.
>
> On your first try, you write this: "Chad appears to be allowing personal problems to affect his work. He needs to get his head out of the clouds and start focusing on finishing his assignments on time."
>
> This is neither objective nor particularly descriptive. An outsider looking at it would be unable to tell what Chad did that warranted discipline. So you try again, this time sticking to what you know: "Chad missed the deadline for handing in his work on the Ascendance project. His assignment was due on Monday, May 1, 20xx. Because he was late, we did not meet our May 3 deadline for presenting the project to our client. Mary Allman, our contact at Ascendance, stated in a telephone conversation with me on May 3 that our lateness has caused them to consider using another company for future projects.
>
> Chad did not inform me ahead of time that he might not meet the deadline. I met with him on May 3 in my office. At that time, I asked him why he was late. He replied that he was swamped with other work."

What you write should clearly convey the facts, so that someone else reading it can understand what happened and why discipline was necessary. Keep in mind that many different people may read your documentation.

In your company, your audience will include the employee, the human resources department, any future managers to whom the employee reports, and possibly your manager. And your records may be read by people outside the company as well: If an employee considers or takes legal action against the company, what you write may wind up in the hands of lawyers, agency investigators, judges, or jurors. You'll want them to know, just by reading the documents, that you had good reasons for the disciplinary action you took.

Avoid Legal Conclusions

Carefully select the terms you use when documenting discipline. In addition to avoiding conclusions about what an employee's thoughts or motivations are, you shouldn't draw any conclusions about what an employee's actions mean legally. That means you shouldn't use any phrases implying that the employee did something illegal, such as violating another employee's legal rights. The reason for this rule is simple: If someone later tries to hold your company legally responsible for the employee's actions, your documentation could be used as proof against the company (or even against you personally).

If your company prohibits the employee's conduct, you can and should indicate that the employee violated company policy. Just steer clear of any discussion of legal violations.

> **EXAMPLE:** Several employees complain that Doug is viewing pornographic images on his computer. Although the employees agree that Doug quickly changes screens when he realizes he is no longer alone, and no one claims that Doug has tried to show them the pictures or discuss the pictures with them, they are uncomfortable with his behavior. When you confront Doug, he admits that he has been viewing these images but says he didn't realize anyone else knew about it. He is deeply embarrassed by the incident and quickly promises that he will no longer view pornography at work.
>
> You decide to issue Doug a written warning. In your documentation, you describe what the employees reported and how Doug responded when you talked to him. Then you state, "Because your behavior qualifies as sexual harassment, I have decided that serious disciplinary measures are in order. I am therefore giving you a written warning."

Several months later, one of the employees who complained about Doug files sexual harassment charges against the company. Her lawyer asks to see all files relating to the incident with Doug. Your company's lawyer wants to argue that, although inappropriate, Doug's conduct does not meet the legal definition of sexual harassment. The problem here is that you've already said, while writing on behalf of the company, that Doug committed sexual harassment. Although your lawyer might be able to argue around this, you've stacked the deck against your company.

Be Thorough

When you document a disciplinary action, you are creating a record for later use. That record should include all of the important facts: what happened, when, where, and so on. Of course, no manager has time to write a novel every time an employee shows up late for work or misses a production goal. But leaving out important details can create major headaches down the road:

- You might not remember exactly what happened later (for example, if you have to discipline the employee again, or review the employee's file to draft a performance appraisal).
- If the employee begins working for another manager, that manager won't know all of the facts.
- You'll be in trouble if you ever have to justify your actions to higher-ups in the company, or in court. You'll either forget what actually happened, or you'll have to say, "This important thing happened, but for some reason I forgot to put it in my notes." Even if you're able to remember the incident, it will look less credible if you didn't make a record of it when it occurred.

EXAMPLE: Kate manages the customer service center for a software company. She fires Francis after he repeatedly fails to meet the company's productivity standards. Customer service representatives are expected to answer or return at least 15 calls per day; Francis averaged nine or ten calls per day. Reps are also expected to complete all of the paperwork for customer orders on the day the customer orders the product. Francis's paperwork was routinely two or three days late.

Francis files a discrimination lawsuit, stating that Kate singled him out for discipline because of his age (he is 55 years old). He claims that Kate told him his numbers were low but never told him how he could improve. He also says that Kate never told him about the same-day requirement for customer orders.

Kate reviews her documentation. If she finds something like "I reviewed customer service productivity requirements with Francis," with no mention of a follow-up plan, she might have a hard time disproving Francis's allegations. On the other hand, if her records say, "I expect you to complete all of the forms for customer orders on the day the orders are placed" and "I will spend one morning next week with you at your workstation; later that day, we will meet to discuss how you can shorten the time you spend on the phone with each customer," she will be able to confidently dispute his statements.

Don't Overdocument

We know, we know: We just told you to be thorough. But it's also important not to go overboard, either by formally documenting minor incidents or by going on for pages and pages about a single incident or disciplinary meeting. You probably don't have time for that kind of documentation, and it won't help your employees' performance much either. If your employees think they will be written up for every tiny misstep, they are likely to stop trying to meet your expectations. They might even decide to look for another job that isn't as stressful.

This type of documentation doesn't provide much legal protection either; in fact, it can actually work against you in court. Overdocumenting minor problems will make you look like a micromanager or a nitpicker. An employee can use extensive documentation to show that you were particularly hard on him or her or that you never gave the employee a real chance to improve.

Also, the more details you write down, the easier it is to contradict yourself or get confused about what happened. If you try to remember every single thing that was said or done, it might be difficult to distinguish the really important facts. And these inconsistencies could give more fuel to a disgruntled employee who wants to challenge your disciplinary decisions.

Don't Make Promises

Because you want to motivate your employees to succeed, you might be tempted to offer rewards to an employee who successfully meets the goals in his or her action plan. However, you should not tell the employee that he or she will receive certain benefits for improving. Similarly, you should not promise to follow a particular disciplinary process with the employee. Either of these mistakes could tie your hands later, if the employee tries to hold you to your promise.

As we explained in Chapter 3, stating or implying that an employee will be fired only for particular types of misconduct could limit the company's right to fire that employee. And, if your documentation states that an employee will receive a promotion, raise, or other benefit for improved performance, you might have created a contract obligating the company to provide that benefit, even if the company cannot afford it or does not want to provide it.

Making promises may also send the wrong message to the employee. Instead of helping the employee understand that there is a problem, promising incentives may lead the employee to believe he or she is meeting expectations and will be given extra benefits for *exceeding* them. You want to stay focused on the disciplinary issue, ensuring the employee understands there is a problem that needs to be fixed.

> **EXAMPLE:** Ben disciplines Jerry for roughhousing on the loading dock. Ben informs Jerry that his actions violate the company's safety rules. To give Jerry an incentive to shape up, Ben writes this in his verbal warning documentation: "You cannot violate this rule again if you wish to be promoted to Fulfillment Manager." If Jerry never roughhouses again, he might argue that he is entitled to the promotion, even if the company later decides someone else should get the job.

Explain the Effects

As we've already discussed, it's very important to communicate to the employee how his or her performance or conduct problems are affecting you, others on your team, and the company as a whole. This is the best way to convince the employee that the problem is important and must change. It also conveys respect for the employee's contribution, because people notice—and suffer—when that contribution isn't made.

To drive the point home, you should not only discuss it with the employee, but also include it in your documentation. Employees are more likely to sit up and take notice when they see, in black and white, exactly how their problems are creating more work for others, costing the company money, leading to lost customers or sales, and so on.

Always Include a Follow-Up Plan

As you know, you and the employee should always come up with a plan for improvement, including deadlines. Always include this plan in your documentation. This will remind you to check in with the employee to make sure these targets are met, and to fulfill any other obligations you have to the employee. This will also help the employee focus on what he or she needs to do, and by when, to meet your expectations.

Informal Documentation

You don't have to fill out formal paperwork every time you meet with an employee to discuss performance improvement. For example, if you have a brief coaching conversation with an employee who seems to be away from her desk frequently or turns in a report that contains a couple of typos, you shouldn't spend the time or energy to document every word you said. Similarly, if you have a quick meeting to check in with an employee whom you had to discipline, you don't have to record the meeting in great detail.

However, you should make a quick written note of these meetings for future reference. After all, what happens if that one report with typos becomes ten? You'll want to remember—and be able to show—that the incident occurred before and that you addressed it. If your first quick coaching session isn't successful, you may have to move into your company's formal discipline process. At that point, you'll need to know (and be able to show) that you already spoke to the employee about the issue. Similarly, your follow-up meeting may become important if the employee later claims that it never happened or does not remember the objectives you created together to improve the problem.

What to Include

For brief meetings and conversations like these, write a short memo—a paragraph or two—summarizing the discussion. Note the date and time you spoke to the employee and the employee's response, if any. Here's a sample memo documenting a follow-up meeting with an employee who was required to take a training program:

Memo

I met with Jennifer Shiu on February 3, 20xx to find out whether she had completed her class on using Excel spreadsheets for accounting. She told me that she finished the class on January 31 and that she learned a lot of helpful tips. I asked her if she would be willing to do a brief presentation on what she learned to the bookkeeping department at our departmental meeting on February 20; she agreed to do so.

Where to Keep Informal Documentation

If your company has a procedure for handling informal documentation, follow it. Some companies require managers to create written records of coaching sessions for the employee's personnel file; others will not allow managers to place anything short of a written warning in the file.

In companies that don't have a policy on this, many managers choose not to put informal coaching memos in the employee's personnel file. Instead, it's a good idea to keep these in your office, in a separate working file for each employee or a single file for ongoing performance issues. If you later have to discipline the employee for the same problem, you can use the memo to complete the "Prior Incidents" portion of the form below.

Unlike more formal documentation, you don't have to show these "coaching logs" to the employee. In fact, the employee probably won't ever find out that you wrote yourself a note. Knowing every incident is documented might make the employee feel micromanaged and afraid of each misstep. Because so many problems can be solved at the coaching level, there's no need to make the employee feel intimidated or watched. The document is really just to remind you to monitor the situation and to give you a basis to progress in the discipline process if that becomes necessary.

> **CAUTION**
>
> **It's all discoverable.** In the best case scenario, your disciplinary sessions will help employees improve their performance, turn attendance problems around, put misconduct behind them, and move on to succeed at your company. Unfortunately, it's also possible that an employee who can't or won't improve will have to be terminated. If that employee takes legal action against your company, all of your documentation will have to be handed over to the employee's lawyer during the legal process of "discovery." Even informal notes and reminders are subject to discovery, not just the formal documents that go into the employee's official personnel file. Remember this unfortunate possibility when you're documenting discipline problems.

Formal Documentation, Step by Step

This section explains exactly what information you should include in your disciplinary records. To make the process clearer, we'll be creating documentation of a written warning for Randy, a fictional employee who is having trouble meeting deadlines.

At the end of this chapter, you'll find a sample discipline form you can use (see Appendix D to access a downloadable copy). You can either use the form electronically, or you can print it out and handwrite the information in the space provided. Of course, if your company has its own forms to document discipline, you should use those instead. You'll see that we prefer to address the employee directly, rather than in the third person. Again, if your company had a different practice, you should follow it.

Once the paperwork is complete and signed by both you and employee, place it in the employee's personnel file.

Heading

At the beginning of your documentation, insert the employee's name, your name, the date, and the purpose of the document (for example, a verbal or written warning). Here's the heading for Randy's written warning:

Employee Disciplinary Notice	
Employee's Name: Randy Clark	
Manager's Name: Sarah Bronson	**Date of Incident:** September 10, 20xx
Type of Warning: ☐ Verbal Warning ☑ Written Warning	

Incident Description

Next, explain the reason you are disciplining the employee. If the employee committed misconduct, describe what happened. For poor performance, describe how the employee is falling short of company requirements or expectations. This is also the place to include information about how the employee's problem is affecting the company. Don't include information about any past incidents or problems for which you've already disciplined the employee. If it belongs in the memo, that information will go in the next section.

Assume that Randy works for a company that owns a chain of stores selling home improvement products. He missed his deadline to finish five articles on kitchen remodeling for the company's website. His manager describes it like this:

Type of Warning: ☐ Verbal Warning ☑ Written Warning

Incident Description:

On August 3, 20xx, I asked you to create five new articles about kitchen remodels for the company's website. As we discussed, these articles were to be descriptions of typical kitchen remodeling projects, with references and links to relevant company products. I informed you that these articles would be the prototype for new website content that ties our products to a detailed description of particular projects, rather than simply listing products by category. I also informed you that I needed to have a final draft of these articles by September 8, so I could present them to our marketing team at a meeting on September 10.

On September 7, you came to my office and told me that you would not make the deadline. You told me that you had completed a draft of three articles but had not yet included references to company products. You also stated that you thought someone in marketing should handle this part of the assignment, as they are more familiar with the products than you are. You did not let me know that you might miss the deadline or that you were having any trouble with the articles until September 7.

As a result of your failure to meet this deadline, Cynthia Bradley, Russell Jenkins, and I all had to drop our other work to complete the three articles you drafted. These articles had to be changed substantially because they were not written to best utilize the company's products. We had to add products to the articles as well. Because I was able to present only three articles at the marketing meeting, we had to postpone the rollout date for this new type of content. Our department's failure to meet its goal may cause other departments to believe we are unreliable. Moreover, because the new content is expected to drive higher sales, this delay will cost the company money.

Prior Incidents

If this is not the first time the employee has had this problem, describe previous incidents here. Include any disciplinary actions or coaching sessions that occurred. Also describe the action plan you and the employee came up with at that time, including any help you made available to the employee. You don't need to go into great detail here, as you've already documented the prior incident. If you kept informal documentation of earlier coaching sessions or discussions, refer back to those notes to complete this portion of the form.

Randy has already received a verbal warning for missing a previous deadline, so his manager completes this section as follows:

Prior Incidents:

I have already issued you a verbal warning, on March 15, 20xx, for missing a deadline. You were assigned to write a list of suggested projects store associates could discuss with customers looking for spring gardening and landscaping ideas. You missed your deadline by a week, and we were unable to present your ideas to associates at the company's quarterly meeting.

When we met to discuss this problem, you told me that you tended to wait until the last minute to complete writing projects. We agreed that you would attend a seminar on time management. We also agreed that you would outline your future writing assignments several days after receiving them, and that you would check in with me immediately if you needed help meeting a deadline. The details of this incident and our plan for improvement are in your personnel file, as is the certificate you received for participating in a seminar entitled "Time Management for Busy Employees," dated March 23, 20xx.

Improvement Plan

In this section, you should first state the improvement you need to see. You should be very specific in this section, giving the employee tangible goals he or she is capable of meeting. For example, you might write, "You must be here when your shift begins at 7:00 a.m. each morning, unless you have called in sick" or, "I need to see you at every district manager's meeting." This is far more useful to the employee than statements such as "Don't be late" or "Attend important meetings."

Next, describe the plan you and the employee have developed. Be specific about the changes you expect and the deadlines for achieving them. Again, this will help the employee understand what is expected, and it will help remind you what you should be evaluating when you revisit the issue.

Even though Randy took a time management course and has been required to submit outlines of his writing assignments, he has still missed another deadline. He and his manager agree that he needs more frequent interim deadlines to prevent him from procrastinating. Here's the plan that Randy and Sarah develop together:

Improvement Plan:

Randy, you must meet your deadlines for writing assignments. When you miss your deadlines, you cause more work for me and your coworkers, and our department's reputation in the company suffers.

You have told me that you are still putting your writing assignments off until the last minute and that you are having trouble estimating how long projects will take. We have agreed that you and I will meet every Friday at 11 a.m. to discuss your writing projects. At the first meeting after I assign you a project, you will show me your outline. At subsequent meetings, you will report on your progress and show me what you have written to date. At the end of each meeting, I will tell you what I expect you to accomplish by the next meeting. I will confirm this expectation in a follow-up email to you every Friday afternoon. If you disagree with my understanding of the expectation, you have agreed to tell me immediately by the end of the day on Friday.

Employee Comments

No matter how carefully you draft your documentation, your employee may not feel that you fully or fairly captured the issue. There is no requirement that you come to a consensus on what the documentation says. In fact, if you disagree with the employee's interpretation of what happened, you should stick to your version of events. Remember, you are focused on communicating the facts. Because the employee may come into the discussion with a lot of emotions, he or she may feel entirely different issues need to be addressed.

To account for this, you should leave room on the form for the employee to comment. If the employee doesn't rebut your statements, it will be very difficult for him or her to claim later that your documentation is incorrect or incomplete. If the employee takes issue with your characterization of the problem, he or she can put those concerns in writing, and the two of you can meet again to hash it out. Sometimes, the employee just needs the opportunity to "vent" to feel that both sides of the issue are accurately reflected (for instance, because the employee failed to perform as required but thinks he or she was justified in doing so).

Of course, even if the employee disputes your characterization of the problem, you'll need to know that the employee is on board about the agreed-upon solution. If the employee's written rebuttal indicates that he or she is not willing to perform the steps required by your written improvement plan, you'll know that your discipline discussion is not over. Otherwise, you're setting the employee up for failure.

Randy knows that he missed the deadline, and he agrees with the proposed action plan. However, he still thinks the project was too difficult in the first place, so he adds his two cents to the written warning:

Employee Comments:

One of the reasons I missed the website deadline is because I was unable to figure out which products to feature. This isn't my responsibility; it should have been done by the marketing people.

In response to these comments, Sarah should probably have a follow-up discussion with Randy. In this case, she could tell Randy that he must do the projects she assigns to him and that he should tell her during their first Friday meeting after a project is assigned if he thinks any part of the project is beyond his abilities. If Randy agrees to this plan, Sarah can write a brief note documenting the meeting for Randy's personnel file.

Dates, Acknowledgments, and Signatures

At the end of the form, you and the employee should sign and date it. Some employees are reluctant to sign a disciplinary form, because they believe that signing it means they agree that they deserve discipline. However, you need to have proof that the employee received a copy of the document so you can show that the employee had notice of his or her problems and the proposed resolution. Most companies get around this problem by requiring the employee only to acknowledge having received and read the document. If the employee is reluctant to sign, explain that doing so is just an acknowledgment of receipt. And if the employee wants to say anything in response, he or she had that opportunity on the form. If the employee still refuses to sign, write a note on the document to that effect ("Delivered to the employee on September 10, 20xx. Employee refused to sign the document.")

The bottom of Randy's form looks like this:

Manager's Signature: *Sarah Bronson*	Date: *September 10, 20xx*
Employee Acknowledgment	
I acknowledge that I have received and understand this document.	
Employee's Signature: *Randy Clark*	Date: *September 10, 20xx*

Sample Employee Disciplinary Form

Employee Disciplinary Notice	
Employee's Name:	
Manager's Name:	**Date of Incident:**
Type of Warning: ☐ Verbal Warning ☐ Written Warning	
Incident Description:	
Prior Incidents:	
Improvement Plan:	
Employee Comments:	
Manager's Signature:	**Date:**
Employee Acknowledgment	
I acknowledge that I have received and understand this document.	
Employee's Signature:	**Date:**

SMART SUMMARY:
Smart Documentation

- **Documenting discipline has many benefits.** It ensures that you and the employee are on the same page, helps you and the company track discipline problems, helps maintain consistency, and provides proof of what you did and why.

- **The documentation you create should be understandable to anyone who reads it.** You must be clear, thorough, and factual. Be sure to include all relevant information, including dates, full names, prior incidents, and an action plan.

- **Stick to the facts.** When documenting, don't interpret the meaning of an employee's actions or word. Just record them. If your documentation is based on fact, it will be hard for the employee to refute what you say.

- **Unless company policy requires otherwise, keep informal documentation in a separate file (such as a manager's log), and use it to remind yourself to follow up with employees.** If the documentation is formal and going into the employee's file, give the employee the opportunity to make comments.

- **Don't overdocument.** That means you shouldn't include information that isn't directly related to the incident you're describing. If you write down too many details, you may have a harder time distinguishing the important facts, which may be confusing later if you have to discuss the decision to discipline with the employee, your manager, your human resources department, or a lawyer.

Smart Collaboration: Involving the Right People at the Right Time

Sometimes, it's necessary to discuss a disciplinary issue with people in the company who are not directly involved in the situation. In particular, you may need to talk with your manager, human resources department, and/or legal counsel to make sure you have handled an issue appropriately and legally and are marshalling all the resources necessary to ensure the employee's success. Additionally, as you work to gather all the facts, you may need to talk with other employees who have witnessed or been affected by the problem.

However, whom to tell and what to reveal can be touchy subjects. On the one hand, you want to respect the employee's privacy. On the other hand, you have a responsibility to appropriately inform certain parties and to gather all the pertinent information. This chapter will show you how to collaborate properly with others in the discipline process, while respecting the employee's privacy.

Involving Management

Often, when small problems persist or grow, you won't be the only one dealing with the issue. You may need to involve your manager, too. There are three major points in the process when it may be necessary to involve your manager: when an issue has an important effect on the business, when you need an alternate perspective, or when company policy or practice dictate it.

Issues That Affect the Business

Earlier chapters explain how discipline problems affect your company, both financially and otherwise. Not only does this analysis help you figure out what level of action is appropriate, it also helps you determine when you should involve your manager.

If an issue has had or will have a significant financial impact on the business, you need to talk to your manager about the problem fairly quickly. What constitutes significant financial impact will vary by the size and nature of the company, but it may include lost sales, internal theft, or lost customers.

What information should you share with your manager? You probably do not need to give every detail. Instead, you only need to give a basic description of the problem, its impact, and the solution you and the employee have developed. You should also provide regular updates on the status of the action plan as it proceeds. This will assure your boss that you are on top of the issue.

> **EXAMPLE:** Aaron, a sales representative, is responsible for maintaining customer relationships and ensuring that customers renew their annual subscriptions to the company's product. His numbers have been falling steadily over the past three months. Renewals are down, and so is revenue. Sharon, his manager, is concerned about his performance, as it affects not only his numbers, but hers as well. Sharon realizes that she needs to address this issue and let her boss know that she is working to fix it.
>
> Sharon sets up a meeting with Richard, her boss and the head of sales for the company. She begins by telling Richard that sales numbers are down and that she has figured out the reason. She tells him she has set up a meeting with Aaron. Knowing that Richard has great ideas for improving renewals, she also asks him for his input. They have a productive 15-minute conversation and come up with some good ideas for bringing the numbers back up.
>
> Sharon concludes the meeting with Richard by telling him the schedule for talking with Aaron, promising to copy Richard on the action plan, and creating an ongoing agenda item of bringing Richard up to date on Aaron's progress as the plan is implemented.

In Sharon's discussion with Richard, she gave him the information he needed to feel confident that she would resolve the problem. She got him invested in Aaron's success by getting his thoughts about an effective action plan. Lastly, she has committed to keeping Richard informed, so he knows he can help redirect the process if it doesn't seem to be working.

Getting an Alternate Perspective

Sometimes, you may be unsure how to handle a performance or conduct issue, or you may just need confirmation that your intended course of action is an appropriate one. Additionally, you might find it helpful just to get another opinion or idea about how to approach the situation. In these instances, your manager can be the perfect person to talk to. The benefits of talking to your manager include:

- **Experience.** Your manager supervises people, too, and probably has experience with many of the same issues that you face.
- **Fresh perspective.** Your manager is generally not as close to the problem as you are, and may be able to offer a fresh, and more objective, perspective. He or she may have questions or answers that you hadn't thought of.
- **Institutional knowledge.** In addition to experience managing others, your manager may know more about how the company, and other managers, have handled similar situations in the past. Your manager may also be able to tell you how the problem and your proposed solution will be viewed by others in the company.

Talking to your manager about a discipline issue has additional benefits. It guarantees that your manager won't be surprised to learn about an issue from someone else. And if you've already discussed the issue together, you'll know you have your manager's support as you carry out the discipline.

Company Policy and Practice

Even if the problem has only a minor effect on the company, and you don't feel like you need an alternate perspective, you might still need to involve your manager. If you are required—or expected—to do so, whether by your manager, company policies, or the human resources or legal departments, you should certainly escalate the problem. Here are some examples where you might need to bring your manager in on a disciplinary matter:

- **Company policy.** Many company policies dictate when managers must be involved, often when a problem has escalated to a serious step in the discipline process, such as a verbal or written warning.
- **Your relationship with your manager.** If you work closely and frequently with your manager and keep him or her updated on your workload, treat the discipline process as one more business issue to discuss. If you don't bring it up, it may look like you are "hiding" something if and when the problem worsens and you need to involve your manager later.
- **If you have involved your human resources or legal departments.** Because the issue is taking up a significant amount of your time, you probably want to keep your manager informed about what you are working on. Additionally, chances are good that the human resources or legal

department may need to raise the issue with your manager, and it's better if he or she hears it from you first.

- **Your level of experience.** If you have seen and successfully dealt with the same issue before, then chances are good you can do the same thing without more assistance. However, if the problem is new to you, and additional input would be valuable, approach your manager for help.
- **The company culture.** While some companies encourage collaborative discussion during the discipline process, others are more focused on driving results. If your company emphasizes the importance of collaboration, ask for additional input and help early on.

If you're not sure what to do in a given situation, you should always talk to your manager. Just as you are a resource for your employees, your manager is a resource and coach for you.

Involving Human Resources

For additional help, you can and should talk to a representative of your human resources department. Human resources professionals have direct experience with and training on most disciplinary issues and can counsel you on applying company policy and handling difficult conversations. They can also partner with you to facilitate the actual discipline process.

Applying Company Policy and Practices

At their best, company discipline policies are based on fairness and legality and will outline the steps in the company's discipline process. At worst, they are confusing, outdated, and dense with legal language and don't tell you what you really need to do. And in some cases, they just don't exist.

The good news is, there is someone in the company who can help you interpret, apply, or even work to change these policies. Your human resources department deals with these policies and practices on a regular basis. They know how the rest of the company is using them, which is important in maintaining consistent, company-wide application (see Chapter 3 for more information). They also know the ins and outs of the policy language and can decipher it for you when it seems unclear.

When your company doesn't have a written policy in place, chances are good that the company has had to deal with the same or a similar issue before. The human resources department is a repository of knowledge about these practices and can let you know how you should proceed based on how it's been done in the past. Again, this helps maintains consistency and fairness.

When You Don't Have a Human Resources Department

Many smaller companies operate without full-time human resource professionals or legal help. For those of you operating in this environment, you are not without resources. For human resources help, you can consult the Society for Human Resources Management (www.shrm.org), who can either set you up with the information you need or help you find a reasonably priced consultant. SHRM has local chapters throughout the country.

For legal help, visit Nolo's website (www.nolo.com), which has information about how to find an attorney, articles and products addressing issues in employment law, and an attorney directory. If you need to hire an attorney, you may also want to ask professional colleagues for referrals.

Getting Advice

As a manager, you may need help when you are dealing with something you have not seen before, or when you simply are not sure how to proceed. This could happen at any step in the discipline process; even if you have experience with a particular type of problem, you might not know what to do when things get worse or the employee just doesn't seem to be improving. In situations like these, your human resources department can provide advice and support, giving you the chance to get feedback on your proposed response, and make sure it is consistent with company policy and practice and the law.

Human resources professionals can also role play difficult conversations, giving you a chance to practice what you will say. They can prepare you for the real conversations by discussing potential employee reactions and how you will deal with them. They often have a good working knowledge of the overall organization, so they can help you consider how your decisions will affect the organization as a whole. Finally, many human resources professionals are trained in conflict resolution and negotiation, as well as employment law, and can help you negotiate murky legal or emotional waters.

Partnership and Facilitation

If you are a new manager, dealing with an issue that you've never experienced before, or worried about a strong reaction from the employee, consider using human resources as your partner or facilitator in the disciplinary process. This means actually having the disciplinary conversations—usually for verbal or written warnings, or even terminations—with a human resources representative in the room, acting as an "in-the-moment" coach for you or as an objective third party who facilitates the discussion. Using human resources as a partner in the process will give you a safety net: They can help clarify any aspects of the process or conversation that get confused, bring up previously discussed points that you may have forgotten, and keep you from saying anything that might put the company in legal hot water.

A human resources professional can also act as a facilitator. In this role, he or she can make sure that that each party is being heard and that you are headed for a successful outcome. This is particularly useful if you have a difficult employee who sinks into silence or is known to be resentful. In this case, the human resources representative maintains objectivity and focuses on getting the issues aired on both sides of the table. This fosters collaboration and encourages the employee and manager to work together to create a successful outcome.

Of course, you need to consider how the employee might perceive having a human resources representative in the room. Involving human resources adds formality to the process. Sometimes you need that formality, for example, when giving a formal written warning. Other times, you may not want that formality, like during a coaching session. Particularly if human resources is involved early in the process, it may even signal to the employee that you do not feel confident in handling things on your own or that you need protection. This can undermine your authority with your employee and may lead him or her to believe that you are not experienced or knowledgeable enough to handle the problem.

If you are trying to decide whether to include a human resources representative in the meeting, consider these factors:

- **Does company policy require it?** If so, you should talk with the representative ahead of time, to explain why he or she needs to be involved.
- **Will the employee feel glad to have an objective listener, or embarrassed by the presence of a third party?** Obviously, this is something you can only speculate about, but if you're fairly certain that having an objective third party will help the discussion, include the human resources representative.
- **Do you need backup?** If you will better communicate your message if a third party is present, ask human resources to participate.

Involving Legal Counsel

Sometimes, you might need some help from a lawyer before you decide how to handle a discipline problem. Whether—and how—you seek this help will depend on your company's structure and policies. If your company has its own legal department or in-house counsel, you might be able to just pick up the phone or walk down the hall for a quick chat. If your company uses outside counsel to handle its legal matters, you will probably need to get authorization from someone—perhaps your manager or the human resources department—to get an attorney involved. Of course, you should follow your company's procedures for when and how to involve legal counsel.

If you have the authority to decide when to consult with a lawyer, however, you should consider using it whenever you believe the company might have some legal exposure. In other words, if you have an inkling that the company might be at fault (or appear to be at fault), or that imposing discipline or terminating employment might violate the employee's legal rights, you would be wise to get some help from a lawyer as you decide how to proceed.

Consider getting some legal advice in these situations (you can find detailed information on each of these issues in Chapter 3):

- **The employee absolutely denies the misconduct for which you are imposing discipline.** In this situation, a lawyer can help you make sure you investigated the facts thoroughly and came to the right conclusion.
- **The employee has hired a lawyer.** In this case, you know that at least one lawyer will be watching your every move; you want to make sure you have someone looking out for your legal interests, too.
- **The employee has a written or oral employment contract that restricts the company's right to fire or discipline.** You'll want to make sure you understand how to comply with that agreement.

> EXAMPLE: Hector is hired as the Director of Marketing for a large Internet service provider. The company has had trouble keeping a marketing director, so it offers Hector a three-year employment contract. The contract provides that Hector's employment can be terminated only for "good cause," which it further defines as "commission of a felony; gross malfeasance; or willful and continued failure to perform the duties of the position."
>
> Toshi is the company's Vice President of Sales and Marketing. He believes Hector is not working out: the marketing initiatives he has rolled out have not been very successful, an advertising campaign Hector spearheaded has flopped, and Hector's staff turnover has increased. Toshi has coached Hector, to no avail. What Toshi really wants is to replace him with someone who is more creative and better able to ignite his team's enthusiasm.
>
> Toshi needs some legal advice. Clearly Hector hasn't committed a felony, but do his actions constitute gross malfeasance or willful and continued failure substantially to perform his duties? If Toshi doesn't have good cause to fire Hector, should he consider breaking the contract or perhaps negotiating a severance? If Toshi decides not to fire Hector, should he discipline him? Is there language he could use in his disciplinary sessions and documentation to show that the company has good cause to fire Hector under the contract? A good lawyer could help provide some answers.

- **The employee recently filed a complaint or claim with a government agency or complained within the company of illegal or unethical activity.** In this situation, disciplining or firing the employee could lead to a retaliation claim.

- **The employee recently revealed that he or she is in a protected class.**
For example, the employee has recently told you that he or she has a
disability or practices a particular religion.
- **You are concerned about the worker's potential for violence, vandalism, or
sabotage.** This is particularly important if the worker has access to the
company's high-level trade secrets or competitive information.

> **EXAMPLE:** Roberto works for a company that makes vitamins and
> nutritional supplements. The company has an extensive website where
> it provides product information, customer testimonials, and articles on
> health and wellness. About one-third of the company's total product sales
> comes through its website. Roberto supervises the team of employees that
> keep the website up and running.
>
> Roberto has already disciplined Camilla for spending work time on
> personal projects; another employee reported that Camilla spent a couple
> of hours each day on her own personal website and blog. Roberto kept
> an eye on Camilla and confirmed the employee's report, then gave her a
> written warning. During their disciplinary meeting, Camilla told Roberto
> that she thought he was being too harsh and that the company should treat
> its technical employees better "because we are the ones who control what
> goes on the company's site."
>
> A month later, Roberto notices that Camilla is still posting to her blog
> from work. Before deciding what to do, he reads through her blog. There,
> he discovers that Camilla has commented extensively on his decision to
> discipline her. She has also written, "This company is crazy. Don't they have
> any idea what kind of havoc I could cause with just a couple of keystrokes?"
>
> Now Roberto is worried. He wants to fire Camilla, but he's concerned that
> she'll sabotage the website. He also has questions about her postings—can
> she write about the company? Can the company discipline her for it? Is it
> legal for her to mention him by name? Is there anything the company can
> do to stop her from writing about it? Again, a knowledgeable employment
> lawyer can help Roberto sort through the alternatives and decide what to do.

- **You are disciplining the employee for excessive absences or leave and are
concerned that the employee's time off might be legally protected.** For
example, the time off might qualify as family and medical leave or
protected military leave.

Involving Other Employees

Through the course of the disciplinary process, it may be necessary to talk to people who have information that is relevant or related to the problem you're dealing with. You may need to talk to people who witnessed or are affected by certain behavior or actions. And if the behavior or action was targeted at a specific person, you will need to let that person know that you are dealing with it.

Involving Other Employees in an Investigation

Determining whom to talk to and what to say as you gather information can have a direct effect on the success of the disciplinary process. As we discussed in earlier chapters, employees often talk about what's happening in the workplace. If you cast your net too wide and involve too many people, you could severely hamper the environment in which the disciplined employee has to work. If a large group of people know about an employee's problem, it may permanently tarnish that person's reputation. This can create an environment where it is difficult to succeed: If everyone believes that the person is a failure, the person may actually fail because he or she feels unsupported, threatened, or overwhelmed by what's happening. And of course, if you reveal too much information to too many people, a disgruntled employee might even bring a lawsuit against you, claiming defamation or invasion of privacy.

As you investigate a problem, avoid inadvertently tainting the environment by:

- **Working consciously to limit the number of people involved.** The fewer people involved, the fewer people can pass judgment on the disciplined employee. Of course, in order to be thorough and fair, you need to involve the pertinent people in an investigation. Just don't troll widely for information; target the people who you know have information you need.

- **Keeping your questions as open ended as possible.** If you make your questions specific and closed ("yes" or "no" questions), you will find yourself giving out information that shouldn't be discussed. An example of this is "Did you see Rafael try to kiss Hope?" versus "Tell me about what you witnessed on Tuesday afternoon in the break room at about 3:00."

- **Keeping your disciplinary decisions private.** You will probably face more than a few questions from the employees you interview. They might want to know all the details of what happened, who was involved, and what you plan to do about it. This curiosity is natural, but you can't satisfy it. Ultimately, any action you decide to take is between the affected employee and the company (that is, you and perhaps your manager or a human resources representative). While other employees will probably be talking about the situation, you shouldn't tell them your conclusions about the problem (in other words, what you think "really" happened) or how you decided to handle it. The most you should say is that the company is looking into the matter and will deal with it appropriately.

EXAMPLE: Vitali is the Quality Assurance Manager for a small software company. One day, Cliff, one of the QA engineers, tells Vitali about a problem with Bruce, another QA engineer. Cliff cites a recent meeting with several other members of the QA team. At the meeting, Bruce talked loudly while others were talking. He also got angry at one of the other engineers, who asked Bruce to stop interrupting. Cliff says the team has noticed that Bruce isn't finishing his work on time and that he seems easily upset. Cliff decided to talk to Vitali when Bruce got frustrated by a problem he was trying to work out and started cursing and throwing books and office supplies in the team's work area. Bruce then left work for the day. Cliff says that the team is concerned for Bruce, but also fearful that his increasing volatility and lack of control could lead to trouble.

Vitali knows that these allegations are serious and must be investigated. He notifies human resources, and they meet to strategize about the investigation. Together they determine that Vitali should talk to the other employees who attended the meeting, as well as someone who saw Cliff's angry outburst in the work room.

Vitali meets with Andrew, the witness in the work room. He asks him, "Andrew, can you tell me what, if anything, you saw this morning in the QA work area?" Andrew replies, "Well, Bruce kind of lost it. Cliff and I were talking to each other, and Bruce suddenly started swearing at the program he was working on. He was yelling really loudly, and when we tried to find out what was going on, he started yelling and swearing at us. Then he threw some of his manuals across the room and threw his stapler and one of his speakers at the wall. At that point, I left because I was afraid of what might happen next. Cliff was trying to calm him down." Andrew then asks, "What's going to happen? Is Bruce in trouble? The whole thing was pretty weird, but it seems so out of character for him. Do you think he's having personal problems?"

Vitali responds, "I'm gathering information now about what happened. I'm also going to ask Bruce to take a day or two off while I investigate. Once I've finished my investigation and talked things over with Bruce, the company will decide how to handle the situation."

By limiting what he tells Andrew, Vitali minimizes the chance that Andrew will draw any improper conclusions. He is also taking care not to poison the investigation (or the work environment for Bruce) by sharing too much unnecessarily. At the same time, Vitali has reassured Andrew that Bruce will not be returning to work until the problem is resolved, which should alleviate Andrew's safety concerns. Vitali has given out just enough information to reassure Andrew that the company knows about the problem and will deal with it.

> **CAUTION**
> Asking employees to maintain confidentiality can lead to legal trouble. You may be tempted to tell your employees to keep your discussions confidential or refrain from discussing ongoing investigations with each other. However, recent decisions by the EEOC and National Labor Relations Board have held that a blanket requirement of confidentiality violates employee rights under antidiscrimination and labor laws. Because this is an evolving area of law, it's best not to make this request of your employees or consult with a lawyer before doing so. You can also learn more about how to conduct a thorough and legal investigation in *The Essential Guide to Workplace Investigations*, by Lisa Guerin (Nolo).

Communicating With Those Affected

During the course of a disciplinary action, you may also need to collaborate and communicate with people directly affected by the problem. This is particularly true when dealing with poor performance that changes the workload or work product of other team members. For example, if a project team has a member whose deliverables have been consistently substandard, and the results are affecting the whole team, then the team is going to want to know what you, the manager, are going to do about it.

The best practices for talking to employees affected by a problem are similar to those for dealing with employees during an investigation:

- Limit your conversation to the pertinent facts.
- Provide assurance that you are aware of and dealing with the situation.
- Don't give so much information that the employee will have a difficult time being successful.

When deciding how much information to share, err on the side of less rather than more.

> **EXAMPLE:** In the example of Bruce and Vitali above, the company has decided to put Bruce on a written warning as Vitali discovered that his actions were due to a personal issue at home: his wife's terminal cancer. Vitali referred Bruce to the company's employee assistance program and talked to him about rearranging his schedule for a while, so he could spend more time with his family. Vitali also arranged for Bruce to meet with a human resources representative, to find out about his right to take leave and care for his wife.
>
> What should Vitali tell the rest of the team? Only that he has spoken to Bruce and taken appropriate action. This assures the team that Vitali knows what's going on and is dealing with it. It also opens the door for team members to provide feedback should they see Bruce continue to create problems. What Vitali should not do is reveal Bruce's personal problems or explain that Bruce has received a written warning. All of this information goes beyond what the team needs to know, and revealing it could make it difficult for Bruce to do his job.

Confidentiality

If you need to discuss a problem with others in the company, you're probably painfully aware of another need: the need to maintain confidentiality, to the extent possible. After all, you don't want the employee to think you can't be trusted, and most employees would prefer not to share their performance and conduct issues with others. In general, that means that it's best to discuss a disciplinary issue only with those people who are directly involved or need to know. By limiting communication, you give your employee a fair chance to improve without a lot of eyes observing and passing judgment.

If you maintain confidentiality when appropriate, you will:

- establish trust between you and your employee
- limit gossip in your workplace, and
- minimize legal problems.

> ⚠ **CAUTION**
>
> **Don't promise absolute confidentiality.** While you want to respect the employee's privacy, you shouldn't promise the employee that you're going to keep everything confidential. There are instances when you will need to talk to others about what has been said or done. This occurs frequently when one employee accuses another of violence, harassment, or other inappropriate behavior. In those cases, you will probably have to talk to several employees—at very least, the accuser and the accused—about the allegations.

Establishing Trust

Successful discipline requires that the manager and the employee have some level of trust. As a manager, you must trust your employee to do all he or she can to improve. In turn, the employee must trust you to help guide the process and provide resources and encouragement when needed.

This trust can be severely undermined if the employee believes that you are talking to others inappropriately about his or her issues. If you have no legitimate reason to tell another person about a disciplinary issue, then don't. While your employees and coworkers may be curious, you risk serious damage to the discipline process if you undermine the employee's trust by talking to others about the problem. If you feel the need to vent or get another perspective, talk about it with an appropriate person, such as your boss.

Limiting Gossip

Another reason it is important to maintain confidentiality is that it allows the employee the room to improve without being scrutinized and criticized by others. While gossip is unavoidable in the workplace, there are a few things you can do to limit it.

As the manager of the group, your own behavior is critical in letting others know what is acceptable. If you engage in gossip about employee problems, the door is open for others to as well. Employees may have a hard time understanding the difference between sharing information on a subject and gossiping about it, which means you have to draw that line clearly. Only share information that the employee needs to know. When you're pushed for more, you can and should tell your employees no. Remember, there are many important reasons—including legal ones—to keep information private if you don't have a good reason to reveal it.

Gossip tends to die away when there is no new news on a subject. Involving only the appropriate people at the right times in the process and maintaining a steadfast tight lip will eventually quell the chatter.

Minimize Legal Problems

Keeping a disciplinary issue private will also help you avoid legal claims for defamation and violation of privacy. A disgruntled employee who believes that people are making untrue or derogatory statements may take action against a company or the individuals making the statements, including you. (See Chapter 3 for more on the legal reasons to maintain confidentiality.)

If your company has a policy addressing confidentiality of employee information, you could also put the company at risk legally if you don't follow that policy. As we discussed in Chapter 3, if you follow the policy in one situation and not another, the employee who didn't get the benefit of the policy might feel he or she wasn't treated fairly. The employee might attribute this unfair treatment to an illegally discriminatory motive on your part.

If your company has such a policy, read it carefully, and ask your human resources department or legal counsel any questions you have about how it applies.

SMART SUMMARY:
Smart Collaboration

- Involve your manager in the process when the problem has a significant effect on the business, when you need an alternate perspective, or when company policy or practice require it.

- Human resources is a partner in the discipline process. Because they're usually trained and experienced, they can help you apply and navigate complex company policies and practices, guide you through the process, or partner with you in your discipline meetings.

- You should work with legal counsel when the discipline process raises possible legal problems, for instance, because the employee denies misconduct, has an employment contract, hires an attorney, or takes a leave that may be legally protected.

- When you include other employees in the discipline process, be careful to involve only those who need to know and to share only the information necessary. Keep things as confidential as you can; it shows respect for the employee, reduces gossip in the workplace, and limits legal liability.

Build Your Skills: Smart Performance Management

Questions

1. If you feel awkward about disciplining an employee, you should:

   a. Ask human resources to deliver the message. They have a lot of experience and will be able to communicate more clearly, anyway.

   b. Accept that it's part of the process. Discipline is awkward, but it's a necessary part of your job.

   c. Just get it over with. Sit down with the employee, say what you need to, and get out.

   d. Talk to other managers about it. Your colleagues have probably dealt with the same thing themselves.

2. Even though workplace gossip about disciplinary issues is inappropriate and wastes time, there isn't really anything you can do to prevent it.

   ☐ True   ☐ False

3. Chelsea, the manager of a clothing store, needs to discipline Evan, a supervisor, for repeatedly forgetting to lock the door to the supervisor's office at the end of his shift. Which of these is the best way to begin the conversation?

   a. "Evan, you keep leaving the door to the supervisor's office unlocked. This has got to stop immediately."

   b. "Hey, Evan! How are things going on the night shift?"

   c. "Evan, you could really get us into trouble by leaving the door to the supervisor's office unlocked. Why do you keep doing that?"

   d. "Evan, I noticed twice last week that the supervisor's office wasn't locked when I came in the morning after your shift. Can you explain why?"

4. Sy, a secretary in a college admissions office, has been sending out letters with numerous typos to prospective students. She explains to her supervisor, Dalia, that she is making the errors because she has too many other competing tasks, and she doesn't feel like she has time to proofread the letters carefully. Which of these is the best response?

a. "Unfortunately, Sy, that is just part of your job. You need to figure out how to get this done. Do you have any suggestions for how you can accomplish that?"

b. "Sounds like you're feeling overwhelmed. What I hear you saying is that you don't feel you have adequate time to proofread these thoroughly. Is that right?"

c. "I'm sorry, Sy, but I just don't agree with you. I really think you need to try and get these done, error free. What will it take?"

d. "So what you're saying is, you're really busy so you think someone else should proofread the letters before they go out?"

5. When you deliver discipline, you should give an employee as many examples of a problem as possible.   ☐ True   ☐ False

6. When you're dealing with an employee who becomes angry, you should:

a. Let the employee know who's in control. Anger isn't appropriate in the workplace. You need to communicate this message strongly, which may mean raising your voice if the employee's voice is raised or telling the employee it's time to walk away if he or she isn't capable of talking about things calmly.

b. Let the employee know that his or her feelings shouldn't enter the discussion. There's no need to get angry; it won't get you anywhere.

c. Encourage the employee to take a break until he or she is ready to talk about it again.

d. Try to slow the meeting down. Acknowledge the anger but tell the employee that he or she needs to calm down before you can proceed.

7. Boris needs to discipline Monica for making inappropriate and demeaning comments to a coworker, Linda. When he confronts her with the problem, Monica replies, "It wasn't me! I never said anything to Linda!" Which of these is the best response?

a. "I know you did it, Monica. Linda told me about it, and Cory verified that it was true."

b. "Well, I know that Linda has a tendency to exaggerate. Let me look into it."

c. "Monica, did you tell Linda at the register last Friday, 'It doesn't take a rocket scientist' when she asked you how to change the receipt tape?"

d. "No one's blaming you, Monica. Just tell me the truth."

8. When an employee commits misconduct that appears to be illegal, and you decide to terminate employment, you should say that the employee broke the law in your termination memo. ☐ True ☐ False

9. You should require your employee to sign your documentation, agreeing with its contents and your decision. ☐ True ☐ False

10. Victoria hears from four different employees that another employee, Deborah, is constantly on the phone, making personal calls to her family, who lives in London. She checks the phone records and finds that it's true and that it's at a cost of almost $1,000. Whom should Victoria talk to about this first?

a. Deborah.

b. All four coworkers.

c. Human resources.

d. Her boss.

Answers

1. B. Sometimes it's uncomfortable or difficult to tell an employee that his or her behavior or performance isn't measuring up. If you accept that it's just part of the process, you can prepare yourself to deal with that reality. While you may want to talk about the problem with others, you should limit that to appropriate individuals like your manager, legal counsel, or human resources department, who can counsel you on how to deliver the difficult message. Ultimately, it's up to you, and you shouldn't push the job off on someone else, even though it's awkward. Otherwise, you might have a hard time finding a collaborative solution with the employee.

2. False. Although there's nothing you can do to prevent gossip altogether, you can limit it by involving only the appropriate people in the discipline process, keeping your employees focused on their own work, and refusing to engage in it yourself.

3. D. When you meet with an employee to administer discipline, it's a good idea to have your opening sentences prepared. In this example, Chelsea should make sure she has all the facts before telling Evan what to do. In Answer D, Chelsea makes sure she has the facts straight, but she's also focused on the problem. If she begins the conversation too informally, Evan might be confused about the purpose of the meeting. On the other hand, if she is too accusatory, Evan might shut down at the very beginning.

4. B. When you get an employee's perspective on a given problem, it's important to show that you're really understanding what the employee is saying. You can do that by playing back what you are hearing and listening empathically. That means paraphrasing what you heard, without judgmental edits, and putting yourself in the employee's shoes. In Answer B, Dalia summarized Sy's words, which let Sy know she was really paying attention, without passing judgment. After listening this way, Dalia can engage Sy in a discussion about what to do about it.

5. False. While it's important to give the employee examples of the problem performance or behavior, it isn't necessary to have an exhaustive list. In fact, it could do more harm than good. If your examples are second-, third-, or fourthhand, or inaccurate, the employee may be so focused on the example that he or she isn't thinking about the problem and how to solve it.

6. D. If an employee is angry, you may be able to slow the meeting down. If that doesn't work, you might need to take a break, but make sure the employee understands it

can't be indefinite. Choose a time to reengage, preferably within the next day or so. You don't want so much time to pass that the employee's anger has time to fester or that you forget the important facts that led you to discipline in the first place.

7. C. In this case, Boris will be best served by going through examples of Monica's problem behavior with her. He shouldn't deny the truth of Linda's allegations or suggest that they're made up. But asking Monica to verify whether specific statements are true shows her that he's prepared and looked into the matter. She'll have a harder time dodging the questions when they're this focused.

8. False. Although you should document the facts that led you to make a discipline decision, and explain what company policy it violates, you shouldn't draw legal conclusions. After all, you don't want those conclusions to be used against you. If the company is sued for the employee's behavior, your disciplinary records might become evidence that the employee broke the law (or, at least, that you thought he or she did) and that the company should be held responsible.

9. False. It's a good idea to ask the disciplined employee to sign formal documentation, but the signature need only acknowledge receipt. Requiring an employee to agree with your description can hamper the disciplinary process if the employee thinks you're being coercive. If the employee doesn't want to sign, you can just note on the form that he or she was asked to but refused to do so. Also, if you leave a blank space on the form for the employee to comment, he or she can include information you didn't record. This gives the employee the opportunity to participate in the documentation process, and it also protects you: If the employee elects not to comment but then later says your documentation was inaccurate, he or she will be hard-pressed to explain why that section of the form is blank.

10. D. Although Victoria will probably eventually discuss this with human resources and with Deborah, she should probably first discuss it with her boss. This could have significant financial impact on the company, or it could mean that she is going to have to deliver some fairly serious discipline. In either case, Victoria doesn't want her boss blindsided by hearing about the problem when the discipline is already well underway or when human resources brings it to the boss's attention. Note that in this case, Victoria doesn't need to discuss it with the four employees who reported it: She was able to verify it independently through phone records, and she can maintain confidentiality and limit gossip by keeping it private.

PART

IV

The Disciplinary Steps

Step 1: Coaching

Sometimes, you know it's time to correct workplace behavior, but the problem isn't serious enough to warrant formal discipline like a verbal or written warning. While you want the employee to resolve the issue, you don't want to come down too hard or make the employee feel attacked or overwhelmed. That's where coaching comes in.

Relatively new to traditional discipline, which tends to be immediately formal in its approach, coaching gives you the chance to correct behaviors and actions before implementing a more serious corrective measure. For this reason, more so than the other steps in the disciplinary process, coaching is an opportunity, rather than a punishment. This chapter will outline what coaching is (and is not), when and how to do it, how you know it's going well, and what to do if it's not working.

What Is Coaching?

As with sports, coaching in the workplace means offering encouragement and direction, so that the employee will accomplish the final goal. Based on your expertise, you help the employee recognize a weakness and find a way to fix it. Then you make sure that the employee is successfully improving, making adjustments if needed. While managing people involves coaching on many levels, here, we use the term "coaching" specifically in the context of improving employee performance and behavior.

One of the big benefits of coaching is that it does not confer the stigma of a formal disciplinary step, such as a verbal or written warning. As a result, the employee usually feels less threatened by coaching, and you are able to work together to correct problems quickly. This often prevents the need to go to the next measure in the progressive discipline process. Other benefits of coaching include:

- **Problems are corrected early.** Coaching allows you to address problems before they have a serious impact on the business.
- **The tone is positive.** Because coaching can be informal, it permits a less serious tone than a more advanced disciplinary measure does, emphasizing the opportunity to improve performance, rather than the consequences for failing to do so.

- **Your documentation is not as formal.** Coaching documentation does not require the same level of detail as more advanced disciplinary measures, where details are more important.
- **You create a record to move forward, if necessary.** With a history of coaching, you have solid justification—and a record of your previous efforts to help the employee improve—to move to a more serious disciplinary measure.
- **Your leadership is established.** Coaching tells your employee that you are invested in the success of your team and that you're actively leading it toward its goals.
- **Communication is improved.** Coaching gives you the opportunity to open lines of communication, preventing future misunderstandings or problems.
- **You learn about how the team is working.** Like one-on-ones, coaching sessions give you the opportunity to see how your team is working together and what roadblocks are keeping you from moving forward.

To Coach or Not to Coach?

With all the benefits of coaching, it's hard to imagine a time when it would not be appropriate. Because coaching prevents problems from growing, keeps the employee engaged, and justifies more serious measures when an employee does not improve, it is an important and valuable step to use whenever possible.

However, as we discussed in Chapter 5, there are times when a more serious disciplinary measure is warranted. You may know this immediately, or you may discover it as you try to coach the employee and meet resistance. To determine whether coaching is the right step, you should consider whether coaching can solve the problem.

Most, but not all, employee discipline problems can be addressed by coaching. Remember that it's important to impose proportionate discipline: discipline that is directly related to the severity of the problem. Unless the problem is serious, or you've already disciplined the employee for the same issue, it's probably appropriate to first try coaching. This notifies the employee that a problem must be fixed before it escalates and has more serious consequences for the business.

When an issue occurs repeatedly, it may indicate that more serious discipline is needed. However, don't immediately assume that an employee's continuing problem means coaching just won't work. It may instead indicate that the employee needs more guidance and that you need to take additional time to discuss the issue. The employee may not understand the problem and may be repeating it unknowingly or unintentionally. Using an alternate coaching technique may also overcome that problem. (Different coaching techniques are discussed in "Types of Coaching," below.)

> **EXAMPLE:** Sandy is a dental hygienist in Dr. Brown's office. She cleans patients' teeth and has a list of daily appointments.
>
> One day, Sandy arrives to the office 20 minutes late. The first patient is kept waiting, and all of Sandy's subsequent appointments run behind, too. "You really need to make it here on time," Dr. Brown tells her.
>
> Twice the next week, Sandy is behind schedule again. This time, although she is in the office on time, she is on the phone, returning patient phone calls from the day before. Dr. Brown takes Sandy aside again. This time, he explains the reason for the previous week's session. "Sandy," he says. "When you have appointments, you need to make them your first priority. That means you need to be in the office and ready to go when they arrive. If patients are kept waiting, they become frustrated and might even choose a different dental office. Do you understand?"

Because Sandy now understands the real problem—keeping patients waiting—she knows what she needs to do to correct the behavior. The additional coaching session should solve the problem. Unless she continues to run behind, no further discipline will be needed.

Types of Coaching

Coaching comes in various forms, from a simple request in the hallway to an actual sit-down session with a clear agenda. Before deciding which is appropriate for your situation, you need to understand the nature and benefits of each.

Simple Requests

Simple requests are made when an employee has tried another method of doing something, but that method hasn't been successful. Because they are very informal, you may not even realize you are coaching. Employees often respond well to this informal approach. Most people prefer to be asked to do something, not told. As a result, simple requests often fix problems without making the employee feel bad.

Simple requests occur throughout the day: during a meeting, in casual conversation, or even via email or voicemail. You make simple requests all the time, when you ask your employees to do or try something new or different. Your comments might start with these phrases:

- "Next time, you might want to …"
- "Hey, try doing it this way …"
- "Did you consider …?"
- "Why don't you give this a try?"

Despite the informality of simple requests, it is still important that you document these incidents. You may use your calendar or tickler log to track them, jotting down a note of when you said what to whom. It can be as brief as one sentence: "Spoke with Luz about frequent interruptions during today's directors meeting." If it is written on a calendar, the date is already noted. If it is in the form of an email, you should archive it. Also write down your plans for following up or making sure the employee fixes the problem. Your notes should be clear enough that you will be able to understand them and remember the incident later, if you need to escalate to a verbal warning.

Corrective Actions

A corrective action is more directive than a simple request. You use it when you want one course of action to stop and to be replaced with another. You use phrases like:

- "Actually you can't do it that way. You need to …"
- "We need to change this. Can you please …?"

Using this language conveys a bit more urgency, indicating that the action or behavior must change immediately.

EXAMPLE: Omar is the floor manager of a packaging plant. He oversees a large assembly line and is responsible for an output target every day. Chris is the new guy on the line.

In his second week on the floor, Chris realizes that he can save time by applying the pricing label in the upper left-hand corner instead of the upper right-hand corner, since it is closer to him. Chris makes this change and indeed sees improvement in his overall station time.

Omar is notified by the Quality Assurance inspector of the misapplication of the labels. He approaches Chris and says, "Hey Chris. Your station times are great and we're happy with your work, but I need you to change the way you are applying these labels. They've got to go in the upper right-hand corner because we have to adhere to the design requirements."

Chris responds, "Oh, sorry, I didn't realize it was a problem. I did it because I thought I could finish applying the labels more quickly that way."

"Thanks for taking that initiative, Chris," Omar replies. "However, the design requirements are more important than the station time." Chris understands and applies the labels correctly.

Omar has provided Chris the direction he needs to solve the problem, while recognizing the value of Chris's contribution. Chris corrects the behavior, remains motivated, and will likely need no further discipline on this issue.

Coaching Sessions

While simple requests and corrective actions are appropriate for problems with quick, easy solutions, more thoughtful measures may be required when the problem is more complex or when you need input from the employee to craft a solution. In the example above, Omar knew objectively what needed to change and communicated it to Chris. But what if the problem was that Chris wasn't producing enough? Omar might have wanted to discuss with Chris why he wasn't able to meet production standards and what he needed to be able to do so.

A coaching session is like a "time out": an opportunity to step away from the situation, communicate that change is necessary, and talk about how to make it happen. Because the session is a little more formal, you should take more time preparing what you will say and do. Set a time and date to meet with the employee to specifically discuss the issue.

> **EXAMPLE:** Jayne is a highway patrol officer. She is praised by everyone she works with for her professionalism and thoroughness. She pays close attention to detail, writes excellent incident reports, and follows up on every loose end.
>
> However, in her focus on detail and procedure, Jayne often deals abruptly with auto accident victims. Jayne's boss, Sergeant Rialto, is concerned that this could affect not only community relations, but also Jayne's ability to get good information when victims are upset. Sergeant Rialto decides that he needs to pull Jayne off the route to address the problem.
>
> Sitting down together in his office, Sergeant Rialto explains the problem: "Jayne, you've been doing really good work out there and the department appreciates it. When you are on an accident site, you are terrific at detailing the accident, getting the right people involved, and clearing the site as soon as possible.
>
> "Another important aspect of our jobs, though, is getting statements from accident victims. Sometimes, that's hard because they're so upset. You may have to spend some time calming them down. If you deal too abruptly with them, they might shut down, which could prevent us from getting the full story. I've seen you get short with accident victims. Do you see how this might affect your ability to do your job?"
>
> "You're right," Jayne replies. "I do get short with some of the victims when they have a hard time telling me what happened. What do you think I can do to make that better?"

Jayne and Sergeant Rialto are now engaged in a discussion about improving Jayne's performance on accident sites. Because the sergeant approached this situation by first praising Jayne's performance and focusing on improving (not correcting) it, Jayne is engaged in working on a solution, instead of building a defense. The sergeant will also be prepared if Jayne doesn't improve: It will be easy to explain why they would now move to the next step in the progressive discipline process.

How Do You Coach?

Now let's focus on how you actually coach. You've already decided that coaching is appropriate, so now you need to:
- prepare to talk with the employee
- meet with the employee
- document, and
- follow up.

Prepare

When you decide coaching is appropriate, there are a couple specific factors you should consider before sitting down with the employee. As with all discipline measures, you should think about when and where to coach, what to say, and how the employee might react.

When and Where Is the Best Place to Coach?

Best practices would have you provide coaching as close to the actual event that precipitated it as possible. Coaching an employee through a recent event that's still fresh in both your minds is a much easier task than conjuring up memories of a past event. While this is often intuitive when you're imposing a more serious disciplinary measure, you may be tempted to put your meeting off when you're facing a minor problem. But you want to give the employee a fair shot to improve as soon as you know there's a problem, which means raising the issue as soon as you become aware of it.

No matter which method of coaching you use, do it in a place that is not threatening for the employee. That means an environment that is confidential, but also where the employee feels comfortable. It might be in your office, in the employee's office, or over a private lunch together. Your regularly scheduled one-on-one is also a great place to engage in informal coaching. As you discuss other issues and status reports, you can work your coaching in at the appropriate time.

When you are in a coaching session, make sure the employee is comfortable and relaxed. After all, you've chosen to coach because you want the employee to engage in the process with some enthusiasm. Treating the session with too much formality could cause the employee to freeze up and become defensive.

How Will You Start the Conversation?

Although it's important to be prepared for any disciplinary discussion, you don't want to script the entire conversation in advance. When coaching, that means you should be prepared to start the conversation by putting the employee at ease but then move on quickly to addressing the problem and finding a solution. With more advanced disciplinary measures, communicating the import of the problem necessitates a serious tone. However, keeping a lighter and more encouraging tone when coaching may help the employee feel motivated to work with you to bring about change, instead of doing it just to avoid further discipline.

Your first couple of sentences should explain the problem, describe how it's affecting the employee's or team's performance, and end with a question designed to immediately find a solution together. Here are a few examples:

- "Thanks for meeting me here, Scott. It's nice to get out of the office every now and then. Listen, I understand that you have been having trouble getting along with Susan. In fact, I've heard that you've even raised your voice at Susan in meetings. I'm worried about what this might do to the team's morale and performance. Do you worry about this?"

- "Hey Samantha, thanks for taking the time to meet with me. You know, overall I'm really happy with your performance; you're doing a great job. And since we've added all that new responsibility, I've seen how hard you've been working to keep up. It seems like you could use some help with that. Is there anything we can do?"

- "Bob, I need to have an uncomfortable conversation with you. I value working with you, but recently, I've received some complaints. I know you're as busy as the rest of the team, but lately you've been providing incomplete information and not following up on questions until matters become urgent. Lara reported this to me on the Brody project, and Allen said it happened on the Meyers case. When this happens, it wastes everyone's time. It's also hurting your working relationships. How can we tackle this problem?"

Make sure you communicate the basic problem right away. If you wait until the middle of your coaching session to finally say that there's a problem, the employee may not understand the real purpose of the meeting or may just feel blindsided. You want the employee to know right away that while the setting may be informal, the message is still important. The more coaching sessions you have, the more comfortable you will become with the process.

How Might the Employee React?

Chapter 8 gives an in-depth look at preparing for and dealing with employee responses. While each employee will respond differently, most don't respond as negatively or as strongly to coaching as to other, more serious discipline measures.

The most common reactions to coaching include:

- **Surprise.** Given that coaching is usually the first step in the discipline process, the employee may well be surprised to hear that there's a problem. Be sure to allow your employee time and space to deal with the surprise before moving on to problem solving, even if it means walking away and coming back later. Otherwise, the employee will have a hard time listening or participating.

- **Defensiveness.** Your employee may not be willing to own the issue right away and may instead blame someone else, refuse to accept your feedback, or shut down and stop talking to you at all. To work through that defensiveness, be sure that you have concrete examples of the problem and can be specific about its effect on the business.

- **Openness.** Most people really do want to improve and embrace the opportunity. Take advantage of this reaction and work together to establish a plan for improvement.

- **False assurances.** Some people will instantly agree with you and promise to immediately improve. This can be an avoidance tactic, used to try and focus your energy elsewhere. If you think the employee hasn't really heard you and committed to improvement, take some time to explain exactly what the problem is and why things need to change. Then, ask the employee what he or she will do to solve the problem. Don't settle for vague statements like "I'll take care of it" or "It won't happen again."

Dealing With Resistance

Most employees are willing to improve when confronted with a discipline problem. Sometimes, however, an employee will not be open to your coaching and will refuse to change. Because coaching may be your first disciplinary encounter with the employee, it is often the first time you see this resistance.

There are many reasons an employee may resist coaching, including:

- The employee has been doing the job for a long time and knows the "right" way to do things.
- The employee has enjoyed great success doing things one way and sees no need to change.
- The employee disagrees with how you want to do things or believes you are not competent.
- The employee does not believe there is a problem in the first place.
- The employee does not believe there is any benefit from improving.

It's hard to recognize up front whether an employee will be resistant to coaching; that's why starting with coaching makes sense whenever the issue calls for it. The communication techniques discussed in Chapter 8 may help you overcome some of this resistance. If the employee's resistance prevents him or her from showing any improvement following your coaching session, you may have to take the discipline process to the next level.

Meet With the Employee

Now that you have set up the discussion, crafted your opening sentences, and considered potential responses, it's time to actually do the coaching. It's also time to listen closely to the employee's responses for information you didn't have before and to understand what caused the behavior.

Explain the Problem

Once you've started your meeting, you should provide the information the employee needs to understand the problem and develop an effective solution. If you're making a simple request or having a corrective action session, this will be a quick discussion. In a coaching session, you'll need to give more detail. You should plan to explain what the problem is (the facts), how it's affecting the company (the impact), and what the company's needs are (the goal). Then, you can determine what you and the employee need to do next (the solution).

- **The facts.** You'll need to communicate this information to the employee:
  - when the problem or incident occurred (date and time)
  - who was involved (if applicable), and
  - how you discovered the problem, including direct quotes, samples of work product, or supporting documentation.
- **The impact.** Explain how the problem affects the workplace or business and why it can't continue. For example, a problem might lead to:
  - poor teamwork
  - low productivity
  - loss of morale
  - low quality, or
  - low customer satisfaction.
- **The goal.** Be very clear about what the company needs. These are not the solutions you and the employee will come up with, but the nonnegotiable standards that must be met. For example:
  - "We need to bring in $15,000 in revenue this month."
  - "Customers must be greeted as soon as they enter the building."
  - "We can't ship this product late; it has to be done by March 1."
- **The solution.** Let the employee know that the solution is collaborative; you must find it together.

Get the Employee to Respond

While getting the employee involved in the discussion is always an important part of the discipline process, it's particularly challenging when coaching. Because the problems you address when coaching may not be as serious as problems that require more advanced measures, your employee may have a hard time even understanding what the problem is or acknowledging that there is a problem in the first place.

On the other hand, because the problem hasn't escalated, an employee's reluctance to deal with a problem can be more easily overcome in a coaching session. If an employee isn't willing to talk in a coaching session, you can push a little harder than you might be able to if dealing with a more serious issue and work harder to get the employee engaged.

Consider the following example:

EXAMPLE: Michael is the CEO of a small startup. The company plans to release a new product and is on a strict schedule to complete development in three months. Michael learns that Dan, the head of engineering, has not required his employees to focus on the product and has instead permitted them to work on less pressing projects.

Michael takes Dan to lunch to discuss this. After brief small talk, Michael begins, "Dan, I am worried about something. Even though you and I went through the milestones of the project plan, and agreed on the dates that we needed to hit in order to meet the release schedule, I've been hearing that not all the engineers are focused on making that happen. Can you tell me why?"

Dan replies, "I have no idea what you are talking about."

Michael is ready with a few examples and the names of the engineers who are working on noncore projects. He says, "Dan, I really want to work with you in coming up with a solution to this problem. If we miss that date, the company will really suffer, and our investors will certainly question our management. Can you help me understand what's happening?"

Dan softens a bit and says, "I know the company priorities. And I know my part in meeting those. You don't have to worry about me."

Michael persists, "Dan, how can we make sure that your team is focused on the same priorities? Tell me about how you communicate goals and allocate projects."

Michael stays focused in this coaching session and does not let Dan's reluctance control the conversation. By continually focusing on coming up with a solution, and giving Dan opportunities to speak, Michael eventually gets Dan to participate.

Find a Solution Together

When you're coaching, you have the liberty to spend more time encouraging the employee to come up with creative ideas to solve the problem. After all, the problem isn't as serious at this point, and it's probably the first time you've discussed the issue with the employee. That means you may be able to come up with some good ideas that can quickly set things on the right track.

One way to work toward a solution is to flip roles, asking the employee what he or she would do in your position: "Betsy, if our roles were reversed, what would you suggest that I do to fix this? How long would you give me to improve?" You can also point the employee to past experience: "Betsy, have you ever experienced this kind of thing before or been told that it was an issue? What did you do then?" You might even try asking the employee to play out what would happen if the problem were to continue: "Betsy, if this problem were to continue, what do you think will happen to the team or to the business? How would you reverse the trend before that happens?" By getting the employee to approach the problem in different ways, you make it easier to come up with ideas for improvement.

Document

Documentation can be less formal when coaching. Nevertheless, it is still important. You may need it in the future if a problem persists. For that reason, make sure you always list the most relevant facts. Documentation of simple requests or corrective actions can be a one-line sentence in your calendar or tickler log:

- "Bridgett was ten minutes late today. Reminded her to be on time."
- "Told Carol she needed to add service revenue to her overall revenue forecast for better accuracy."

These simple reminders will help you remember what you said and when you said it, as well as give you the opportunity to see if there is a pattern of behavior emerging. If Bridgett repeats the same problem after you have coached her, you might need to move to the next level of progressive discipline; if all of your employees are having a hard time understanding customer priorities, it might be that you need to explain them more thoroughly to the whole team.

Likewise, you can use the calendar to schedule future check-ins. If the employee promises change or action, write yourself a note to discuss the employee's progress at some reasonable date in the future. If you don't think you can fit all the relevant facts into your calendar, do a more detailed coaching log or memo, like the one described below.

Because a coaching session deals with more complex issues, and it will be both harder and more important to remember the details, spend a little more time documenting this conversation. At minimum, the memo must have:

- date and time of the occurrence
- date and time of the coaching session

- a description of the issue and how it was communicated to the employee
- a brief recap of previous disciplinary history for the issue (you might have to look back at your calendar or tickler if you've coached informally)
- what the employee said or did in response, and
- the action plan, with deadlines.

These details will help refresh your memory when you want to see how an action plan is progressing, or if you need to move to another step in the discipline process.

EXAMPLE: Here's how Michael, the CEO, wrote up his coaching session with Dan, who wasn't setting priorities properly for his department:

> Met with Dan today, August 31, 20xx, to discuss the product release. I told Dan that I'd heard Dylan was working on a database project, and that Sasha was updating the department's internal communications protocols, rather than working on the new product. I told Dan I was concerned that his group might not hit the milestones and release schedule.
>
> Dan informed me that he had sent the team an email outlining the due dates but had not followed up and met with each team member to assign interim deadlines and establish priorities. We agreed that Dan would write up a plan by tomorrow afternoon, detailing how his team would complete the remaining work. I'll review that plan, then Dan will meet with each team member and explain the priorities and due dates. If any problems come up, Dan will discuss them with me immediately.

For additional examples of coaching memos, see Appendix B.

Follow Up

Often overlooked, following up is the most important, fruitful step in the coaching exercise. It will help you make sure that coaching is succeeding, and redirect the process when it isn't.

How will you know if coaching is successful? In some cases, it will be obvious. An employee will automatically correct behavior or improve performance, and you'll see the difference. For example, when Omar told Chris to place the labels in the upper right-hand corner, he could look at the boxes that followed to see if Chris did as he was told.

Other times, however, coaching will require ongoing evaluation. The employee may need continued feedback and praise from you. For example, in Jayne's situation, she might need to know whether her attempts to be more compassionate toward auto accident victims were successful. Because she has no objective way to measure this, and it was not an intuitive behavior for her, she needs Sergeant Rialto to observe and then tell her what she's doing right and wrong. If he continues to do this and sees improvement each time, they'll both know that the process is working.

You may not be in direct contact with your employee every day, or you may not always see his or her work product. If that's the case, make it a part of the coaching plan to look at the employee's work product on a regular basis. If you are working with a geographically remote person, it is important to establish check-in times and discuss how the work is going. If you don't do this, you won't be able to see whether the employee is responding to your coaching.

When Coaching Is Over

If coaching is successful, you have just one step left: Document the success. If you wrote a coaching memo, add a new section briefly describing the outcome. If you are using a tickler log or your calendar, jot another one-liner noting the success.

If your employee is not responding well to coaching, and you're sure the employee has had ample opportunity to identify and correct the problem, you will need to progress to the next step in the discipline process. In the next chapter, we'll discuss how to issue a verbal warning.

PODCAST
You can listen to podcasts with sample coaching conversations at this book's online companion page. See Appendix D for details.

SMART SUMMARY:
Coaching

- When you're dealing with a problem for the first time, and the problem isn't very serious, try coaching before going to more-serious disciplinary measures. Because coaching is less formal, problems can often be corrected early, and employees are less threatened by the process.

- Coaching can occur three different ways: through simple requests to change straightforward problem actions or behaviors, through corrective actions intended to have immediate effect, or through coaching sessions when problems are more serious or complex.

- If coaching isn't working, don't immediately assume it can't. It may be that your message wasn't clear to the employee, especially if you used one of the more informal coaching techniques to address the problem.

- Even though coaching is informal, it still requires documentation. You may need it to remind yourself to check in with the employee later or may need to refer to your documentation when you impose more serious discipline if coaching doesn't work.

Step 2: Verbal Warnings

Perhaps you've had a coaching session or two with an employee, but he or she hasn't improved as expected. Or, maybe an employee has committed obvious misconduct or had a significant slip in performance that merits an immediate, more formal intervention. Either way, it's time to take progressive discipline to the next level: the verbal warning.

Giving a verbal warning is similar to a coaching session in many ways. In either case, you meet with the employee, explain the problem, make sure the employee acknowledges and understands the problem, listen to what the employee has to say about it, and work together to come up with a solution.

However, a verbal warning is also a more serious disciplinary measure, and it requires you to use—and communicate to the employee—a higher degree of formality. Although coaching is the first step in progressive discipline, the employee doesn't really enter the disciplinary system in a formal way—with official notification, documentation, and company involvement—until a verbal warning is issued. Because the problem is more serious, you will need to spend more time preparing for the meeting, conveying that the issue must be dealt with, going over why previous efforts to improve (if any) have failed, and collaboratively solving the problem. You'll also need to spend more time on documentation, and you might need to involve your human resources department or your boss.

What Is a Verbal Warning?

Sometimes called a "verbal reprimand," an "oral reminder," a verbal warning gives the employee fair notice that there is an important problem that must be dealt with. A verbal warning is formally documented, commonly in the employee's personnel file. Even if an employee has already received coaching on a particular performance or behavior issue, a verbal warning often serves as the first true wake-up call. It lets the employee know that the issue is now on the company's radar, not just a matter to be resolved between the employee and his or her manager.

When to Give a Verbal Warning

To figure out whether a verbal warning is the appropriate way to deal with a particular problem, you'll need to follow the steps outlined in Chapter 5. You'll have to review your company's policy, check in with your human resources department, consider how similar issues have been handled in the past, and weigh how serious the problem is.

For serious misconduct, immediate termination might be the appropriate response. In contrast, many first-time performance and attendance problems are best handled in a coaching session. So where on this spectrum does the verbal warning fall? And how do you know when to use one?

A verbal warning is probably appropriate if:

- The employee has not responded to your efforts to coach a performance problem or a relatively minor conduct problem.

> EXAMPLE: Ken works the deli counter in a large grocery store. His manager, Clark, notices that Ken doesn't talk to the customers much. Rather than making chitchat, offering information about various items, or asking if they'd like anything else, Ken simply calls the next number and waits for the customers to tell him what they want.
>
> Clark has a coaching session with Ken, telling him that the company expects employees who interact with customers to be friendly and engaging. Clark works with Ken for an hour, demonstrating the welcoming conversation and positive demeanor he expects. By the end of the hour, Ken is chatting a bit with customers and appears to be getting the hang of things.
>
> A week later, however, Clark once again sees Ken standing silent behind the counter. Clark reminds Ken of their discussion, and Ken improves, but only temporarily. The next day, and the day after that, Clark has to keep reminding Ken to talk to the customers. Because Clark has already coached Ken and the reminders don't seem to be helping, Clark decides to issue a verbal warning. Clark hopes that having a formal disciplinary session with Ken will convey to him that his behavior must change.
>
> If a few facts were different here or there, Clark should have chosen a different response. For example:
>
> - If Ken had taken Clark's coaching to heart and was consistently demonstrating the kind of customer interaction Clark expected, the best response would be praise. When employees improve, you can encourage continued success with positive reinforcement, such as "Ken, I've noticed that you're really engaging the customers as we discussed, and it's having a great effect. Yesterday, Mrs. Santiago told me that she really appreciates your positive attitude and courtesy. Keep up the good work!"

- If Ken was being more friendly toward the customers but was working too slowly as a result, the best response probably would be another coaching session. Ken responded positively to the first session and probably doesn't know that his efforts to improve resulted in a different problem.

- If Ken went beyond his lack of socializing and was actually rude to the customers, a written warning might have been appropriate. Rudeness is a much more serious offense: It can lead to extreme customer dissatisfaction, and it demonstrates a major attitude problem.

- The employee has violated a company rule, but it does not appear to be deliberate or malicious, and has not caused significant harm to the company.

> **EXAMPLE:** Nguyen is a carpenter who works for a major construction company. When hired, every employee receives training in the use of safety equipment and rules for the proper operation of company machinery. The company also makes a point of enforcing these rules, so employees know that they must be followed.
>
> The site manager, Jennifer, notices that Nguyen is not wearing his safety gear when using a power saw. Because this could cause major injuries, and because of the company's position on safety violations, Jennifer decides to give him a verbal warning.

- The employee's behavior or poor performance is causing some problems for the company, but the employee seems to be unaware of the issue and genuinely interested in improvement.

> **EXAMPLE:** Marcus was recently hired as a paralegal for a large law firm. Juan, Marcus's manager, tells him that the firm is not pleased with its case management software—the software it uses to keep track of clients, billing, court dates, case data, and so on—and will soon consider some alternative programs.
>
> Marcus has used some of the other software programs and is eager to please his new boss. He decides to put together a brief comparison of the most popular programs. He asks a friend who works for another law firm to lend him the disks for that firm's software, which he loads onto his computer at work. He also downloads another program from the Internet; this program

isn't available for free from the software company, but he finds a pirated version on the Web. He puts together his report and shows it to Juan.

At first, Juan is pleased with Marcus's initiative in preparing the report, but he quickly becomes upset when he learns how Marcus acquired the software he used to put it together. The firm's employee handbook clearly states that employees may not download software from the Internet or load programs onto their computers without the permission of the IT department. Software piracy is illegal (not to mention embarrassing for a major law firm). To remedy Marcus's error, the firm will probably have to pay for the legal right to use these programs.

Juan plans to give Marcus a written warning for blatantly violating a company rule and costing the firm money. But when he sits down to talk to Marcus about the problem, Marcus says, "I wasn't going to actually use any of the programs, just look at them so I could report on their features. I thought the rule applied only to programs I was going to use as part of my job. I'm sorry I made such a stupid mistake." Although Marcus has used poor judgment, his explanation makes sense. When Juan considers the circumstances, including the fact that Marcus only got into trouble because he was being resourceful and doing extra work, he decides to give Marcus a verbal warning instead.

How to Give a Verbal Warning

Now that you've decided a verbal warning is in order, it's time to get down to business. Like any other disciplinary measure, giving a verbal warning requires you to prepare, meet with the employee, document, and follow up. But the details are a bit different when you're using a verbal warning. You'll want to communicate that there's a real problem, but at the same time make clear that you believe the employee can and will improve. And you'll need to prepare documentation and plan to follow up in a way that's more structured than you would use for a coaching session, maximizing the employee's opportunity to succeed and creating a more detailed history that justifies your decisions and actions.

If you're dealing with a recurring problem, consider what went wrong with your coaching and how you can better bring about improvement this time around. Did you explain the problem clearly to the employee? Was your plan for improvement feasible? Why do you think the employee has failed to improve? (Of course, you can—and should—ask the employee the same questions when you meet.) Did you check in with the employee to make sure he or she was on the right track?

Prepare

Begin preparing by consulting with others in the company. Many companies require managers to get some guidance from their human resources department—or from a particular higher-up in the company, such as their own managers or a company officer—if they are considering issuing a verbal warning. Some companies don't require you to check in first but require you to talk to human resources or someone else before you actually give the warning. Typically, the purpose of this type of requirement is to make sure that individual managers know how to discipline, what to say, how to document the conversation, and what to do next.

If your company doesn't require you to collaborate this way, that doesn't mean you can't. If you have any questions about whether a verbal warning is appropriate, what to say, how to deal with the employee's reactions, what types of action plans to consider, or anything else, go to your human resources department or manager. Chances are good that they can help you brainstorm the issues and develop some strategies for dealing with the problem.

Once you've done some collaboration, you're ready to plan the meeting itself. You'll need to gather necessary information, decide when and where to meet, and think through what you will say.

Gather Information

As explained in Chapter 1, you should always gather information before you meet with the employee. You'll want to make sure that you have your facts straight, so you can use those facts to successfully communicate to the employee that this is a real problem and must be corrected.

Often, you will be giving a verbal warning because your coaching efforts didn't work. In this situation, you'll need to make sure the employee understands the problem and why it must be solved. If you haven't tried coaching but have jumped to a verbal warning because the situation warrants more formal discipline, you'll need to explain why a verbal warning is appropriate. In either case, be ready with facts demonstrating the severity of the problem and the importance of immediate improvement.

- **Look at the facts.** As always, you should start by reviewing the facts of the situation that led you to decide a verbal warning was appropriate, including what actually happened, how the employee's poor performance or other problem affected the company, and so on.
- **Review past conversations.** Next, review any prior conversations you've had with the employee on this issue. If you've coached the employee, go over your notes. How often have you had to talk to the employee about this problem? What did you say about it? What was the action plan?
- **Consider what didn't work.** What specific things did the employee do or not do that caused the action plan to fail? Be prepared to discuss specifically what went wrong.

Having these facts at your fingertips will help you make your position clear and help you evaluate the likely success of any new plans for improvement.

> **CAUTION**
>
> **If you skipped straight to a verbal warning because the employee violated a rule or committed misconduct, review your employee handbook or other written company policies.** What does the rule require? Did the employee know about the rule or know that his or her conduct was not appropriate? What's the purpose of the rule? Being able to point to the rule and explain its importance will help you communicate why the employee's problem warrants a verbal warning, and, hopefully, help you ward off a defensive reaction.

Set Up Logistics

Now it's time to plan where and when you will have the meeting and who should be there. Once you've decided that a verbal warning is in order, it's a good idea to meet with the employee right away: ideally, within a day or two. Holding a meeting immediately after the incident lets the employee know that the issue is important and has captured your full attention. Also, the quicker you step in, the quicker the employee will have an opportunity to improve.

Unlike a coaching meeting, which might take only ten or 15 minutes, you should plan at least half an hour to discuss a verbal warning. Because the employee will be facing a formal disciplinary intervention, he or she is more likely to have questions and concerns. You are also more likely to see emotional or angry reactions, which you and the employee may need some time to sort through. And, particularly if you have already coached the employee on the problem, you should budget extra time to analyze and discuss what went wrong with your previous action plan and how you can do better this time around.

Although an offsite meeting may be appropriate for a coaching session, you should stay at work to administer a verbal warning. While you want to emphasize informality in a coaching session, it's important to be more formal with a verbal warning, to demonstrate that the company is getting involved. If your office is private (that is, you have walls that reach to the ceiling and a door that closes), you can hold the meeting there. If not, book a conference room or another space where you can talk comfortably. If you have concerns about office gossip, you should coordinate a time and place with the employee that maximizes privacy.

If You're Managing an Offsite Employee

If you manage employees who work offsite, you may have a hard time following the suggestions above. Here are a few options for delivering a verbal warning:

Bring the employee into the office. Set up a formal meeting time and date. Even if that delays your meeting by a couple of days, it's better to have the meeting face to face.

Go to the employee's worksite. This may be feasible if the employee's location isn't very far away. Be sure that there is a private place to have your discussion, however.

If you must discipline remotely, don't do it in an email. Set up a formal phone conference, or a videoconference if you can. Conduct the meeting sitting at a desk, well prepared to have the same discussion you would engage in if the employee were in the room.

Some companies require you to have a witness at formal disciplinary meetings, typically, a human resources representative or a higher-level manager. If your company is one of them, you should arrange to have the appropriate person attend. If your company doesn't require you to bring a witness, consider the pros and cons of having a third person present (these are covered in Chapter 10).

Allowing the Employee to Bring a Witness

There are two situations in which you must allow the employee to bring a witness to a disciplinary meeting:

- If your company policy states that employees may bring witnesses, then you must allow them to do so.
- If the employee is represented by a union, he or she is entitled to bring a union representative to any meeting that could lead to discipline. These rights are called "*Weingarten* rights," after the name of the U.S. Supreme Court case that created them.

If the employee asks to bring a witness or support person but you aren't required to allow it, check with your human resources department (if you have one) to find out how this type of request has been handled in the past.

There are pros and cons to allowing the employee to bring a witness. The employee might feel more comfortable—and therefore, better able to discuss the problem and possible solutions—with another person there, particularly if the employee has an emotional reaction. And allowing a witness will help the employee feel supported.

On the other hand, having an extra person in the room will probably make it more difficult to establish a rapport with the employee. If an employee brings a witness, you may also want to bring a representative from human resources, to help provide balance and perspective to the conversation.

Plan the Conversation

As always when delivering discipline, you can't script the whole discussion in advance. But you should consider how to begin the conversation and the tone you'd like to set.

Unlike a coaching session, which an employee might not even recognize as discipline, a verbal warning is a formal disciplinary step. If you've decided to issue a verbal warning, you are dealing with either a recurring problem or a first-time event that is serious enough to move past the coaching step in the disciplinary system. Either way, you should begin the conversation in a way that conveys the seriousness of the matter to the employee, without making the employee feel like he or she is under attack.

> EXAMPLE: Charles supervises Peggy, who has left work early a couple of times. The first time Charles noticed that Peggy wasn't at her workstation, he sat down with her the next day for a quick reminder. She told him it wouldn't happen again. But two weeks later, Charles actually saw Peggy gathering her belongings and heading out 20 minutes before she was supposed to leave. The next day, he calls her into his office, where he plans to issue a verbal warning.
>
> Charles is angry that Peggy has blatantly disregarded company rules and his previous effort to coach her. As soon as she sits down, he says, "What were you doing, leaving early after I told you not to? I think I've made it clear that this is completely unacceptable, and I'm not going to let you get away with it. If this keeps up, you're going to be let go."
>
> If Peggy responds that she left early because her husband was in a serious car accident, Charles is going to feel pretty bad. But even if Peggy doesn't have a good excuse, Charles's angry approach has essentially foreclosed any possibility of collaborative discussion. Peggy will feel that Charles has his mind made up, and it doesn't matter what she says or does. She is likely to respond defensively and will probably either clam up entirely or get angry. She might improve her attendance, at least temporarily, but her dedication to the job and the company is likely to take a sharp downturn (along with her performance, most likely). Charles has lost an opportunity to develop loyalty and improved performance and has probably made an enemy.
>
> This would have been a better approach:
>
> "Peggy, I asked you to meet with me today to discuss an important issue that has come up more than once: leaving work early. We talked about this a couple of weeks ago, and I thought we agreed that it wouldn't happen again. But yesterday, I saw you leaving your workstation at 4:40 in the afternoon, and you didn't return. What's going on?"

When you plan your opening sentences, remember that you want to briefly describe the problem, convey that it is serious, and mention any prior conversations about it. Here are some more examples:

EXAMPLE: "Martina, please come in and sit down. I want to talk about the way you spoke to Eric this afternoon about the Jones account. I heard you raise your voice to him and tell him that he was incompetent. I spoke to Eric about the conversation, and he told me that you said some other negative things, as well. He is upset about it, and I'm concerned. That is not how we talk to each other at this company. Tell me what happened."

EXAMPLE: "Brad, you are continuing to miss your project deadlines. We've talked about this before, and I've explained that your coworkers have to pick up the slack when you aren't finished with your work on time. We also came up with a more detailed schedule so you could complete and hand in your work a little bit at a time. However, you've been missing those interim deadlines as well. We need to get things back on track right away."

EXAMPLE: "I know that you're having a hard time arranging child care, Maurice, but you were late by more than 20 minutes twice last week. As we've discussed twice in the past month, you have to be here, on time, every day, in order to help open the store. This is a job requirement, and there are good reasons for it. We need to get this problem solved."

CAUTION

Save the small talk for happier times. Don't start a formal disciplinary meeting with casual chatter or questions about the employee's weekend. This will only give the employee the wrong idea about the purpose of the meeting. It could even make the employee feel tricked when the real agenda is revealed. This isn't a good way to begin a conversation that you hope will be open and collaborative. Likewise, don't allow the employee to avoid the discipline discussion by sidetracking you with small talk. Say something like "I wish we could use our time today to catch up, but we are really here to address this issue." This will keep your discussion on track.

Meet With the Employee

During the meeting, you should clearly communicate what the problem is, why it's a problem, and what needs to happen next. Although the meeting will be similar to a coaching session, there are some important differences, which stem from the more formal nature of a verbal warning. Here is the basic agenda your meeting should follow (each of these steps is covered more fully below):

- State the problem.
- Review past efforts to correct, if any.
- Make sure the employee acknowledges the problem.
- Listen to the employee's explanation.
- Tell the employee that you are issuing a verbal warning.
- Develop a solution.
- Discuss next steps.

State the Problem

At the outset, tell the employee exactly why you are meeting. Explain the facts that lead you to believe there is a problem: what you saw or heard, or what was reported to you by others. Let the employee know why his or her performance, behavior, or misconduct is causing a problem for the company, and clearly state that things need to change.

> EXAMPLE: Steve's manager, Jerry, begins a verbal warning discussion like this: "Steve, I've asked you to meet with me today to talk about our process for managing deals. As we discussed several weeks ago, while we expect all of our account representatives to close at least three new deals each month, we also expect you to follow the processes and procedures established for implementing those deals. While your sales numbers are improving, and we want to encourage continued progress, your deal implementation memos are incomplete and often have significant errors. This means the support teams scramble around asking you to clarify what should have been clearly stated in the first place. What's more, you often don't answer their questions in a timely way, though everything you send to them is marked 'urgent.' This lack of attention to detail and process management means that the support teams spend three times the usual amount of time implementing your deals, which makes for bad feelings on the team. It also costs the company money, because we can't invoice until everything is satisfactorily delivered. While you are meeting the sales goals, these sales are coming at a high internal price."

Review Past Discussions

If you have already coached the employee on this issue, talk briefly about those conversations. You don't have to go into great detail; after all, the employee was at the coaching session with you. The purpose of this review is to gently remind the employee that he or she already had an opportunity to discuss and resolve the problem informally, and it didn't work. It also acknowledges that the employee didn't meet the commitments he or she made in that earlier conversation. This makes it easier for the employee to accept that a verbal warning is necessary and puts him or her in the right frame of mind to talk honestly about what happened.

> **EXAMPLE:** Jerry says, "When we talked several weeks ago about this problem, you told me that you thought it was more important to bring in deals than worry about 'mindless paperwork.' I explained then that it was vital to product delivery and asked you to reread the process handbook. We also discussed that you'd complete all deal memos fully. If anything confused you, you were to ask me about it before you turned in the memo. I haven't heard a single question from you, but I have had continued complaints about your deal memos."

Seek the Employee's Acknowledgment

At this point, the employee will probably start talking. Before you get too involved in a conversation about what happened and why, however, it's very important to make sure that the employee understands exactly what the problem is. If the employee starts off by acknowledging the problem, you can cross this off your list. If the employee denies the problem or admits the behavior but claims that it isn't a problem or makes excuses, however, you'll need to make sure that you're both on the same page before you continue.

To do this, go back to the beginning and state the facts: what the employee did (or didn't do) and why it's a problem. If necessary, lay out the facts one by one. For example, if an employee responds to your conversation about tardiness by saying, "It's not that big of a deal. Anyway, I've hardly been late at all this month," you might respond by saying, "In fact, you were late twice last week alone—20 minutes late on Tuesday and 15 minutes late on Friday. And, as we've discussed, it is a big deal, because when you're late, you are not available to serve our customers."

> **EXAMPLE:** Steve responds to Jerry's statements by saying, "Why are you riding me so hard? My job is to bring in the business. Let the clerks do the paperwork."
>
> Jerry replies, "Steve, I'm not coming down especially hard on you. Your job isn't just to bring in the deals: It's also to manage your accounts and help the company profit

from those deals. If your deal memos are incomplete, a lot of time is wasted figuring out what needs to be done, who needs to do it, and when it needs to be done. That costs the company a lot of employee time, and it also creates resentment on your team.

"We'll talk about why you haven't completed your deal memos correctly in a minute; first, I need to make sure that we agree about the facts. You signed four new deals this month, right?" Steve says, "Yeah, that sounds about right." Jerry responds, "And you were contacted by Claire last Friday, April 27, because the deal memo on the Briggs account was incomplete and had some incorrect information, right?" Steve agrees. Jerry continues, "Claire told me you didn't respond until the following Wednesday. Does that sound right to you?" Steve again agrees. Jerry then moves the conversation along by saying, "Okay, now that I know we're both on the same page about what actually happened, let's talk about why."

TIP

A detailed investigation can help. Sometimes, you might have to discipline an employee for behavior that you haven't witnessed first-hand, such as being rude to customers or harassing a coworker. In these situations, talking to witnesses and gathering any other evidence before you meet with the employee can help you head off a flat denial. Once the employee sees that you know (or at least, have a pretty good idea) about what happened, he or she will be less likely to stonewall.

Listen to the Employee's Explanation

Pay very careful attention to the employee's comments about what happened and why. Of course, you'll need to listen well to understand where the employee is coming from and develop an action plan to solve the problem. But you also need to make sure that a verbal warning is the appropriate disciplinary measure. You might not have the full story, or some other employee might really be to blame, which might dictate that you make the meeting a coaching session or simply a conversation. On the other hand, the incident might be worse than you feared: The employee might have done something wrong intentionally, for example, to sabotage the company or endanger a coworker.

EXAMPLE: After Jerry makes sure Steve understands the problem, Steve has the chance to explain: "It takes all my energy just to bring in new clients, so the last priority on my list is filling out paperwork. You can see my new client numbers are improving but I have to tell you, not having secretarial help really handicaps me when it comes time to implement the deals. And I admit, I'm still not that comfortable with the internal process. At my old job, I just handed the deal off to administrative staff, and my numbers were great. I think that if I understood the process and technology here better, I'd have better results."

Jerry responds, echoing what Steve has said to show that he's listening carefully: "I'm glad you think that you're progressing with new accounts. That's important. And it sounds like you're still having trouble making the move from selling benefit programs to selling boxed software, partly because the implementation system is new to you. Does that sound right?"

Explain the Verbal Warning

This can be the most awkward part of the conversation, but it's absolutely necessary: You must tell the employee explicitly that you are issuing a verbal warning (unless, of course, the employee has told you something that changes your mind about giving the warning). The employee needs to be on notice that he or she has entered the disciplinary system, that the issue will be documented, and that further problems could result in more serious discipline.

If you don't tell the employee that you're giving a warning, the employee might later be surprised to see the warning in his or her personnel file or to have it come up later, when it's time for bonuses, promotions, raises, and the like. What's more, it denies the employee the opportunity to improve: If the employee doesn't understand the seriousness of the problem, he or she might not understand the pressing need to immediately alter behavior.

Managers are often hesitant to announce that they're issuing a formal warning during a disciplinary meeting, because they're concerned that this will turn the employee against them and poison the rest of the conversation. But there are ways to break the news while still maintaining a positive note. For example, you might emphasize that you will continue to help the employee improve and that you hope further discussions and discipline won't be necessary.

EXAMPLE: Jerry tells Steve, "I need to let you know that I'm giving you a verbal warning, based on your problem managing deals effectively. I made that decision because we've already discussed the issue and I haven't yet seen an improvement in your deal memos or your deal management generally. But I'm hopeful that we'll come up with some good ideas today that will help you understand our deal management process, so we won't have to talk about this again. In fact, I already have some ideas kicking around in my head, so let's start brainstorming on how we can resolve this problem."

💡 TIP

Let the employee know if the warning will "expire." Many companies put a time limit on how long a verbal or written warning will remain in an employee's file. After that time has passed, the warning is removed, and the employee has a clean slate from that point forward. If your company has this type of policy, tell the employee that the warning will be removed if he or she has no further problems while the warning is active. This provides a strong incentive for improvement and lets the employee know that you really want him or her to succeed.

Develop Solutions

This is most managers' favorite part of the meeting: looking ahead to positive change in the future. Hopefully, your employee will have some ideas of what might help. Some of these ideas might be too expensive or otherwise impractical, but don't be dismissive. Instead, tell the employee why his or her idea won't work, and keep the conversation moving. Share your own ideas as well, but stay open to the employee's input. After all, the employee is the one who will ultimately have to carry out the plan, and he or she knows best what is feasible and what is not.

> **EXAMPLE:** Steve says, "I'd like to talk about solutions, too. What I'd really like is to lower my sales targets for a few months, just until I get a handle on how the deal management process works. Can we do that?" Jerry knows this is a nonstarter, and responds, "I'm afraid not, Steve. These numbers are set specifically for newer sales reps, and your coworkers are meeting them successfully. We have to come up with some ways to improve your deal management, not lower your sales goals."
>
> Steve says, "I see your point, I guess. What I really need help with is learning what the relevant information is. I want to make sure I get it in there the first time, because right now, I feel like these memos are taking up too much time. But it's really hard for me to tell what it is exactly that the support staff need from me."

Jerry replies, "I can see that if you don't understand how the information is used, you won't know what to include in your memos. Have you spent a few hours listening to the customer support inbound calls, to hear the kinds of questions they get from customers?"

Steve responds, "No, I haven't. I've never thought about the deals from the back end."

Jerry offers, "What I'd like to do is set up a schedule, so you can spend a couple of hours with each department that helps to implement your deals. That way, you can see what information really needs to be spelled out in your deal memos, and why it's important to manage the process very carefully. It will show you how properly managing deals really impacts their profitability, and it will give you a chance to foster better relationships with the 'back office' team. And I'd also like you to spend a couple of hours with Celia. She's our top closer and also works great with the back office."

Steve says, "That sounds great. If it's all right with you, I'd also like to show you my draft deal memos, after I've had a chance to hear from everyone else what's really important. Then you can tell me how well they meet the company's needs. Would that be okay?" Jerry agrees.

Agree on Next Steps

Once you've developed an action plan, discuss exactly what will happen next. Start by spelling out what you and the employee have committed to do. Make your action plan concrete by setting dates and specific targets for improvement. Especially if you are dealing with a recurring issue, you will want to set fairly tight deadlines and regular check-ins. If this is a recurring issue, this employee hasn't been able (or willing) to improve after notice of the problem, which means you will need to keep a closer eye on the situation.

Because you will be documenting the meeting afterward, you should also let the employee know when the paperwork will be ready. Give the employee an opportunity to read the documentation and raise any questions or concerns. It's a good idea to schedule a brief follow-up meeting the next day (assuming you can complete the paperwork by then) to review the documentation.

EXAMPLE: Jerry says, "Okay Steve, it sounds like we have a plan. I'll let the back office leads know that you'll be spending some time with them. Why don't you give me some dates and times that work for you by the end of the day, then I'll set up a schedule by the beginning of next week. After you've met with them to understand the process from their end, and you've completed another sale, you can get the draft deal memo together and we can go over it together. How does that sound?" Steve agrees to the plan.

Jerry also talks to Steve about paperwork: "As we discussed, this is a formal verbal warning, so I need to summarize our conversation in writing, for your file. As I told you, the documentation will be removed from your file after one year, as long as we don't have any further problems with this. I'll write that up by the end of the day; I'd like you to read it and make sure you agree with it. There's a space on the form for you to comment and sign, so I know we're both on the same page. I'll email you the paperwork later today. If you'd like to talk about it after you look it over, let me know and we can talk again. If not, you can just print it out, sign it, and return it to me."

Make sure to close the meeting on a positive note. After all, you and the employee have successfully developed a solution and are both looking forward to improvement in the future. Say something like "I'm glad we talked about this and developed an action plan. I'm confident that you'll be able to follow through and get this resolved."

> ⓘ **CAUTION**
>
> **Don't make promises for the future.** It's important to say something positive to an employee who's just received a warning: It reinforces that you want to help, are focused on what happens next, and believe in the employee. But don't take it a step further and promise a reward for improved performance (or further discipline if things don't get better). These kinds of statements might have to be followed later, even if the company can't or doesn't want to. See Chapter 3 for more information on why it's smart to avoid specific promises.

Document

After the meeting—preferably on the same day—complete your paperwork. If your company requires you to use a particular form or follow certain rules for documentation, by all means do so. If not, you can use the form we provide at this book's online companion page (see Appendix D for details).

Here's a sample form, which Jerry used to document his verbal warning to Steve:

Sample Verbal Warning

Employee Disciplinary Notice	
Employee's Name: Steve Hinds	
Manager's Name: Jerry Martinez	**Date of Incident:** May 3, 20xx
Type of Warning: ☑ Verbal Warning ☐ Written Warning	

Incident Description:

On May 1, 20xx, I received a complaint from administrative assistant Claire Stewart that your deal memo on the Briggs sale was incomplete and contained numerous errors that slowed implementation of the deal significantly. I investigated whether this was true by reviewing the deal memo (attached) and talking with the administrative staff responsible for assisting you in completing this deal.

The deal memo did not have all the information the staff needed to complete the deal. For example, the memo did not explain the shipping method or the shipping date. Additionally, the memo had errors including incorrect prices and the wrong delivery address.

On April 27, Claire tried to contact you via both email and phone to correct these errors, but you did not respond. As a result of these errors, three administrative assistants spent approximately eight extra hours trying to resolve the discrepancies. Claire also informed me that a similar problem occurred on the Edwards deal earlier in the month.

While your gross sales numbers have been improving, these errors are reducing profit margin on your deals significantly and causing extra work for other team members.

When you and I met to discuss this issue earlier today, you told me that you believed this was the responsibility of administrative staff and that you were not comfortable with the company process.

Prior Incidents:

Customer support, clerical, and fulfillment have each complained about incorrect or incomplete information on your deal memos at least three times. We discussed this in my office on April 5. At that time, I tasked you with rereading the process handbook, which you told me that you did. I also told you to ask me if you had questions about writing deal memos. Since April 5, you have not asked me any questions about deal memos.

Sample Verbal Warning, continued

Improvement Plan:

We agreed that you will meet with each back office department and spend a couple of hours learning what information they need from you to implement your deals. You will also spend a couple of hours with Celia, who will show you one of her deal memos and explain how she decides what to include in it. You will let me know some dates and times that are good for you by tomorrow; I will set up a schedule for these visits by the beginning of next week, May 7.

We also agreed that we will review your next deal memo together. I will tell you whether that memo includes the relevant information. When you have closed your next deal, please inform me and we can schedule that review.

Employee Comments:

Manager's Signature:	Date:

Employee Acknowledgment	
I acknowledge that I have received and understand this document.	
Employee's Signature:	Date:

Remember, you might need to meet with the employee again, if he or she takes issue with anything you wrote or wants to discuss things further. You'll want to secure the employee's signature, whether or not the employee adds comments to the form. If the employee resists, remind him or her that it is only an acknowledgment, not an agreement. For more information on preparing documentation, see Chapter 9. You can also find other examples of verbal warnings in Appendix B.

Follow Up

What happens after you meet with the employee will make or break your action plan. Don't wait until a month or two has passed before you get involved: Check in often, offering any advice or assistance you can. Make sure that you provide the resources and other help you promised during your meeting.

You should have your calendar out as you complete your paperwork, to record important dates and commitments. For example, if you agreed to meet with the employee once a week, schedule those appointments. If you told the employee you'd make any changes—for example, by putting the employee on a particular project, giving a troublesome account to a coworker, or arranging for the employee to attend a training program—write a note to remind yourself to do it, and schedule check-ins to make sure those changes have the desired effect.

If your company removes discipline documentation from the personnel file after a certain amount of time has passed without further problems, mark that date on your calendar as well. You must keep this commitment: Chances are good that it's providing a strong incentive to your employee. If someone else (for example, the human resources department) is responsible for actually removing this documentation from the file, write yourself a note to send a reminder email a couple of days before the deadline. Check the file yourself to make sure the paperwork is no longer there after the deadline has passed.

And don't forget the power of positive reinforcement: Even if the employee doesn't turn things all the way around, it's important to praise improvement. Teachers and trainers tells us that everyone learns more quickly through praise for appropriate behavior than through punishment for doing things wrong. Look for things that you can praise, then make a point of doing it.

EXAMPLE: One week after their meeting, Jerry sees Steve in the hallway and says, "Steve, I just want to let you know that Mary and Sam both made a point of telling me that they appreciated the time you took to understand how their departments functioned and that you asked some good questions. I appreciate that you're taking those meetings so seriously, and I wanted to thank you for that. Here's to smooth deals in May!"

You should offer the employee praise for improvement even if he or she isn't yet performing up to your standards, but only if the employee is on an upward trajectory. This is most often an issue when dealing with performance problems: The employee's performance improves but is still short of the mark. As long as the employee is still getting better and you foresee fully acceptable performance in the near future, you should praise the improvement while noting that there's still some room for growth.

EXAMPLE: In May, Steve makes his sales targets, but his revenues dip slightly. However, all his deal memos are flawless, and Steve has expressed to Jerry that he now feels more comfortable with the implementation process and more appreciative of the contribution of other staff members. He has met with Jerry a couple of times to hone his memos, and Jerry is confident that he'll keep getting better. Rather than criticizing his lowered sales numbers, Jerry tells him, "Steve, I'm happy that you understand the deal implementation process. Although your sales numbers were a little low this month, I'm confident that you'll turn that around as you get more comfortable with the implementation process and it starts taking up less of your time. Let's sit down in a couple of weeks and make sure you're still on target."

If, on the other hand, the employee doesn't seem to be improving much or at all, even after you've lived up to the commitments you made in the action plan, it's time to consider giving a written warning. Chapter 13 explains how.

PODCAST
If you'd like to hear a sample verbal warning discussion, check out this book's online companion page. Appendix D provides the link.

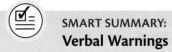

SMART SUMMARY:
Verbal Warnings

- A verbal warning is the first "formal" step in the disciplinary process: the employee is officially notified of the discipline, it is documented, and the company is involved.

- A verbal warning is appropriate when an employee hasn't responded to previous coaching efforts, when an employee has violated a company rule inadvertently or unknowingly, or when an employee's performance or behavior has caused problems for the company but the employee seems unaware of the issue and genuinely interested in improvement.

- A verbal warning is more formal than a coaching session. Take more time to prepare what you will say—including a review of any previous discussions on topic—and allow at least a half hour for the discussion. The discussion should take place in a more formal setting that gives the employee privacy and communicates to the employee that the problem is serious.

- When you meet with an employee to issue a verbal warning, state the problem, review past efforts to correct it, make sure the employee acknowledges the problem, listen to the employee's explanation, tell the employee you are issuing a verbal warning, develop a solution, and discuss next steps.

- Although a verbal warning is given orally, it must be followed up by documentation that acknowledges the discipline, the reason for it, whether there were any prior incidents, and the action plan. The employee should be given a copy of the documentation, invited to make comments and asked to sign it, acknowledging receipt.

Step 3: Written Warnings

We all hope for the best in the disciplinary process: to have positive, productive conversations with our employees that motivate them to improve and resolve problems before they become critical. But if you're facing a problem that's ongoing, serious, or both, a written warning may be your only choice, because either company policy or common sense dictates it.

Typically, a written warning is given when an employee doesn't improve after coaching and a verbal warning. However, you may also give a written warning for a first-time problem, if the behavior or consequences are serious enough to justify a forceful response but not so serious as to call for immediate termination of employment.

Giving a written warning can be difficult. Because a written warning is—and will be viewed by the employee as—a serious disciplinary measure, you should anticipate that the employee might become defensive or emotional. Particularly if you're revisiting an issue that you and the employee have discussed before, the employee might feel more frustrated, angry, or embarrassed that there hasn't been sufficient improvement. Typically, written warnings come with some serious job consequences—such as ineligibility for merit raises and promotions or lowered performance appraisals—which can also lead to heightened emotions and anger.

And the employee might not be the only person who's upset about the situation. Because you're dealing with someone who has either committed serious misconduct or failed to improve after you've tried to help, you might be frustrated and angry yourself. This can make it tough to get down to the business at hand: communicating, clearly and objectively, why the situation is not acceptable and how it will need to change. If you're dealing with one-time, serious misconduct, you'll need to keep close tabs on the employee in the future, to make sure your written warning puts the problem in the past. If you're dealing with an ongoing problem, the action plan you develop at this stage might have to include more detail, oversight, and direction from you.

This chapter explains how to give a written warning, from start to finish. You'll learn when a written warning is appropriate, how to plan to meet with the employee, and what to say during the meeting. You'll also learn how to document the situation—that is, how to actually write your written warning—and how to follow up afterwards, to make sure that the employee stays on track.

A Written Warning Is Both a Conversation and a Document

It used to be standard practice for a written warning to simply appear on a worker's desk or locker, unaccompanied by any discussion. (Pink slips—notices that the employee had been fired—often showed up in the same, silent way.) In today's modern workplace, however, the term "written warning" generally refers both to the actual written document and to the conversation that accompanies it. Giving a written warning doesn't simply mean handing over a piece of paper: It also means explaining the warning to the employee and talking about what will happen next.

At some companies, managers are told to draft the written warning before they meet with the employee, then hand it over during the meeting. There are several problems with this approach, however:

- You can't be sure that the facts warrant a written warning until you meet with the employee and hear him or her out. If you were wrong in your assessment of the situation, you'll have to go back on what you've said, get your piece of paper back from the employee, and start all over again.
- You won't be able to include the employee's response in your documentation. Sometimes, the employee says something during your meeting that should be memorialized, for example, admitting to wrongdoing or providing an explanation for poor performance.
- Once you hand over the written warning, the employee will start reading and stop listening to you. The employee might also be upset that you decided how to handle the situation without even asking for his or her side of the story.

For all of these reasons, we recommend that you write your written warning after you meet with the employee, just like any other disciplinary documentation.

What Is a Written Warning?

A written warning is the second formal step in most discipline systems (following a verbal warning) and is typically reserved for fairly serious problems. Often, a written warning affects an employee's opportunities for advancement and eligibility for merit raises, bonuses, and consideration for special projects. Because a written warning has significant consequences, it gives the employee an extra incentive to make a change for the better. If the employee can't or won't improve, it also lays the groundwork for a fair and legally defensible termination.

When to Give a Written Warning

To figure out whether a written warning is the appropriate way to deal with a particular problem, you'll need to follow the steps outlined in Chapter 5. You'll have to review your company's policy, check in with your human resources department, consider how similar issues have been handled, and weigh how serious the problem is.

Because a written warning is a severe disciplinary measure, it isn't the right response to minor problems or many first-time offenses. At the other end of the spectrum, some problems—almost always misconduct—are so serious that they justify immediate termination of employment. So when is a problem serious enough to warrant a written warning, but not so serious that the employee should be fired? Here are some examples:

- The employee has not improved a performance, attendance, or misconduct problem, even after you've provided coaching and given a verbal warning. In this situation, a written warning is appropriate; it is simply the next step in the discipline process.

  > EXAMPLE: Cora answers phones at the help desk of a large company. Cora and the other customer service representatives answer basic customer questions, but they forward most calls on to other departments or outside technicians. If the customer wants to purchase a product or receive a refund, Cora or one of her coworkers processes the transaction.
  >
  > Customer service representatives are expected to answer an average of 20 calls a day, return all messages left since the previous business day, and process all paperwork for orders and refunds on the same day they are made. Cora averages about 14 calls a day and often waits several days before processing paperwork or returning customer calls.
  >
  > Cora's manager had a coaching session with her and asked her to spend a morning observing a more experienced coworker handling calls. The manager also reviewed the ordering and refund paperwork with Cora, to

make sure she understood what was required. When Cora didn't improve, the manager gave her a verbal warning. Because Cora said that it was hard for her to budget her time properly to get everything done, the manager sent her to a time management seminar. Cora still hasn't improved, so the manager decides to give her a written warning.

> **CAUTION**
>
> **Make sure the employee had a fair opportunity to improve.** Before you decide to give a written warning for an ongoing problem, take a look at the action plan you came up with in your last disciplinary meeting with the employee. Were the goals you set feasible? Did you provide the resources necessary for the employee to succeed? Did you hold follow-up meetings as promised? If your review reveals flaws in the action plan, you might want to scale back and give another verbal warning. This time, make sure you have agreed on a fair and achievable action plan.

- The employee has taken an extended unexcused absence that is not legally protected, failed to turn up at a mandatory event, or otherwise engaged in a serious and/or flagrant violation of the company's attendance rules. Typically, managers handle first-time attendance problems through coaching. If that first absence is prolonged or causes extreme hardship, however, stronger discipline might be appropriate.

  EXAMPLE: Josephine is a driver for a company that delivers documents and packages. Each driver is responsible for pickups and deliveries in a particular region. The company requires drivers to request vacation time at least three weeks in advance and requires drivers to call in before taking a sick day, so it can line up substitute drivers.

  Josephine doesn't show up for work on a Wednesday. Her supervisor, Hank, calls her home; when no one answers, Hank leaves a message asking Josephine to call in right away. Josephine doesn't show up or call in until Friday afternoon, when she calls Hank and tells him that she will return to work on Monday morning. Josephine explains that she has been out of town since Tuesday evening, when her sister called from out of state and said that she had been evicted. Josephine went to help her sister find a new place to live and move into it.

  Because Hank didn't know whether Josephine was coming in, he had to find a driver at the last minute for three days in a row. Some of the customers on Josephine's regular route complained about late service, and one important delivery didn't get made on time. Hank knows that Josephine understood the company's attendance policy, because he explains it to all drivers when they are hired. Even though Josephine had a compelling reason to be out, she didn't call or ask for permission. All in all, Hank decides that this conduct merits a written warning.

- The employee has committed misconduct that is serious but does not warrant termination. Examples typically include horseplay, violations of safety rules, problems dealing with customers or clients, or mistreatment of coworkers.

  EXAMPLE: Dave asked Crystal, his coworker, out a month ago, but she told him she was seeing someone else. Since then, Dave has asked Crystal questions about her boyfriend, what they do together, how she feels about him, and so forth. Although they are friendly with each other, Crystal is uncomfortable about Dave's interest in her love life. When she tells him she doesn't want to talk about her relationship, Dave responds, "Why won't you tell me anything about this guy? You don't seem very excited about him; are you sure you don't want to go out with me instead?"

  Claude, their manager, overhears the end of this conversation as he's walking by Crystal's cubicle. He also sees that Crystal looks upset, so he asks her to come to his office. Claude asks Crystal what's going on, and she says, "I don't want to get Dave in trouble, but he's kind of creeping me out. He asked me to go on a date with him, and when I told him I had a boyfriend, he just started in with all of these questions. I don't want to go out with him and I don't want to talk about my relationship, but he just doesn't seem to be getting the message."

  After conferring with the human resources department and considering the situation carefully, Claude decides to give Dave a written warning. Discipline is clearly in order: Dave's behavior is out of line, upsetting to his coworker, and skirting close to the edge of sexual harassment. On the other hand, Dave hasn't had any disciplinary problems before; he hasn't touched, threatened, or made crude comments to Crystal (any of which could well be grounds for immediate termination); and there's a good possibility that he doesn't understand why his behavior is inappropriate. All in all, it looks like Dave needs a serious wake-up call, and Claude decides that a written warning is the right way to deliver it. Claude also realizes that he will have to monitor the situation very carefully, to make sure Dave changes his ways.

How to Give a Written Warning

Now that you've decided to give a written warning, it's time to get started. As when you coach or give a verbal warning, you'll need to prepare, meet with the employee, document the discussion, and follow up. When you give a written warning, however, things are more formal. At this point, you're usually dealing with an employee who can't or won't meet basic standards of performance or conduct. Giving a written warning conveys that things must change if the employee wants to keep working for your company.

If you've already coached and given a verbal warning for the same behavior, you'll have to spend some time analyzing, and then discussing with the employee, why your previous action plan hasn't worked. Your first step should be to make sure that the employee had a fair chance to succeed: that your action plan was clear and achievable, that you provided any resources and training you promised, and so on. Assuming the action plan was fair, you'll need to emphasize that the employee did not do as he or she agreed to do and that this is unacceptable.

You should also spend extra time coming up with a new plan for improvement, with more frequent follow-up meetings and tight deadlines that will allow you to stay on top of the situation. Although this might feel like micromanagement, you've already given the employee the opportunity to improve, and it hasn't worked. If your employee needs more involvement or direction from you in order to succeed, that's what you should provide.

If you're handling a first-time problem, the purpose of the written warning is to administer a powerful wake-up call. You must communicate why the employee's behavior was serious enough to warrant an immediate written warning and explain exactly what you expect in the future.

Prepare

Many companies require managers to get permission—from the human resources department, legal counsel, or a higher-level manager or officer—before giving a written warning. Even if your company doesn't require it, however, you should still consult with others in the company before taking action. A written warning is a serious step, and it's a good idea to get input from those who know how the company has handled similar problems in the past, to make sure that you are acting consistently with past practice. You can also use this meeting to practice what you plan to say and how you might react to various responses by the employee.

Once you've obtained permission—or at least some feedback—from human resources, your legal counsel, and/or your manager, plan for your meeting with the employee. As is true of other disciplinary measures, you'll need to gather necessary information, decide when and where to meet, and think through what you will say.

Gather Information

As you would before giving a verbal warning, you must get the information you need to hold a productive meeting with the employee. You should be prepared to discuss exactly what happened, why it is a serious problem, any prior disciplinary discussions you've had with the employee, and what needs to happen going forward. You might need to investigate the facts and review your documentation from previous discussions to get ready for the conversation.

The way you prepare will depend, in part, on whether or not you have previously disciplined the employee for the same behavior.

Written Warnings for a Recurring Problem

If you are giving a written warning for an ongoing problem, you should be prepared to discuss very specifically what went wrong with the previous action plan. After all, you and the employee have already discussed this issue more than once, agreed that it's a problem, and come up with a solution that you both thought would be effective. If the employee still hasn't improved, you need to understand why.

Before you meet with the employee, you should sit down with the documentation from your previous meeting(s) and review that action plan. Think carefully about why the action plan wasn't successful and further discipline is necessary. Did the employee have the necessary resources? Did the employee follow through on the specific commitments he or she made by, for example, attending training, meeting with you, handing in assignments, and so on? Did the employee improve in some areas but not others? If so, does this indicate more clearly where the weaknesses in the employee's abilities might lie?

When you give the written warning, you'll need to redouble your efforts to convince the employee that things need to change and that the employee must commit to improving. Spend some extra time preparing to talk about how the employee's ongoing problem is affecting the company. Think through every possible impact, and make sure you have the necessary data—dollar amounts, hours lost, and so on—to make your case. Even though it may be uncomfortable, you're going to have to show the employee that the consequences for the company are simply too great to permit the problem to continue any longer.

Controlling Your Emotions

If you have to give a written warning for an ongoing problem, you're probably wrestling with some tough emotions of your own. You might feel angry that the employee hasn't responded to your earlier efforts or appreciated all the time you have taken to try and resolve the problem, sad that the employee just doesn't seem to be working out, worried about backlash you might experience as a result of discipline, or insecure that you weren't sufficiently "skilled" as a manager to solve this problem already. And you probably aren't looking forward to sitting down with the employee to talk about the issue, yet again.

These are perfectly natural responses, but you can't let them dictate the tone or content of your meeting with the employee. If you speak in anger, you risk alienating the employee forever. You also make it more likely that the employee will try to take action against you, whether through poisoning your relationships with other employees, sabotage, or legal action. On the other hand, if you allow your sympathy for the employee to hold sway, you might try too hard to soften the blow. As a result, the employee might not really understand exactly what the problem is and how serious his or her situation has become. The employee might therefore not take advantage of this opportunity to improve.

To keep your emotions in check, focus squarely on the facts: How have the employee's problems affected the company? What did the action plan require, and how did the employee do on each item? What improvement do you need to see in each area, and by when? What resources can you offer that might help? By sticking to the facts, you should be able to avoid emotional responses that could get you into trouble.

If the employee appears to be trying hard but isn't getting any better despite your efforts to help, you might want to consider whether the employee would be more successful in another position at your company. Once you reach the written warning stage, employees who fall into this category may be starting to realize that they don't have the necessary skills and aptitudes to do the job well. In fact, some employees will raise this issue at the disciplinary meeting and ask about other positions at the company. If this happens, you'll want to be prepared to discuss the issue.

Written Warnings for a First-Time Problem

If you have skipped straight to a written warning, that means the employee's conduct was pretty serious. Typically, managers move directly to a written warning to deal with misconduct or a serious violation of attendance rules. Especially if you have a written discipline policy or follow one in practice, you're going to have to explain to the employee why you aren't proceeding through the earlier measures in the process. At the same time, you don't need to justify your actions to the employee. Remember, you're not the one who has the problem here. You're only explaining why a written warning is a logical and necessary reaction to the employee's behavior.

To prepare to discuss this with the employee, start by reviewing the rule or policy the employee violated; you'll probably want to bring a copy to the meeting. What's the purpose of the rule? Why is it important enough to enforce with a written warning? If there wasn't a written rule, but the employee's actions were contrary to common sense or company practice, be prepared to explain why that justifies the discipline you're imposing. Thinking through these issues ahead of time will help you state your reasons for discipline confidently. It will also help you deflect—or at least, shorten—arguments with the employee over the meaning or clarity of the rule, or whether it was broken.

You should also be prepared to tell the employee exactly what you expect going forward, whether it's no further violations of the rule, attending antiharassment or anger management training, an apology to a coworker, or checking in with you before taking a sick or vacation day.

Arrange Logistics

Once you have gathered the necessary facts, it's time to set up the meeting itself: when and where you will hold it and who will be there. Ideally, you should hold a written warning meeting within a day or two of learning of the incident or problem that merits discipline. Acting quickly communicates urgency: It shows the employee that this type of behavior is serious and and must change immediately. It also demonstrates to your other reports (and the rest of the company) that you are aware of the situation and taking steps to correct it. If you manage employees who are offsite, try to set up meetings either at your office or at the employee's. If that's not feasible, deliver the discipline by phone. Set up a date and administer the discipline as you would if the employee were present in the room. For more information on disciplining offsite employees, see Chapter 12.

If you are meeting to discuss an ongoing problem, you should budget 30 to 45 minutes for the meeting. You'll have to cover your previous conversations, talk about why the previous resolution didn't work, and come up with a fairly detailed plan for improvement. Because written warnings are a serious disciplinary step, you may also have to spend some extra time explaining the consequences of the written warning (on the employee's performance evaluation, merit raises, opportunities for promotion, and so on) and the reasons why you decided it was necessary to give one.

Many companies require managers to bring another person to a written warning meeting (typically, a higher-level manager or a representative from the human resources department). If your company has this type of rule, of course you must follow it. Even if your company doesn't require you to bring someone else along, though, you might want your manager or a human resources representative present. Although it can make it difficult to build rapport and trust with the employee, it might be a good idea if:

- **The employee doesn't seem to be getting the message that recurring behavior is a problem.** If you've already disciplined the employee and you feel that you aren't getting your message across, bringing an authority figure to the meeting conveys that the problem is serious.
- **The employee has issues with you (or vice versa).** If you think that the employee doesn't trust you, has personal problems with you, or is likely to later deny what the two of you discuss, bring a third person to serve as a witness. This also demonstrates that you are imposing discipline because the employee is causing problems for the company, not because of your own personal feelings.

- **The employee is angry or volatile.** If you think the employee may become angry or make threats, by all means bring a witness along. Having a third party present may remind the employee to act professionally and help defuse the situation. If the employee's reaction becomes dangerous, you will more readily be able to seek outside assistance.

> RELATED TOPIC
>
> **Letting the employee bring a witness.** For information on allowing the employee to have a witness at the meeting, see Chapter 12.

Hold the meeting in your office (as long as it's relatively soundproof) or a private conference room. Don't meet offsite or in a public area such as the lunchroom. You want to communicate a serious, respectful, and professional tone, and maintain control of the meeting. If you decide—or are required—to bring a human resources representative or a higher-level manager to the meeting, you could also hold it in that person's office. This might be a good idea if the employee seems to blame you for the problem or has resisted your guidance in the past. It suggests that the problem is a company problem that goes beyond you.

Plan the Conversation

As with any disciplinary measure, before you actually meet with the employee, you should think about how to start the conversation and the main points you want to cover. Because written warning discussions are often more emotionally charged, you might even want to take some notes to bring to the meeting, so you don't forget anything if the discussion becomes heated. Just don't spend so much time and energy consulting your notes that you aren't able to be fully present in your conversation with the employee.

When you give a written warning, you are dealing with a serious problem. You should start the meeting in a manner that communicates this clearly. At the same time, however, you'll want to let the employee know that you are committed to resolving the situation and to helping him or her improve, if possible. When you plan your opening sentences, remember that you want to briefly describe the problem, convey that it is serious, and mention any prior conversations about it. If you've discussed the issue before, you'll need to acknowledge what's happened or failed to happen since the last time the issue was raised, and why or how the previous action plan didn't work. Here are some examples:

- "Mike, please come in and sit down. I need to talk to you about a very serious customer complaint I received this morning. A woman named Mrs. Daglian told me that she tried to ask you a question while you were stocking the shelves and that you ignored her. When she asked you again, you interrupted her and said loudly, "I heard you the first time, lady. I'm busy. Ask the front desk." Mrs. Daglian said you then turned your back on her and walked away. LeShawn was working with you at the time, and he confirmed what Mrs. Daglian said. He had to apologize for your behavior. This is not an acceptable way to treat our customers."

- "Carl, you are continuing to take long lunches and breaks, even though we've discussed this before. When we last spoke, you promised that you would keep your breaks to 15 minutes and your lunches to half an hour, as company policy requires. But twice last week, you took breaks that were more than half an hour long each. I've already explained that this is causing resentment among your coworkers, who are putting in more work time than you and having to deal with more customers in your absence. I've looked at your numbers, and you process fewer orders than any of your coworkers. This situation needs to change, right away. The company pays you to work a full eight-hour day, and right now, we are not getting our money's worth."

- "We need to talk about your work product, Mariah. As we've already discussed, the presentations you are creating for our clients are too long, and the main points aren't emphasized adequately. Since we last discussed this issue, two salespeople have complained that they don't like using your materials, because the audience gets confused. This has a serious effect on our reputation and our brand. We've sent you to the Writing for Maximum Impact seminar, and I've spent time going over your presentations with you, but these problems aren't improving. We need to come up with a plan today that will resolve this issue once and for all."

You should anticipate that the employee might have a defensive reaction to receiving a written warning. The employee will now suffer real consequences—and may be on the verge of losing his or her job—so you may be challenged on your reasons for acting. Before the meeting, prepare to answer such a challenge with factual statements, like "Milo, I know this is not a surprise to you. You and I have met twice in the last few months to talk about missed deadlines. I sent you to a time management class, worked with you to prioritize your projects, and met with you every week to gauge your progress. As you know, the Abbot report was a day late, and you didn't run the weekly financials until Monday. You agreed to get things in on time, and you haven't lived up to that agreement."

Meet With the Employee

As when you give a verbal warning, you'll need to state the problem, explain its impact, discuss the issue with the employee, and come up with an action plan. When you give a written warning, however, you'll need to deliver your message a bit more forcefully. You might also face more pushback from the employee.

State the Problem

Start the meeting by letting the employee know what the issue is and why it's a problem. Briefly describe the facts, then explain how the employee's behavior is affecting the company. Explicitly state that the employee's behavior is not acceptable and needs to change.

> **EXAMPLE:** Let's continue with the example involving Dave, above, the employee who wouldn't take no for an answer. After investigating, Claude calls Dave into his office and says, "Hi Dave, please sit down. I have a serious problem I need to discuss with you. As you know, I caught part of your conversation with Crystal earlier today, and what I heard bothered me. I asked Crystal about it, and she told me you had asked her out and asked her a number of questions about her boyfriend, even after she told you she didn't want to discuss it. When I asked you about this earlier, you confirmed what Crystal said. This kind of behavior is inappropriate, it's making Crystal uncomfortable, and it needs to stop."

> **CAUTION**
>
> **Investigate serious misconduct.** Especially if one employee reports misconduct by another, you need to investigate before you decide what to do. In this example, Claude already spoke to Dave, who agreed with Crystal's version of events. It

wouldn't be fair (or legally defensible) to simply discipline Dave without hearing his side of the story. For detailed information on investigating misconduct, see *The Essential Guide to Workplace Investigations*, by Lisa Guerin (Nolo).

If you're dealing with a recurring problem, think carefully about how you phrase what you say, starting with how you present the problem. If you've dealt with this issue before, either the employee didn't fully understand the problem, or the employee can't or won't fix it. If the employee didn't understand, saying the same thing again isn't going to make the problem any clearer. You may need to walk through the issues more slowly to make sure the employee gets it.

Review Past Discussions

If you're giving a written warning for an ongoing problem, briefly summarize your previous discussions with the employee on the topic. You don't have to give all of the details, but you should mention the prior conversations, restate the action plan you came up with at that time, and explain how the employee has not lived up to his or her commitment. If you've been following the discipline process and documenting thoroughly, this should be pretty easy to do. Moreover, it will help the employee contextualize the discipline.

> **EXAMPLE:** Christine is giving a written warning to Sheila for continuing to hand in substandard work reports, even after being coached and receiving a verbal warning. After stating the problem and the impact it's continuing to have on the company, Christine says, "Sheila, I'm especially concerned because we've talked about this problem before. We met in March, and again last month, to talk about the weekly reports. I agreed to tell you exactly what I expect in those reports and provide detailed comments on how you can improve your work. I've lived up to those commitments, but you haven't done what you promised: hand in reports that are complete, cover all of our accounts, and provide the information the rest of the company needs to understand how our department is doing."

If you are imposing discipline for a serious first-time problem, you may not have had previous discussions with the employee. However, you should mention any workplace policies, training sessions, or announcements that demonstrate the employee's behavior was inappropriate. For example, if an employee takes several days off and doesn't call in, you could say, "The employee handbook states that you must receive permission from your manager before taking a vacation day."

Get the Employee's Agreement

Before you continue, make sure the employee understands the problem and agrees with you on the basic facts. By doing this, you'll ensure that you're on the same page and talking about the same issues. You'll also set the stage for the employee to take responsibility for the problem, something that can't happen as long as the employee is arguing with you about what occurred and whose fault it was.

> **EXAMPLE:** Tanya is giving Gerard a written warning for missed deadlines. She has already told him which deadlines were missed and reviewed their prior disciplinary conversations. Gerard says, "Yeah, but I've had a lot of other things to do in the past few weeks. You can't expect me to get everything done on time. Anyway, I was hardly late."
>
> Tanya responds by saying, "As we've discussed before, Gerard, I do expect you to get your work done on time. It's an essential part of your job, and our whole department is set back when you're late. And each of your last three reports has been at least two days late; the one you just handed in was four days late, and I was unable to use it at the company meeting. We'll talk about why you're missing deadlines in a minute. For right now, I want to make sure that we agree that your reports are due each Monday afternoon and that the last three reports have been late. Isn't that correct?"

Listen to the Employee's Explanation

If the employee doesn't offer an explanation, ask for one. What the employee says will help you figure out what went wrong and why, and it will help you come up with an appropriate plan for improvement. Listening carefully engages the employee and shows that you're interested. It also gives the employee a chance to vent a bit, if necessary.

Listening will also help you make sure that a written warning is appropriate. After all, the employee might have had good reason for committing what looked like misconduct or may have a good excuse for an ongoing attendance or performance problem. In this situation, you might want to use a lesser disciplinary measure or forgo discipline altogether. And, of course, if the employee's actions were even worse than they appeared to be, you might want to consider a more serious response.

> **EXAMPLE:** Rob is meeting with Jonelle, who has already been coached and received a verbal warning for tardiness. Rob and Jonelle agreed, at their last meeting, that Jonelle would check in with him each morning when she arrived, before attending to anything else. This morning, Jonelle was a half hour late checking in with Rob. Rob was in a meeting when Jonelle arrived, but he sat down with her as soon as he was finished. After reviewing their earlier agreement, Rob asked, "Why were you late this morning?"
>
> Jonelle replied, "I actually got to work a bit early, but a customer had a seizure in the lobby. I helped take care of him—you know I used to be a nurse—until the EMTs got there. I also called his wife and let her know what happened. Once he was taken away, I took a little time to clean myself up, then I came right up here."
>
> Rob realizes that Jonelle should not be disciplined for being late and thanks her for the explanation and the customer care.

Explain the Written Warning

As with a verbal warning, you must tell the employee that you are giving a written warning. You don't want the employee to be surprised to find a written warning in the personnel file later or to be blindsided when the warning gets in the way of a promotion or raise. Explicitly stating that you are giving a written warning also reinforces the message that the situation is serious.

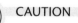 **CAUTION**

Make sure the employee's performance appraisal is consistent with your reasons for discipline. If you give an employee a written warning for poor performance, the employee's next performance appraisal should reflect the problem. It should note the employee's performance difficulties and mention the written warning. If the appraisal instead gives the employee high marks for performance and suggests a merit raise, the employee will likely be confused about what constitutes good performance. And you will have trouble justifying your decision to discipline (and a later decision to terminate employment, if it comes to that).

If company policy dictates specific consequences for receiving a written warning, explain them briefly to the employee. For example, an employee who has received a written warning might be ineligible for certain job benefits or opportunities, might not be considered for promotions or performance-based bonuses, or might receive a lower performance appraisal. Remember, it is important to impose these criteria consistently among your employees, too.

> **EXAMPLE:** "Corinne, I'm giving you a written warning for mishandling customer checks. I decided a written warning was called for because this is the second time you haven't deposited checks on time, and this affects our cash management. I also need to tell you that a written warning makes you ineligible for an overall rating of 'exceeds expectations' on this year's performance appraisal, which could affect your eligibility for raises and bonuses, if they are offered this year. I know these are serious consequences, and I think they are justified by your actions. But I'm confident that you can solve this problem and get back on the right track."

> **TIP**
>
> **Let the employee know if the warning will "expire."** As with a verbal warning, many companies put a time limit on how long a written warning will remain in an employee's file, or how long it will continue to affect the employee's opportunities at the company. If your company has this type of policy, tell the employee that the warning will be removed if he or she has no further problems while the warning is active. This provides a strong incentive for improvement.

Develop Solutions

Now it's time to talk about how to solve the problem. If you're dealing with one-time misconduct, the solution is usually quite clear: The employee has to stop the behavior. In this situation, an employee might need some training or perhaps even a referral to your company's employee assistance program (EAP), if you have one. But there's no need to spend lots of time brainstorming ideas for the future.

> **EXAMPLE:** Back to Dave and Claude's meeting, about getting too personal with a coworker. Claude says, "Dave, this behavior needs to stop. You may not ask Crystal out on dates or ask her about her personal life. She has made clear to you that these conversations make her uncomfortable, and they cannot continue. Do you understand?"

If Dave says that he understands, this portion of the meeting is over. But what if Dave responds, "You mean I can't talk to her, ever again? She and I are kind of friends. I mean, I didn't realize she was taking all of this so seriously, but it seems weird that I can never even say hello to her."

Claude might say, "Dave, that isn't what I said. You can say hello to Crystal or ask how she's doing, and you can have regular conversations with her about work. What you can't do is ask her out, ask her about her boyfriend, comment about her appearance, or other things like that. Do you understand the difference?"

If Dave indicates that he understands, the session has addressed the issue. If not, or if Dave continues to argue the point, Claude should probably send him to more detailed sexual harassment training.

If, on the other hand, you're dealing with an ongoing problem, you'll really need to go deep in this part of the conversation. You and the employee have already discussed this problem and come up with a solution, which didn't work. At this point, you'll need to talk about why that happened and what needs to change in the future for the employee to improve.

EXAMPLE: Melanie is a member of a cross-departmental team tasked with developing and implementing new branding for a company that makes shampoo, lotion, and other toiletries. Melanie's own department handles the product packaging. They determine what goes on the labels for various products and various markets, contract with vendors to produce the packaging, and oversee the entire packaging process.

Carly, Melanie's boss, has heard from other team members that Melanie doesn't contribute at the meetings. Carly has met with Melanie to discuss this twice, and Melanie promised to be more actively involved in the conversation. But Melanie still hasn't spoken up. Carly decides to give her a written warning and tells her, "Melanie, if you don't give the team input from our department, they won't know how expensive various redesigns might be, how particular types of logos and verbiage might affect our costs, and so on. We already discussed this problem, and you told me you would be more vocal during the meetings, but it hasn't happened. Why haven't you played a more active role?"

Melanie responds, "You know, I really don't like Travis, who runs the meetings. I feel like he always looks down on me, and I'm self-conscious about saying anything. Also, I'm just naturally kind of shy, I guess."

Carly says, "Melanie, all of us have personal feelings about the people we work with, but you can't let that get in the way of doing your job. I need for you to represent our department at these meetings. And that requires you to speak up. Is that going to be a problem?"

Melanie at last admits, "I guess it might be, just because of my shyness. I feel weird that everyone is looking at me, and I can't remember what I want to say."

Carly responds, "It's common for people to feel fearful of speaking in front of a group. But again, you're letting that get in the way of doing your job. I'd like for you to do two things. First, before the meeting scheduled for next month, I'd like you to meet with me and go over what you plan to say at the meeting. I understand the group will be discussing color options, and you are the only one who knows what those options cost. We'll review what you want to say about it, and I'll help you iron out the kinks.

"In the meantime, I'd like you to go to a workshop on public speaking. It's something our company representatives attend when they start here, and I think it will do you a lot of good. I'll check the schedule for upcoming workshops and sign you up. I think that will help you stop allowing this problem to hold you back at work. What do you think?"

Carly had to dig a bit to get to the real root of the problem. Before, she thought Melanie just didn't know that she should be speaking up. Then, Melanie raised Travis as a possible issue. But another aspect of the problem—Melanie's fear of speaking in public—was something that she found more difficult to admit. Once Carly understood all the causes of the problem, she was able to come up with some detailed solutions that should help Melanie feel more comfortable with this aspect of her job.

Summarize the Action Plan

End the meeting by summing up what you and the employee have agreed to. Unless you were dealing with serious misconduct—to which the resolution is typically "stop doing that"—you'll also want to set some dates and goals for improvement. Especially if you're dealing with an ongoing problem, you should make the schedule fairly tight, with frequent follow-up meetings and progress checks. This will show your employee that you're serious about needing to see immediate improvement and will help you keep a close eye on the problem. If you don't see a change after giving the employee a fair chance, you know that the employee either can't or won't improve. At that point, it's time to consider termination.

If your company uses a performance improvement plan (PIP) or similar approach, in which the action plan is in place for a set amount of time (three or six months, for example), let the employee know how long it will last. You might say, "For the next six months, you are to complete every recap report on time. This means I have to have the finished report, with no mistakes, on my desk by Thursday afternoon. If you meet this goal for the next six months, you will be taken off the performance improvement plan and the written warning will be removed from your file."

It's best to complete your documentation right after the disciplinary meeting, while it's still fresh in your mind. You will also want to schedule another brief meeting—preferably in the next day or two—to go over the paperwork. As explained in Chapter 9, you'll want to give the employee a chance to review your written documentation and talk to you about any questions or concerns.

Try to close the meeting on a positive note. Although this can be tough to do, especially if you feel like you're dealing with the same problem over and over again, it's very valuable for the employee, who probably needs encouragement. Remember, though, not to make any promises for the future: Leave yourself (and your company) the leeway to handle future problems or achievements as you see fit when the time comes. Try a simple statement like "This was a productive discussion, and I think we've come up with some good ideas to resolve this situation."

Document

Once your meeting is over, it's time to actually write your written warning. If your company requires you to use a particular form or follow certain rules, by all means do so. If not, you can use the sample form we provide in Chapter 9 to create the written warning. (For an electronic copy, see Appendix D.)

Here is Claude's written warning to Dave:

Sample Written Warning

Employee Disciplinary Notice	
Employee's Name: Dave Costello	
Manager's Name: Claude Washington	**Date of Incident:** February 12, 20xx
Type of Warning: ☐ Verbal Warning ☑ Written Warning	

Incident Description:

On February 11, 20xx, I overheard part of a conversation you had with Crystal Cavalier in her cubicle. I heard you questioning her about her boyfriend, then saying something like "Are you sure you don't want to go out with me instead?" I also observed that Crystal did not respond. Instead, she turned away from you and focused on her computer screen.

I called Crystal into my office and asked her what happened. She said you had asked her out and persisted in asking her questions about her relationship with her boyfriend, even after she told you she didn't want to discuss it. She confirmed that you said, "Are you sure you don't want to go out with me instead?" even though she previously turned down your request for a date. She told me that she felt very uncomfortable about your interest in her, and that she felt you were not getting the message that she does not want to have a romantic relationship with you.

When I talked to you later that same day, you confirmed that you had said these things to Crystal.

Prior Incidents:

None.

Improvement Plan:

Dave, your conduct violates company policies on appropriate workplace behavior. Specifically, your conduct violates our policy on Professional Behavior (p. 23 of the Employee Handbook) and Harassment (p. 12). Your comments and requests for a date made Crystal very uncomfortable. She has stated that clearly to you, but you have persisted.

You are not to talk to Crystal about her personal life or ask her out on dates. In addition, because you seem unclear about what constitutes appropriate workplace behavior, I have scheduled you to attend a sexual harassment training workshop on February 19. Following this training, we will meet again to make sure that you understand the types of comments and behavior that are inappropriate in the workplace.

Sample Written Warning, continued

Employee Comments:	
Manager's Signature:	**Date:**
Employee Acknowledgment	
I acknowledge that I have received and understand this document.	
Employee's Signature:	**Date:**

For help preparing documentation, see Chapter 9. For additional samples of written warnings, see this book's online companion page. (You can find the link in Appendix D.)

Follow Up

Because you are dealing with a serious problem, you should plan to check in with the employee regularly to make sure the situation is improving. You might also need to check in with others in the company. While this may seem to take an inordinate amount of time and energy, the consequences of failing to correct the problem are very serious now, and it's imperative that you do everything you can to help the employee succeed.

> **EXAMPLE:** The day after Claude meets with Dave, he calls Crystal into his office. Claude says, "I want you to know that I've spoken to Dave and told him his behavior is inappropriate. I've given him clear instructions that he may not ask you out or talk to you about your relationship. Please come to me right away if Dave says or does anything to make you uncomfortable."
>
> Notice that Claude did not tell Crystal that he gave Dave a written warning; that isn't any of Crystal's business. However, it's very important for Claude to ask Crystal to bring future problems to his attention immediately. Because harassment happens in private, this might be the only way Claude can find out whether Dave really got the message. And, now that Claude knows about Dave's behavior, the company is legally liable for any harassment Crystal suffers. If Dave continues to question Crystal inappropriately even after being disciplined and going to sexual harassment training, the company will probably have to fire him.

> **TIP**
>
> **There's still room for positive reinforcement.** Even though you're dealing with a major problem, don't forget to praise the employee if you see improvement. The employee might have a long way to go, but it's important to mark any progress in that direction. Unless you're dealing with a really bad egg, your employee probably

feels pretty bad about letting you and the company down. By giving praise, you are communicating that you still support the employee and want him or her to do well.

Schedule Important Dates

After the disciplinary meeting, schedule your follow-up meetings, the employee's goals, and so on in your calendar. If you've agreed to provide training, equipment, or other resources, write yourself a note and follow through right away. And, if your company removes written warnings from an employee's file after a certain amount of time, mark that date on your calendar. You'll want to make sure that the documentation is removed if the employee has no further problems.

When the Action Plan Is Complete

Sometimes, particularly for serious misconduct, the action plan will be as simple as "stop it." For example, if an employee left the store safe open—and full of cash and valuables—overnight, your action plan might say, "You are to check the safe each night before you leave to make sure it is closed and locked." This type of action plan doesn't have a start and end date: You don't really need to follow up unless the employee leaves the safe open again. If that happens, termination is probably appropriate.

Other action plans call for the employee to do discrete, one-time tasks, such as attending a training seminar, getting a certification, giving an apology, or completing a report. For these plans, you should give the employee a date by which he or she must complete these items, then follow up to make sure the employee did what was required. If the employee doesn't meet one of these goals, you should meet immediately to find out why; if the employee doesn't have a good reason or excuse, it might be time to consider termination. If the employee does meet the goal, you should document that briefly.

EXAMPLE: Penny gave Jessie a written warning for poor performance. Among other things, the action plan they developed required Jessie to take a class on how to use PowerPoint. Jessie took the class by the required date. Penny documents this as follows:

Date: September 25, 20xx

On September 1, 20xx, I gave Jessie Pitt a written warning. In his action plan, I required him to complete a training class on using PowerPoint, among other things. He was to complete this class by October 1, 20xx.

Jessie informed me today that he completed the class "PowerPoint Basics: Presentations, Graphics, and More!" on September 24. He gave me a copy of his certificate of completion (attached) as well as a syllabus from the class. I have asked him to do a brief presentation, using PowerPoint, at the next department meeting on October 15. He has agreed to do so.

Signed: *Penny Meyer*

If you put a time limit on the entire action plan, you must decide, at the end of that time, whether the employee has done as you agreed. For example, if you have a proofreader who is not catching grammatical errors, your action plan might say, "You will review each document for errors two times, with a minimum of a one-hour break between each review. Additionally, you will reduce your weekly average error rate from 4 per document to 2 per document. You and I will meet each week on Monday morning to discuss your progress." If the employee successfully completes this type of action plan, you should also write a memo to the file.

PODCAST
To hear a sample written warning meeting visit this book's online companion page. (You can find the link in Appendix D.)

SMART SUMMARY:
Written Warnings

- Written warnings are difficult because employees usually recognize them as a serious disciplinary measure and may become defensive or emotional. Additionally, if you've dealt with the same issue with the employee before, you might also be frustrated or angry. Control these emotions by preparing thoroughly and focusing the discussion on the problem and how to improve it.

- A written warning is usually the right response when an employee hasn't improved a problem after coaching and a verbal warning, the employee has flagrantly violated the company's attendance rules, or the employee has committed serious misconduct that does not warrant immediate termination.

- When you give a written warning, focus on creating a very detailed, thorough, and clear action plan, particularly if you've already coached or given a verbal warning. If the employee needs more involvement or direction from you to succeed, provide it.

- You should write the written warning after you've had a chance to meet with the employee and get his or her input or perspective. Complete the documentation right after the meeting, when it's still fresh in your mind. You might want to schedule another brief meeting to go over the written document with the employee. And, be sure to ask the employee to sign in acknowledgment.

Build Your Skills: The Disciplinary Steps

Questions

1. What are the three types of coaching?

   _____

   _____

   _____

   _____

2. Which of these is a common reaction to coaching?

   a. Surprise

   b. Anger

   c. Denial

   d. Blame

3. Verbal warnings don't require formal documentation—after all, they're just oral reminders to shape up.　　☐ True　　☐ False

4. Which of these situations probably calls for a verbal warning?

   a. For the first time, Sarah, a long-time budget analyst, shows up to work 15 minutes late.

   b. Imran, a new transfer to the mail room, violates a company policy that prohibits wearing ear plugs or headphones while operating a mail sorting machine; he'd never read the policy, though it was given to him.

   c. Pamela, a new clerk, sends the entire department's time sheets to payroll a few hours late because she misread the policy and thought they were due on the fifteenth, when actually that's the date checks are issued.

   d. Greg, a veteran supervisor, tells one of his employees, Jim, all the details of the investigation into a coworker's harassment suit.

5. When you give a verbal warning, you should tell the employee explicitly that you are doing so.

   　　☐ True　　☐ False

6. When you decide to issue a written warning, how should you deliver it?

   a. Carry it to the meeting you have with the employee. Give it to the employee at the start of the meeting.

   b. Have a discussion with the employee about it, then draft the warning and place it in the employee's personnel file.

   c. Carry it to the meeting you have with the employee. Give it to the employee at the end of the meeting.

   d. Meet with the employee, then draft the written warning, send it to the employee for acknowledgment, and place it in the employee's file.

7. Because employee discipline is a serious matter, it should be delivered in a serious setting. Whenever possible, you should meet with the employee in your office.

   ☐ True   ☐ False

8. Which of these steps will help you prepare for a written warning?

   a. Consult with your boss, human resources, or your legal department to get input on how similar problems have been handled in the past.

   b. Review the employee's previous disciplinary history.

   c. Think about why the previous action plan, if there was one, didn't work.

   d. All of the above.

9. In which situation might it be appropriate for you to bring a witness to a discipline meeting?

   a. You're in an informal coaching session, and you want to make the employee feel more at ease, so you grab lunch with the employee and a human resources representative the employee is friendly with.

   b. You are issuing a written warning, and it seems the employee is really resisting your guidance. In fact, the employee hasn't done anything to follow the action plan you two have outlined together.

   c. You don't feel comfortable issuing the discipline; even though company policy calls for it, the employee is your friend. You'd rather bring your boss along to deliver the tough message.

    d. You're issuing a verbal warning to an employee for an attendance policy violation. The employee was late three times in two weeks; you've dealt with the same issue many times before and have even coached this employee about it.

10. What is the purpose of a written warning?

    a. To make sure you communicate very clearly—on paper—what the problem is, so that the employee understands it and you have a written record of it.

    b. To make sure that the employee is given a fair opportunity to improve performance or behavior.

    c. To make sure you treat employees consistently, issuing similar discipline for similar problems.

    d. All of the above.

Answers

1. The three types of coaching are simple requests, corrective actions, and coaching sessions. You make simple requests when a method of doing something hasn't been successful, and you ask the employee to try something new or different. Corrective actions are a little more serious; they occur when you tell an employee how something must be done or done differently. You can deal with more complex problems with coaching sessions: opportunities to sit down with employees to discuss problems and find solutions together, before things get worse.

2. Because coaching is the first step in the disciplinary process, employees are often surprised by it. Sometimes you may need to allow the employee a little time to deal with that reaction. The more serious reactions—anger, denial, and blame—typically happen later in the process, when discipline becomes more serious.

3. False. Verbal warnings are the first formal entry into the discipline process, when the employee is made aware that discipline is happening. They need to be formally documented so that the manager will have a record of what's happened in the event that further discipline—or even termination—becomes necessary.

4. B. In this case, Imran inadvertently violated a company rule that was implemented for his own safety. Imran should have read the policy, but his failure to follow it here appears inadvertent, so a verbal warning is probably appropriate. Answers A and C probably call for coaching. The employees there have correctable problems that don't appear extremely serious. And in Answer D, Greg is creating serious problems for the company, not to mention acting extremely inappropriately and insensitively, by revealing this information. More serious discipline is probably necessary.

5. True. Even though it might be uncomfortable, when you issue a verbal warning, you should state explicitly that that's what you're doing. That way, the employee is on notice that he or she has entered the formal disciplinary system and won't be surprised to come across the documentation later.

6. D. The best way to make sure you fully capture all the facts is to meet with the employee, draft the documentation, and then ask the employee to acknowledge that he or she received it (often in a separate, brief meeting). This ensures you hear the whole story, and that the whole story is accurately captured in the documentation, before the warning is issued.

7. False. The appropriate setting for a disciplinary discussion will vary based on the type of discipline being administered. For example, if you're going to coach an employee, it might be more comfortable to do so in an informal setting. If you and the employee need to brainstorm possible action plans, it might be appropriate to work in a neutral space, like a conference room, with a whiteboard.

8. D. In this case, all these steps will help you get ready to deliver a written warning. Talking to an appropriate third party will help you gain perspective (but make sure it's someone whom you should be talking to about the issue, not a peer or subordinate). Likewise, if you review the employee's disciplinary history, don't give undue weight to things that happened in the distant past. And finally, as you think about the former action plan and why it didn't work, think about your responsibility for that, too, not just the employee's.

9. B. When an employee resists your guidance, it may mean that you need the help or intervention of a third party. You probably wouldn't want a third party involved in an informal coaching session (Answer A), especially if it could keep the employee from understanding the purpose of the discussion: to improve behavior. And while you should definitely talk to your boss if you don't feel comfortable issuing discipline (Answer C), you can cause confusion for the employee—and appear weak or unsure of yourself—if you ask the boss to issue the discipline directly. Finally, if you're carefully following a clear company policy, and you've dealt with the issue before, you probably won't need outside assistance (Answer D).

10. D. All of the answers are benefits that result from a fair, consistent discipline system. Answer B speaks to what is probably the most basic reason to use it: You want the employee to succeed. At the same time, you will be communicating clearly to the employee, and you'll have a written record in case you have to impose further discipline or terminate employment (Answer A). You'll also be imposing consistent discipline (Answer C).

PART

V

If Discipline Fails

Termination

Even if you faithfully follow the disciplinary strategies in this book, chances are good that you'll one day be faced with a manager's least favorite task: firing an employee. The discipline and communication techniques explained in the previous chapters will help you get most employees back on track, but there will still be a few who are simply unable—or unwilling—to do the job. Whether the employee has failed to resolve an ongoing problem or has committed egregious misconduct, it's time to consider termination of employment.

This chapter explains how to decide whether it's time to fire someone and how to handle every step of the termination process. Before we get to those details, however, we should acknowledge a basic fact about terminations: They are difficult for everyone involved. The employee who is being fired will be out of work and may face financial, emotional, and family troubles as a result. As the agent of this unhappiness, you will almost certainly feel some sadness, anxiety, or even guilt about your role in the process.

Only the most hard-hearted person could avoid feeling at least a little bit bad about firing someone. But, if you find these emotions overwhelming, remember this: If you followed the strategies we've explained, you gave the employee every opportunity to improve. The employee either wasn't capable of improvement or chose not to take advantage of those opportunities. Either way, an employee who isn't able or willing to do what the job requires should not be holding that job.

You may also be concerned about how your team might react to the news that one of their coworkers has been fired. If you fear that your team will be angry or blame you for the fired employee's woes, you might be pleasantly surprised. Often, coworkers are relieved to see a problem employee go. If the employee has committed serious misconduct, coworkers aren't likely to miss the fighting, harassment, or theft. If the employee has had ongoing performance or attendance problems, coworkers have probably grown pretty tired of having to pick up the slack. They may feel frustrated that the employee seems to have been "getting away with it," while they toil away. This generally holds true even if the employee was otherwise well liked and coworkers feel sad about the situation on a personal level.

Is It Time for Termination?

There are two scenarios when termination might be appropriate. In the first, the employee commits misconduct so serious that it's incompatible with continued employment at your company. (We list many of these firing offenses in Chapter 5.) An employee who threatens others, acts violently, makes racist comments, commits blatant sexual harassment, steals from the company, or otherwise demonstrates serious disregard for the legal rights of others or the company should be fired.

What About Final Warnings?

Some companies have discipline policies that give employees a final warning before firing them. The final warning might take a number of forms. It might be called a suspension, probationary period, performance improvement plan (PIP), last-chance agreement, decision-making leave, or something else. Regardless of its name, the message conveyed by the final warning is this: One more strike and you're out.

We advise against final warnings. From a practical standpoint, an employee who has already had three chances to improve is unlikely to turn things around on the fourth try. It's far more sensible to cut your losses (in time and energy) rather than to keep trying to inspire improvement.

Using a final warning also creates legal risks. Because any type of final warning typically is accompanied by an explicit statement that the employee will be fired if the problem continues, it can lead the employee to believe that he or she will not be fired otherwise. That is, a final warning can undo a company's at-will rights (explained in Chapter 3). What if the employee develops another problem or improves somewhat but, you ultimately decide, not enough? What if there is a targeted layoff due to lack of work or location transfer? The language found in a typical final warning could tie the company's hands in these situations.

In the second scenario, the employee has a performance, attendance, or misconduct problem that you've addressed through your company's disciplinary policy. You've provided coaching and given a verbal warning and a written warning, but the situation has not improved. At this point, you know that it's time to replace the employee. An employee who either cannot or will not do what the job requires, even after several constructive interventions, is unlikely to improve at this late date.

In either situation, there are a number of factors you should consider when you're deciding whether to fire the employee. Carefully weighing each of the factors below before you take action will help you confirm that you're making the right decision. It will also help you minimize the possibility of legal trouble down the road and ensure that you're being fair and impartial, rather than allowing emotions to influence your decision.

Here is a checklist that will help you consider every angle before you fire an employee (each item is explained in more detail below):

- Make sure you know the facts.
- Check the employee's personnel file.
- Review company policies.
- Consider past statements to the employee.
- Examine how other employees have been treated.
- Consider the timing.
- Get a second opinion.

> **TIP**
>
> **Don't be afraid to ask for help.** Termination is the aspect of your job that's most likely to lead to legal trouble. It's also the most likely to cause you stress and emotional discomfort. The information we provide below should help alleviate your concerns, but don't hesitate to call on your human resources department or legal counsel for advice. They can help you troubleshoot your decision, consider other courses of action, practice delivering the message to the employee, and more.

Make Sure You Know the Facts

As always, your first step is to gather information. When you are terminating employment, it is especially important to get your facts straight. If there's any question about what has happened, the company must investigate and come to a conclusion. No matter how serious the offense, you must take the time to gather facts, even if you catch the employee apparently "in the act." There is always the possibility, no matter how slim, that things are not as they appear to be. And the employee might have an explanation for the misconduct that is not immediately apparent.

If you are dealing with serious misconduct, you might want to put the employee on paid suspension while the investigation takes place. This will get the employee out of the workplace and give you some time to proceed carefully. For step-by-step instructions on investigating, see *The Essential Guide to Workplace Investigations*, by Lisa Guerin (Nolo).

CAUTION

Don't use unpaid investigative suspensions. If you suspend an employee while you investigate an issue, the suspension should be paid. As a practical matter, paying the employee demonstrates that you have not yet made up your mind and plan to conduct an impartial investigation. Legally, you can create problems if you dock the pay of exempt employees—those who are not entitled to earn overtime— for reasons that are not allowed by the Fair Labor Standards Act. You might even convert these employees into nonexempt employees, which means your company would probably be faced with hefty overtime claims. It's much easier, more fair, and less expensive in the long run to suspend employees with pay while you investigate.

If you are dealing with an ongoing problem, a full-blown investigation is probably unnecessary. However, you should still take whatever steps are necessary to make sure that you understand what happened and that the employee is responsible. Once you are satisfied that you have the facts you need, move on to the next step.

EXAMPLE: Lindsey is facing termination for poor performance. Her manager, Jason, has coached and given warnings, but Lindsey has continued to spend at least an hour a day talking to friends on the phone, looking at catalogs, and otherwise goofing off. As a result, Lindsey doesn't finish her work on time.

Several weeks ago, Jason put Lindsey on a performance improvement plan (PIP) and told her that she had to meet every requirement in the plan. One of the requirements was that Lindsey finish everything assigned to her for the week before she leaves on Friday afternoon, then send Jason an email detailing every completed assignment. Jason was on a business trip last week, and he didn't get an email from Lindsey last Friday. He notices, when he arrives on Monday morning, that Lindsey's desk is littered with papers, which looks like she didn't finish everything before she left.

Jason is ready to fire Lindsey as soon as she arrives for work. But before he does, he needs to find out what happened. Of course, one possibility is that Lindsey simply blew off the PIP and left for the weekend without finishing her work. In this case, termination would be entirely appropriate. On the other hand, maybe Lindsey didn't finish her work because she had to leave early for a legitimate emergency, such as a sudden illness or a family crisis. Maybe Lindsey finished her work but couldn't send Jason an email because the computers were down. Maybe Lindsey finished most of her work but couldn't complete an assignment because she needed guidance from Jason, who was traveling on Friday afternoon when she tried to reach him. Before Jason makes a final decision, he needs to find out exactly what happened and why.

Check the Employee's Personnel File

Next, read the employee's personnel file, even if you think you already know what's in it. If you are dealing with persistent problems with performance, attendance, or conduct, these issues should be documented in the file. The employee's performance evaluations should note these deficiencies and suggest goals for improvement. There should also be notes from your disciplinary meetings with the employee.

Of course, if you have carefully followed the procedures outlined in this book, you will have documented the employee's problems appropriately. However, if other managers have supervised the employee, or you weren't fully aware (until reading this book) of how to use and document disciplinary measures, you might find that the file is a bit thin. In this situation, you should consult your human resources department for guidance. If, together, you conclude that the file doesn't include sufficient documentation of the problem and your efforts to help the employee improve, you might need to hold off on the termination and give the employee another, well-documented chance.

Weigh Your Disciplinary Documentation Against Evidence of Good Performance

When you review the employee's personnel file, pretend you're a lawyer representing the employee. Are there documents you could use to show that the employee should not have been fired? If so, consult with your human resources department—or legal counsel—before proceeding.

A file that contains glowing performance appraisals, merit raises, commendations, and promotions could spell trouble, especially if they contradict your reasons for firing. An employee who is fired for poor performance should not be able to point to positive reviews and merit increases. Similarly, an employee who is fired for insubordination and attitude problems should not have a recent evaluation praising the employee's teamwork, collegiality, and willingness to go the extra mile.

EXAMPLE: Julius is considering firing Kathy for ongoing attendance problems. Julius just took over managing Kathy's group a month ago. When he began, Marc—the team's former manager—told him that Kathy often came in late, despite his repeated conversations with her about it over the last year. Since Julius has been her manager, Kathy has continued the trend. Julius gave her a verbal warning because it has been an ongoing problem, but Kathy hasn't improved at all.

Now Julius thinks it's probably time to replace Kathy. After all, she has had an attendance problem for more than a year and has shown no signs of improvement after repeated efforts by two managers. But when he looks at Kathy's personnel file, Julius realizes that he might not be able to fire her without some legal risk. His verbal warning is in the file, but there are no other disciplinary documents. Apparently, Marc didn't keep a record of his conversations with Kathy, nor did he use the company's disciplinary system. What's more, Kathy's last appraisal rates her overall performance as "outstanding" and makes no mention of her attendance problem. After talking to the human resources director, Julius decides to give Kathy a written warning.

If the employee has committed a single act of serious misconduct, the file probably won't contain any mention of prior problems. That's fine. Of course, if this isn't the employee's first major blunder, you should find documentation of the prior incident(s) in the file.

Does the Employee Have a Contract?

As you review the employee's paperwork, look for a written employment contract. As explained in Chapter 3, an employment contract doesn't necessarily protect the employee from termination, but it may limit your options. The language of the contract governs when you can fire an employee. For most contracts, this means you need only have a good business reason (good cause) to end the employment relationship. However, if the company agreed to different restrictions (for example, that the employee could be fired only for committing a criminal act or for defrauding the company), consult with your human resources department or legal counsel to make sure that your reasons for firing fit within these limits.

Review Company Policies

Next, take a look at your company's employee handbook and other written policies. As you review these materials, ask yourself a few questions:

- **Did you follow the company's discipline policy?** Make sure you've followed the rules to the letter before you fire anyone.
- **Did the employee have notice that his or her behavior was a problem?** Of course, if you've been dealing with ongoing issues, your conversations and documentation have made this clear to the employee. For egregious misconduct, make sure the employee's actions are either prohibited by company policy or so obviously wrong that no explicit notice is necessary. (For more on this, see Chapter 5.)
- **Is your right to fire limited?** As explained in Chapter 3, most companies are at-will employers, which reserve the right to fire employees at any time, for any reason that is not illegal. However, companies can forfeit this right by making promises of continued employment in their

employee handbooks (among other things). If you see something in your company's written policies that makes you think you might not be able to fire at will, talk to your human resources department or legal counsel.

Consider Statements Made to the Employee

Consider whether you have said anything that might have led the employee to believe he or she would be fired only for specific reasons. As you'll recall from Chapter 3, if you promise an employee continued employment or say that he or she will be fired only for certain reasons, you may have created an implied contract. In this situation, you must make sure that your decision to fire is in keeping with your earlier statements. For example, if you told an employee (before reading this book) that you would never fire someone who was doing a good job, that statement wouldn't prevent you from firing the employee for poor performance. If, on the other hand, the employee has an attendance problem but performs well when at work, your earlier statement might limit your options. If you have any concerns about prior statements you've made to an employee, consult your human resources department or legal counsel.

Consider How Others Employees Have Been Treated

In Chapter 3, we explained the importance of being consistent. A fired employee's most effective argument to a jury is that you've acted unfairly, by treating the employee differently from others who have been in the same position. An employee who makes this argument can even risk admitting misconduct or poor performance. The employee's complaint is not that he or she is perfect, but that you've come down harder on him or her than you have on others who have committed the same transgression.

Before you fire an employee, make sure that your actions are consistent with the way you've handled similar offenses or misconduct by other workers. Have you always fired for this type of behavior? Or have you given other employees another chance or helped them try to improve? Also consider how others in your company have handled similar problems. Is your plan to fire the employee consistent with your company's treatment of other workers with similar issues?

If you have treated other employees differently, there may be a good reason for the difference. Perhaps one person's conduct was worse, was more intractable, lasted longer, or caused the company more trouble. Make sure that your choice to fire this employee, while allowing others to remain, will make sense to a jury as a valid business decision.

Consider the Timing

If an employee recently complained of illegal activity in the workplace, such as discrimination or harassment, firing that person may lead to a retaliation claim. Firing someone shortly after he or she exercised a legal right or complained of improper or illegal activity could also lead to legal trouble. Even if you have a good reason to terminate employment, the employee might think that you are acting out of illegal motives. Similarly, if you fire someone who just told you that she is pregnant, has a disability that requires accommodation, or holds certain religious beliefs, the employee could decide that the firing and the disclosure are linked.

Of course, this doesn't mean that you can never fire someone who has a disability, for example, or that complaining of sexual harassment makes an employee "fire-proof." In this situation, however, you must make very certain that your reasons for firing are beyond reproach. You must also be able to show, through documentation, that the employee's problems preceded his or her protected activity. If you are considering firing an employee in these circumstances, talk to your human resources department and/or legal counsel.

Get a Second Opinion

If possible, have a second person from within your company review the decision to terminate. (Many companies require managers to have a higher-level manager or human resources representative review firing decisions.) The purpose of this review is to make sure that your decision is legitimate, reasonable, and well supported. The reviewer should consider how the termination would look to someone outside the company. The reviewer should also make sure that the decision is based on objective, work-related concerns, not favoritism, discrimination, or other subjective factors.

Ideally, the person who does this review should be removed from the situation and have no stake in the outcome, such as a human resources representative. The less contact the reviewer has had with the people involved, the more likely his or her decision will be objective.

Take the reviewer's comments seriously. If the reviewer finds that your decision could be challenged, find out the basis for the problem. Is there insufficient documentation in the file? Have other employees committing similar misconduct been retained? Was your decision colored by your dislike of the worker or—worse—by prejudice? Use the reviewer's comments to figure out how you can either salvage the employment relationship or properly document and support your decision.

Prepare for the Meeting

If you decide, after carefully considering each of the factors discussed above, that you should fire the employee, it's time to plan the termination meeting. You'll be tempted to put this off, but don't. Even though you might feel bad about having to fire someone, if you've followed the guidelines explained in earlier chapters, you also probably know that the time has come. Once the employee has demonstrated an inability or unwillingness to meet the company's expectations, it's time to cut your losses and find someone who can do the job.

The 15 minutes or so it takes you to break the bad news to an employee you have to fire may be the most important of the employment relationship. The way you handle this meeting could well determine whether the employee moves on to greener pastures without hard feelings or whether the employee harbors ill will towards the company that manifests itself in malicious gossip, litigation, or even violence or sabotage. It follows, then, that it's well worth spending some time planning the meeting, so you can make sure that you're ready to handle it well.

Where to Meet

If the employee has a private office, that's a good place to hold the termination meeting. The employee will be most comfortable there and won't have to take a "walk of shame" through the building after being fired. Also, you will be able to end the meeting easily, simply by leaving the room. This can be an important advantage if the employee wants to argue with you about the termination. If the employee doesn't have an office, choose somewhere neutral, like a conference room

If you fear that the employee may become violent, however, there are some different factors to consider. In this situation, you'll want to hold the meeting in an area that is as far away from other employees as possible. You should choose a private space that is also close to a building exit, so the employee can be escorted out of the building, if necessary. You might also arrange to have security standing by, close to where you will meet but not visible to the employee.

When to Meet

There are many different theories about which day—and time of day—is best for firing an employee. Some say employees should be fired first thing Monday morning, to give them time to get on with life and ramp up their job searches right away. Others say Friday afternoon is best, because fewer employees will still be at work to see the employee leave with his or her possessions.

Our advice is to let the schedule of the employee and your workplace guide your decision. If the employee is completing an assignment on a Wednesday, it makes more sense (and is kinder) to fire that employee right away than to assign busy work just to carry the employee to a Friday termination. If you know that important customers will be in the office on Monday, it's probably better to wait until Tuesday to fire someone. Usually, there's no need to follow a hard-and-fast rule; do what makes sense.

Again, however, different considerations apply if you are firing someone from whom you fear violence or sabotage. In this situation, you'll want to fire the employee at the end of the workday and end of the workweek. You will want to get this employee out the door as soon as possible (and the fewer employees around when that happens, the better.).

Who Should Attend the Meeting

Many companies require managers to bring another person—usually a higher-level manager or someone from human resources—to a termination meeting, to act as a witness. If your company doesn't require this, you should bring another company representative only if there's a good reason.

Bringing someone to act as a witness could make the employee feel embarrassed and humiliated, and it's not necessary if you're dealing with a reasonable, relatively trustworthy employee.

On the other hand, if the employee has already talked about hiring a lawyer, has made threats, or had done anything else that makes you uncomfortable about handling the meeting on your own, by all means bring another company representative along.

What You Can Offer the Employee

You should anticipate that the employee will be concerned about the future. Money, benefits, continued use of company property (such as a car or laptop), and finding another job will all be front and center in the employee's mind as soon as you announce your decision.

Do any preparation necessary to find out what you can tell the employee about the following:

- **Final paychecks.** State law governs how much time a company has to hand over that final check. Some states (including California) require companies to pay a fired employee at the time of termination; others allow several days or more. (Appendix C includes a chart with information about each state's law.) If you have to—or your company is willing to—provide the check right away, make arrangements to have it cut and bring it to your meeting.

- **Continued insurance benefits.** A federal law called the Consolidated Omnibus Budget Reconciliation Act (COBRA) requires employers with at least 20 employees that offer health insurance benefits to allow an employee to continue those benefits for a period of time after he or she quits or is fired (at the employee's expense); similar state laws may apply to smaller employers. If the employee is entitled to continued benefits, talk to your human resources department to find out exactly what to tell the employee. There may also be paperwork you can give the employee that explains the issue.

- **Severance pay.** If your company will offer severance to the employee, find out what the package will be. Today, companies don't necessarily offer severance as a matter of course but do provide some benefits to certain employees. In the case of an employee you have to fire for disciplinary reasons, you will probably be offering severance only if the company believes that the employee might have a valid legal claim against it. As a condition of receiving a severance package, an employee in this situation is typically asked to sign a release, agreeing not to sue the company in the future.

Giving References

Many companies no longer give detailed references because they are afraid of being sued for defamation by the former employee. If the employee can prove that the employer said something false that harmed the employee's reputation, caused a prospective employer not to hire the employee, or otherwise caused the employee damage, the employee might have a viable case. Even though most employers don't—and certainly don't intend to—say things about a former employee that are not true, companies have generally decided to play it safe and just say as little as possible.

However, there are also good reasons to provide a more detailed reference. First off, it might help a fired worker find a new job more quickly, particularly if the worker had good qualities that might be a better fit for a different type of job. The sooner the employee gets a new job, the sooner he or she will be able to move on and, hopefully, get over any negative feelings about you and your company. Giving a reference will also help out your counterparts at other companies. After all, you probably call around for references when you hire. Where would you be if no one gave you any information?

Of course, you'll need to follow your company's procedures for references, if it has established some. If not, however, we think the best way to reconcile these competing interests is to give a more detailed reference, but only if the employee signs a release agreeing not to sue you or the company for anything you say. You should also let the employee know exactly what you plan to say, so the employee can decide whether to list you as a reference or not.

- **Company property.** Sometimes, an employee who is using company property will really be left in the lurch if he or she has to hand that property over right after being fired. To take an obvious example, an employee who drove a company car to work might have no way to get home. And certainly, an employee who has been using a company-issued cell phone or computer might need some time to buy a replacement. If it's not too much of a hardship, and you don't suspect that the employee will take advantage of the situation, it can be a very kind gesture to allow the employee to continue using company property for a short period of time. Decide how you will handle this issue ahead of time, so you can let the employee know.

- **References.** Be ready to explain your company's policy about references. This is likely to be a major concern for the employee. If your company (like many, these days) follows a strict "name, rank, and serial number" approach, let the employee know. If the company is willing to give a fuller reference in exchange for a release—a practice we recommend (see "Giving References," above)—explain the procedure and provide a form for the employee to sign.

- **Contact person.** You should give the employee someone to contact with further questions. Often, it makes sense to provide a contact in the human resources department who can help with questions about benefits, company property, and so on. Write down this person's name and number on a piece of paper, so you can hand it to the employee during the meeting.

> **RELATED TOPIC**
>
> **Want more information on termination procedures?** Take a look at *Dealing With Problem Employees*, by Amy DelPo and Lisa Guerin (Nolo), which includes detailed information on giving references, severance and releases, continuing insurance, and other important topics.

What You Need From the Employee

Before the employee leaves the building, you'll want to get back any company property in the employee's possession (unless, for example, you are planning to let the employee use a computer or phone for a while). This includes not only things like a phone, car, or computer, but also client files, keys or access cards to the building, corporate credit cards, and so on. Make a list of everything the employee might have, then bring it with you to the meeting so you can make sure you collect every item.

In addition to property, the employee might have information you need, too. Depending on the employee's position, you might want to ask about the status of various projects or accounts, find out where the employee keeps things in his or her desk or computer, and so on. Make a list of these things, too, and bring it to the meeting.

> ⓘ **CAUTION**
>
> **Don't go overboard.** Although you are probably thinking about how the company will cover the employee's job in the future, that is not what the employee is thinking about. Don't ask too many detailed questions about work during the termination meeting. If you do, you risk appearing to be insensitive to the employee's plight (and too eager to move on). Stick to the bare minimum you need. If you absolutely need more information later, you can ask the company's contact person to get in touch with the employee and get more information.

The Termination Meeting

Now that your preparation is complete, it's time to sit down and deliver the news. No matter how carefully you plan the other aspects of the meeting, what you say and how you say it will be the most important thing to the employee. More than anything else, your words and demeanor will determine whether the employee leaves on a positive or a negative note.

Before you enter the meeting room, remember that your goal is to terminate employment, not to denigrate or hurt the employee. Choose your words carefully, and maintain your self-control. The employee might become angry or upset, but you shouldn't. Treating the employee disrespectfully at this crucial point could damage your reputation with your other employees and even prod the fired employee to take legal action against you and/or the company.

Remember, too, that the employee is losing a lot. Most of us look at our jobs as more than just a source of income: They might also be a source of self-esteem, companionship, identity, and more. Even an employee who has had several chances to improve—and probably saw this day coming—is likely to be upset when you actually announce the termination. Don't expect the employee to make your job any easier or go out of his or her way to ease the transition.

State Your Business

It's especially important during a termination meeting to get right to the point, without any small talk or pleasantries. While you might think you are easing the blow by asking about the employee's kids or hobbies, you are really just setting both of you up for an extremely awkward transition to the real reason for the meeting.

Start the meeting by saying that you are terminating the employee's employment and why. Don't hide behind vague phrases like "We've decided to make a change" or "This might not be the best fit." The best approach is to actually say that you are terminating employment.

> ⓘ CAUTION
>
> **Don't hide behind the company.** You might be tempted to distance yourself from the situation by claiming that "the company" or "senior management" made the decision to fire. In the typical discipline scenario that results in termination, this type of statement would not be entirely true: You will have been making these decisions yourself for the employees you supervise. What's more, acting as if you didn't make the decision allows the employee to believe that you might not agree with it, which can lead to suspicions about the true reasons for the termination (and lead to a discrimination or other lawsuit). This is particularly true if you take your "I'm not the bad guy" routine a step further and claim to actually disagree with the termination decision. It's much more respectful—and safer, from a legal point of view—to make it clear that you made the decision.

EXAMPLE: Christine manages vendor accounts for a large catering company. Unbeknownst to her manager, Christine and her husband started their own linen supply service, "Tablecloths & More," solely to provide linens to the company for its events. Christine hired "Tablecloths & More" to provide linens for every large company event and paid herself a hefty markup, well higher than what the company was paying its other linen vendors. When Lily, Christine's manager, found out about this blatant conflict of interest, she asked Christine about it. After a long, uncomfortable meeting, Christine finally admitted to the scheme. After considering the factors listed above, Lily decides to fire her.

Lily goes to Christine's office, along with the director of human resources (as her company requires when an employee is fired). Lily starts the meeting this way:

"Christine, I've decided to terminate your employment, effective immediately. Directing company business to your own company is a violation of company policy prohibiting conflicts of interest. I can't have someone working here who puts the interests of her own business ahead of the company's interests."

Don't Be Drawn Into a Debate

Sometimes, an employee will respond to being fired by trying to argue the issue. You can help avoid this by being very clear when you announce the termination, as explained above. But if the employee tries to change your mind, simply say, "I'm sorry you feel that way, but the decision is final." Don't undermine your decision by getting in an argument with the employee about whether or not termination is justified.

It's also very important to avoid responding in kind to an angry or upset employee. For example, imagine that the employee says, "I can't believe you're doing this to me! How am I going to support my family?!" If you respond with "If you really cared about your family, you wouldn't have downloaded pornography on your company PC," what happens next will be a yelling match. It's far better to say, "I'm sorry, but my decision is final. Now, let's talk about what will happen next."

You may feel sorry for the employee, which is perfectly natural. But if you've followed the procedures we've described in this book, you've already given the employee every opportunity to improve. Ultimately, the employee was not able to do the job for which he or she was hired and being paid. It's important to keep this in mind when you fire someone, to make sure that you don't backpedal at the last minute. Your natural instinct to feel sad for someone who's lost a job shouldn't translate into changing your mind, offering to reconsider, or saying things that will undermine the decision.

Explain What Happens Next

Once you've announced your decision (and headed off any effort to change your mind), let the employee know about anything that's coming to him or her: a final paycheck, continued health insurance benefits, severance (if applicable), and so on. Also, explain your company's position on references. If your company provides references and the employee is interested, talk about what you might say to a prospective employer.

> **EXAMPLE:** Christine knew that she would probably be fired if she got caught, so she doesn't argue with Lily about her termination. Lily continues the meeting like this: "Here is your final paycheck. It covers from the first of the month until the end of the day today. We won't require you to work the rest of the day, but we are going to pay you for it. Also, I've brought some forms with me that give you the option of continuing your health insurance, if you pay the full premium. You can read those at your leisure; if you have any questions about them, you can ask Scott in Human Resources.
>
> "Our company provides references only if the employee who's leaving signs a release agreeing not to take any action against the company for anything said by the person providing the reference. Scott can explain that to you further, if you're interested. You should know that, although there are some positive things I can say about your work, I would also have to reveal the reason you were fired."

Review Property and Paperwork

After explaining what happens next, it's time to get back company property, such as keys, phones, credit cards, and so on. If you've decided to allow the employee to use any of these items for a while, explain what will happen and how and when you will get the property back.

If the employee will have any ongoing obligations to the company, discuss those now, as well. For example, if the employee has signed a valid noncompete agreement (these are not allowed in some states, including California), promising not to work for a competitor for a set period of time after leaving your company, you should bring that agreement with you and remind the employee of its terms. If the employee has had access to company trade secrets during his or her employment, you should let the employee know that he or she has an obligation not to reveal that information.

EXAMPLE: Because Christine committed misconduct that involved deception and defrauding the company, Lily doesn't want to allow her to keep any company property. Lily also wants to make very sure that Christine doesn't use the company's confidential information, particularly about its clients, after she leaves. Lily starts this part of the conversation this way: "Christine, I need to get back any company property in your possession. I'll need your keys to the building, the company credit card, and your cell phone. If there are any personal numbers you need to get off your cell phone, I'll give you a few minutes to write them down now."

Lily continues, "I'd also like to talk to you about your obligations to the company. As you may know, we consider information about our clients—including their names, preferences, and specifications, and the prices we charge them for various services—to be company trade secrets. This means that you may not reveal or use this information, even after your employment here is over. If you do use this information, the company can sue you for damages. Do you have any questions about this?"

> **CAUTION**
>
> **You might want to have passwords and access codes turned off during the meeting.** If you fear violence, sabotage, or other angry actions against the company, you should arrange to have the employee's access to the workplace, computer and email system, phone system, company credit card accounts, and so on blocked while you are in the termination meeting. This removes many opportunities for the employee to do damage. At the same time, of course, this tactic clearly demonstrates that you don't trust the employee, so use it only when warranted.

Tie Up Loose Ends

Once you've finished with all of the details, find out whether the employee has any questions. You should also explain how you will handle the employee's ongoing work.

EXAMPLE: Lily tells Christine, "Tammi is going to take over your accounts until we hire someone new. Tammi will be instructed to tell any vendors who inquire that you're no longer with the company. That's the same thing I'm going to tell your coworkers.

"Do you have any questions about anything I've said?"

Close on a Positive Note

When you've covered everything, end the meeting cordially. Give the employee the name of a contact person to call with any questions, then wish the employee good luck. Don't say anything that undermines or contradicts your decision to terminate employment, however.

> EXAMPLE: Lily is rather angry at Christine, who has not only betrayed her trust but also ripped the company off. Lily also feels worried that Christine might try to take client files or other company information with her. So, Lily decides to keep her closing remarks very brief and to leave her witness behind while Christine cleans out her desk and office.
>
> "Christine, I've asked Scott to make himself available to answer any questions that might come up later. I've written his number down for you. I'm going to leave now, to give you some time to gather your things together. Scott will be here to assist you with anything you need and to walk you out when you're ready to leave. Best of luck in the future, Christine."

Does the Employee Need an Escort?

Unless you have a legitimate fear of violence, sabotage, or theft, it's best to avoid the strong-arm tactic of having the fired employee escorted through the building by a guard. In most situations, this is simply unnecessary and is likely to embarrass and humiliate the fired worker. It could also make the rest of your team feel that you are heartless or unkind.

At the same time, however, it is a good idea to get a fired employee out of the building as soon as possible. You don't want the employee stopping at every desk to tell the sad tale of being fired. For these reasons, it's a good idea to escort the employee out yourself. Let the employee stop to say goodbye to friends along the way, and offer to help carry things to the employee's car. This is a humane approach that is also effective at getting the employee out of the building relatively quickly.

Documentation

The last step in the termination process is to document your decision in an internal memorandum to the employee's personnel file. The purpose of this memo is quite different from a disciplinary memo. When you document discipline, you have a number of goals: to make sure you and the employee agree on what happened and what will happen next; to memorialize your decision so the employee will know what's expected in the future; and to help the employee's future managers at the company understand what took place, to name a few. When you document a termination, your goal is simply to make a written record of what happened, so you can defend it later if necessary.

Keeping this goal in mind, your documentation should completely and accurately describe the reason or reasons you decided to terminate employment. If the employee committed a one-time serious offense, write down what happened and why it is cause for termination. Whenever possible, specify the policy the worker violated. If the worker engaged in persistent misconduct or poor performance over a period of time, specify not only the problem but also your efforts to remedy it. Write down the dates of disciplinary meetings and warnings.

Below is a sample termination memo, written by Lily from the example above. You can find additional samples in Appendix B.

If you have followed the advice in this book, you should already have a lot of documentation about the employee's problem and your response (if you are dealing with an ongoing problem). As a result, this memo can be fairly short and to the point, as long as it is also accurate and complete. For a one-time firing offense (such as Christine's), you might need to include a few more details.

Once the employee is gone and you've filed your termination memo, you still have one important job to do: Get yourself and your team focused on the work ahead. Chapter 15 explains how to share the difficult news with your staff, figure out the lessons you need to learn from this disciplinary experience, and move on.

Termination Memorandum

By: Lily Lamont
Date: November 13, 20xx
Re: Christine Coleman

I terminated Christine Coleman's employment today. Yesterday, November 12, 20xx, Martin Yarrow told me that Christine was routing work to a company she owns with her husband, "Tablecloths & More." I looked over the vendor records for the past year and saw that Tablecloths & More had received every contract for linens in the last four months. I also saw that we were paying Tablecloths & More $0.50 more per tablecloth, and $0.10 more per napkin, than we paid to any other linen vendor in the past year. These higher charges added up to almost $5,000 in the last quarter.

I met with Christine this morning to talk about this. When I presented her with the facts described above, Christine admitted that she had been routing all of the company's linen contracts to the company she owned with her husband. She also admitted that she gave these contracts to her company even though other vendors were available to provide the same service for less.

Based on these facts and my conversation with Christine, I decided to terminate her employment. Christine's behavior violates our company policy on conflicts of interest. I informed Christine that her employment was terminated in a meeting this afternoon, which Scott McPhee from Human Resources also attended.

Signed: *Lily Lamont*   **Dated:** Nov. 13, 20xx

SMART SUMMARY:
Termination

- Termination is a serious step: It indicates that the discipline process hasn't worked. For that reason, you should carefully review the facts, the employee's personnel file, company policies, past statements made to the employee, how other employees have been treated, and the timing before making the decision. You might also want to get a second opinion from an appropriate person like your manager, human resources, or your legal counsel.

- When you prepare to meet with the employee, have administrative issues—like the final paycheck, continued insurance benefits, severance pay, the return of company property, references, and a contact person—sorted out. This will save you and the employee potential embarrassment and discomfort.

- Your goal when documenting termination is different from your goals when documenting discipline: You simply want to make a written record of what happened, so you can defend it later if necessary. Note former discipline and also what specific policy was violated, if applicable.

- If you feel guilty about the decision to terminate, remember this: You only got to this point because either the employee committed egregious and obviously unacceptable misconduct, or the employee was given the opportunity to improve and was unwilling or unable to do so.

15

Life After Discipline

You're at the end of a long, arduous journey. Maybe you went through the entire discipline process with the employee, coaching, encouraging, and monitoring along the way. Or perhaps, you were forced to take immediate action to deal with a really serious issue.

In either case, the discipline process can take a toll on all those involved: the manager, coworkers, and even the company itself. It takes time, effort, and commitment. It can take you away from your core work, and it can be highly emotional. After the stress of disciplining and terminating the employee, you're probably just ready to wash your hands of the whole affair.

Unfortunately, it's not quite time to do that. First, you'll want to spend some time wrapping up. This is an opportunity to learn from your experience and decide how to move forward. It's a multistep process that requires you to:

- evaluate what went right and wrong
- communicate an appropriate amount of information to your team, and
- update other relevant people in the company, including managers and coworkers.

Conduct a Process Evaluation

Before you explain to others what happened, how you dealt with it, and how you plan to proceed, take some time to think about it privately. The discipline process stirs up all kinds of emotions: You may feel angry, defeated, or saddened by what's occurred. Taking some time alone gives you the opportunity to separate those emotions from actual events, so that you can figure out whether there is anything you, or someone else, could have done differently. In business—and discipline is no different—this step is often referred to as conducting a "postmortem."

The postmortem may well be the key to preventing future problems. It gives you a chance to reflect on what preventive steps could have been taken, what went well, and what could have been done better. If others were involved in the process, it allows you to evaluate the success of each person's role. The idea isn't to lay blame, but to learn and improve or eliminate these issues in the future.

The overarching question that should be ever present in the postmortem process is: *What could I have done differently?* No one is perfect, and the only person's behavior and actions you control is your own. Focus on the things you have the ability to change to make the process work better the next time around.

To do this, you can think about the following questions:

- **Did you impose discipline fairly?** That means that you made sure the response was proportionate to the problem, applied discipline according to company policy, and responded consistently to similar problems.

- **Did you communicate clearly?** At every step, the employee should have understood your expectations: what specific tasks were required, when they were required, and how they were to be accomplished. Ideally, your emotions were in check, and you kept communications as confidential and factual as possible. At the same time, you showed respect and empathy for the employee's thoughts and feelings.

- **Did you get help when you needed it?** Sometimes, you might not have known the answers or how to solve the problem. Did you ask for help when you needed it? If the employee (or you) needed help from outside sources, did you get those people involved at the appropriate juncture?

- **How do you think the employee felt?** Although most employees won't feel happy (and may not like you), it is important that the employee feels he or she got a fair shake.

- **What did you do right?** Make sure to think about the things that went well, so that you can repeat them in the future.

When you conduct a postmortem, you'll also want to think more specifically about opportunities you had to prevent, discover and investigate, respond to, and follow up on the problem. Next, we'll go through some of the specific questions you should ask yourself to evaluate how well you took advantage of your opportunities.

RELATED TOPIC

Check out the "Discipline Review Checklist." To make it easier for you to ask yourself these questions, we've included a "Discipline Evaluation Checklist" in Appendix A and at this book's online companion page. You can use the checklist to brainstorm and prepare yourself to talk about the problem with others. Although a lawsuit is unlikely, if there is one, you don't want the terminated employee privy to your innermost thoughts. For that reason, we don't recommend responding to these questions on paper. Simply use the list to collect your thoughts and assess the process.

Looking at all these factors doesn't mean that you won't have any problems in the future. After all, you can't force employees to behave or perform a certain way. However, you can make sure that you were not the reason the employee didn't live up to expectations.

Could You Have Prevented the Problem?

Hindsight is 20/20. Looking back, you may be able to see exactly what you could have done to prevent the problem in the first place. It might even be recognizing that you hired the wrong person. Or it might be that there was nothing you could do, that a problem was sudden and completely unanticipated.

In trying to evaluate whether there was anything you could have done to prevent the problem, consider these questions:

- **Were you checking in with the employee?** Most employees want to succeed, but not all employees will tell you when they realize they're failing. As we discussed in Chapter 4, it's your responsibility to touch base with the employee, and that's your opportunity to see if there are any concerns that could create problems down the road.

- **Were you checking in with your team?** Remember, your team members offer information and perspectives you won't otherwise get. Sometimes, listening to what your team members have to say is the first step to heading off performance or conduct problems. If you haven't been taking the time to sit down with your employees—saying "good morning" in the elevator doesn't count—you're probably losing the opportunity to gain some valuable information. Refer back to Chapter 4 to see if you were doing your best to sit down with employees regularly, listen empathically, and follow up when appropriate.

- **Did you make a mistake in assigning duties or tasks to the employee?** Sometimes, problems occur because managers hire underqualified candidates, ignore troublesome history or experience (or the lack thereof), or give employees duties that go beyond their level of expertise. It may be that you pushed an employee into a position or duty that wasn't appropriate for that person's skill level.

Did You Recognize the Problem?

Even if you couldn't have prevented a problem, you might have been able to recognize it earlier in the process. As we've already discussed, when managers fail to recognize problems early, everyone loses. The company, the manager, and the employee waste valuable time and resources trying to undo mistakes that could have been avoided.

Sometimes, it's difficult to pinpoint exactly when you became aware of a problem. Here are some questions to ask yourself to see whether you were clued in to the problem at the first opportunity:

- **Were there any signs that something wasn't right?** Often, you have indications that something might not be right, which you might only be able to describe as a "gut feeling." An employee with a performance problem may have been underqualified when you compare the job's requirements to the person's résumé, or an employee with an attendance problem might have started arriving a couple of minutes late months ago, showing up later and later as weeks went by. Did you see those things at the time and take them into account? If you did, you might handle future situations differently, getting involved earlier in the process. On the other hand, if you only see those signs in retrospect, what can you do to make sure they're more visible next time?

- **Did you speak up as soon as you had reason to believe there was a problem?** Often, we don't speak up because we think a problem is "no big deal." An employee is ten minutes late, for example, and we don't want to make a fuss. Remember, though, that sometimes very simple conversations and coaching techniques make it possible to nip problems in the bud. Refer back to Chapter 11 to see how you might have coached an employee through a minor problem.

Did You Respond Appropriately to the Problem?

Once you decided to deal with the problem, how did you handle it? Consider these questions:

- **Did you respond immediately?** Doing so keeps the facts fresh and relevant. Catching it early also minimizes the impact of the problem and maximizes the chance that your employee will improve.

- **Did you investigate?** It's not fair to take action against an employee until you know the whole story, and sometimes, that means a lot of investigative work on your part. This includes research, like looking at your company's relevant policies to make sure you are applying them fairly and consistently, reviewing the employee's discipline history, and looking at how others in the company have handled the same or similar problems.
- **Did you plan?** Did you sit down and think about where you were going to meet with the employee, what you would say, and how the employee might respond? This planning allows you to get the most important points across, without getting sidetracked by the employee's emotions.
- **Did you get the right people involved?** Did you involve your manager, human resources, or legal counsel in the discipline at the right time in the process?
- **Did you work with the employee to create an action plan?** Did the employee know what was expected next? If your action plan was unclear, nonexistent, or prepared just by you, you didn't give the employee a fair shot at owning and fixing the issue.

Did You Follow Up?

After the meeting ended, what did you do to ensure the employee's continued success? Here are a few things to consider:

- **Did you document?** Documenting does more than protect the company—and you—if there is a dispute. Documenting reminds you of important facts, including what the employee's concerns were and what you agreed to do to solve the problem.
- **Did you check in with the employee?** The employee needed to hear the message that the problem was correctable. If you weren't checking in with the employee—praising successes, offering further direction or encouragement, and voicing concerns about continued problems—you might not have provided every available resource for success.
- **Did you hold up your end of the bargain?** If there were tasks you were supposed to do in the action plan, did you do them?

Talk to Your Team

After you've spent some time evaluating what happened, you should move on to thinking about what to share with your team and how to share it. Although you have handled the discipline issue based on a thorough analysis of the facts and arrived at a fair and reasoned conclusion, most likely your team has not been privy to the whole process as it unfolded. Instead, the situation may have become fodder for gossip, and incomplete stories may have been shared.

Change itself can be alarming for employees. William Bridges, a noted change management guru, says, "That decision [(to make a change)] and the first steps taken to implement it are [(management's)] beginning, but for the people who haven't been in the transition process up to this point, that same decision and those same steps represent an ending to the way things were."

As with any change, termination is an ending to the way things were and can cause confusion and even fear in the workplace. Your employees need some way to "catch up" in the process you have already gone most of the way through: What felt like a long process for you may feel very sudden for them. You need to communicate a delicately balanced message that employees must meet the company's expectations, without creating an environment of fear and dread.

Decide How Much to Share

When you've determined that a disciplinary issue has affected the team's morale or overall performance, you must take immediate steps to address it. You'll want to talk to the team about what happened, why, and where to go next, without sharing all the gory details.

Here are some of the most important issues to consider when deciding how much information to share with employees:

- **The need to know.** What your team members want to know may be very different from what they need to know. Often all a team needs to know is that an employee is no longer with the company. You may need to say only that the employee has departed and identify who will handle his or her job tasks. If more detail is needed, limit it to issues that affect the employees' ability to get their jobs done.

- **Confidentiality.** There are a couple of reasons to maintain confidentiality, when possible: It assures your team members that they will be afforded the same respect, and it avoids legal trouble, including possible defamation or invasion of privacy claims if word gets back to the former employee. (See Chapter 3 for more information about potential legal problems that can result from unnecessarily breaching confidentiality.) Keep in mind that while you and the company must maintain confidentiality, you shouldn't ask your employees not to discuss ongoing investigations or other issues in the workplace. (See Chapter 10 for more information on confidentiality.)

- **Your role.** Although you want to assure employees that the situation was handled fairly, you don't want to spend time explaining what you did and why. This could lead you to say negative things about the employee to justify the actions you took. Those statements could get back to the employee, but they could also cause coworkers to worry about whether you'd say the same kinds of things about them.

- **Morale.** Understand that employees feel insecure about their own jobs when a coworker is terminated. Although you can't share details about what happened, you can reiterate your commitment to treating employees fairly. If your company has a written discipline policy, you can also emphasize your commitment to following that policy.

EXAMPLE: Joseph supervises a team of 12 customer service representatives in a call center. He receives a report that one of the representatives, Greg, shouted profanity at a customer on the phone. The report is verified by a telephone recording of the call.

Joseph calls Greg into his office to discuss the incident. Greg begins to yell at Joseph, calling him a liar and making obscene gestures. Joseph asks Greg to leave the office for the rest of the afternoon to cool down. Later that day, Greg calls Joseph and threatens to harm him physically. Because of the seriousness of the behavior, Joseph terminates Greg's employment immediately.

Employees have heard about Greg's behavior and threats but don't know the details. Joseph can hear his team members whispering about it. He quickly calls a team meeting and explains, "As you may have heard, Greg exhibited some inappropriate behavior today, including threats. Because of safety concerns, we had to terminate his employment. The front desk and security have been alerted that Greg is not allowed in the building, and security guards are available to escort you to your car when you leave the building. We're sorry that the situation came to this, but we hope you understand that employee safety is a priority in this company, and we want to make sure you all feel secure.

"For now, we'll all take on a little extra work until we can find a replacement for Greg. I'll work with human resources to get the opening posted as soon as possible, hopefully this week. If you have safety concerns, please talk to me or human resources."

Decide How to Share It

Once you've decided that you need to talk to your employees, and you know what you want to say, you must decide how you will share the message. You'll have to decide:

- **When to talk to employees.** Talk to your employees as close to the end of the process as possible. Waiting two or three weeks for things to "cool down" makes you look like you are avoiding something or that you don't value your employees enough to inform them of important issues. Plus, you want to end all the speculation and chatter and get everyone focused back on work as soon as you can.

- **Whether to talk to employees together or individually.** If the issue has affected everybody equally, talk to your employees together. In the example above, Greg's behavior was equally dangerous for everyone involved, and Joseph saved time and sent a consistent message by talking to everyone at once, while still giving the employees the opportunity to come to him individually. If the issue affects only a more limited number of employees, or might embarrass someone (for example, an employee who was sexually harassed by a coworker), you might want to talk only to the affected employees, individually. You might also choose to talk individually to employees who are more directly affected by the problem, for instance, because they will be responsible for assuming some of the former employee's duties.

- **How to respond to questions.** While it's good to communicate openly, your team also needs to know that you're going to be conscious of each employee's privacy and communicate only appropriate facts. Field questions all day long about the work going forward, but steer clear of probing questions that go beyond what the employees need to know.

Focus Your Team on the Work Ahead

While it's important to tell your team what happened so you can eliminate the mystery and intrigue, it's even more important to communicate what must happen going forward. Gathering your team and outlining the work that needs to be done will get your team members focused on their jobs and put the distracting issue to rest. To do this, you'll need to decide what needs to be accomplished and then focus on what steps have to occur for that to happen.

Step One: What Needs to Be Accomplished?

You'll first need to decide what needs to be done in the absence of the former employee. It may be that you just need to reassign his or her duties. If you aren't familiar with everything your employee did, you may need to research or discuss with individual employees what needs to get done.

However, it's also possible that other team members lost focus on their own goals as a result of the discipline process. It's inevitable that, as a manager, something had to give as you dedicated time to dealing with the discipline and termination. It may be that other employees were left spinning their wheels without a clear idea of what they should have been doing. You'll want to reevaluate where things are and do whatever's necessary to get the team back on track.

Step Two: Set Targets

Now that you know what work needs to be done, give your employees new work targets–deadlines, milestones, or measurements—to refocus them on their work. This narrow concentration will allow little time for conversing about the past. It also reaffirms that you are personally committed to the team's performance. After all, you probably haven't spent as much time managing them as you would have under normal circumstances.

> **EXAMPLE:** Louise manages a team of analysts who are responsible for implementing new record-keeping software within the company. The implementation is a multi-step process, with team members working with different departments to implement the software by a target date. During actual implementation of the software within each department, several team members assist a project leader who is primarily responsible for that department.

Chad is responsible for implementing the new system in the accounting department. As his implementation date comes closer, it becomes evident that Chad has not done the work necessary to make it happen. In fact, he has lied to Louise about his accomplishments. After much investigation and discipline, Louise terminates Chad's employment.

Louise's team members were planning on helping Chad with the implementation in accounting and have set other projects aside in preparation. Louise realizes that considerable work needs to be done before Chad's project can be implemented, though. She gathers together the team that was going to help Chad and works with them to set new, more appropriate deadlines for implementing the software in accounting. She decides to keep the other teams on track, given that they were not as affected by Chad's performance.

In this example, Louise is not only focused on the practical issue of completing the software rollout in the accounting department, but she is also giving that team something to focus on other than Chad's termination.

When the tasks or projects you have assigned have been completed, celebrate that accomplishment. While largely symbolic, this celebration signifies to your team that you all have indeed moved on and worked together to accomplish goals despite prohibitive challenges.

Tell Others Who Need to Know

Even after you've shared the necessary information with your team, you might not be done. Although you may have involved various people in your company as you went through the disciplinary process (human resources, legal counsel, or the management team), there may be additional people who need to be involved now that the issue has been resolved. These include people who worked closely with the employee and others in the management chain.

Whom Do You Tell?

As with all communication in the disciplinary process, you should tell only those in your company who need to know about the termination. First, consider whether you need to tell people who worked closely with the employee but were outside your own team, or people who relied on his or her function to complete their own jobs. For example, a salesperson is not only a member of the sales team, but has a set of customers and support staff. If the salesperson is terminated, support staff might need to know whether that changes their job duties, or what to tell customers about the former employee.

Second, identify other managers or departments who need to know about the specific issue you've faced. While your boss has probably already gotten involved, the impact may have reached others if it has caused your team to miss deadlines or has affected the company's bottom line. In those circumstances, you may need to explain to other managers who depend on your work or those who have set company-wide goals based on your deliverables.

What Do You Say?

Just as with your own team, you want to thoughtfully communicate relevant information to the people that need to know. What you say will be dictated by your audience. An employee from another department probably only needs to know how the discipline impacts his or her job; your boss might need to know how the details are going to affect your ability to meet goals and deadlines; and upper management may need to know only the "big picture" financial effect and plan for the future.

That means that you need to plan what you say based on your audience. To do that, be prepared to acknowledge the issue, explain the issue's impact, and outline the plan going forward.

Acknowledge the Issue

How you acknowledge the issue will be depend on your reasons for sharing the information. For example, if you are talking to an employee who worked with the terminated employee, you need share only information that relates to the working relationship, which may mean saying very little about what actually happened.

On the other hand, if you're talking to someone up the chain of command, you will probably have to provide more detail. You should be prepared to explain how you recognized the problem and how you handled it. Those concerned with the bottom line may wonder how or why the problem escalated, but if you imposed discipline fairly, that's something you'll be able to explain.

EXAMPLE: Morgan works in the office of a small architecture firm. One of her job duties is processing payroll. Once checks are issued, Libby, a mailroom employee, picks them up from Morgan and delivers them to employees.

Hannah, Morgan's boss, discovers that Morgan has been making errors in the payroll. After Hannah utilizes the discipline process, Morgan is unable to improve her performance. Hannah terminates Morgan's employment and assigns payroll processing to another employee, Darrin. Hannah calls Libby. She states, "Libby, I know you usually pick up paychecks from Morgan. I just wanted to let you know that Morgan's no longer with the company, and Darrin will be processing the payroll now. Please pick up the checks from him, and direct any questions you have about payroll to him as well."

Hannah has taken care to make sure that the people who work closely with Morgan are not left wondering whom they now need to work with.

> 💡 **TIP**
>
> **Remember what you learned from your postmortem.** When you have to explain what happened to upper management, the lessons you learned in your process evaluation are handy: You can preempt most of management's concerns since you have already thought it through so well, and you can provide a thorough analysis of what you did and why. Likewise, documenting your disciplinary actions pays off here, too. You'll be able to respond to more specific questions if they arise, because you will have written down the most pertinent details.

Explain the Impact

In addition to acknowledging the issue, you're going to have to explain the impact. This will indicate to others that you've thought of a solution, not just recognized the existence of a problem.

When you're dealing with coworkers, you probably need to explain only the impact on that person's job. When dealing with higher-ups, you might have to explain the fiscal impact or how it affects your ability to meet target goals or deadlines. Again, this can often be one brief sentence such as "This has set back our product release timeline three weeks" or "Our customer satisfaction in the Southeast has declined as a result."

The meat of any discussion you have with others who work closely with your team, or the larger management team, should be the plan you have put in place to recover from the discipline issue. This brief sentence should focus on the business steps you are taking to address the issue (as opposed to the disciplinary steps you took in addressing it with the individual). So if your issue was an employee with an apparent dismal attitude and your customer satisfaction in the Southeast declined as a result, you would add a sentence that says, "We have implemented a customer satisfaction recovery operation and trained each person on how to achieve it. We expect to have the issue fixed by the next reporting period." You are using a brief sentence or two to describe what's been done to address the business issue that might arise and to assure your audience that you have things under control.

EXAMPLES:

To the direct team: "As many of you know, John has left the company. I know his leaving may cause more work for some of you, but here is the plan for short-term coverage …. We also have some rebuilding work to do with John's former customers, and the plan for that is …."

To the upper management chain: "We recently let John go due to substandard performance. This will put a strain on the team in the short term, but I believe it will help the team overall in the long run. To cover for John, I have asked Mary, Patricia, and Susan to each take one of his regions for now. To account for that new workload, I've extended their deadlines for completing the customer survey analysis. In the meantime, we will actively search for John's replacement."

To the Board of Directors: "We recently terminated an employee, John, for failure to uphold our standards of customer service. He was responsible for the loss of two long-term customers, and this may have ongoing revenue impact. I have put my top three people on the three regions that John formerly covered and directed them to rebuild these lost relationships. The overall impact to revenue will be $500,000 initially, but I expect to recoup about $300,000 of that through these focused efforts."

Moving Forward

Once you've evaluated the discipline process, focused your team on forward-looking objectives, and communicated the necessary information to others in the company, you're ready to move on. Hopefully, you've learned steps, tools, and tips that will help you either avoid or control the discipline process in the future. And you can continue to utilize the skills you've learned here to make each encounter with your employees more successful and more positive. Remember that all new concepts take practice to turn into habits, so don't let frustration or qualified success keep you from doing the right thing. Stay the course, practice discipline smartly, and watch your team flourish under your care.

Build Your Skills: If Discipline Fails

Questions

1. Termination of employment is usually not a manager's favorite task. What's something important about a well-run process that you should remember as you prepare yourself to give the bad news?

   _____

   _____

   _____

   _____

2. When an employee is accused of serious misconduct, and you need to investigate, it's a good idea to put the employee on an unpaid leave.

   ☐ True   ☐ False

3. On what day or at what time of day should you terminate employment?

   a. It depends on the situation and your workplace.

   b. At the beginning of the workweek.

   c. On Friday, after everyone has gone home.

   d. As soon as you're able to wrap up the employee's final projects.

4. Employees are often angry about being fired. To be safe, whenever you decide to terminate employment, you should have an employee's passwords and access codes turned off during the termination meeting.

   ☐ True   ☐ False

5. Nora is getting ready to fire Stuart for serious misconduct; he has given away several thousands of dollars' worth of the company's products to friends and family for free, in violation of company policy. Which of these reasons should cause Nora to reconsider that decision?

   a. Stuart's file shows he has always been an exemplary performer; this is his first discipline problem.

   b. Stuart tells Nora when they meet that he did not know this was prohibited and thought it was "not a big deal."

   c. At the termination meeting, Stuart tells Nora that he was sexually harassed by a coworker.

   d. The prior week, Stuart complained to the human resources department that he was sexually harassed by a coworker.

6. When you have to fire an employee, what are some of the benefits of conducting a postmortem?

_____

_____

_____

_____

7. Which of these factors indicate that you could have done more to prevent a discipline problem?

   a. You didn't meet regularly with your employees.

   b. You didn't speak up as soon as you saw a problem.

   c. You didn't create an action plan with the employee.

   d. You didn't document.

8. When an employee is terminated, it's best not to say anything to coworkers; after all, you want to respect that person's privacy.

                                ☐ True   ☐ False

9. What is the most important method for getting beyond a termination, as a team?

   a. Spend some time together talking about the termination and how everyone feels about it.

   b. Focus your team on the work that needs to be done by setting and meeting identified targets.

   c. Get away from the office for a team-building exercise or break.

   d. Meet regularly with your team members to reinforce the rules or expectations that the terminated employee failed to meet.

10. Chrissy had to terminate Lloyd's employment. She crafts this statement: "Lloyd is no longer with the company. From now on, when you have questions about the Stow-rite line of products, please contact Evelyn." To whom should Chrissy deliver such a message?

    a. Holly, her boss.

    b. The whole company.

    c. The customer service team who usually call Lloyd when they need help with customer inquires about Stow-rite products.

    d. Sidney and Leny, who Chrissy knows usually eat lunch with Lloyd.

Answers

1. Remember: If you followed the strategies explained in this book, you've given the employee every opportunity to improve. The employee either wasn't capable of improvement or chose not to take advantage of those opportunities. Either way, the employee isn't willing or able to do what the job requires.

2. False. Whether called "leave" or "suspension," it's a bad idea to put an employee on an involuntary, unpaid break while you conduct an investigation into that person's conduct. While a suspension may be necessary—so that you can gather information without the employee's presence and make sure you know the facts—the time off should be paid. An unpaid suspension looks like you're penalizing the employee and might send the message that you've already made up your mind about the truth of the allegations. Moreover, if you suspend an exempt employee without pay, you could run into legal wage and hour problems.

3. A. It's best to let the workplace guide your decision. However, if you fear violence or sabotage from an employee, you should terminate employment at the end of the workweek or workday and get the employee out the door as soon as you can.

4. False. Although you may wish to disable passwords, access codes, and the like if you fear violence, sabotage, or theft of company secrets, it isn't necessary in every case. In many instances, the employee will feel grief, disappointment, frustration, or humiliation. There's no need to compound that by also making the employee feel like you don't trust him or her.

5. D. In this instance, firing Stuart after he complained of illegal activity could look like retaliation. Nora will want to talk to her human resources department or legal counsel to first make sure that the firing is beyond reproach. Here, it doesn't matter that Stuart had a great performance record (Answer A), because his problem is serious misconduct that justifies immediate termination. It's also fair to terminate Stuart for stealing the company's products even though he didn't know it violated company policy. He *should* have read it because it was accessible to him, and common sense should tell him that it's not okay to take things without paying for them (Answer B). Finally, although Nora should sit up and take notice of Stuart's claim that he was sexually harassed (Answer C), if she'd already made and communicated the decision to terminate employment, Stuart will have a hard time arguing that her decision was made *because* of his complaint.

6. The postmortem gives you an opportunity to separate your emotions from actual events so that you can figure out whether there is anything you could have done differently or better. It allows you to reflect on what preventive steps could have been taken and what you could have changed to get a different result.

7. A. While all these factors indicate steps you might have taken to help the discipline process succeed, most involve actions you could have taken *after* you knew there was a problem. However, if you'd been meeting with your employees regularly, you might have been turned on to discipline problems early on, either because the employees themselves would have told you about their problems, or because being in touch with your team would have clued you in to areas of weakness.

8. False. While you should respect the terminated employee's privacy, you will probably want to acknowledge that the employee isn't with the company any longer. After all, the termination process is a big transition point for your employees, and they may be feeling nervous or confused. It's a good idea to let them know that the employee is gone, but be tight-lipped about the details.

9. B. The best method to move beyond the termination is to get your employees focused on the work that needs to be done. This provides the opportunity for everyone to think about something other than the termination and to set and meet their own targets. Doing this sets your employees up for the opportunity to succeed, something they may badly need. Don't forget to praise them when they accomplish their goals.

10. C. In this case, Chrissy needs to tell those who used to work with Lloyd that he is no longer with the company, but that doesn't mean she needs to go into great detail. Instead, she just needs to let them know how it will affect their jobs. So here, it's probably enough to just tell them that they can now direct their calls to Evelyn.

Appendixes

Sample Forms and Checklist

Sample Workplace Discipline Policy

Workplace Discipline Policy

Any employee conduct that violates company rules or that, in the opinion of the company, interferes with or adversely affects our business is sufficient grounds for disciplinary action.

Disciplinary action can range from coaching to immediate discharge, depending on the severity of the offense. Our general policy is to take disciplinary steps in the following order:

- coaching
- verbal warning(s)
- written warning(s), and
- termination.

However, this is not a guarantee of any particular treatment in a given circumstance. We reserve the right to alter the order described above, to skip disciplinary steps, to eliminate disciplinary steps, or to create new disciplinary steps.

In choosing the appropriate disciplinary measure, we may consider any number of factors, including:

- the seriousness of the offense
- any history of misconduct
- your employment record
- your length of employment
- the strength of the evidence against you
- your ability and willingness to correct the behavior
- your attitude about the behavior
- actions taken by the company in the past for similar behavior by other employees
- how the behavior affects the company, its customers, and your coworkers, and
- any other circumstances related to the nature of the behavior, your employment with this company, and the effect of your behavior on the company.

We will give these considerations whatever weight we deem appropriate.

Sample Workplace Discipline Policy, continued

Depending on the circumstances, we may give some considerations more weight than others, or no weight at all.

Some conduct may result in immediate termination of your employment. Here are some examples:

- theft of company property
- excessive tardiness or absenteeism
- arguing or fighting with customers, coworkers, managers, or supervisors
- bringing a weapon to work
- threatening the physical safety of customers, coworkers, managers, or supervisors
- physically or verbally assaulting someone at work
- any illegal conduct at work
- using or possessing alcohol or illegal drugs at work
- working under the influence of alcohol or illegal drugs
- failing to carry out reasonable job assignments
- insubordination
- making false statements on a job application
- violating company rules and regulations, and
- discrimination or harassment.

Of course, it is impossible to compile an exhaustive list of the types of conduct that will result in immediate termination. The above examples are merely illustrations; other conduct may also qualify as an immediately terminable offense.

You should remember that your employment with this company is at will. This policy does not change that fact. This means that you or the company can terminate the employment relationship at any time, with or without cause, and with or without advance notice.

Sample Employee Disciplinary Notice

Employee Disciplinary Notice	
Employee's Name:	
Manager's Name:	**Date of Incident:**
Type of Warning: ☐ Verbal Warning ☐ Written Warning	
Incident Description:	
Prior Incidents:	
Improvement Plan:	
Employee Comments:	
Manager's Signature:	**Date:**
Employee Acknowledgment	
I acknowledge that I have received and understand this document.	
Employee's Signature:	**Date:**

Sample Discipline Evaluation Checklist

Discipline Evaluation Checklist

General Considerations

- Did you impose discipline fairly?
  - Was the discipline proportionate to the problem?
  - Did you apply company policy?
  - Did you discipline consistently for similar problems?
- Did you communicate clearly?
  - Did the employee know what specific tasks were required?
  - Did the employee know when each task was to be completed?
  - Did the employee understand how each task was to be accomplished?
  - Did you keep your emotions in check?
  - Did you keep your communications as factual and confidential as possible?
  - Did you respect the employee's thoughts and feelings?
- Did you get help when you needed it?
  - If you didn't know what to do or wanted a fresh perspective, did you ask your boss, human resources, or your legal department for help?
  - If the employee needed additional training, accommodation, or instruction, did you get the right people involved?
- How do you think the employee felt?
  - Did the employee feel fairly treated?
  - Did the employee feel blindsided?
- What did you do right?

Preventing the Problem

- Were you checking in with the employee?
- Were you checking in with your team?
  - Did you have regular one-on-ones?
  - Did you have team meetings?
  - Did you set your expectations clearly?

Sample Discipline Evaluation Checklist, continued

- Did you assign appropriate tasks and duties to the employee?
  - Was the employee qualified for the job?
  - Were the tasks you assigned appropriate for the position?

Recognizing the Problem

- Were there indicators something wasn't right?
  - If yes, did you take them into account in deciding when to discipline?
  - If no, what can you do to make sure you see the indicators next time?
- Did you speak up as soon as you had reason to believe there was a problem?

Responding to the Problem

- Did you respond to the problem immediately?
- Did you investigate?
  - Did you talk to relevant people?
  - Did you research relevant company policy, the employee's disciplinary history in the company, and how others have been disciplined for similar infractions?
- Did you plan?
  - Did you think about what you were going to say and where you would meet?
  - Did you prepare yourself for the employee's responses?
- Did you collaborate with the employee to create an action plan?

Follow Up

- Did you document?
- Did you check in with the employee?
  - Did you praise successes?
  - Did you offer further direction when needed?
  - Did you voice concern about continued problems?
- Did you complete any tasks that you agreed to in the action plan?

Sample Documentation

Sample Coaching Memo 1

To: File
From: Michael Norris
Date: August 31, 20xx
Re: Dan Warburg

Met with Dan today, August 31, 20xx, to discuss the product release. I told Dan that I'd heard Dylan was working on a database project and that Sasha was updating the department's internal communications protocols, rather than working on the new product. I told Dan I was concerned that his group might not hit the milestones and release schedule.

Dan informed me that he had sent the team an email outlining the due dates but had not followed up and met with each team member to assign interim deadlines and establish priorities. We agreed that Dan would write up a plan by tomorrow afternoon, detailing how his team would complete the remaining work. I'll review that plan, then Dan will meet with each team member and explain the priorities and due dates. If any problems come up, Dan will discuss them with me immediately.

Sample Coaching Memo 2

To: File
From: Eileen Wilkins
Date: December 14, 20xx
Re: Grace Hernandez

Grace and I met yesterday, December 13, 20xx, to talk about errors in the customer records database. I told Grace that I had received several reports from the sales team that some of the information entered in the last three months—including phone numbers and names—is incorrect. I also told Grace that these errors make it difficult for salespeople to make their calls and track sales, which results in lost time and revenue.

Grace initially denied that she was responsible for these errors but eventually agreed that she was the only one who made entries in the database during the last three months. Grace also told me that since we rented out some of our office space, she has been very busy answering phones and assisting visitors to the tenant company and has not had as much time to see to her job responsibilities.

I told Grace that our new tenant is entitled only to basic reception services under our lease, and that I would talk to them about getting their own receptionist if they were taking up too much of her time. Grace wasn't sure exactly how much time she was spending on them, so she suggested that she would keep a log of her hours for the next week. We will meet again on December 22 to review her log and come up with an action plan. In the meantime, I have authorized Grace to work up to an hour of overtime each day (if necessary) to complete her own duties. We have also agreed that Grace will double-check customer information before entering it into the database. On December 22, we will also come up with a plan to review the information currently in the database for accuracy.

Sample Coaching Memo 3

To: File
From: Sergeant Rialto
Date: March 21, 20xx
Re: Meeting With Jayne Thomas

I pulled Jayne off the route today to discuss her demeanor with accident victims. I told Jayne that her work has been good, particularly at detailing accidents, involving the appropriate people, and clearing the scene quickly. I also told Jayne that I have seen her deal with accident victims too abruptly, which could cause them to clam up and not provide as much detail as they otherwise might.

Jayne agreed that she is sometimes abrupt and said that she sometimes gets impatient when victims have a hard time explaining what happened. Jayne asked whether we had a class that would help her with this, but we do not. I suggested that Jayne could ride along with Janet Singh a couple of days next week and see how she handles accident victims; Jayne agreed that this would be helpful. I also told Jayne that I would observe her next few interactions with accident victims carefully and give her detailed feedback on her tone and demeanor.

Sample Verbal Warning 1

Employee Disciplinary Notice

Employee's Name: Steve Hinds

Manager's Name: Jerry Martinez | **Date of Incident:** May 3, 20xx

Type of Warning: ☑ Verbal Warning ☐ Written Warning

Incident Description:

On May 1, 20xx, I received a complaint from administrative assistant Claire Stewart that your deal memo on the Briggs sale was incomplete and contained numerous errors that slowed implementation of the deal significantly. I investigated whether this was true by reviewing the deal memo (attached) and talking with the administrative staff responsible for assisting you in completing this deal.

The deal memo did not have all the information the staff needed to complete the deal. For example, the memo did not explain the shipping method or the shipping date. Additionally, the memo had errors including incorrect prices and the wrong delivery address.

On April 27, Claire tried to contact you via both email and phone to correct these errors, but you did not respond. As a result of these errors, three administrative assistants spent approximately eight extra hours trying to resolve the discrepancies. Claire also informed me that a similar problem occurred on the Edwards deal earlier in the month.

While your gross sales numbers have been improving, these errors are reducing profit margin on your deals significantly and causing extra work for other team members.

When you and I met to discuss this issue earlier today, you told me that you believed this was the responsibility of administrative staff and that you were not comfortable with the company process.

Prior Incidents:

Customer support, clerical, and fulfillment have each complained about incorrect or incomplete information on your deal memos at least three times. We discussed this in my office on April 5. At that time, I tasked you with rereading the process handbook, which you told me that you did. I also

Sample Verbal Warning 1, continued

told you to ask me if you had questions about writing deal memos. Since April 5, you have not asked me any questions about deal memos.

Improvement Plan:

We agreed that you will meet with each back office department and spend a couple of hours learning what information they need from you to implement your deals. You will also spend a couple of hours with Celia, who will show you one of her deal memos and explain how she decides what to include in it. You will let me know some dates and times that are good for you by tomorrow; I will set up a schedule for these visits by the beginning of next week, May 7.

We also agreed that we will review your next deal memo together. I will tell you whether that memo includes the relevant information. When you have closed your next deal, please inform me and we can schedule that review.

Employee Comments:

Manager's Signature: *Jerry Martinez*	**Date:** May 3, 20xx
Employee Acknowledgment	
I acknowledge that I have received and understand this document.	
Employee's Signature: *Steve Hinds*	**Date:** May 3, 20xx

Sample Verbal Warning 2

Employee Disciplinary Notice

Employee's Name: Luis Guerrero

Manager's Name: Pedro Salazar **Date of Incident:** July 18, 20xx

Type of Warning: ☑ Verbal Warning ☐ Written Warning

Incident Description:

On July 11, Ken Schwarz complained to me that the tables at your station often are still dirty and/or have dirty dishes on them when he seats customers. Since receiving that complaint, I have checked the entire restaurant a few times each day and have noticed that only your tables are left unbussed for more than a minute or two. When you do not bus your tables promptly, our customers have to wait longer to be seated or have to sit at tables that have not been cleaned properly. This reflects badly on all of us.

I met with you earlier today to discuss this problem. You told me that you were working as quickly as you can and that you believe you have improved since our last discussion.

Prior Incidents:

We met on June 12, 20xx to discuss this issue. At that time, I told you that I had received complaints from customers that your tables were not properly cleaned and that I had noticed that you were not bussing your tables as quickly as the other staff. We agreed that you would clear and wipe down each table within a few minutes after customers leave. We also agreed that you were spending too much time hanging out with the dishwashers in the kitchen, and that your speed would improve if you waited at your station in the dining room, with the other bussers.

During the last week, I have observed that you are still spending time in the kitchen, rather than with the other bussers in the dining room. I also noticed that you do not bus tables immediately after customers leave. During the dinner rush last Friday, for example, one of your tables was not bussed for eight minutes after the customers left.

Sample Verbal Warning 2, continued

Improvement Plan:

We have agreed that I will spend 15-20 minutes with you each day for the next two weeks, observing your work and giving you feedback on how to improve. At the end of that time, I expect you to bus each table in your section within two minutes after the customer leaves.

To do your job properly, you must be at your station. Therefore, we have also agreed that you will remain at your station in the dining room at all times, unless you are on break.

Employee Comments:

Manager's Signature: *Pedro Salazar* | **Date:** July 18, 20xx

Employee Acknowledgment

I acknowledge that I have received and understand this document.

Employee's Signature: *Luis Guerrero* | **Date:** July 18, 20xx

Sample Verbal Warning 3

Employee Disciplinary Notice

Employee's Name: Sharon Osmond

Manager's Name: Ed Washington | **Date of Incident:** April 18, 20xx

Type of Warning: ☑ Verbal Warning ☐ Written Warning

Incident Description:

On April 11, 20xx, I received a complaint from June Kulau that you had pushed her to accept one of the candidates (Robert McAdams) you recruited for the product development team. June told me that she raised concerns about Robert's qualifications, but you told her she was not being creative and had to learn to "think outside the box." June also told me that you said you didn't think you'd be able to find another candidate for several months, and that she should accept Robert rather than leave the position open. June has provided me with the emails in which these exchanges took place.

Based on your advice, June interviewed Robert for the position. However, June learned that Robert did not meet some of the essential job requirements. He was not familiar with basic market research techniques and had no experience with children's products. He was also unaware of the "Healthy Back Packs" line of ergonomic bookbags and backpacks for kids— our bestselling, signature product in this area. Based on this, June decided that she could not hire Robert.

After hearing from June, I contacted the other managers for whom you recruit. Sam Montenegro, in the legal department, informed me that you had strongly recommended a paralegal (Duane Mitchell) several months ago, although Sam was not comfortable with Duane's limited experience. Sam told me that you said Duane had "intangibles" that made him an attractive candidate and asked him to "trust me on this one." Sam hired Duane based on your comments. To date, Duane's performance has been satisfactory, but Sam told me that he was uncomfortable with the process because of your lack of regard for the position's advertised requirements.

We met today to discuss these issues. I informed you that your actions in recommending possibly unqualified candidates and pressuring managers to hire them could cause other departments to view the recruiters poorly.

Sample Verbal Warning 3, continued

When you recommend candidates who are not qualified, we also risk making hiring mistakes, which are very costly—in time and money—to correct. These are serious issues that must be addressed immediately.

Prior Incidents:

None.

Improvement Plan:

We have agreed that you will recommend only those candidates who meet the job requirements as stated in the job description. If you believe that a particular candidate warrants the manager's consideration, even though he or she does not meet every job requirement, you will write me a memo explaining why you believe the candidate should be considered before you make that recommendation to the manager.

In addition, you will copy me on your emails to managers for the next two months. You have told me that you do not intend to pressure managers to hire your candidates, but that your enthusiasm for the candidates you find may be causing you to seem overbearing or unwilling to hear any criticism of the candidates you present. Seeing your emails will help me give you feedback on how to appropriately communicate with managers.

We will meet every Friday at 3:00 p.m. for the next two months to review your communications and candidate selections during the previous week. I will be talking to the managers with whom you worked during the week to get their feedback, and I will present this to you during our meetings. After two months, we will decide whether to continue meeting on a weekly basis.

Employee Comments:

Manager's Signature: *Sharon Osmond* | **Date:** April 18, 20xx

Employee Acknowledgment

I acknowledge that I have received and understand this document.

Employee's Signature: *Ed Washington* | **Date:** April 18, 20xx

Sample Written Warning 1

Employee Disciplinary Notice

Employee's Name: Dave Costello

Manager's Name: Claude Washington | **Date of Incident:** February 12, 20xx

Type of Warning: ☐ Verbal Warning ☑ Written Warning

Incident Description:

On February 11, 20xx, I overheard part of a conversation you had with Crystal Cavalier in her cubicle. I heard you questioning her about her boyfriend, then saying something like "Are you sure you don't want to go out with me instead?" I also observed that Crystal did not respond. Instead, she turned away from you and focused on her computer screen.

I called Crystal into my office and asked her what happened. She said you had asked her out and persisted in asking her questions about her relationship with her boyfriend, even after she told you she didn't want to discuss it. She confirmed that you said, "Are you sure you don't want to go out with me instead?," even though she previously turned down your request for a date. She told me that she felt very uncomfortable about your interest in her, and that she felt you were not getting the message that she does not want to have a romantic relationship with you.

When I talked to you later that same day, you confirmed that you had said these things to Crystal.

Prior Incidents:

None.

Improvement Plan:

Dave, your conduct violates company policies on appropriate workplace behavior. Specifically, your conduct violates our policy on Professional Behavior (p. 23 of the Employee Handbook) and Harassment (p. 12). Your comments and requests for a date made Crystal very uncomfortable. She has stated that clearly to you, but you have persisted.

You are not to talk to Crystal about her personal life or ask her out on dates. In addition, because you seem unclear about what constitutes appropriate workplace behavior, I have scheduled you to attend a sexual

Sample Written Warning 1, continued

harassment training workshop on February 19. Following this training, we will meet again to make sure that you understand the types of comments and behavior that are inappropriate in the workplace.	
Employee Comments:	
Manager's Signature: *Claude Washington*	**Date:** February 12, 20xx
Employee Acknowledgment	
I acknowledge that I have received and understand this document.	
Employee's Signature: *Dave Costello*	**Date:** February 12, 20xx

Sample Written Warning 2

Employee Disciplinary Notice

Employee's Name: Melanie Cohen

Manager's Name: Carly Genrette

Date of Incident: October 21, 20xx

Type of Warning: ☐ Verbal Warning ☑ Written Warning

Incident Description:

On October 20, I spoke to Travis, who leads the new branding team, to find out whether you were contributing at the team's meetings. He informed me that he did not remember you saying anything during the last few meetings. I also spoke to Jenya, who confirmed that you had not contributed at these meetings.

As we have discussed previously, when you don't participate in the branding meetings, the team is deprived of our department's perspective on the pros and cons of the proposed redesigns. Because we handle all of the packaging, this means that the team might choose branding that has undisclosed costs, affects our ability to make required disclosures on the product box, negatively impacts our ability to use particular vendors, and so on. You are on the team to give our department's input on the redesign proposals; because you have not provided this input, the redesign might be more expensive or difficult to implement than necessary.

When I talked to you about this problem today, you let me know that you feel shy about speaking up at the meetings. You also told me that you are nervous and uncomfortable talking to a group and that you are concerned that Travis looks down on you.

Prior Incidents:

We have discussed this problem twice before, on August 14, and again on September 30, when I gave you a verbal warning. On each occasion, I informed you that you needed to speak up at the branding team meetings. We have reviewed the type of information you should be bringing to the meeting and sharing with the team. I have also reviewed your written notes from the meetings. However, you have not spoken up at these meetings.

Sample Written Warning 2, continued

Improvement Plan:

We have agreed that you will attend a workshop on public speaking. Our company representatives attend a training class to develop their skills as public speakers. The next class begins on November 1 and lasts for six weeks. I have enrolled you in this class. The company will pay for you to attend, and we will arrange your work around the class sessions.

We have also agreed that you and I will meet before the next three meetings to review what you plan to say. At the next meeting, the team will be discussing color options for the branding, and they must have our input on cost. You will present our department's information as if you were speaking to the team, and I'll give you feedback. We will also meet after each team meeting, to review what you said and how it was received.

Employee Comments:

Manager's Signature: *Carly Genrette*	Date: October 21, 20xx
Employee Acknowledgment	
I acknowledge that I have received and understand this document.	
Employee's Signature: *Melanie Cohen*	Date: October 21, 20xx

Sample Written Warning 3

Employee Disciplinary Notice

Employee's Name: Randy Clark

Manager's Name: Sarah Bronson

Date of Incident: September 10, 20xx

Type of Warning: ☐ Verbal Warning   ☑ Written Warning

Incident Description:

On August 3, 20xx, I asked you to create five new articles about kitchen remodels for the company's website. As we discussed, these articles were to be descriptions of typical kitchen remodeling projects, with references and links to relevant company products. I informed you that these articles would be the prototype for new website content that ties our products to a detailed description of particular projects, rather than simply listing products by category. I also informed you that I needed to have a final draft of these articles by September 8, so I could present them to our marketing team at a meeting on September 10.

On September 7, you came to my office and told me that you would not make the deadline. You told me that you had completed a draft of three articles but had not yet included references to company products. You also stated that you thought someone in marketing should handle this part of the assignment, as they are more familiar with the products than you are. You did not let me know that you might miss the deadline or that you were having any trouble with the articles until September 7.

As a result of your failure to meet this deadline, Cynthia Bradley, Russell Jenkins, and I all had to drop our other work to complete the three articles you drafted. These articles had to be changed substantially because they were not written to best utilize the company's products. We had to add products to the articles as well. Because I was able to present only three articles at the marketing meeting, we had to postpone the rollout date for this new type of content. Our department's failure to meet its goal may cause other departments to believe we are unreliable. Moreover, because the new content is expected to drive higher sales, this delay will cost the company money.

Prior Incidents:

I have already issued you a verbal warning, on March 15, 20xx, for missing a deadline. You were assigned to write a list of suggested projects store

Sample Written Warning 3, continued

associates could discuss with customers looking for spring gardening and landscaping ideas. You missed your deadline by a week, and we were unable to present your ideas to associates at the company's quarterly meeting.

When we met to discuss this problem, you told me that you tended to wait until the last minute to complete writing projects. We agreed that you would attend a seminar on time management. We also agreed that you would outline your future writing assignments several days after receiving them, and that you would check in with me immediately if you needed help meeting a deadline. The details of this incident and our plan for improvement are in your personnel file, as is the certificate you received for participating in a seminar entitled "Time Management for Busy Employees," dated March 23, 20xx.

Improvement Plan:

Randy, you must meet your deadlines for writing assignments. When you miss your deadlines, you cause more work for me and your coworkers, and our department's reputation in the company suffers.

You have told me that you are still putting your writing assignments off until the last minute and that you are having trouble estimating how long projects will take. We have agreed that you and I will meet every Friday at 11 a.m. to discuss your writing projects. At the first meeting after I assign you a project, you will show me your outline. At subsequent meetings, you will report on your progress and show me what you have written to date. At the end of each meeting, I will tell you what I expect you to accomplish by the next meeting. I will confirm this expectation in a follow-up email to you every Friday afternoon. If you disagree with my understanding of the expectation, you have agreed to tell me immediately by the end of the day on Friday.

Employee Comments:

Manager's Signature: Sarah Bronson	**Date:** July 18, 20xx
Employee Acknowledgment	
I acknowledge that I have received and understand this document.	
Employee's Signature: Randy Clark	**Date:** October 21, 20xx

Sample Follow Up 1

To: File
From: Donald Briggs
Date: February 3, 20xx
Re: Jennifer Shiu

I met with Jennifer Shiu on February 3, 20xx to find out whether she had completed her class on using accounting software. She told me that she finished the class on Excel spreadsheets on January 31, and she had learned a lot of helpful tips. I asked her if she would be willing to do a brief presentation on what she learned to the bookkeeping department at our departmental meeting on February 20; she agreed to do so.

Signed: *Donald Briggs*
Date: February 3, 20xx

Sample Follow Up 2

To: File
From: Penny Myer
Date: September 25, 20xx
Re: Jessie Pitt

On September 1, 20xx, I gave Jessie Pitt a written warning. In his action plan, I required him to complete a training class on using PowerPoint, among other things. He was to complete this class by October 1, 20xx.

Jessie informed me today that he completed the class "PowerPoint Basics: Presentations, Graphics, and More!" on September 24. He gave me a copy of his certificate of completion (attached) as well as a syllabus from the class. I have asked him to do a brief presentation, using PowerPoint, at the next department meeting on October 15. He has agreed to do so.

Signed: *Penny Myer*
Date: 9-25-xx

Sample Follow Up 3

To: File
From: Vitali Marcuse
Date: May 31, 20xx
Re: Bruce Bohannon

On April 30, I gave Bruce Bohannon a written warning for inappropriate workplace behavior (see file). I informed Bruce that the company would not tolerate any further angry outbursts and advised him to consult the EAP program if he wanted assistance in dealing with personal issues.

Today, Bruce informed me that he has been meeting with one of the EAP counselors on a regular basis and plans to continue to do so. Bruce also told me that he would like to leave half an hour early each Wednesday for the next six weeks, so he can attend a support group at the hospital for partners of cancer patients. I said this would be fine; Bruce will take personal time for these absences.

Signed: *Vitali Marcuse*
Date: 5-31-xx

Sample Termination 1

Termination Memorandum

By: Lily Lamont
Date: November 13, 20xx
Re: Christine Coleman

I terminated Christine Coleman's employment today. Yesterday, November 12, 20xx, Martin Yarrow told me that Christine was routing work to a company she owns with her husband, "Tablecloths & More." I looked over the vendor records for the past year and saw that Tablecloths & More had received every contract for linens in the last four months. I also saw that we were paying Tablecloths & More $0.50 more per tablecloth, and $0.10 more per napkin, than we paid to any other linen vendor in the past year. These higher charges added up to almost $5,000 in the last quarter.

I met with Christine this morning to talk about this. When I presented her with the facts described above, Christine admitted that she had been routing all of the company's linen contracts to the company she owned with her husband. She also admitted that she gave these contracts to her company even though other vendors were available to provide the same service for less.

Based on these facts and my conversation with Christine, I decided to terminate her employment. Christine's behavior violates our company policy on conflicts of interest. I informed Christine that her employment was terminated in a meeting this afternoon, which Scott McPhee from Human Resources also attended.

Signed: *Lily Lamont*
Date: Nov. 13, 20xx

Sample Termination 2

Termination Memorandum

By: Joseph Farradeh
Date: September 5, 20xx
Re: Greg Johnson

I terminated Greg Johnson's employment today. This morning, Marion Samuels told me that Greg was shouting loudly on the phone in the customer service center. Marion heard him say, "Bitch, I already told you we don't have a record of that! Leave me the fuck alone."

I asked Greg to come to my office and told him that I had heard he may have used profanity with a customer earlier today. Greg immediately jumped out of his chair and screamed, "You're a liar! I never did anything like that!" He also raised the middle fingers of both hands in the direction of the call center and said, "They're all a bunch of jerks. I swear, when I find out who told you that, I'm going to deal with it."

At this point, I asked Greg to sit down immediately and summoned Tom Grady, head of security. I told Greg that he should take the rest of the day off, so I would have a chance to find out what happened. I also told him that he was not to return to work or contact any of his coworkers until he heard from me. Tom escorted Greg from the building and alerted the rest of the security team that he was not to be allowed back on company premises until further notice.

At 1:30 p.m., Greg called me. He asked what the company was planning to do, and I told him that I was still investigating. Greg said, "If you know what's good for you, you won't take someone else's word over mine. You seem like a nice enough guy, but I bet you can't handle yourself in a fight. And you never know when you might turn around and find me right behind you."

Shortly after this conversation, the IT department delivered the records of Greg's calls for the morning. The recordings confirmed that Marion correctly heard Greg's statements and that Greg was speaking to a customer at the time.

Sample Termination 2, continued

Based on these facts, I decided to terminate Greg's employment immediately. I did so in a conference call to his home, with Tom Grady and Elizabeth Durkheim from human resources sitting in. I also told Greg that he was not to return to the building for any reason and that I had informed the local police of his threats against me.

Signed: *Joseph Faradeh*

Date: 9-5-xx

Sample Termination 3

Termination Memorandum

By: Louise Salk
Date: December 10, 20xx
Re: Chad Chang

I terminated Chad Chang's employment today. Chad was responsible for implementing our new record-keeping software in the accounting department. On October 15, 20xx, I met with each of the analysts on the team to find out how they were progressing with their implementation milestones. During my meeting with Chad, he informed me that he was on track for our January 30 deadline. He told me that he had met with Charlotte Holmes and Jonathan McBryde about the project and given each a schedule of tasks to be completed before the rollout.

During my meetings with Charlotte and Jonathan, however, both expressed concern about Chad's project. Charlotte said that Chad didn't seem to have a clear sense of how much time the project would take and had met only two of the project milestones thus far. Jonathan said that he had never met with Chad or received any tasks from him and that he was worried about meeting the January 30 deadline.

Following these meetings, I met with Chad again. After some discussion, Chad admitted that he had not met with Jonathan and had not yet met with anyone in accounting to discuss the project. He also told me that he might be a bit further behind than he initially had reported to me. Chad also admitted that he had met only the initial two milestones, but the remaining items were not completed. I gave him a verbal warning (attached) and asked him to update me on his progress on a weekly basis.

On November 15, I gave Chad a written warning for performance (attached). In the month since our verbal warning, Chad had not met any of his project milestones. Although he had made some progress in catching up on the work he had already missed, he was falling further behind. I assigned an extra member to Chad's team and asked Chad to come to me if he needed

Sample Termination 3, continued

additional resources to meet the January 30 deadline. I continued to meet with Chad every week thereafter.

On November 29, during our weekly meeting, Chad informed me that he did not think he could meet the deadline. Chad told me that he would need at least three more team members and another month to complete the implementation in the accounting department.

During the first week of December, I met with each member of Chad's team. Charlotte informed me that Chad could not answer her questions about the project and that she was unsure how to proceed. Jonathan informed me that several employees in accounting had complained that Chad's instructions to them were not clear and that they were confused about how and when the implementation would proceed. And Corinne, whom I assigned to Chad's team two weeks earlier, told me that Chad had given her a very heavy workload, making her primarily responsible for meeting the project milestones going forward.

Based on these facts, I decided to terminate Chad's employment. I did so in a meeting earlier today, which Gail Richards also attended.

Signed: *Louise Salk*
Date: December 10, 20xx

State Laws

State Laws Prohibiting Discrimination in Employment

Note: Federal law makes it illegal to discriminate on the basis of race, color, national origin, sex (including pregnancy, childbirth, and related medical conditions), age (40 and over), disability (including AIDS/HIV), religion, and genetic information. The following states have their own laws protecting certain classes from discrimination.

Alabama

Ala. Code §§ 25-1-20, 25-1-21

Law applies to employers with: 20 or more employees

Private employers may not make employment decisions based on:
- Age (40 and older)

Alaska

Alaska Stat. §§ 18.80.220, 18.80.300, 47.30.865

Law applies to employers with: One or more employees

Private employers may not make employment decisions based on:
- Age
- Ancestry or national origin
- Physical or mental disability
- Gender
- Marital status, including changes in status
- Pregnancy, childbirth, and related medical conditions, including parenthood
- Race or color
- Religion or creed
- Mental illness

Arizona

Ariz. Rev. Stat. §§ 41-1461, 41-1463, 41-1465

Law applies to employers with: 15 or more employees

Private employers may not make employment decisions based on:
- Age (40 and older)

- Ancestry or national origin
- Physical or mental disability
- AIDS/HIV
- Gender
- Race or color
- Religion or creed
- Genetic testing information

Arkansas

Ark. Code Ann. §§ 11-4-601, 11-5-403, 16-123-102, 16-123-107

Law applies to employers with: Nine or more employees

Private employers may not make employment decisions based on:
- Ancestry or national origin
- Physical, mental, or sensory disability
- Gender
- Pregnancy, childbirth, and related medical conditions
- Race or color
- Religion or creed
- Genetic testing information

California

Cal. Gov't. Code §§ 12920, 12926.1, 12940, 12941, 12945; Cal. Lab. Code § 1101

Law applies to employers with: Five or more employees

Private employers may not make employment decisions based on:
- Age (40 and older)
- Ancestry or national origin
- Physical or mental disability
- AIDS/HIV
- Gender
- Marital status
- Pregnancy, childbirth, and related medical conditions
- Breastfeeding
- Race or color

State Laws Prohibiting Discrimination in Employment, continued

- Religion or creed
- Sexual orientation
- Genetic testing information
- Gender identity, gender expression
- Medical condition
- Political activities or affiliations
- Status as victim of domestic violence, sexual assault, or stalking
- Military and veteran status

Colorado

Colo. Rev. Stat. §§ 24-34-301, 24-34-401, 24-34-402, 24-34-402.5, 27-65-115; Colo. Code Regs. 708-1:60.1, 708-1:80.8

Law applies to employers with: One or more employees; 25 or more employees (marital status only)

Private employers may not make employment decisions based on:

- Age (40 and older)
- Ancestry or national origin
- Physical, mental, or learning disability
- AIDS/HIV
- Gender
- Marital status (only applies to marriage to a coworker or plans to marry a coworker)
- Pregnancy, childbirth, and related medical conditions
- Race or color
- Religion or creed
- Sexual orientation, including perceived sexual orientation
- Lawful conduct outside of work
- Mental illness
- Transgender status

Connecticut

Conn. Gen. Stat. Ann. §§ 25-4-1401, 46a-51, 46a-60, 46a-81a, 46a-81c

Law applies to employers with: Three or more employees

Private employers may not make employment decisions based on:

- Age
- Ancestry or national origin
- Present or past physical, mental, learning, or intellectual disability
- Gender
- Marital status, including civil unions
- Pregnancy, childbirth, and related medical conditions
- Race or color
- Religion or creed
- Sexual orientation (includes having a history of such a preference or being identified with such a preference)
- Genetic testing information
- Gender identity or expression
- Arrests or convictions that have been erased, pardoned, or rehabilitated

Delaware

Del. Code Ann. tit. 19, §§ 710, 711, 724

Law applies to employers with: Four or more employees

Private employers may not make employment decisions based on:

- Age (40 and older)
- Ancestry or national origin
- Physical or mental disability
- AIDS/HIV
- Gender
- Marital status
- Pregnancy, childbirth, and related medical conditions
- Race or color
- Religion or creed
- Sexual orientation
- Genetic testing information
- Gender identity

State Laws Prohibiting Discrimination in Employment, continued

- Status as victim of domestic violence, sexual offense, or stalking
- Family responsibilities
- "Reproductive health decisions"

District of Columbia

D.C. Code Ann. §§ 2-1401.01, 2-1401.02, 2-1401.05, 2-1402.82, 7-1703.03, 32-131.08

Law applies to employers with: One or more employees

Private employers may not make employment decisions based on:
- Age (18 and older)
- Ancestry or national origin
- Physical or mental disability
- Gender, including reproductive health decisions
- Marital status, including domestic partnership
- Pregnancy, childbirth, and related medical conditions, including parenthood and breastfeeding
- Race or color
- Religion or creed
- Sexual orientation
- Genetic testing information
- Enrollment in vocational, professional, or college education
- Family duties
- Source of income
- Place of residence or business
- Personal appearance
- Political affiliation
- Victim of intrafamily offense
- Gender identity or expression
- Status as unemployed
- Tobacco use
- Reproductive health decisions
- Any reason other than individual merit

Florida

Fla. Stat. Ann. §§ 448.075, 760.01, 760.02, 760.10, 760.50

Law applies to employers with: 15 or more employees

Private employers may not make employment decisions based on:
- Age
- Ancestry or national origin
- "Handicap"
- AIDS/HIV
- Gender
- Marital status
- Pregnancy, childbirth, and related medical conditions
- Race or color
- Religion or creed
- Sickle cell trait

Georgia

Ga. Code Ann. §§ 34-1-2, 34-5-1, 34-5-2, 34-6A-1 and following

Law applies to employers with:
- 15 or more employees (disability)
- 10 or more employees (gender) (domestic and agricultural employees not protected)
- One or more employee (age)

Private employers may not make employment decisions based on:
- Age (40 to 70)
- Physical, mental, or learning disability
- Gender (wage discrimination only)

Hawaii

Haw. Rev. Stat. §§ 378-1, 378-2, 378-2.5; Hawaii Admin. Rules § 12-46-182

Law applies to employers with: One or more employees

State Laws Prohibiting Discrimination in Employment, continued

Private employers may not make employment decisions based on:

- Age
- Ancestry or national origin
- Physical or mental disability
- AIDS/HIV
- Gender
- Marital status
- Pregnancy, childbirth, and related medical conditions, including breastfeeding
- Race or color
- Religion or creed
- Sexual orientation
- Genetic testing information
- Arrest and court record (unless there is a conviction directly related to job)
- Credit history or credit report, unless the information in the individual's credit history or credit report directly relates to a bona fide occupational qualification
- Gender identity and gender expression
- Status as a victim of domestic or sexual violence (if employer has knowledge or is notified of this status)

Idaho

Idaho Code §§ 39-8303, 67-5902, 67-5909, 67-5910

Law applies to employers with: Five or more employees

Private employers may not make employment decisions based on:

- Age (40 and older)
- Ancestry or national origin
- Physical or mental disability
- Gender
- Pregnancy, childbirth, and related medical conditions
- Race or color
- Religion or creed
- Genetic testing information

Illinois

410 Ill. Comp. Stat. § 513/25; 775 Ill. Comp. Stat. §§ 5/1-102, 5/1-103, 5/1-105, 5/2-101, 5/2-102, 5/2-103; 820 Ill. Comp. Stat. §§ 105/4, 180/30; Ill. Admin. Code tit. 56, § 5210.110

Law applies to employers with: 15 or more employees; one or more employees (disability only)

Private employers may not make employment decisions based on:

- Age (40 and older)
- Ancestry or national origin
- Physical or mental disability
- Gender
- Marital status
- Pregnancy, childbirth, and related medical conditions
- Race or color
- Religion or creed
- Sexual orientation
- Genetic testing information
- Citizenship status
- Military status
- Unfavorable military discharge
- Gender identity
- Arrest record
- Victims of domestic violence
- Order of protection status
- Lack of permanent mailing address or having a mailing address of a shelter or social service provider

Indiana

Ind. Code Ann. §§ 22-9-1-2, 22-9-2-1, 22-9-2-2, 22-9-5-1 and following

Law applies to employers with: Six or more employees; one or more employees (age only); 15 or more employees (disability only)

State Laws Prohibiting Discrimination in Employment, continued

Private employers may not make employment decisions based on:

- Age (40 to 75)
- Ancestry or national origin
- Physical or mental disability
- Gender
- Race or color
- Religion or creed
- Off-duty tobacco use
- Status as a veteran
- Sealed or expunged arrest or conviction record

Iowa

Iowa Code §§ 216.2, 216.6, 216.6A, 729.6

Law applies to employers with: Four or more employees

Private employers may not make employment decisions based on:

- Age (18 or older)
- Ancestry or national origin
- Physical or mental disability
- AIDS/HIV
- Gender
- Pregnancy, childbirth, and related medical conditions
- Race or color
- Religion or creed
- Sexual orientation
- Genetic testing information
- Gender identity
- Wage discrimination

Kansas

Kan. Stat. Ann. §§ 44-1002, 44-1009, 44-1112, 44-1113, 44-1125, 44-1126, 65-6002(e)

Law applies to employers with: Four or more employees

Private employers may not make employment decisions based on:

- Age (40 or older)

- Ancestry or national origin
- Physical or mental disability
- AIDS/HIV
- Gender
- Race or color
- Religion or creed
- Genetic testing information
- Military service or status

Kentucky

Ky. Rev. Stat. Ann. §§ 207.130, 207.135, 207.150, 342.197, 344.010, 344.030, 344.040

Law applies to employers with: Eight or more employees

Private employers may not make employment decisions based on:

- Age (40 or older)
- Ancestry or national origin
- Physical or mental disability
- AIDS/HIV
- Gender
- Pregnancy, childbirth, and related medical conditions
- Race or color
- Religion or creed
- Occupational pneumoconiosis with no respiratory impairment resulting from exposure to coal dust
- Off-duty tobacco use

Louisiana

La. Rev. Stat. Ann. §§ 23:301 to 23:368

Law applies to employers with: 20 or more employees; 25 or more employees (pregnancy, childbirth, and related medical condition only)

Private employers may not make employment decisions based on:

- Age (40 or older)
- Ancestry or national origin
- Physical or mental disability
- Gender

State Laws Prohibiting Discrimination in Employment, continued

- Pregnancy, childbirth, and related medical conditions
- Race or color
- Religion or creed
- Genetic testing information
- Sickle cell trait
- Being a smoker or nonsmoker

Maine

Me. Rev. Stat. Ann. tit. 5, §§ 19302, 4552, 4553, 4571 to 4576; tit. 26, § 833; tit. 39-A, § 353

Law applies to employers with: One or more employees

Private employers may not make employment decisions based on:

- Age
- Ancestry or national origin
- Physical or mental disability
- AIDS/HIV
- Gender
- Pregnancy, childbirth, and related medical conditions
- Race or color
- Religion or creed
- Sexual orientation, including perceived sexual orientation
- Genetic testing information
- Gender identity or expression
- Past workers' compensation claim
- Past whistleblowing
- Medical support notice for child

Maryland

Md. Code, [State Government], §§ 20-101, 20-601 to 20-608; Md. Code Regs. 14.03.02.02

Law applies to employers with: 15 or more employees

Private employers may not make employment decisions based on:

- Age
- Ancestry or national origin

- Physical or mental disability
- AIDS/HIV
- Gender
- Marital status
- Pregnancy, childbirth, and related medical conditions
- Race or color
- Religion or creed
- Sexual orientation
- Genetic testing information
- Civil Air Patrol membership
- Gender identity

Massachusetts

Mass. Gen. Laws ch. 149, § 24A, ch. 151B, §§ 1, 4; Code of Massachusetts Regulations 804 CMR 3.01

Law applies to employers with: Six or more employees

Private employers may not make employment decisions based on:

- Age (40 or older)
- Ancestry or national origin
- Physical or mental disability
- Gender
- Marital status
- Race or color
- Religion or creed
- Sexual orientation
- Genetic testing information
- Military service
- Arrest record
- Gender identity
- Status as a veteran

Michigan

Mich. Comp. Laws §§ 37.1103, 37.1201, 37.1202, 37.2201, 37.2202, 37.2205a, 750.556

Law applies to employers with: One or more employees

State Laws Prohibiting Discrimination in Employment, continued

Private employers may not make employment decisions based on:

- Age
- Ancestry or national origin
- Physical or mental disability
- AIDS/HIV
- Gender
- Marital status
- Pregnancy, childbirth, and related medical conditions
- Race or color
- Religion or creed
- Genetic testing information
- Height or weight
- Misdemeanor arrest record
- Civil Air Patrol membership

Minnesota

Minn. Stat. Ann. §§ 144.417, 181.81, 181.974, 363A.03, 363A.08

Law applies to employers with: One or more employees

Private employers may not make employment decisions based on:

- Age (18 to 70)
- Ancestry or national origin
- Physical, sensory, or mental disability
- Gender
- Marital status
- Pregnancy, childbirth, and related medical conditions
- Race or color
- Religion or creed
- Sexual orientation, including perceived sexual orientation
- Genetic testing information
- Gender identity
- Member of local commission
- Receiving public assistance

- Familial status (protects parents or guardians living with a minor child)

Mississippi

Miss. Code Ann. § 33-1-15

Law applies to employers with: One or more employees

Private employers may not make employment decisions based on:

- Military status
- No other protected categories unless employer receives public funding

Missouri

Mo. Rev. Stat. §§ 191.665, 213.010, 213.055, 375.1306

Law applies to employers with: Six or more employees

Private employers may not make employment decisions based on:

- Age (40 to 70)
- Ancestry or national origin
- Physical or mental disability
- AIDS/HIV
- Gender
- Race or color
- Religion or creed
- Genetic testing information
- Off-duty use of alcohol or tobacco

Montana

Mont. Code Ann. §§ 49-2-101, 49-2-303, 49-2-310

Law applies to employers with: One or more employees

Private employers may not make employment decisions based on:

- Age
- Ancestry or national origin
- Physical or mental disability
- Gender

State Laws Prohibiting Discrimination in Employment, continued

- Marital status
- Pregnancy, childbirth, and related medical conditions
- Race or color
- Religion or creed

Nebraska

Neb. Rev. Stat. §§ 20-168, 48-236, 48-1001 to 48-1010, 48-1102, 48-1104

Law applies to employers with: 15 or more employees; 20 or more employees (age only)

Private employers may not make employment decisions based on:

- Age (40 or older)
- Ancestry or national origin
- Physical or mental disability
- AIDS/HIV
- Gender
- Marital status
- Pregnancy, childbirth, and related medical conditions
- Race or color
- Religion or creed
- Genetic testing information (applies to all employers)

Nevada

Nev. Rev. Stat. Ann. §§ 613.310 and following; 2017 Nevada Laws Ch. 271 (A.B. 113), 2017 Nevada Laws Ch. 496 (S.B. 361)

Law applies to employers with: 15 or more employees

Private employers may not make employment decisions based on:

- Age (40 or older)
- Ancestry or national origin
- Physical or mental disability
- AIDS/HIV
- Gender

- Pregnancy, childbirth, and related medical conditions, including breastfeeding
- Race or color
- Religion or creed
- Sexual orientation, including perceived sexual orientation
- Genetic testing information
- Use of service animal
- Gender identity or expression
- Opposing unlawful employment practices
- Credit report or credit information (with some exceptions)
- requesting leave or reasonable accommodation due to status as victim of domestic violence (applies to all employers).

New Hampshire

N.H. Rev. Stat. Ann. §§ 141-H:3, 354-A:2, 354-A:6, 354-A:7

Law applies to employers with: Six or more employees

Private employers may not make employment decisions based on:

- Age
- Ancestry or national origin
- Physical or mental disability
- Gender
- Marital status
- Pregnancy, childbirth, and related medical conditions
- Race or color
- Religion or creed
- Sexual orientation
- Genetic testing information
- Victims of domestic violence, harassment, sexual assault, or stalking
- Off-duty use of tobacco products

State Laws Prohibiting Discrimination in Employment, continued

New Jersey

N.J. Stat. Ann. §§ 10:5-1, 10:5-4.1, 10:5-5, 10:5-12, 10:5-29.1, 34:6B-1, 43:21-49

Law applies to employers with: One or more employees

Private employers may not make employment decisions based on:

- Age (18 to 70)
- Ancestry or national origin
- Past or present physical or mental disability
- AIDS/HIV
- Gender
- Marital status, including civil union or domestic partnership status
- Pregnancy, childbirth, and related medical conditions
- Race or color
- Religion or creed
- Sexual orientation, including affectional orientation and perceived sexual orientation
- Genetic testing information
- Atypical heredity cellular or blood trait
- Accompanied by service or guide dog
- Military service
- Gender identity
- Unemployed status

New Mexico

N.M. Stat. Ann. §§ 24-21-4, 28-1-2, 28-1-7, 50-4A-4; N.M. Admin. Code 9.1.1

Law applies to employers with:

- Four or more employees
- 50 or more employees (marital status only)
- 15 or more employees (sexual orientation and gender identity only)

Private employers may not make employment decisions based on:

- Age (40 or older)
- Ancestry or national origin

- Physical or mental disability
- Gender
- Marital status
- Pregnancy, childbirth, and related medical conditions
- Race or color
- Religion or creed
- Sexual orientation (including perceived sexual orientation)
- Genetic testing information
- Gender identity
- Serious medical condition
- Domestic abuse leave

New York

N.Y. Exec. Law §§ 292, 296; N.Y. Lab. Law § 201-d

Law applies to employers with: Four or more employees; all employers (sexual harassment only)

Private employers may not make employment decisions based on:

- Age (18 and over)
- Ancestry or national origin
- Physical or mental disability
- Gender
- Marital status
- Pregnancy, childbirth, and related medical conditions
- Race or color
- Religion or creed
- Sexual orientation, including perceived sexual orientation
- Genetic testing information
- Lawful recreational activities when not at work
- Military status or service
- Observance of Sabbath
- Political activities
- Use of service dog
- Arrest or criminal accusation

State Laws Prohibiting Discrimination in Employment, continued

- Domestic violence victim status
- Familial status
- Gender identity and transgender status

North Carolina

N.C. Gen. Stat. §§ 95-28.1, 95-28.1A, 127B-11, 130A-148, 143-422.2, 168A-5

Law applies to employers with: 15 or more employees

Private employers may not make employment decisions based on:

- Age
- Ancestry or national origin
- Physical or mental disability
- AIDS/HIV
- Gender
- Race or color
- Religion or creed
- Genetic testing information
- Military status or service
- Sickle cell or hemoglobin C trait
- Use of lawful products off site and off duty

North Dakota

N.D. Cent. Code §§ 14-02.4-02, 14-02.4-03, 34-01-17

Law applies to employers with: One or more employees

Private employers may not make employment decisions based on:

- Age (40 or older)
- Ancestry or national origin
- Physical or mental disability
- Gender
- Marital status
- Pregnancy, childbirth, and related medical conditions
- Race or color
- Religion or creed
- Lawful conduct outside of work
- Receiving public assistance

- Keeping and bearing arms (as long as firearm is never exhibited on company property except for lawful defensive purposes)
- Status as a volunteer emergency responder

Ohio

Ohio Rev. Code Ann. §§ 4111.17, 4112.01, 4112.02

Law applies to employers with: Four or more employees

Private employers may not make employment decisions based on:

- Age (40 or older)
- Ancestry or national origin
- Physical, mental, or learning disability
- AIDS/HIV
- Gender
- Pregnancy, childbirth, and related medical conditions
- Race or color
- Religion or creed
- Military status
- Caring for a sibling, child, parent, or spouse injured while in the armed services

Oklahoma

Okla. Stat. Ann. tit. 25, §§ 1301, 1302; tit. 36, § 3614.2; tit. 40, § 500; tit. 44, § 208

Law applies to employers with: 1 or more employees

Private employers may not make employment decisions based on:

- Age (40 or older)
- Ancestry or national origin
- Physical or mental disability
- Gender
- Pregnancy, childbirth, and related medical conditions (except abortions where the woman is not in "imminent danger of death")

State Laws Prohibiting Discrimination in Employment, continued

- Race or color
- Religion or creed
- Genetic testing information
- Military service
- Being a smoker or nonsmoker or using tobacco off duty

Oregon

Ore. Rev. Stat. §§ 25-337, 659A.030, 659A.122 and following, 659A.303

Law applies to employers with: One or more employees; 6 or more employees (disability only)

Private employers may not make employment decisions based on:
- Age (18 or older)
- Ancestry or national origin
- Physical or mental disability
- Gender
- Marital status
- Pregnancy, childbirth, and related medical conditions
- Race or color
- Religion or creed
- Sexual orientation
- Genetic testing information
- Parent who has medical support order imposed by court
- Domestic violence victim status
- Refusal to attend an employer-sponsored meeting with the primary purpose of communicating the employer's opinion on religious or political matters
- Credit history
- Whistleblowers
- Off-duty use of tobacco products

Pennsylvania

43 Pa. Cons. Stat. Ann. tit. 43 §§ 954–955

Law applies to employers with: Four or more employees

Private employers may not make employment decisions based on:
- Age (40 to 70)
- Ancestry or national origin
- Physical or mental disability
- Gender
- Pregnancy, childbirth, and related medical conditions
- Race or color
- Religion or creed
- Relationship or association with a person with a disability
- GED rather than high school diploma
- Use of service animal

Rhode Island

R.I. Gen. Laws §§ 12-28-10, 23-6.3-11, 28-5-6, 28-5-7, 28-6-18, 28-6.7-1

Law applies to employers with: Four or more employees; one or more employees (gender-based wage discrimination only)

Private employers may not make employment decisions based on:
- Age (40 or older)
- Ancestry or national origin
- Physical or mental disability
- AIDS/HIV
- Gender
- Pregnancy, childbirth, and related medical conditions
- Race or color
- Religion or creed
- Sexual orientation, including perceived sexual orientation
- Genetic testing information
- Domestic abuse victim
- Gender identity or expression
- Homelessness

State Laws Prohibiting Discrimination in Employment, continued

South Carolina

S.C. Code §§ 1-13-30, 1-13-80

Law applies to employers with: 15 or more employees

Private employers may not make employment decisions based on:

- Age (40 or older)
- Ancestry or national origin
- Physical or mental disability
- AIDS/HIV
- Gender
- Pregnancy, childbirth, and related medical conditions
- Race or color
- Religion or creed

South Dakota

S.D. Codified Laws Ann. §§ 20-13-1, 20-13-10, 60-2-20, 60-12-15, 62-1-17

Law applies to employers with: One or more employees

Private employers may not make employment decisions based on:

- Ancestry or national origin
- Physical or mental disability
- Gender
- Race or color
- Religion or creed
- Genetic testing information
- Preexisting injury
- Off-duty use of tobacco products

Tennessee

Tenn. Code Ann. §§ 4-21-102, 4-21-401 and following, 8-50-103, 50-2-201, 50-2-202

Law applies to employers with: Eight or more employees; one or more employees (gender-based wage discrimination only)

Private employers may not make employment decisions based on:

- Age (40 or older)
- Ancestry or national origin
- Physical, mental, or visual disability
- Gender
- Race or color
- Religion or creed
- Use of guide dog
- Volunteer rescue squad worker responding to an emergency

Texas

Tex. Lab. Code Ann. §§ 21.002, 21.051, 21.082, 21.101, 21.106, 21.402

Law applies to employers with: 15 or more employees

Private employers may not make employment decisions based on:

- Age (40 or older)
- Ancestry or national origin
- Physical or mental disability
- Gender
- Pregnancy, childbirth, and related medical conditions
- Race or color
- Religion or creed
- Genetic testing information

Utah

Utah Code Ann. §§ 26-45-103, 34A-5-102, 34A-5-106

Law applies to employers with: 15 or more employees

Private employers may not make employment decisions based on:

- Age (40 or older)
- Ancestry or national origin
- Physical or mental disability

State Laws Prohibiting Discrimination in Employment, continued

- AIDS/HIV
- Gender
- Pregnancy, childbirth, and related medical conditions, includes breastfeeding
- Race or color
- Religion or creed
- Sexual orientation
- Genetic testing information
- Gender identity

Vermont

Vt. Stat. Ann. tit. 21, §§ 495, 495d; tit. 18, § 9333

Law applies to employers with: One or more employees

Private employers may not make employment decisions based on:
- Age (18 or older)
- Ancestry or national origin
- Physical, mental, or emotional disability
- AIDS/HIV
- Gender
- Race or color
- Religion or creed
- Sexual orientation
- Genetic testing information
- Gender identity
- Place of birth
- Credit report or credit history

Virginia

Va. Code Ann. §§ 2.2-3900, 2.2-3901, 40.1-28.6, 40.1-28.7:1, 51.5-41

Law applies to employers with: One or more employees

Private employers may not make employment decisions based on:
- Age
- Ancestry or national origin

- Physical or mental disability
- AIDS/HIV
- Gender
- Marital status
- Pregnancy, childbirth, and related medical conditions
- Race or color
- Religion or creed
- Genetic testing information

Washington

Wash. Rev. Code Ann. §§ 38.40.110, 49.12.175, 49.44.090, 49.44.180, 49.60.030, 49.60.040, 49.60.172, 49.60.180, 49.76.120; Wash. Admin. Code § 162-30-020

Law applies to employers with: Eight or more employees; one or more employees (gender-based wage discrimination only)

Private employers may not make employment decisions based on:
- Age (40 or older)
- Ancestry or national origin
- Physical, mental, or sensory disability
- AIDS/HIV
- Gender
- Marital status
- Pregnancy, childbirth, and related medical conditions, including breastfeeding
- Race or color
- Religion or creed
- Sexual orientation
- Genetic testing information
- Hepatitis C infection
- Member of state militia
- Use of service animal
- Gender identity
- Domestic violence victim

State Laws Prohibiting Discrimination in Employment, continued

West Virginia

W. Va. Code §§ 5-11-3, 5-11-9, 15–1K–4, 16-3C-3, 21-5B-1, 21-5B-3

Law applies to employers with: 12 or more employees; one or more employees (gender-based wage discrimination only)

Private employers may not make employment decisions based on:

- Age (40 or older)
- Ancestry or national origin
- Physical or mental disability, or blindness
- AIDS/HIV
- Gender
- Race or color
- Religion or creed
- Off-duty use of tobacco products
- Membership in the Civil Air Patrol (for employers with 16 or more employees).

Wisconsin

Wis. Stat. Ann. §§ 111.32 and following

Law applies to employers with: One or more employees

Private employers may not make employment decisions based on:

- Age (40 or older)
- Ancestry or national origin
- Physical or mental disability
- Gender
- Marital status
- Pregnancy, childbirth, and related medical conditions
- Race or color
- Religion or creed
- Sexual orientation, including having a history of or being identified with a preference
- Genetic testing information
- Arrest or conviction record
- Military service
- Declining to attend a meeting or to participate in any communication about religious matters or political matters
- Use or nonuse of lawful products off duty and off site

Wyoming

Wyo. Stat. §§ 27-9-102, 27-9-105, 19-11-104

Law applies to employers with: Two or more employees

Private employers may not make employment decisions based on:

- Age (40 or older)
- Ancestry or national origin
- Disability
- Gender
- Pregnancy, childbirth, and related medical conditions
- Race or color
- Religion or creed
- Military service or status

State Laws That Control Final Paychecks

Note: Some states are not included in this chart because they do not have laws specifically controlling final paychecks. Contact your state department of labor for more information. (See appendix for contact list.)

Alaska
Alaska Stat. § 23.05.140(b)

Paycheck due when employee is fired: Within 3 working days after termination.

Paycheck due when employee quits: Next regular payday that's at least 3 days after employee gives notice.

Unused vacation pay due: Only if agreed to by employer or required by company policy or practice.

Arizona
Ariz. Rev. Stat. §§ 23-350, 23-353

Paycheck due when employee is fired: Next payday or within 7 working days, whichever is sooner.

Paycheck due when employee quits: Next regular payday or by mail at employee's request.

Unused vacation pay due: No provision.

Arkansas
Ark. Code Ann. § 11-4-405

Paycheck due when employee is fired: Upon request, within 7 days of discharge; otherwise, next regular payday.

Paycheck due when employee quits: No provision.

Unused vacation pay due: No provision.

Special employment situations: Railroad or railroad construction: day of discharge.

California
Cal. Lab. Code §§ 201 to 202, 227.3

Paycheck due when employee is fired: Immediately.

Paycheck due when employee quits: Immediately if employee has given 72 hours' notice; otherwise, within 72 hours.

Unused vacation pay due: Yes.

Special employment situations:

Motion picture business: next payday.

Oil drilling industry: within 24 hours (excluding weekends and holidays) of termination.

Seasonal agricultural workers: within 72 hours of termination.

Colorado
Colo. Rev. Stat. § 8-4-109

Paycheck due when employee is fired: Immediately. (Within 6 hours of start of next workday, if payroll unit is closed; 24 hours if unit is off-site.) When paycheck is not due immediately, employer may make the check available at the worksite, the employer's local office, or the employee's last-known mailing address.

Paycheck due when employee quits: Next payday.

Unused vacation pay due: Yes.

Connecticut
Conn. Gen. Stat. Ann. §§ 31-71c, 31-76k

Paycheck due when employee is fired: Next business day after discharge.

Paycheck due when employee quits: Next payday.

Unused vacation pay due: Only if policy or collective bargaining agreement requires payment on termination.

State Laws That Control Final Paychecks, continued

Delaware

Del. Code Ann. tit. 19, § 1103

Paycheck due when employee is fired:
Next payday.

Paycheck due when employee quits:
Next payday.

Unused vacation pay due: Only if required by employer policy or agreement, in which case vacation must be paid within 30 days after it becomes due.

District of Columbia

D.C. Code Ann. §§ 32-1301, 32-1303

Paycheck due when employee is fired:
Next business day unless employee handles money, in which case employer has 4 days.

Paycheck due when employee quits: Next payday or 7 days after quitting, whichever is sooner.

Unused vacation pay due: Yes, unless there is an agreement to the contrary.

Hawaii

Haw. Rev. Stat. § 388-3

Paycheck due when employee is fired:
Immediately or next business day, if timing or conditions prevent immediate payment.

Paycheck due when employee quits: Next payday or immediately, if employee gives one pay period's notice.

Unused vacation pay due: No.

Idaho

Idaho Code §§ 45-606, 45-617

Paycheck due when employee is fired: Next payday or within 10 days (excluding weekends and holidays), whichever is sooner. If employee makes written request for earlier payment, within 48 hours of receipt of request (excluding weekends and holidays).

Paycheck due when employee quits:
Next payday or within 10 days (excluding weekends and holidays), whichever is sooner. If employee makes written request for earlier payment, within 48 hours of receipt of request (excluding weekends and holidays).

Unused vacation pay due: No provision.

Illinois

820 Ill. Comp. Stat. § 115/5

Paycheck due when employee is fired: At time of separation if possible, but no later than next payday. Employer must comply with employee's written request to mail final paycheck.

Paycheck due when employee quits: At time of separation if possible, but no later than next payday. Employer must comply with employee's written request to mail final paycheck.

Unused vacation pay due: Yes.

Indiana

Ind. Code Ann. §§ 22-2-5-1, 22-2-9-1, 22-2-9-2

Paycheck due when employee is fired: Next payday.

Paycheck due when employee quits: Next payday. (If employee has not left address, (1) 10 business days after employee demands wages or (2) when employee provides address where check may be mailed.)

Unused vacation pay due: If employer agrees to vacation pay, absent an agreement to the contrary, employer must pay out accrued unused vacation upon termination.

Special employment situations: Does not apply to railroad employees.

State Laws That Control Final Paychecks, continued

Iowa
Iowa Code §§ 91A.4, 91A.2(7)(b)

Paycheck due when employee is fired:
Next payday.

Paycheck due when employee quits:
Next payday.

Unused vacation pay due: Yes.

Special employment situations: If employee is owed commission, employer has 30 days to pay.

Kansas
Kan. Stat. Ann. § 44-315

Paycheck due when employee is fired:
Next payday.

Paycheck due when employee quits:
Next payday.

Unused vacation pay due: Only if required by employer's policies or practice.

Kentucky
Ky. Rev. Stat. Ann. §§ 337.010, 337.055

Paycheck due when employee is fired: Next payday or within 14 days, whichever is later.

Paycheck due when employee quits: Next payday or within 14 days, whichever is later.

Unused vacation pay due: Yes.

Louisiana
La. Rev. Stat. Ann. § 23:631

Paycheck due when employee is fired: Next payday or within 15 days, whichever is earlier.

Paycheck due when employee quits: Next payday or within 15 days, whichever is earlier.

Unused vacation pay due: Yes.

Maine
Me. Rev. Stat. Ann. tit. 26, § 626

Paycheck due when employee is fired:
Next payday.

Paycheck due when employee quits:
Next payday.

Unused vacation pay due: Yes, accrued vacation is considered wages and must be paid out upon termination.

Special employment situations: Employer must pay employees all wages due within two weeks of the sale of a business.

Maryland
Md. Code Ann., [Lab. & Empl.] § 3-505

Paycheck due when employee is fired:
Next scheduled payday.

Paycheck due when employee quits:
Next scheduled payday.

Unused vacation pay due: Yes.

Massachusetts
Mass. Gen. Laws ch. 149, § 148

Paycheck due when employee is fired:
Day of discharge.

Paycheck due when employee quits:
Next payday. If no scheduled payday, then following Saturday.

Unused vacation pay due: Yes.

Michigan
*Mich. Comp. Laws §§ 408.471 to 408.475;
Mich. Admin. Code § 408.9007*

Paycheck due when employee is fired:
Next payday.

Paycheck due when employee quits:
Next payday.

Unused vacation pay due: Only if required by written policy or contract.

Special employment situations: Hand-harvesters of crops: within one working day of termination.

State Laws That Control Final Paychecks, continued

Minnesota

Minn. Stat. Ann. §§ 181.13, 181.14, 181.74

Paycheck due when employee is fired: Within 24 hours.

Paycheck due when employee quits: Next regular payday. If next payday is less than 5 days after employee's last day, employer may delay payment until payday after that. But in no event may payment exceed 20 days from employee's last day.

Unused vacation pay due: Only if required by written policy or contract.

Special employment situations: If employee was responsible for collecting or handling money or property, employer has 10 days after termination or resignation to audit and adjust employee accounts before making payment.

Commissions must be paid to sales employees within 3 days if employee is fired or quits with at least 5 days' notice. Otherwise, commissions must be paid within 6 days.

Migrant agricultural workers who resign: within 5 days.

Missouri

Mo. Rev. Stat. § 290.110

Paycheck due when employee is fired: Day of discharge.

Paycheck due when employee quits: No provision.

Unused vacation pay due: No.

Special employment situations: Requirements do not apply if employee is paid primarily based on commission and an audit is necessary or customary to determine the amount due.

Montana

Mont. Code Ann. § 39-3-205; Mont. Admin. Code § 24.16.7521

Paycheck due when employee is fired: Immediately if fired for cause or laid off (unless there is a written policy extending time to earlier of next payday or 15 days).

Paycheck due when employee quits: Next payday or within 15 days, whichever comes first.

Unused vacation pay due: Yes.

Nebraska

Neb. Rev. Stat. §§ 48-1229 to 48-1230

Paycheck due when employee is fired: Next payday or within 2 weeks, whichever is earlier.

Paycheck due when employee quits: Next payday or within 2 weeks, whichever is earlier.

Unused vacation pay due: Only if required by agreement.

Special employment situations: Commissions due on next payday following receipt.

Nevada

Nev. Rev. Stat. Ann. §§ 608.020, 608.030

Paycheck due when employee is fired: Immediately.

Paycheck due when employee quits: Next payday or within 7 days, whichever is earlier.

Unused vacation pay due: No.

New Hampshire

N.H. Rev. Stat. Ann. §§ 275:43(v), 275:44

Paycheck due when employee is fired: Within 72 hours. If laid off, next payday.

Paycheck due when employee quits: Next payday, or within 72 hours if employee gives one pay period's notice.

Unused vacation pay due: Yes.

State Laws That Control Final Paychecks, continued

New Jersey

N.J. Stat. Ann. § 34:11-4.3

Paycheck due when employee is fired: Next payday.

Paycheck due when employee quits: Next payday.

Unused vacation pay due: Only if required by policy.

New Mexico

N.M. Stat. Ann. §§ 50-4-4, 50-4-5

Paycheck due when employee is fired: Within 5 days. 10 days for commission or piece-based workers. § 50-4-4(A).

Paycheck due when employee quits: Next payday.

Unused vacation pay due: No provision.

Special employment situations: If paid by task or commission, 10 days after discharge.

New York

N.Y. Lab. Law §§ 191(3), 198-c(2)

Paycheck due when employee is fired: Next payday.

Paycheck due when employee quits: Next payday.

Unused vacation pay due: Yes, unless employer has a contrary policy.

North Carolina

N.C. Gen. Stat. §§ 95-25.7, 95-25.12

Paycheck due when employee is fired: Next payday.

Paycheck due when employee quits: Next payday.

Unused vacation pay due: Yes, unless employer has a contrary policy.

Special employment situations: If paid by commission or bonus, on next payday after amount calculated.

North Dakota

N.D. Cent. Code § 34-14-03; N.D. Admin. Code § 46-02-07-02(12)

Paycheck due when employee is fired: Next payday.

Paycheck due when employee quits: Next payday.

Unused vacation pay due: Yes. However, if an employer provides written notice at the time of hire, employer need not pay out vacation that has been awarded, but not yet earned. And, if an employee quits with less than 5 days' notice, employer may withhold accrued vacation, as long as the employer gave written notice of the limitation at the time of hire and the employee was employed for less than one year.

Ohio

Ohio Rev. Code Ann. § 4113.15

Paycheck due when employee is fired: First of month for wages earned in first half of prior month; 15th of month for wages earned in second half of prior month.

Paycheck due when employee quits: First of month for wages earned in first half of prior month; 15th of month for wages earned in second half of prior month.

Unused vacation pay due: Yes, if company has policy or practice of making such payments.

Oklahoma

Okla. Stat. Ann. tit. 40, §§ 165.1(4), 165.3

Paycheck due when employee is fired: Next payday.

Paycheck due when employee quits: Next payday.

Unused vacation pay due: Yes.

Oregon

Ore. Rev. Stat. §§ 652.140, 652.145

State Laws That Control Final Paychecks, continued

Paycheck due when employee is fired:
End of first business day after termination.

Paycheck due when employee quits:
Immediately, with 48 hours' notice (excluding weekends & holidays); without notice, within 5 business days or next payday, whichever comes first (must be within 5 days if employee submits time records to determine wages due).

Unused vacation pay due: Only if required by policy.

Special employment situations: Seasonal farmworkers: fired or quitting with 48 hours' notice, immediately; quitting without notice, within 48 hours or next payday, whichever comes first. If the termination occurs at the end of harvest season, the employer is a farmworker camp operator, and the farmworker is provided housing at no cost until wages are paid, employer must pay by noon on the day after termination.

Pennsylvania
43 P.S. §§ 260.2a, 260.5

Paycheck due when employee is fired:
Next payday.

Paycheck due when employee quits: Next payday.

Unused vacation pay due: Only if required by policy or contract.

Rhode Island
R.I. Gen. Laws § 28-14-4

Paycheck due when employee is fired:
Next payday. Paycheck is due within 24 hours if employer liquidates, merges, or disposes of the business, or moves it out of state.

Paycheck due when employee quits:
Next payday.

Unused vacation pay due: Yes, if employee has worked for one full year and the company has verbally or in writing awarded vacation.

South Carolina
S.C. Code Ann. §§ 41-10-10(2), 41-10-50

Paycheck due when employee is fired: Within 48 hours or next payday, but not more than 30 days.

Paycheck due when employee quits: No provision.

Unused vacation pay due: Only if required by policy or contract.

South Dakota
S.D. Codified Laws Ann. §§ 60-11-10, 60-11-11, 60-11-14

Paycheck due when employee is fired:
Next payday (or until employee returns employer's property).

Paycheck due when employee quits:
Next payday (or until employee returns employer's property).

Unused vacation pay due: No.

Tennessee
Tenn. Code Ann. § 50-2-103

Paycheck due when employee is fired: Next payday or within 21 days, whichever is later.

Paycheck due when employee quits: Next payday or within 21 days, whichever is later.

Unused vacation pay due: Only if required by policy or contract.

Special employment situations: Applies to employers with 5 or more employees.

Texas
Tex. Lab. Code Ann. §§ 61.001, 61.014

Paycheck due when employee is fired:
Within 6 days.

Paycheck due when employee quits:
Next payday.

Unused vacation pay due: Only if required by policy or contract.

State Laws That Control Final Paychecks, continued

Utah

Utah Code Ann. §§ 34-28-5; Utah Admin. Code § 610-3

Paycheck due when employee is fired:
Within 24 hours.

Paycheck due when employee quits:
Next payday.

Unused vacation pay due: Only if required by policy or contract.

Special employment situations: Requirements do not apply to commissioned sales employees if audit is necessary to determine the amount due.

Vermont

Vt. Stat. Ann. tit. 21, § 342(c)

Paycheck due when employee is fired:
Within 72 hours.

Paycheck due when employee quits:
Next regular payday or next Friday, if there is no regular payday.

Unused vacation pay due: No provision.

Virginia

Va. Code Ann. § 40.1-29(A.1)

Paycheck due when employee is fired:
Next payday.

Paycheck due when employee quits:
Next payday.

Unused vacation pay due: Only if agreed to in a written statement.

Washington

Wash. Rev. Code Ann. § 49.48.010

Paycheck due when employee is fired:
End of pay period.

Paycheck due when employee quits:
End of pay period.

Unused vacation pay due: No provision.

West Virginia

W.Va. Code §§ 21-5-1, 21-5-4

Paycheck due when employee is fired:
Next regular payday.

Paycheck due when employee quits:
Next regular payday.

Unused vacation pay due: Only if required by policy or contract.

Wisconsin

Wis. Stat. Ann. §§ 109.01(3), 109.03

Paycheck due when employee is fired:
Next payday or within 1 month, whichever is earlier. If termination is due to merger, relocation, or liquidation of business, within 24 hours.

Paycheck due when employee quits:
Next payday.

Unused vacation pay due: Yes.

Special employment situations: Does not apply to managers, executives, or sales agents working on commission basis.

Wyoming

Wyo. Stat. Ann. §§ 27-4-104, 27-4-501, 27-4-507(c)

Paycheck due when employee is fired:
Next regular payday.

Paycheck due when employee quits:
Next regular payday.

Unused vacation pay due: No, if employer's policies state that vacation is forfeited upon termination of employment and the employee acknowledged the policy in writing.

Special employment situations: Requirements do not apply to commissioned sales employees if audit is necessary to determine the amount due.

Using the Downloadable Forms

This book comes with downloadable files that you can access at this book's online companion page:

www.nolo.com/back-of-book/SDHB.html

Here is a list of the types of files provided by this book, as well as the software programs you'll need to access them:

- **RTF.** You can open, edit, print, and save these form files with most word processing programs, including *Microsoft Word*, *Windows WordPad*, and recent versions of *WordPerfect*.
- **PDF.** You can view these files with Adobe *Reader*, free software available at www.adobe.com.
- **MP3.** You can listen to these podcasts through your computer's sound system. Most computers come with a media player that plays MP3 files, or you may have installed one on your own.

Editing RTFs

Here are some general instructions about editing RTF forms in your word processing program. Refer to the book's instructions and examples for help about what should go in each blank.

- **Underlines.** Underlines indicate where to enter information. After filling in the needed text, delete the underline. In most word processing programs you can do this by highlighting the underlined portion and typing CTRL-U.
- **Bracketed and italicized text.** Bracketed and italicized text indicates instructions. Be sure to remove all instructional text before you finalize your document.
- **Signature lines.** Signature lines should appear on a page with at least some text from the document itself.

Every word processing program uses different commands to open, format, save, and print documents, so refer to your software's help documents for assistance using your program. Nolo cannot provide technical support for questions about how to use your computer or your software.

CAUTION

In accordance with U.S. copyright laws, the forms and audio files provided by this book are for your personal use only.

List of Forms and Podcasts

The following files can be accessed at: **www.nolo.com/back-of-book/SDHB.html**

Form in rich text format (RTF)	File Name
Employee Disciplinary Notice	DisciplinaryNotice.rtf
Workplace Discipline Policy	DisciplinePolicy.rtf
Forms in Adobe *Reader* PDF format	**File Name**
Discipline Evaluation Checklist	Checklist.pdf
Build Your Skills: An Overview of Employee Discipline	Overview.pdf
Build Your Skills: Is it Time for Discipline?	Time.pdf
Build Your Skills: Smart Performance Management	Smart.pdf
Build Your Skills: The Disciplinary Steps	Steps.pdf
Build Your Skills: If Discipline Fails	Fail.pdf
Skills Enhancement 1: Setting Expectations	Expect.pdf
Skills Enhancement 2: Opening Discussions	Discuss.pdf
Skills Enhancement 3: Choosing Tone of Voice	Tone.pdf
Skills Enhancement 4: Brainstorming an Action Plan	Action.pdf

Podcasts in MP3 format (available for listening online)	File Name
Segment 1: Coaching Session	Segment1-Coaching.mp3
Segment 2: Verbal Warning Session	Segment2-VerbalWarning.mp3
Segment 3: Written Warning Session	Segment3-WrittenWarning.mp3
Interview With Margie Mader-Clark	Interview-Mader-Clark.mp3
Interview With Lisa Guerin	Interview-Guerin.mp3

BONUS

Minimizing Legal Risk When Firing an Employee

Avoiding Wrongful Termination Lawsuits

F iring an employee is one of the toughest tasks you'll face as a manager. And because of the emotional stakes involved, it's also the task most likely to land your company in legal trouble. When you fire a worker, some amount of his or her dignity, self-esteem, and livelihood is on the line; it's understandable that a poorly handled termination might lead a disgruntled employee to the courthouse door.

Because firing an employee poses considerable risks to your company, it pays to consider the decision carefully. In this chapter, we will explain some of the legal rules that govern employment terminations, discuss some factors to consider in deciding whether to fire, and give you advice on how to break the news. We cover:

- legal and illegal reasons for firing
- special rules for employees with contracts
- how to decide whether to fire workers, and
- how to conduct the termination meeting.

(For information on your company's obligations to departing workers, see Section 2 of this bonus chapter.)

Illegal Reasons for Firing Employees

If your company employs workers at will, you don't need good cause to fire them. You can generally let them go at any time for any reason. (For a discussion of at-will employment, see Chapter 3.) However, you can't fire them for illegal reasons. Here, we list some of the most common illegal reasons for firing an employee.

Discrimination

Federal law makes it illegal for most employers to fire an employee because of the employee's race, color, gender, national origin, disability, religion, genetic information, age (if the person is at least 40 years old), or pregnancy (including birth or a pregnancy-related medical condition).

Most states also have antidiscrimination laws that protect the same characteristics listed in the federal law. Many state laws also protect additional characteristics, such as sexual orientation or marital status. Some laws apply to a wider range of employers; for example, they might cover employers with fewer employees than those covered by federal law. (For more information on how to avoid discrimination, see "Be Consistent" in Chapter 3.)

Retaliation

It is illegal for employers to fire employees for asserting their rights under the state and federal antidiscrimination laws described above. You cannot fire an employee for complaining of discrimination or harassment, for filing a lawsuit or a charge with a government agency alleging discrimination or harassment, or for testifying on behalf of a coworker who was discriminated against or harassed. (For more, see "Don't Retaliate" in Chapter 3.)

Refusal to Submit to a Lie Detector Test

A federal law called the Employee Polygraph Protection Act prohibits most employers from firing employees for refusing to take a lie detector test. The law has a few limited exceptions, including one that allows an employer to require a lie detector test when an employee is reasonably suspected of committing a workplace theft or other crime that causes economic loss to the company. Many states have similar laws prohibiting the use of lie detector tests in screening applicants or during employment, except in limited circumstances.

Citizenship Status

Under the federal Immigration Reform and Control Act (IRCA), an employer cannot fire an employee based on lack of citizenship. As long as the employee is legally authorized to work in the United States, the employer cannot discriminate against the worker based on his or her status as a noncitizen.

Whistleblowing

Generally, you may not fire an employee for complaining about illegal or unethical conduct in the workplace. A number of laws protect an employee's right to complain to a government agency or to company management about potential workplace illegalities. Some of these types of whistleblowing are covered by the laws that prohibit retaliation. For example, an employee who files an OSHA complaint or a charge of discrimination with the EEOC cannot be fired for doing so.

However, protections for whistleblowers go quite a bit further. For example, an employee who complains about financial irregularities or improprieties relating to a government contract cannot be fired for doing so. A number of laws protect the right to blow the whistle on improper employer conduct, including the Sarbanes-Oxley Act of 2002, which protects employees who complain of accounting irregularities and potential shareholder fraud.

Frequently Asked Questions About Firing Employees

Can at-will employees be fired for any reason?

In general, an employer may fire an at-will employee at any time, for any reason (or for no reason at all). But there's one big exception to this rule: An employer may not fire an at-will employee for an illegal reason. Federal and state laws establish a number of illegal reasons, including discrimination based on a protected characteristic and retaliation for an employee exercising a legal right. (See "Illegal Reasons for Firing Employees," above, for more information.)

Does a written employment contract limit our right to fire?

Typically, yes. If an employee has a written contract, the terms of the contract will dictate the circumstances under which the worker can be fired. (See "Firing Employees With Employment Contracts," below, for more on written agreements.)

How can I protect our company from lawsuits when firing workers?

Make sure you always have a legitimate, business-related reason—known in the legal world as "good cause"—to fire. (While this is not required to fire an at-will employee, it is always a good idea.) And make sure you have documented evidence that the worker didn't meet company standards, in the form of performance reviews, disciplinary warnings, and so on. (For more tips, see "Making the Decision to Fire," below.)

Does it really matter how we fire workers?

In a word, yes. Surveys have shown that the manner in which an employee is fired plays a very important role in determining whether that employee decides to file a wrongful termination lawsuit. (For more information on how to break the bad news, see "How to Fire," below.)

Because so many types of whistleblowing are protected, the safest course of action is to never fire an employee for complaining of illegal or unethical behavior. Before you take any disciplinary action against an employee who has made this type of complaint, talk to an experienced employment lawyer.

Lessons From the Real World

Kaaren Yarborough worked as a manager in the recruiting department of PeopleSoft, Inc., a software maker in California. Because PeopleSoft has significant contracts with the Department of Defense and other federal agencies, it was required to comply with federal guidelines relating to the recruiting and hiring of women and minority workers.

In 1995, Yarborough saw reports that management sent to the Office of Federal Contract Compliance, a government agency that monitors companies with government contracts. According to Yarborough's lawyer, these reports falsely claimed that the company had a significantly higher percentage of female and minority workers than it actually did. Although the company claimed that 60% of its workforce was female and 21.7% were racial minorities, the true figures were 45% and 13%, respectively.

Yarborough reported these problems but was fired two days before she was scheduled to meet with auditors from the federal agency. Although PeopleSoft claimed it fired Yarborough for poor performance, the Alameda County jury that heard the case thought otherwise. The jury awarded Yarborough $5.45 million in damages on August 16, 2001.

John Roemer, "Wrongful Termination Suit Brings $5.45M," *The Daily Journal*, August 17, 2001; "PeopleSoft Whistleblower Awarded $5.4 Million," Reuters, August 16, 2001.

Violations of Public Policy

Most states prohibit employers from firing an employee in violation of public policy (that is, for reasons that most people would find morally or ethically wrong). Of course, morals and ethics are relative things, so the range of prohibited reasons for firing varies from state to state. Some state and federal laws explicitly prohibit employers from firing workers for taking advantage of certain rights, like taking family and medical leave or supporting a union. In some states, a worker can also successfully argue that he or she was fired in violation of public policy even if no statute spells out exactly what the employer can and cannot do.

Although the laws and rules vary from state to state, most states agree that firing an employee for any of the following reasons would violate public policy:

- refusing to commit an illegal act (like falsifying insurance claims or submitting false tax returns)
- complaining about illegal workplace conduct (see "Whistleblowing," above), and
- exercising a legal right (such as voting or filing a workers' compensation claim).

To find out more about the law regarding public policy in your state, contact your state labor department or your state fair employment office. (You'll find contact information in the appendix.)

Firing Employees With Employment Contracts

If an employee has an employment contract—whether written or oral, express or implied—that contract might limit your ability to fire the employee. Usually, if an employment contract exists (which is not always easy to figure out), the company must treat the employee fairly and fire him or her only for "good cause."

Is There a Contract?

Before you fire someone, you have to determine whether your company has an employment contract with that worker. This might be as simple as looking in the employee's personnel file for a document labeled "employment contract," but it's often not.

Employment contracts can be created orally—for example, if you and an employee come to an agreement in person or over the phone—even if you never commit the terms to writing. Employers can even create employment contracts without meaning to or even knowing they are doing so. These types of contracts are called implied contracts because they are not written down, but instead are inferred from your actions and statements. Oral and implied contracts are every bit as binding as signed, written contracts.

Employers create implied contracts when they promise an employee something, usually job security. You might inadvertently make these promises in all sorts of circumstances, such as during a casual conversation with an employee or as part of a discussion in an employee handbook. No matter how the promise is made, if the promise has enough weight and the employee has relied on that promise (usually by taking the job or staying there), a court might decide that the promise is a contract that your company must honor.

Figuring out whether the company has unintentionally created an implied contract can be a tricky business. However, past court decisions provide some guidance. Courts have found implied contracts in the following circumstances:

- While trying to convince a prospective employee to take a job, an employer promises the employee that he or she will be fired only if he or she does not do the job well.
- An employee handbook states that once new workers successfully complete a 90-day probation period, they become "permanent" employees.
- A progressive discipline policy in an employee handbook states that employees will not be fired until the company has gone through all steps of its disciplinary process (for example, a verbal warning, a written warning, suspension, and so on).
- During an evaluation, a supervisor gives an employee a glowing review and tells the employee he or she has a long future at the company unless he or she really messes up. (See Chapter 3 for more on creating implied contracts.)

Don't let the specter of implied contracts worry you too much, however. The vast majority of employees in this country are working without a contract—written, oral, or implied. If you are dealing with an employee who has only been with your company for a short time (say, a year or two) and you are sure no one ever promised the employee job security, chances are good that the employee does not have an implied contract. This means that the employee works at will and that you can fire the employee for any reason that isn't illegal. (See "Illegal Reasons for Firing Employees," above).

Remember, too, that a contract doesn't mean you can never fire a worker. It just limits the circumstances under which the worker can be terminated. For workers with implied contracts, this generally means that you must have good cause—such as poor performance or violation of important workplace rules—to fire the employee.

Firing Employees With Written Contracts

If your company has a formal written contract with an employee, it will usually list the reasons for which the employee can be fired. If you want to terminate that employee, you must follow what the contract says. Often, contracts simply state that an employee can only be terminated for good cause. Sometimes, however, the contract will be more detailed. For example, some contracts say that a worker can be fired only for gross misconduct, for committing a crime, or in connection with a sale of the company. Either way, you must follow the contract terms or risk a lawsuit.

Good Cause

As explained above, many employment contracts allow employers to terminate the employee only for good cause. What exactly constitutes good cause varies from state to state, but generally it means what it says: You must have a legitimate, business-related reason for firing the employee. Firing an employee because you want to hire your niece or nephew, for example, isn't good cause. Firing an employee because of excessive absenteeism is.

Examples of good cause include the following:
- poor job performance
- low productivity
- refusal to follow instructions
- habitual tardiness
- excessive absences from work
- possession of a weapon at work
- threats of violence
- violating reasonable company rules
- stealing or other criminal activity
- dishonesty

- endangering the health and safety of others
- revealing company trade secrets
- harassing coworkers
- disrupting the work environment
- conviction of a felony or a crime involving "moral turpitude"
- preventing coworkers from doing their jobs, and
- insubordination.

Lessons From the Real World

If an employee has a contract, you must abide by the terms of the agreement or face a breach of contract lawsuit. That's the very expensive lesson learned by Metris Companies, a credit card issuer that fired its CEO, Ronald Zebeck.

Zebeck claimed that he was fired in anticipation of a sale of the company, which triggered the generous severance provisions of his employment contract; Zebeck also argued that he was fired because he was planning to report financial improprieties to government regulators. Metris claimed that Zebeck was fired for cause, so he forfeited the right to receive severance. Ultimately, the jury sided with Zebeck and ordered Metris to pay him more than $30 million in damages.

Good Faith and Fair Dealing

If your company has a contract with an employee, then it has an obligation to be fair and honest in its dealings with that employee. Although this rule might seem to override your company's ability to terminate employees under contract, it really doesn't. To breach this obligation, employers have to engage in very egregious conduct, such as:

- firing employees to prevent them from collecting sales commissions
- firing employees just before their retirement benefits vest, or
- fabricating evidence of poor performance to fire workers when the real motivation is to replace them with employees who will work for lower pay.

Making the Decision to Fire

Most employers start thinking about firing a worker in one of two situations. In the first, a worker commits a single act of serious misconduct that's dangerous or potentially harmful to the business, such as threatening or committing violence, stealing from the company, violating major safety rules, or revealing important company information to a competitor. These problems require a quick and careful response.

More commonly, though, an employer is facing a "problem" employee who has persistent (but less severe) performance or conduct problems. An employee who is repeatedly absent or tardy, is insubordinate, or simply can't seem to meet reasonable performance and productivity goals falls into this category. Though not as urgent, these problems can also threaten your company's well-being. Left unchecked, they will eventually erode productivity and employee morale.

No matter what your reasons are, consider all the angles before you take action. Remember, firing is the one decision you will make as a manager that is most likely to land your company in court. Stay out of legal trouble by making sure you give the worker a fair shake before showing him or her the door. We provide some suggestions below.

Questions to Ask Yourself Before Firing

If you're contemplating firing an employee, ask yourself these important questions:

- **Do we have a legitimate reason?** Make sure you have good cause— that is, a solid, business-related reason—to fire the worker. (While this is not required for at-will employees, it is always a good idea. Having a solid business reason for the firing will help your company defend against claims that the true motivation behind the firing was discriminatory or otherwise illegal. If the employee has had multiple performance or misconduct issues, or has committed a serious act of misconduct, you probably have good cause. However, you should also consider the timing of the firing and whether there could be an appearance of an illegitimate reason for the firing. For example, if the employee recently disclosed a disability, it might look like the firing is discriminatory, even if you have other legitimate reasons for the firing.

- **Should we investigate first?** If the incident has already been investigated or if the accused worker admits to the misconduct in question, you can skip this step. But if the situation is not so clear-cut, you have to figure out what happened. Take the time to investigate, even when the employee is caught "in the act." There is always the possibility, no matter how slim, that things are not what they appear to be. And the worker might have an explanation or reason for the misconduct that is not immediately apparent. (For an in-depth look at how to perform an investigation, see *The Essential Guide to Workplace Investigations*, by Lisa Guerin (Nolo).)

- **Does the worker's personnel file support the reasons for firing?** Always review the employee's personnel file before firing. If you are considering firing for persistent problems (poor performance or attendance, for example), make sure these problems are documented in evaluations and disciplinary warnings. And make sure the file does not contradict your reason for firing: An employee fired for poor performance should not be able to point to merit increases and glowing performance reviews, for example. If you are firing for a single serious offense, the worker's file might not mention any problems. That's fine as long as there haven't been any.

- **Have we followed company policy?** If your company has written work rules or disciplinary policies, make sure they have been followed to the letter. Was the worker notified that the conduct could result in termination? Did the worker receive any warnings or opportunities to improve, if promised? Be sure to follow any unwritten policies that were communicated to employees orally or that workers have come to expect because of the company's past behavior.

- **Does the worker have a contract?** If the worker has a written employment contract, you can fire only for the reasons stated in the contract. If the worker doesn't have a written contract, consider whether a company representative made any promises or statements that the worker would be fired only for certain reasons. Also, check to see if your company's employee handbook or other written policies include promises of job security—for example, that employees will be fined only for serious misconduct or that they will receive a certain disciplinary process before being fired. If promises like these have been made, make sure you have honored them. (See "Firing Employees With Employment Contracts," above, for more information.)

- **Would firing this worker be consistent with the way the company has handled similar problems?** Think about how your company has dealt with other employees who have committed similar offenses. Have they always been fired? Or have some of them been given a second chance? If your company isn't consistent with discipline, it could be at risk for a claim of discrimination or unfair treatment.

- **Is this worker likely to sue?** Although it's always hard to predict what another person will do, you should take some time to consider whether this worker seems likely to sue. Has he or she threatened to sue, thrown legal terms around with ease, or talked about hiring a lawyer? Does the employee have a history of butting heads with people—such as neighbors or previous employers—and running to the courthouse? Will the employee have difficulty finding another job? Does the employee consistently see himself or herself as a victim? Has your company treated the employee unfairly? If your answer to any of these questions is "yes," your company might be at higher risk for a lawsuit, so handle the termination very carefully.

- **Is there an alternative to firing?** Would less extreme discipline be effective? Do you think it's likely that the employee will be able and willing to improve? If so, you might want to give the employee some time to fix things instead of firing him or her immediately. Just make sure you don't play favorites or bend the rules without a good reason. In particular, you might want to consider an alternative to termination if the worker's problems are due to difficulties outside of work, increased work responsibilities that the employee can't handle, or trouble working with a particular supervisor, or if your company has made some managerial missteps with the worker.

- **Is the firing decision impartial and fair?** Make sure your decision makes sense, is well supported, and can be defended if necessary. Ask a colleague to review your decision to make sure it is based on objective, work-related concerns and has not been influenced by favoritism, discrimination, or other subjective factors.

- **Should we talk to a lawyer?** If it's a close call, or if the company has made some management mistakes, consider talking to a lawyer before firing the employee. For example, getting legal help is probably a good idea if the firing would dramatically change workplace demographics, if the worker recently complained of discrimination or harassment, if the worker has an employment contract that strictly limits your company's right to fire, if the worker is due to vest pension or other benefits soon, if the worker has recently revealed a disability or taken family and medical leave, or if the worker denies the acts for which you are firing him or her.

Once you have run through these questions and are satisfied with the answers, the only thing left to do is to document your decision. Write an internal memo to the worker's personnel file explaining why you have decided to fire the worker. It doesn't have to be a novel; a concise statement of your reasons for firing is enough. Describe any misconduct the worker has committed and, if the worker has had ongoing performance or other problems, the dates and details of any prior evaluations or warnings and any efforts the company has made to try to help the worker improve.

How to Fire

The 15 minutes or so you spend telling an employee that you are terminating his or her employment might be the most important in your company's relationship with that worker. And they will certainly be the most unpleasant: Surveys have shown that managers dread this aspect of their jobs more than any other.

Although you might be tempted to rush the process—a hurried review of the employee's personnel file, a quick check-in with other managers to make sure they're on board with the decision—this isn't the best approach. While you might want to get the task off your plate as soon as possible, the time you spend planning this meeting (such as where it will be held, who will break the news, and what will be said) will pay off in the long run. Prior planning helps ensure that you treat the employee with respect, provide all necessary information, and avoid doing or saying anything unnecessarily cruel or provocative, all of which will make the meeting a bit easier and help you avoid future legal trouble.

Who Should Break the News

The person who actually fires the employee should be someone with whom the worker has a positive, or at least a neutral, relationship. Don't assign someone who has clashed frequently with the worker or who is emotionally involved in the decision to fire the employee. This means the employee's supervisor may not always be the right person for the job. If you have a human resources manager, that person might be another good option.

Where and When to Hold the Meeting

There are many different theories about when an employee should be fired. Some say it's best to fire a worker early in the week, to give him or her the chance to immediately begin the job search and hook up with outplacement services. Others advise waiting until Friday, reasoning that this will give the worker a chance to exit quietly and use the weekend to let the news sink in. Unless you fear violence from a fired worker, you should do whatever feels right. (If you think an employee might get violent, it's best to break the news at the end of the day on a Friday, when fewer people are around. You should also have security present.)

Whichever day you choose, it's usually best to tell the worker earlier in the day. This will give him or her the chance to pack, tie up loose ends, and say goodbye to coworkers. However, holding the meeting first thing on Monday morning might not be the best option, especially if the worker has a long commute to work. (The employee might feel resentful for the waste of his or her time.)

Above all, respect the worker's privacy. Hold the meeting in a private, quiet place away from prying eyes. An open cubicle is a lousy spot for a termination meeting, as is a glass conference room, a lunchroom, or any other area where coworkers can see or hear what's going on. If possible, avoid holding the meeting in a location that will require the worker to make a long, embarrassing march past coworkers after the meeting is over. The best place to break the news is probably the worker's own office, if it is private. This will allow you to end the meeting when you wish (by getting up and leaving), and it will give the fired worker a chance to process the news privately before having to face coworkers.

What to Say

At the meeting, be firm but kind. Don't joke around or make pleasant small talk with the employee to put off the inevitable. It will ring hollow or, worse, seem cruel once the real purpose of the meeting becomes apparent.

Start the meeting by telling the employee that his or her employment is being terminated and why. Long explanations or justifications will only draw the worker into an argument or a plea to change your mind, so keep it brief. It can be tough to strike the right tone in giving this information: If you're too direct, you risk seeming cold. But if you sugarcoat it, the worker won't understand why he or she is being fired and might use your sympathetic words in a lawsuit claiming that the termination wasn't justified. It's a difficult line to walk; the best you can do is to try for an honest, professional tone.

Once the deed is done, explain what will happen next and tie up loose ends. Give the worker his or her final paycheck and any accrued vacation pay (if your state or company policies require it). Although not all states require you to hand over the final paycheck at the time of termination, it's usually best to take care of this right away. (To find out your state's requirements for final paychecks, see "State Laws That Control Final Paychecks," in Appendix C.) Explain the worker's severance package, if you will offer one. (See "Severance " in Section 2 of this Bonus Chapter.) Let the worker know whether you will continue to pay for benefits for any period of time, or of his or her right to continued health insurance coverage under COBRA. Explain your company's reference policy. (See "References" in in Section 2 of this Bonus Chapter.) This is also a good time to review any confidentiality or noncompete agreements the worker has signed, to make sure those obligations are clear.

Finally, try to end the meeting on a positive note. Shake hands, wish the worker good luck, and give him or her the name of someone at the company to contact with any questions.

Company Property

Figuring out when and how to collect company property and block the employee's access to the building and computer system is a matter of judgment and tact. If you trust the employee and don't fear violence or sabotage, don't treat the employee like a criminal, especially at a time when he or she is apt to be feeling pretty low. Unless you have a good reason, you shouldn't march the worker off the premises. Give the worker time to digest the termination before you start cancelling passwords and collecting company property.

If you do fear violence, theft, or sabotage—or if the employee held a highly sensitive position in your company (such as managing your computer system)—act quickly to block the employee's access to the computer system, confidential files, trade secrets, and the building. If you can arrange it, the best time to have access blocked is while you are in the termination meeting with the employee. If you choose this route, explain it to the employee during the meeting. Offer to help the employee retrieve any personal information that might be located on your computer network or in his or her email account. After the meeting, forward the employee's incoming emails and voicemails to someone else in the company and remove the employee's name from the company's website and contact lists.

Documenting the Meeting

As soon as possible after the meeting, write down what happened. Note what you said and how the employee responded. Also keep a record of any issues left up in the air (for example, if the employee wants to negotiate a different severance package or to have the termination messaged in a certain way to others).

Checklist: Things to Do Before the Termination Meeting

- [ ] Cut a final paycheck for the employee that includes all unused accrued vacation time (if required by company policy or your state's law). Also include earned commissions.

- [ ] Issue any outstanding expense reimbursements.

- [ ] Have the employee dropped from payroll.

- [ ] Determine who else needs to know about the termination and inform them.

- [ ] Choose someone (if not you) to conduct the termination meeting.

- [ ] Choose someone to be the employee's contact after the meeting.

- [ ] Make sure that the person who conducts the meeting is familiar with the employee's work history, personnel file, and benefits status.

- [ ] Plan an exit interview, if you choose to conduct one.

- [ ] Decide whether the employee will be offered a severance package.

- [ ] Create an action plan for handing off the employee's current projects.

- [ ] Decide how the company will handle calls from prospective employers seeking a reference for the employee.

- [ ] Decide what you will tell the employee's coworkers about the termination.

- [ ] If you think the employee might turn violent, arrange for security personnel and an escort for the employee.

- [ ] Make arrangements to have the employee's computer privileges turned off.

- [ ] If the employee has an assigned parking space, remove the employee's name from the list and reassign the space.

- [ ] Cancel the employee's company credit card.

- [ ] Identify someone to handle any mail that comes in for the employee after his or her departure.

- [ ] Remove the employee's name from the company's website, email lists, and telephone rosters. Also remove the employee's name from the company's letterhead, if applicable.

Legal Dos and Don'ts: Firing Employees

Do:

- **Document everything.** We can't say it enough: You should always have a written record to back up your reasons for firing an employee. If you are firing someone for ongoing problems, the employee's personnel file should reflect that the employee has had notice of those problems and an opportunity to correct them. Nothing in the file should contradict your reasons for firing.

- **Consider your decision carefully.** It's important to think through your decision to fire. Are your reasons legitimate and documented? Are you sure you know the facts? Have you followed company policy and past practice? Is there any reason why it might make sense to talk to a lawyer? Taking the time to troubleshoot your decision now will save your company a lot of time (and money) down the road.

- **Fire only for good cause.** Although your company has the right to fire an at-will worker for any reason that is not illegal, you shouldn't exercise that right very often. If you fire only for legitimate business reasons, you give workers an incentive to perform well and follow workplace rules. And your company will gain a reputation for being fair and reasonable, which will help in recruiting new workers, retaining employees, and fending off wrongful termination lawsuits.

Don't:

- **Treat fired employees like criminals.** The way you fire someone has a big impact on whether your company will face a lawsuit over that termination. Unless you have legitimate concerns about violence, sabotage, or other extreme behavior, let workers gather their thoughts and belongings, say goodbye to coworkers, and exit your company for the last time on their own accord.

- **Take workers by surprise.** A firing should never come as a complete surprise to the employee who gets the bad news. A worker fired for cause should have been on notice that his or her actions or performance were unsatisfactory and might lead to termination.

- **Postpone the inevitable.** We know that it's difficult to fire an employee. But it's often the best thing for your company. Once an employee has proven that he or she can't meet the company's expectations or has committed serious misconduct, it's time to terminate. The longer you put it off, the more intractable the employee's problems will become.

Test Your Knowledge

Questions

1. An at-will employee can be fired for any reason. ☐ True ☐ False

2. If an employee has an employment contract, he or she can be fired only for good cause. ☐ True ☐ False

3. As long as an employee works at will, you don't need to bother reviewing the personnel file before you fire him or her. ☐ True ☐ False

4. It's a good idea to give an employee an in-depth explanation as to why he or she is being fired. ☐ True ☐ False

5. An employee's direct supervisor should always be the one to do the firing. ☐ True ☐ False

6. You should always ask security to escort someone you've fired off the premises, just in case. ☐ True ☐ False

7. You might have to pay a fired employee on the spot, rather than issuing a final paycheck on your usual payroll schedule. ☐ True ☐ False

8. As long as you have a good reason to fire an employee, it doesn't really matter how other managers handle similar problems. ☐ True ☐ False

9. An employee can have a valid legal claim for breach of contract even without a written employment agreement. ☐ True ☐ False

10. To avoid sabotage, you should always turn off an employee's access to the company's network and computer system before the termination meeting. ☐ True ☐ False

Test Your Knowledge (continued)

Answers

1. False. At-will employees cannot be fired for reasons that are illegal, such as discrimination or retaliation.

2. It depends on the contract. Many written and oral contracts (and virtually all implied contracts) require good cause for termination, but some contracts might impose different requirements. For example, a contract might say the employee can be fired only for committing a crime or for serious financial mismanagement.

3. False. A terminated employee's personnel file should support the reasons for firing. An employee who is fired for persistent performance problems or misconduct should have been on notice that the problems could lead to termination.

4. False. Although you should tell an employee why his or her employment is being terminated, you should keep it brief. Getting into the details will only encourage arguments.

5. It depends on the relationship between the employee and the supervisor. If the relationship is generally good, the supervisor should handle the firing. If there is friction, however, another manager might be better suited to the task.

6. False. Unless you have a legitimate concern about violence or sabotage, don't have the worker escorted off the premises. This only leads to bad feelings, for the employee you fired and the employees who see how you treated him or her.

7. True. This issue is governed by state law, and some states require you to give a fired employee a final paycheck right away. See "State Laws That Control Final Paychecks," in Appendix C, for information on your state's rules.

8. False. Inconsistent treatment can lead to claims of unfairness and discrimination. You should make sure that all managers at your company are handling employee problems according to the same set of rules.

9. True. The employee could have an oral contract or an implied contract (based on the company's actions or statements) that limits the company's right to fire, even if nothing was ever put in writing.

10. False. If you turn off access before the termination meeting, the employee will already know that there's a problem before you have a chance to fire him or her. If you fear sabotage, you can arrange to have access turned off while you are meeting with the employee.

Dealing With Departing Employees

Whether an employment relationship is good or bad, odds are it will end one day, and perhaps sooner than you think. Employment statistics show that the days of an employee staying with a company until retirement are long gone: According to a 2014 study by the U.S. Bureau of Labor Statistics, workers spend a median of 4.5 years with a company before moving on.

Observing legal rules is especially important at the end of the employment relationship. Departing workers (especially those who are leaving involuntarily) may be unhappy, angry, or dissatisfied with the way they've been treated by your company. If you show respect to departing employees, and observe all of their legal rights, you have a much better chance of averting lawsuits and other problems.

In this chapter, we look at some common issues you'll face when workers leave, paying special attention to trouble spots. Regardless of why a worker leaves—whether he or she was fired, was laid off, or quit—you'll face many of the same issues as the employment relationship wraps up. These issues include how to give references, how to extend health benefits, whether to dispute unemployment benefits, and whether to provide severance.

References

Whenever an employee leaves, your company will have to decide what to say to prospective employers that call for a reference. The decision is pretty straightforward if the employee left on good terms: You and the former employee can come up with a mutually agreeable statement to explain the departure. Or, you can simply tell the whole glowing truth to any prospective employer who calls for a reference. But if the employee was fired, or left on bad terms, you face a more difficult task.

Defamation

If you're not careful in your statements about former employees, your company might find itself facing a defamation lawsuit. And, because defamation is a personal injury claim that can be brought against individuals as well as organizations, you could even be sued personally for your comments.

Frequently Asked Questions About Departing Workers

Do we have to give references for every worker who leaves?
No law requires employers to give a reference for a former employee, just as no law prohibits employers from telling the truth about a former employee. However, there are some steps you should take to make sure you don't create unnecessary legal problems when you provide a reference. (For more about this issue, see "References," above.)

What should we say to our remaining workers when an employee leaves?
It depends on why the employee is leaving. If the employee is separating on good terms, you can let other workers know where and when the employee is going. For employees who are fired, however, you should probably be less forthcoming. (See "What to Tell Coworkers When an Employee Leaves," below, for more information.)

Do we have to continue to pay a former employee's health insurance premiums?
No. Under federal and state health insurance continuation laws, employees have the option of continuing coverage at their own expense. Employers are not required to pay for any portion of the premium. However, some employers choose to continue paying for health insurance premiums for a period of time as part of a severance package.

Are we legally required to pay severance?
Probably not. Unless your company has promised severance, or has led employees to believe that they are entitled to severance, there is no obligation to provide it. (For more information, see "Severance," below.)

Is there anything we can do to protect the company from lawsuits by former employees?
Yes. In exchange for something of value, you can ask employees to sign a release in which they agree not to sue the company. Some companies routinely ask employees to sign a release as a condition of receiving a severance package. (For more about this, see "Releases," below.)

Are all departing workers entitled to unemployment compensation?
No. Unemployment laws vary from state to state, but in general, workers who quit voluntarily or who lose their jobs because of misconduct are not entitled to receive benefits. (For more information, see "Unemployment Benefits," below.)

To prove defamation, a former employee typically must show that company representatives intentionally damaged his or her reputation by making harmful statements about the employee that they knew or should have known to be false.

At first glance, it might seem like only the most spiteful manager would get caught in this trap. But, if you make an unflattering statement that you don't absolutely know to be true, it could happen to you. Let's face it: Most reasons for firing make the employee look bad. And managers often cannot prove what they strongly believe to be true: that an employee is stealing from the company, is incompetent, or lied about job qualifications, for example. A manager who makes such statements about a former employee could get into trouble. Your best policy is to say as little as possible and stick to facts you can prove.

Rules for Giving References

When a potential employer calls for a reference, you may feel trapped between wanting to tell the truth and fearing a lawsuit if you say anything unflattering. Unfortunately, this fear is not unfounded. Plenty of defamation lawsuits have been filed over negative references. And, even if a former employee can't successfully prove that you defamed him or her, your company (and possibly you) will have to spend precious time and money fighting the allegation.

Here are some tips to help you avoid problems:

- **Warn a difficult employee that your reference won't be good.** Yes, the employee should know this already. But you can avoid problems at the outset by stating the obvious: "I cannot provide a positive reference for you." Smart employees will leave your company off their reference lists.

- **Keep it brief.** Some companies adopt a policy of only giving out dates of employment, job title, and final salary to prospective employers. If your company chooses to tell more, keep it to a minimum.

- **Stick to the facts.** Now is not the time to speculate about a former employee's bad qualities or to opine on the reasons for his or her failures. Limit your comments to accurate, verifiable facts.

Lessons From the Real World

Randi was a female student at a California middle school when she was called into the vice principal's office one day in 1992. Later, she claimed that the vice principal, Robert Gadams, sexually molested her while she was in his office.

As it turned out, the school hired Gadams after receiving positive recommendations from another school district where Gadams had worked. Even though supervisors in his former school district knew that Gadams had been accused of sexual misconduct and impropriety with students, it failed to mention these claims when the new middle school asked for a reference. In fact, the former district gave letters of recommendation for Gadams that contained unconditional praise. One letter recommended Gadams "for an assistant principalship or equivalent position without reservation."

When Randi sued Gadams's previous school district, the district claimed that she had no legal grounds for suit. After all, it argued, it didn't have any sort of obligation to her, a student in a different district. The California Supreme Court disagreed. It said that Randi could sue because the school district had a duty to not misrepresent the facts when describing the character and qualifications of an employee to a prospective employer (in this case, the middle school that Randi attended).

Randi W. v. Muroc Joint Unified School District, et al., 14 Cal.4th 1066 (1997).

- **Don't be spiteful.** Many states offer some protection for former employers that are called upon to provide a reference. These laws generally shield employers from defamation lawsuits as long as they provide information in good faith. This is a fairly nebulous legal standard, but it clearly does not cover nasty or mean-spirited gripes.
- **Don't give false flattery.** If you had to fire a real bad egg (for example, a worker who was violent in the workplace or threatened coworkers), don't lie about it. You may choose to give only name, rank, and serial number, but, if you give a more expansive reference, don't hide the bad news. If you fail to warn the new employer about serious problems, and the employee ends up harming coworkers or the public, you and your company could be held responsible.

- **Designate one person to give references.** Choose one trusted person in the company to be responsible for all references, and tell employees to direct inquiries to that person. Make sure that your company keeps a record of every request for a reference and every response, in case of trouble down the road. Some companies provide only written references, to make sure they have proof of exactly what was said.
- **Insist on a written release.** To make absolutely sure your company is protected against lawsuits, require former employees to sign a release: an agreement that gives you permission to provide information to prospective employers and that promises the former employee not sue over the information you provide.

What to Tell Coworkers When an Employee Leaves

Before a departing employee walks out the door, sit down and discuss what you will tell coworkers about the situation. If the employee is leaving on good terms, this decision shouldn't be difficult. You'll probably want to thank the worker for his or her service, tell coworkers where the worker is going, and express high hopes for the worker's future.

You'll need to take extra steps if a worker is fired, however. Imagine how other employees will feel when they learn that a coworker—perhaps even a friend—has been fired. Not only will they want to know why that person was fired, but they might also start to fear for their own jobs. Rumors will circulate. Morale might drop. This is especially true if you're terminating a popular employee or someone who's been with the company for a number of years.

You might be tempted to say nothing to other workers about the termination. Although this instinct is understandable, it's not a good one. Employees are not going to ignore or forget about the termination, no matter how much they may have wanted the employee gone. Every employee secretly fears being fired, so it is unsettling at best when it happens to a coworker.

So what should you do? You can keep other workers informed, boost morale, and avoid any legal missteps by following these tips:

- **Call a meeting.** Consider calling a meeting with employees to announce the termination, so you can acknowledge the event on behalf of the company and encourage workers to move past it.
- **Relay the facts.** At the meeting, tell employees who has been terminated and as of what date. Do not explain why the employee was fired.
- **Keep it neutral.** Do not express anger or relief. Be professional and calm. Tell workers that you can't go into details because you must respect the fired employee's privacy.

Of course, this doesn't mean managers can never discuss the reasons for termination with anyone. If there is a compelling business need to tell an employee why a coworker was terminated (for example, an employee is taking on the terminated worker's projects and needs to know how to fix the worker's mistakes), then do it one on one, in a private and confidential setting. Instruct the employee not to reveal anything you say to anyone else in the organization.

Health Insurance

With the astronomical increases in the costs of medical care, health insurance has become a coveted—if not essential—employee benefit. The importance of health care coverage means that this will be one of the first issues a terminated employee will ask about.

Many companies offer to foot the bill for continued insurance coverage—at least for a while—as part of an employee's severance package. Often, this benefit helps give former workers peace of mind and makes them feel more kindly disposed toward a former employer. (See "Severance," below, for more about this issue.)

Federal and state laws often require employers to make continued coverage available to former employees, although it is generally at the employees' own cost.

Federal Law

A federal workplace law, called the Consolidated Omnibus Budget Reconciliation Act (COBRA), 29 U.S.C. § 1162, applies to companies with 20 or more employees that offer a group health care plan. Among other things, it requires companies to offer departing employees the option of continuing their health care coverage for up to 18 months, if they quit or are fired for any reason other than gross misconduct. Companies must also make this opportunity available to the employee's spouse and dependents.

Former employees are responsible for paying the full cost of continuing coverage under COBRA, including both the employee's and the company's share of the premiums. To learn more about COBRA, go to www.dol.gov/dol/topic/health-plans/cobra.htm.

State Laws

Most states have laws similar to COBRA that give former employees the right to continue group health insurance after they leave a job. Your company must comply with both state and federal law. In other words, you must follow whichever law is more generous to employees. State laws are generally more detailed and more generous to workers than COBRA. In addition, even small businesses (those with fewer than 20 employees) that escape COBRA may have to comply with state laws.

To learn more about your state's law, see "State Health Insurance Continuation Laws," at the end of this chapter.

Severance

Some employers assume they have to offer a severance package—some combination of money and continuing benefits—to fired employees. In most cases, however, a company is not legally required to pay employees severance. (A few states require some employers to pay a small amount of severance when they lay off a significant number of workers at one time.)

The law requires a company to provide severance to former employees only if it led them to believe they would receive it by:

- signing a written contract agreeing to pay severance
- promising employees severance pay in an employee handbook or personnel policy
- having a history of paying severance to other employees in the same position, or
- verbally promising severance to the employee.

Even if not required to by law, many employers routinely give severance packages to long-term employees, unless they were terminated for serious misconduct. Many employers do this to soften the blow of being fired or laid off and to buy a little insurance against lawsuits. A severance package may help sweeten the sour grapes workers feel about losing their jobs. And, a happier former employee is a less litigious former employee.

If your company decides to pay severance, the most important rule is to be consistent. The amount of severance can vary depending on how long the employee has worked for the company and on the employee's job category. But be sure to treat similarly situated employees equally. A company that is evenhanded and uniform in paying severance is less likely to face claims of discrimination (for example, that men received higher severance pay than women).

What to Include in a Severance Package

There are no hard-and-fast rules about what should be included in a severance package. The idea is to ease the burden on the soon-to-be-jobless employee. You might consider including any or all of the following benefits:

- **Pay.** Realistically, this is what is most important to employees. Many employers pay a set amount—a week or two of salary, for example— for every year of employment.
- **Insurance benefits.** Some employers offer to continue to pay for insurance coverage for a period of time after an employee leaves the company. Although COBRA requires most employers to allow their employees to continue their health insurance, it does not require employers to foot the bill. (For more about COBRA, see "Health Insurance," above.)

An employer may also want to continue other benefits, such as life or disability insurance.

- **Uncontested unemployment compensation.** Employees can apply for unemployment benefits if they were fired for reasons other than misconduct. After an employee applies for benefits, the employer has the opportunity to contest the employee's claim. By agreeing not to contest an employee's claim, a company makes it more likely that the employee will receive benefits. (For more information about how unemployment works, see "Unemployment Benefits," below.)

- **Outplacement services.** Outplacement programs help employees find new jobs. They may offer counseling on career goals and job skills, tips on résumé writing, leads for potential jobs, practice interview sessions, and help in negotiating with potential employers.

- **References.** You might agree to come up with a mutually agreeable letter of reference for an employee to use in job hunting. But proceed with caution here: Giving references carries with it some possible risks. (For more about this issue, see "References," above.)

- **Other benefits.** Certain benefits or items may be particularly important to a departing employee. If possible, have an honest discussion to find out what the worker would like in a severance package. You might want to consider allowing the employee to keep advances or money paid for moving expenses, giving the employee equipment such as a cell phone or computer, or releasing an employee from contractual obligations, like a covenant not to compete.

As you can see, severance means more than just money. If you think creatively and communicate with the employee, you should be able to come up with some valuable benefits that won't break the bank.

Releases

Firing or laying off a worker is never pleasant. But sometimes, it's actually risky. Perhaps the employee complains a lot or stirs up trouble in the workplace. Or maybe you've made some mistakes in your management of the employee and are concerned how a judge or jury might view your decisions.

Checklist: Collecting Company Property

Before a departing worker walks out the door for the last time, you'll need to disable the employee's passwords and security codes to the company's computers, telephone system, and workplace. You'll also need to get back any company property in the employee's possession; it's much easier to do this before the employee leaves rather than to try to track the employee (and the property) down later. Here are some of the things you may need to collect:

- ☐ company car
- ☐ keys and security cards that allow access to the workplace
- ☐ company credit card (you should also call the credit card issuer to cancel the account)
- ☐ computer password
- ☐ confidential files, client lists, manuals, and other company documents
- ☐ laptop computer, and
- ☐ cell phone.

Either way, if your company is worried about a lawsuit, you might want to ask the employee to sign a release: an agreement not to sue the company in exchange for receiving something of value. Some employers routinely ask employees to sign a release as a condition of receiving a severance package. After all, if they are voluntarily providing a benefit, they might as well get some security out of it. The downside to this approach, however, is that it may get an employee thinking about a lawsuit when that was the furthest thing from his or her mind. For that reason, other employers ask for releases only from employees who might have legitimate legal claims against the company or who seem especially motivated to sue.

The employee might even have legal claims unrelated to the firing that could cause trouble for your company. This often happens with wage and hour claims. For example, suppose you improperly classified an employee as exempt when he or she should have been a nonexempt employee who earns overtime. Even if you had more than enough reason to fire the employee, the employee can file an overtime claim worth several thousands of dollars. In this case, you might want to offer some severance in exchange for a release, even if the employee's behavior was egregious and clearly grounds for termination. An employee's on-the-job conduct generally doesn't matter when it comes to wage and hour violations.

Because some states have specific requirements about what language must go into a release, you should consult an attorney for help in crafting a legal agreement that will hold up in court. Here are some general considerations to keep in mind:

- **Give the employee something in exchange for the release.** You are asking the employee to waive the right to sue the company, and that right is worth something. A signed release will be worthless if you don't give the employee something in exchange for the promise not to sue. This means that if your company is already obligated to provide severance (for example, by a written employment contract), or your company is offering severance packages to employees who don't sign releases, it will have to give something extra on top of the severance (for example, more money or other benefits).

- **Be clear about the rights the employee is waiving.** The release might state that the employee is waiving the right to sue for any claims arising out of the employment relationship, including the termination of that relationship. Make sure the agreement is specific enough to prevent employees from later claiming that they didn't know what rights they were giving up.

- **Give the employee plenty of time to decide whether to sign.** It's reasonable for an employee to take a week or two to decide whether to give up the right to sue. You might even suggest that the employee consult with a lawyer to review the agreement.

- **Avoid any hint of coercion.** An employee must sign the release voluntarily or courts will not enforce it. Don't threaten or talk tough with employees to convince them to sign; a release that gets thrown out of court won't do your company any good.

- **Special rules apply to older workers.** If the employee is 40 years of age or older, a federal law—the Older Workers' Benefit Protection Act (OWBPA)—dictates what language must be included in a release. Among other things, these employees must have a longer period of time to review the release, be able to revoke the agreement (change their minds) for a limited time after they sign, and be advised in writing to consult with an attorney.

Unemployment Benefits

Not everyone who's out of work is entitled to unemployment benefits. A couple of factors dictate whether a former employee will receive unemployment: the circumstances of the employee's departure and whether the former employer decides to contest the employee's claim. This means your company has a lot of power over whether the worker will receive unemployment benefits.

Employee Eligibility

Employees are eligible for unemployment benefits only if they are out of work through no fault of their own. Whether an employee is "at fault" depends on whether the employee quit, was laid off, or was fired.

If an employee quits. An employee who quits or resigns from a job will be eligible for benefits only if he or she did so for "good cause." Good cause means that the reason for quitting was "compelling": that is, the worker would have suffered some sort of harm or injury by staying. Put another way, the reason must be of the sort that would have made any reasonable person leave.

A good reason for quitting a job isn't necessarily good cause. For example, leaving a job because it doesn't offer opportunities for career advancement might be a good reason, but it won't make a worker eligible for unemployment benefits. Similarly, regular job dissatisfaction does not amount to good cause.

In many states, the compelling reason must be job related. If an employee leaves the job because of intolerable working conditions (such as being sexually harassed) or because he or she was offered the opportunity to quit in lieu of being fired, most states would allow the worker to collect unemployment. Similarly, leaving a job because it poses a serious threat to the worker's health or safety is usually good cause. In some states, compelling personal reasons will also qualify as good cause (for example, quitting to relocate with a spouse or to care for an ill family member).

If an employee is laid off. An employee who loses a job through a layoff or reduction in workforce is eligible for benefits.

If an employee is fired. Fired employees can generally claim unemployment benefits if they were terminated because they lacked the necessary skills to do the job or because they were not a good fit. They can also receive benefits if the employer had a good reason to fire but the infractions were relatively minor, unintentional, or isolated.

In most states, however, an employee who is fired for misconduct will not be able to receive unemployment benefits. Although you might think that any action that leads to termination should constitute misconduct, the unemployment laws don't look at it that way. Not all actions that result in termination are serious enough to qualify as misconduct.

So, what qualifies as misconduct? Generally speaking, an employee engages in misconduct by willfully doing something that injures the company's interests. Revealing trade secrets or sexually harassing coworkers is misconduct; simple inefficiency or an unpleasant personality is not. Other common types of misconduct include extreme insubordination, chronic tardiness, numerous unexcused absences, intoxication on the job, and dishonesty.

Common actions that often result in firing —but do not constitute misconduct—are poor performance because of lack of skills, good-faith errors in judgment, off-duty conduct that does not have an impact on the employer's interests, and poor relations with coworkers.

It is important to remember that what qualifies as misconduct is a matter of interpretation and degree. Annoying one coworker might not be misconduct, but intentionally bothering an entire department even after repeated warnings might be.

Should Your Company Contest the Claim?

Your state's unemployment office—not your company—will ultimately decide whether the former employee can receive unemployment benefits. You do, however, have the option of contesting the employee's application— which gives your company a great deal of power. In California, for example, the unemployment board presumes that a terminated employee did not engage in misconduct unless the employer contests the claim. Thus, in California, terminated employees who claim unemployment benefits receive them unless the former employer intervenes.

Anatomy of an Unemployment Compensation Claim

Although the unemployment compensation system is different in each state, some general principles apply in most cases. An unemployment claim will typically proceed through the steps described below.

Step 1: Claim filing. The process starts when the former employee files a claim with the state unemployment office. Your company will receive written notice of the claim and an opportunity to file a written objection.

Step 2: Eligibility determination.
The state agency makes an initial determination of whether the former employee is eligible for unemployment benefits. Usually there's no hearing at this stage.

Step 3: Hearing. Your company or the former employee can appeal the initial eligibility decision, which results in a hearing before a referee: a hearing officer who is on the staff of the state agency. Normally conducted in a private room at the unemployment office, this is the most important step in the process. At the hearing, the company and the former employee will each have an opportunity to speak. In addition, you are entitled to have a lawyer there and to present witnesses and any relevant documents, such as employee evaluations or disciplinary warnings.

Step 4: Administrative appeal. Either your company or the former employee can appeal the referee's decision to an administrative agency, such as a board of review.

Step 5: Judicial appeal. Either side can appeal through the state court system, but this is rare.

Remember, there are no grounds to contest an unemployment claim if the employee was laid off. There are also typically no grounds to contest the claim for run-of-the-mill performance or conduct issues.

Even if an employee does engage in misconduct, your company might want to give up its right to contest an unemployment claim as part of a severance package. This is especially true if the fired employee seems likely to sue. (See "Severance," above, for more about severance packages and unemployment claims.)

Your company should contest a claim only if it has grounds to do so (because the employee engaged in misconduct or quit without a compelling reason). And even then, your company should also have a good, practical reason to contest it. Employers typically fight unemployment claims for one of two reasons:

- **Increase in unemployment insurance rates.** The employer—not the employee—pays for unemployment insurance. The amount the employer pays is often based in part on the number of claims made against the employer by former employees.
- **Anticipating a wrongful termination lawsuit.** The unemployment application process can be a valuable time to discover the employee's side of the story, and it can also provide an excellent opportunity for gathering evidence, both from the employee and from witnesses. (It's a good idea to get a lawyer involved at this stage.)

If your company plans to contest an unemployment claim, proceed with caution. These battles not only cost time and money, but they also ensure that the former employee will become an enemy. The employee might even file a wrongful termination lawsuit that otherwise could have been avoided. If the fired worker has friends who remain on the job, they too may doubt and distrust your company's tactics.

Before making any decisions, you might want to do some research by contacting your state's unemployment office for specific information about the law in your state. This office can tell you what effect a successful claim will have on your company's rates. If it's relatively small, backing off might be a good idea.

Legal Dos and Don'ts: Departing Workers

Do:

- **Fight fair.** As a practical matter, it makes sense to contest an unemployment claim only in limited circumstances, such as when you know the employee plans to file a lawsuit (your company can use the information you gather at the unemployment hearing to help build a defense). Otherwise, let it go: Pursuing a vendetta against a former employee will only take up time and money. It might even convince the employee to sue.

- **Negotiate creatively.** If you can offer a fired or laid-off worker something —anything—to ease the pain of losing a job, you will reduce the risk of a lawsuit. You don't have to break the bank to offer a meaningful severance package; the employee might want something that you hadn't considered, such as keeping a company laptop.

- **Show respect for departing employees.** Even if an employee leaves on bad terms, you shouldn't trash the employee to other workers or prospective employers. Bad-mouthing a former employee can lead to defamation lawsuits, and it will give remaining workers a sour taste of what they can expect should they ever leave the company.

Don't:

- **Ask every employee who leaves to sign a release.** There's a big downside to using releases: Some employees who otherwise wouldn't consider a lawsuit might start thinking about it when faced with a document that asks them to give up their legal rights. Reserve releases for employees who you suspect might sue or for situations in which your company's conduct has been questionable.

- **Play favorites.** You might be tempted to treat some departing workers better than others. However, treating workers differently can lead to resentment and discrimination claims. Make sure you have legitimate, business-related reasons for your actions.

- **Make life difficult for terminated employees.** If you treat former employees fairly, they are much less likely to sue your company. Remember this simple rule when deciding whether to contest an unemployment claim, give an angry reference, or deny a fired employee a simple benefit or two, such as paying for a couple of months of continued health insurance.

Test Your Knowledge

Questions

1. Your company can be sued for giving an honest but negative reference about a former employee, if the reference prevents the employee from getting another job. ☐ True ☐ False

2. The best reference policy is to say only positive things, even if a former employee was truly dreadful. ☐ True ☐ False

3. Managers should not go into detail when telling workers that an employee has been terminated. ☐ True ☐ False

4. Companies must continue to pay for health insurance for former employees for up to 18 months. ☐ True ☐ False

5. Employers are legally required to pay one week of severance for every year an employee has worked for the company. ☐ True ☐ False

6. A company might have to pay severance to a fired employee if it has always paid severance to employees who held that position in the past. ☐ True ☐ False

7. A company can refuse to pay an employee severance unless he or she signs a release agreeing not to sue the company. ☐ True ☐ False

8. A release is valid only if the employee has talked to a lawyer before signing it. ☐ True ☐ False

9. Employees who are fired cannot collect unemployment benefits. ☐ True ☐ False

10. Companies should always contest unemployment claims. ☐ True ☐ False

Test Your Knowledge (continued)

Answers

1. False. To sue for defamation, an employee must be able to prove that your statements were false. As long as you are honest, stick to facts, and aren't motivated by malice or ill will toward the employee, a defamation lawsuit will fail.

2. False. If you give a detailed reference (that is, you go beyond name, salary, and position) for an employee who was dangerous, violent, or otherwise posed a risk to others but you omit that information, the prospective employer (or its employees or customers) may have a legal claim against you if that employee goes on to cause harm. If you choose to be expansive, you must give the bad news as well as the good.

3. True. The safest course is simply to say that the employee has been terminated and explain who will be responsible for that employee's projects going forward.

4. False. Although most companies are required to allow departing employees to continue their health insurance benefits, the company is not required to foot the bill.

5. False. Except for the few states that require employers that conduct mass layoffs to pay a small amount of severance, employers are not legally required to pay severance unless they led employees to believe that they would receive it (for example, through a written contract or company policies).

6. True. If your company has always paid severance to employees who are fired from certain positions, an employee could argue that this is company policy, and that your failure to adhere to it constitutes a breach of contract or discrimination.

7. It depends on your company's severance policies. If employees at your company are already entitled to receive severance, you cannot require them to sign a release to get it. If, however, an employee is not entitled to receive severance, you can condition a severance package on the employee's agreement not to sue.

Test Your Knowledge (continued)

Answers

8. False. In some circumstances—for example, if your company is firing an older worker or your state's law requires it—you might have to advise workers of their right to talk to a lawyer before signing a release. However, if the worker decides not to heed this advice, the release will still be valid.

9. False. A worker who is fired for misconduct is probably not entitled to benefits, but a worker who is fired for poor performance or being a poor fit generally is.

10. False. In fact, there are very few situations when it makes sense to contest an unemployment claim. Fighting an employee's effort to collect unemployment will take time and money. It could also convince the employee to try to get money out of your company through a lawsuit.

State Laws

State Health Insurance Continuation Laws

Alabama

Ala. Code § 27-55-3(a)(4)

Special Situations: 18 months for subjects of domestic abuse who have lost coverage they had under abuser's insurance and who do not qualify for COBRA.

Arizona

Ariz. Rev. Stat. §§ 20-1377, 20-1408

Employers affected: All employers that offer group disability insurance.

Length of coverage for dependents: Insurer must either continue coverage for dependents or convert to individual policy upon death of covered employee or divorce. Coverage must be the same unless the insured chooses a lesser plan.

Qualifying event: Death of an employee; change in marital status; any other reason stated in policy (other than failure to pay premium).

Time employer has to notify employee: No provisions for employer. Insurance policy must include notice of conversion privilege. Clerk of court must provide notice to anyone filing for divorce that dependent spouse entitled to convert health insurance coverage.

Time employee has to apply: 31 days after termination of existing coverage.

Arkansas

Ark. Code Ann. §§ 23-86-114 to 23-86-116

Employers affected: All employers that offer group health insurance.

Eligible employees: Employees continuously insured for previous 3 months.

Length of coverage for employee: 120 days.

Length of coverage for dependents: 120 days.

Qualifying event: Termination of employment; change in insured's marital status. Employer may—but is not required to—continue benefits on death of employee.

Time employee has to apply: 10 days.

California

Cal. Health & Safety Code §§ 1373.6, 1373.621; Cal. Ins. Code §§ 10128.50 to 10128.59

Employers affected: Employers that offer group health insurance and have 2 to 19 employees.

Eligible employees: All covered employees are eligible.

Length of coverage for employee: 36 months.

Length of coverage for dependents: 36 months.

Qualifying event: Termination of employment; reduction in hours; death of employee; change in marital status; loss of dependent status; covered employee's eligibility for Medicare (for dependents only).

Time employer has to notify employee: 15 days.

Time employee has to apply: 60 days.

Special situations: Employee who is at least 60 years old and has worked for employer for previous 5 years may continue benefits for self and spouse beyond COBRA or Cal-COBRA limits (also applies to COBRA employers). Employee who began receiving COBRA coverage on or after 1/1/03 and whose COBRA coverage is for less than 36 months may use Cal-COBRA to bring total coverage up to 36 months.

Colorado

Colo. Rev. Stat. § 10-16-108

Employers affected: All employers that offer group health insurance.

Eligible employees: Employees continuously insured for previous 6 months.

Length of coverage for employee: 18 months.

State Health Insurance Continuation Laws, continued

Length of coverage for dependents: 18 months.

Qualifying event: Termination of employment; reduction in hours; death of employee; change in marital status.

Time employer has to notify employee: 60 days.

Time employee has to apply: 30 days after termination; 60 days if employer fails to give notice.

Connecticut

Conn. Gen. Stat. Ann. §§ 38a-512a, 31-51n, 31-51o

Employers affected: All employers that offer group health insurance.

Eligible employees: All covered employees are eligible.

Length of coverage for employee: 30 months, or until eligible for Medicare benefits.

Length of coverage for dependents: 30 months, or until eligible for Medicare benefits; 36 months in case of employee's death, divorce, or loss of dependent status.

Qualifying event: Layoff; reduction in hours; termination of employment; death of employee; change in marital status; loss of dependent status.

Special situations: When facility closes or relocates, employers with 100 or more employees must pay for insurance for employee and dependents for 120 days or until employee is eligible for other group coverage, whichever comes first. (Does not affect employee's right to conventional continuation coverage, which begins when 120-day period ends.)

Delaware

18 Del. Code Ann. § 3571F

Employers affected: Employers that offer group health insurance and have 1 to 19 employees.

Eligible employees: Employees continuously insured for previous three months.

Length of coverage for employee: 9 months.

Length of coverage for dependents: 9 months.

Qualifying event: Employee's death; termination of employment; divorce or legal separation; employee's eligibility for Medicare; loss of dependent status.

Time employer has to notify employee: Within 30 days of the qualifying event.

Time employee has to apply: 30 days.

District of Columbia

D.C. Code Ann. §§ 32-731 to 32-732

Employers affected: Employers with fewer than 20 employees.

Eligible employees: All covered employees are eligible.

Length of coverage for employee: Three months **Length of coverage for dependents:** Three months

Qualifying event: Any reason employee or dependent becomes ineligible for coverage, except employee's termination for gross misconduct.

Time employer has to notify employee: Within 15 days of termination of coverage.

Time employee has to apply: 45 days after termination of coverage.

Florida

Fla. Stat. Ann. § 627.6692

Employers affected: Employers with fewer than 20 employees.

Eligible employees: Full-time (25 or more hours per week) employees covered by employer's health insurance plan.

Length of coverage for employee: 18 months.

State Health Insurance Continuation Laws, continued

Length of coverage for dependents: 18 months.

Qualifying event: Layoff; reduction in hours; termination of employment; death of employee; change in marital status.

Time employer has to notify employee: Carrier notifies within 14 days of learning of qualifying event (beneficiary has 63 days to notify carrier of qualifying event).

Time employee has to apply: 30 days from receipt of carrier's notice.

Georgia
Ga. Code Ann. §§ 33-24-21.1 to 33-24-21.2

Employers affected: All employers that offer group health insurance.

Eligible employees: Employees continuously insured for previous 6 months.

Length of coverage for employee: 3 months plus any part of the month remaining at termination.

Length of coverage for dependents: 3 months plus any part of the month remaining at termination.

Qualifying event: Termination of employment (except for cause).

Special situations: Employee, spouse, or former spouse, who is 60 years old and who has been covered for previous 6 months may continue coverage until eligible for Medicare. (Applies to companies with more than 20 employees; does not apply when employee quits for reasons other than health.)

Hawaii
Haw. Rev. Stat. §§ 393-11, 393-15

Employers affected: All employers required to offer health insurance (those paying a regular employee a monthly wage at least 86.67 times state hourly minimum—about $542).

Length of coverage for employee: If employee is hospitalized or prevented from working by sickness, employer must pay insurance premiums for 3 months or for as long employer continues to pay wages, whichever is longer.

Qualifying event: Employee is hospitalized or prevented by sickness from working.

Idaho
Idaho Code § 41-2213

Employers affected: All employers that offer group disability insurance

Eligible employees: Employees or dependents who are totally disabled at the time the policy ends. (Applies to policies that provide benefits for loss of time during periods of hospitalization, benefits for hospital or medical expenses, or benefits for dismemberment.)

Length of coverage for employee: Must provide a reasonable extension of coverage (in the case of medical and hospital expenses, a reasonable extension is at least 12 months).

Length of coverage for dependents: Must provide a reasonable extension of coverage (in the case of medical and hospital expenses, a reasonable extension is at least 12 months).

Illinois
215 Ill. Comp. Stat. §§ 5/367e, 5/367.2, 5/367.2-5

Employers affected: All employers that offer group health insurance.

Eligible employees: Employees continuously insured for previous 3 months.

Length of coverage for employee: 12 months.

Length of coverage for dependents: Upon death or divorce, 2 years' coverage for spouse under 55 and eligible dependents who were on employee's plan; until eligible for Medicare or other group coverage for spouse over 55 and

State Health Insurance Continuation Laws, continued

eligible dependents who were on employee's plan. A dependent child who has reached plan age limit or who was not already covered by plan, is also entitled to 2 years' continuation coverage.

Qualifying event: Termination of employment; reduction in hours; death of employee; divorce.

Time employer has to notify employee: 10 days.

Time employee has to apply: 30 days after termination or reduction in hours or receiving notice from employer, whichever is later, but not more than 60 days from termination or reduction in hours.

Iowa

Iowa Code §§ 509B.3, 509B.5

Employers affected: All employers that offer group health insurance.

Eligible employees: Employees continuously insured for previous 3 months.

Length of coverage for employee: Nine months.

Length of coverage for dependents: Nine months.

Qualifying event: Any reason employee or dependent becomes ineligible for coverage.

Time employer has to notify employee: 10 days after termination of coverage.

Time employee has to apply: 10 days after termination of coverage or receiving notice from employer, whichever is later, but not more than 31 days from termination of coverage.

Kansas

Kan. Stat. Ann. § 40-2209(i)

Employers affected: All employers that offer group health insurance.

Eligible employees: Employees continuously insured for previous 3 months.

Length of coverage for employee: 18 months.

Length of coverage for dependents: 18 months.

Qualifying event: Any reason employee or dependent becomes ineligible for coverage.

Time employer has to notify employee: Reasonable notice.

Kentucky

Ky. Rev. Stat. Ann. § 304.18-110

Employers affected: All employers that offer group health insurance.

Eligible employees: Employees continuously insured for previous 3 months.

Length of coverage for employee: 18 months.

Length of coverage for dependents: 18 months.

Qualifying event: Any reason employee or dependent becomes ineligible for coverage.

Time employer has to notify employee: Employer must notify insurer as soon as employee's coverage ends; insurer then notifies employee.

Time employee has to apply: 31 days from receipt of insurer's notice, but not more than 90 days after termination of group coverage.

Louisiana

La. Rev. Stat. Ann. §§ 22:1045, 22:1046

Employers affected: All employers that offer group health insurance and have fewer than 20 employees.

Eligible employees: Employees continuously insured for previous 3 months.

Length of coverage for employee: 12 months.

Length of coverage for dependents: 12 months.

Qualifying event: Termination of employment; death of insured; divorce.

Time employee has to apply: By the end of the month following the month in which the qualifying event occurred.

State Health Insurance Continuation Laws, continued

Special situations: Surviving spouse who is 50 or older may have coverage until remarriage or eligibility for Medicare or other insurance.

Maine

Me. Rev. Stat. Ann. tit. 24-A, § 2809-A

Employers affected: All employers that offer group health insurance and are not subject to COBRA.

Eligible employees: Employees employed for at least 6 months.

Length of coverage for employee: One year.

Length of coverage for dependents: One year.

Qualifying event: Temporary layoff; permanent layoff if employee is eligible for federal premium assistance for laid-off employees who continue coverage; loss of employment because of a work-related injury or disease.

Time employee has to apply: 31 days from termination of coverage.

Maryland

Md. Code Ann., [Ins.] §§ 15-407 to 15-409

Employers affected: All employers that offer group health insurance.

Eligible employees: Employees continuously insured for previous 3 months.

Length of coverage for employee: 18 months.

Length of coverage for dependents: 18 months upon death of employee; upon change in marital status, 18 months or until spouse remarries or becomes eligible for other coverage.

Qualifying event: Termination of employment; death of employee; change in marital status.

Time employer has to notify employee: Must notify insurer within 14 days of receiving employee's continuation request.

Time employee has to apply: 45 days from termination of coverage. Employee begins application process by requesting an election of continuation notification form from employer.

Massachusetts

Mass. Gen. Laws ch. 175, §§ 110G, 110I; ch. 176J, § 9

Employers affected: All employers that offer group health insurance and have fewer than 20 employees.

Eligible employees: All covered employees are eligible.

Length of coverage for employee: 18 months; 29 months if disabled.

Length of coverage for dependents: 18 months upon termination or reduction in hours; 29 months if disabled; 36 months upon divorce, death of employee, employee's eligibility for Medicare, or employer's bankruptcy.

Qualifying event: Involuntary layoff; death of insured employee; change in marital status.

Time employer has to notify employee: Carrier must notify beneficiary within 14 days of learning of qualifying event.

Time employee has to apply: 60 days.

Special situations: Termination due to plant closing: 90 days' coverage for employee and dependents, at the same payment terms as before closing.

Minnesota

Minn. Stat. Ann. §§ 62A.17; 62A.20; 62A.21

Employers affected: All employers that offer group health insurance and have 2 or more employees.

Eligible employees: All covered employees are eligible.

State Health Insurance Continuation Laws, continued

Length of coverage for employee: 18 months; indefinitely if employee becomes totally disabled while employed.

Length of coverage for dependents: 18 months for current spouse or child after termination of employment; divorced or widowed spouse can continue until eligible for Medicare or other group health insurance. Upon divorce or death of employee, dependent children can continue until they no longer qualify as dependents under plan.

Qualifying event: Termination of employment; reduction in hours.

Time employer has to notify employee: Within 14 days of termination of coverage.

Time employee has to apply: 60 days from termination of coverage or receipt of employer's notice, whichever is later.

Mississippi

Miss. Code Ann. § 83-9-51

Employers affected: All employers that offer group health insurance and have fewer than 20 employees.

Eligible employees: Employees continuously insured for previous 3 months.

Length of coverage for employee: 12 months.

Length of coverage for dependents: 12 months.

Qualifying event: Termination of employment; divorce; employee's death; employee's eligibility for Medicare; loss of dependent status.

Time employer has to notify employee: Insurer must notify former or deceased employee's dependent child or divorced spouse of option to continue insurance within 14 days of their becoming ineligible for coverage on employee's policy.

Time employee has to apply: Employee must apply and submit payment before group coverage ends; dependents or former spouse must elect continuation coverage within 30 days of receiving insurer's notice.

Missouri

Mo. Rev. Stat. § 376.428

Employers affected: All employers that offer group health insurance and are not subject to COBRA.

Eligible employees: All employees.

Length of coverage for employee: 18 months.

Length of coverage for dependents: 18 months if eligible due to termination or reduction in hours; 36 months if eligible due to death or divorce.

Qualifying event: Termination of employment; death of employee; divorce; reduction in hours; employee's eligibility for Medicare; loss of dependent status.

Time employer has to notify employee: Same rules as COBRA.

Time employee has to apply: Same rules as COBRA.

Montana

Mont. Code Ann. §§ 33-22-506 to 33-22-507

Employers affected: All employers that offer group disability insurance.

Eligible employees: All employees.

Length of coverage for employee: One year (with employer's consent).

Qualifying event: Reduction in hours.

Special situations: Insurer may not discontinue benefits to child with a disability after child exceeds age limit for dependent status.

State Health Insurance Continuation Laws, continued

Nebraska

Neb. Rev. Stat. §§ 44-1640 and following, 44-7406

Employers affected: Employers not subject to federal COBRA laws.

Eligible employees: All covered employees.

Length of coverage for employee: Six months.

Length of coverage for dependents: One year upon death of insured employee. Subjects of domestic abuse who have lost coverage under abuser's plan and who do not qualify for COBRA may have 18 months' coverage (applies to all employers).

Qualifying event: Involuntary termination of employment (layoff due to labor dispute not considered involuntary).

Time employer has to notify employee: Within 10 days of termination of employment must send notice by certified mail.

Time employee has to apply: 10 days from receipt of employer's notice.

Nevada

Nev. Rev. Stat. Ann. § 689B.0345

Employers affected: All employers that offer group health insurance.

Eligible employees: Employees who are on unpaid leave due to total disability.

Length of coverage for employee: Coverage must continue for 12 months, unless one of the following events occurs sooner: the employee is terminated, the employee obtains another health insurance policy, or the group health insurance policy is terminated.

Length of coverage for dependents: Coverage must continue for 12 months, unless one of the following events occurs sooner: the employee is terminated, the employee obtains another health insurance policy, or the group health insurance policy is terminated.

New Hampshire

N.H. Rev. Stat. Ann. § 415:18

Employers affected: All employers that offer group health insurance.

Eligible employees: All insured employees are eligible.

Length of coverage for employee: 18 months; 29 months if disabled at termination or during first 60 days of continuation coverage.

Length of coverage for dependents: 18 months; 29 months if disabled at termination or during first 60 days of continuation coverage; 36 months upon death of employee, divorce or legal separation, loss of dependent status, or employee's eligibility for Medicare.

Qualifying event: Any reason employee or dependent becomes ineligible for coverage.

Time employer has to notify employee: Carrier must notify beneficiary within 30 days of receiving notice of loss of coverage.

Time employee has to apply: Within 45 days of receipt of notice

Special situations: Layoff or termination due to strike: 6 months' coverage with option to extend for an additional 12 months. Surviving, divorced, or legally separated spouse who is 55 or older may continue benefits available until eligible for Medicare or another employer-based group insurance.

New Jersey

N.J. Stat. Ann. §§ 17B:27-51.12, 17B:27A-27

Employers affected: Employers with 2 to 50 employees.

Eligible employees: Employed full time (25 or more hours).

State Health Insurance Continuation Laws, continued

Length of coverage for employee: 18 months; 29 months if disabled at termination or during first 60 days of continuation coverage.

Length of coverage for dependents: 18 months; 36 months upon death of employee, divorce or legal separation, loss of dependent status, or employee's eligibility for Medicare.

Qualifying event: Termination of employment; reduction in hours; change in marital status; death.

Time employer has to notify employee: At time of qualifying event.

Time employee has to apply: Within 30 days of qualifying event.

Special benefits: Coverage must be identical to that offered to current employees.

Special situations: Total disability: Employee who has been insured for previous 3 months and employee's dependents entitled to continuation coverage that includes all benefits offered by group policy (applies to all employers).

New Mexico

N.M. Stat. Ann. § 59A-18-16

Employers affected: All employers that offer group health insurance.

Eligible employees: All insured employees are eligible.

Length of coverage for employee: Six months.

Length of coverage for dependents: Six months for termination of employment. May continue group coverage or convert to individual policies upon death of covered employee or divorce or legal separation.

Qualifying event: Termination of employment.

Time employer has to notify employee: Insurer or employer must give written notice at time of termination.

Time employee has to apply: 30 days after receiving notice.

New York

N.Y. Ins. Law § 3221(m)

Employers affected: All employers that offer group health insurance.

Eligible employees: All covered employees are eligible.

Length of coverage for employee: 36 months.

Length of coverage for dependents: 36 months.

Qualifying event: Termination of employment; death of employee; divorce or legal separation; loss of dependent status; employee's eligibility for Medicare.

Time employee has to apply: 60 days after termination or receipt of notice, whichever is later.

North Carolina

N.C. Gen. Stat. §§ 58-53-5 to 58-53-40

Employers affected: All employers that offer group health insurance.

Eligible employees: Employees continuously insured for previous 3 months.

Length of coverage for employee: 18 months.

Length of coverage for dependents: 18 months.

Qualifying event: Termination of employment.

Time employer has to notify employee: Employer has option of notifying employee as part of the exit process.

Time employee has to apply: 60 days.

North Dakota

N.D. Cent. Code §§ 26.1-36-23, 26.1-36-23.1

Employers affected: All employers that offer group health insurance.

Eligible employees: Employees continuously insured for previous 3 months.

State Health Insurance Continuation Laws, continued

Length of coverage for employee: 39 weeks.

Length of coverage for dependents: 39 weeks; 36 months if required by divorce or annulment decree.

Qualifying event: Termination of employment; change in marital status, if divorce or annulment decree requires employee to continue coverage.

Time employee has to apply: Within 10 days of termination or of receiving notice of continuation rights, whichever is later, but not more than 31 days from termination.

Ohio
Ohio Rev. Code Ann. §§ 3923.38, 1751.53

Employers affected: All employers that offer group health insurance.

Eligible employees: Employees continuously insured for previous 3 months who were involuntarily terminated for reasons other than gross misconduct on the part of the employee.

Length of coverage for employee: 12 months.

Length of coverage for dependents: 12 months.

Qualifying event: Involuntary termination of employment.

Time employer has to notify employee: At termination of employment.

Time employee has to apply: Whichever is earlier: 31 days after coverage terminates; 10 days after coverage terminates if employer notified employee of continuation rights prior to termination; 10 days after employer notified employee of continuation rights, if notice was given after coverage terminated.

Oklahoma
Okla. Stat. Ann. tit. 36, § 4509

Employers affected: All employers that offer group health insurance.

Eligible employees: Employees insured for at least 6 months; (all other employees and their dependents entitled to 30 days' continuation coverage).

Length of coverage for employee: 63 days for basic coverage; 6 months for major medical at the same premium rate prior to termination of coverage (only for losses or conditions that began while group policy in effect).

Length of coverage for dependents: 63 days for basic coverage; 6 months for major medical at the same premium rate prior to termination of coverage (only for losses or conditions that began while group policy in effect).

Qualifying event: Any reason coverage terminates (except employment termination for gross misconduct).

Time employer has to notify employee: Carrier must notify employee in writing within 30 days of receiving notice of termination of employee's coverage.

Time employee has to apply: 31 days after receipt of notice.

Special benefits: Includes maternity care for pregnancy begun while group policy was in effect.

Oregon
Ore. Rev. Stat. §§ 743B.343 to 743B.347

Employers affected: Employers not subject to federal COBRA laws.

Eligible employees: Employees continuously insured for previous 3 months.

Length of coverage for employee: 9 months.

Length of coverage for dependents: 9 months.

Qualifying event: Termination of employment; reduction in hours; employee's eligibility for Medicare; loss of dependent status; termination

State Health Insurance Continuation Laws, continued

of membership in group covered by policy; death of employee.

Time employer has to notify employee: 10 days after qualifying event.

Time employee has to apply: Within the time limit determined by the insurer, which must be at least 10 days after the qualifying event or employee's receipt of notice, whichever is later.

Special situations: Surviving, divorced, or legally separated spouse who is 55 or older and dependent children entitled to continuation coverage until spouse remarries or is eligible for other coverage; must include dental, vision, or prescription drug benefits, if they were offered in original plan (applies to employers with 20 or more employees).

Pennsylvania

Pa. Stat. 40 P.S. § 764j

Employers affected: Employers that offer group health insurance and have 2 to 19 employees.

Eligible employees: Employees continuously insured for at least 3 months.

Length of coverage for employee: 9 months.

Length of coverage for dependents: 9 months.

Qualifying event: Termination of employment; reduction in hours; death of employee; change in marital status; employer's bankruptcy.

Time employer has to notify employee: 30 days after qualifying event.

Time employee has to apply: 30 days after receiving notice.

Rhode Island

R.I. Gen. Laws §§ 27-19.1-1, 27-20.4-1 to 27-20-4-2

Employers affected: All employers that offer group health insurance.

Eligible employees: All insured employees are eligible.

Length of coverage for employee: 18 months (but not longer than continuous employment); cannot be required to pay more than one month premium at a time.

Length of coverage for dependents: 18 months (but not longer than continuous employment); cannot be required to pay more than one month premium at a time.

Qualifying event: Involuntary termination of employment; death of employee; change in marital status; permanent reduction in workforce; employer's going out of business.

Time employer has to notify employee: Employers must post a conspicuous notice of employee continuation rights.

Time employee has to apply: 30 days from termination of coverage.

Special situations: If right to receiving continuing health insurance is stated in the divorce judgment, divorced spouse has right to continue coverage as long as employee remains covered or until divorced spouse remarries or becomes eligible for other group insurance.

South Carolina

S.C. Code Ann. § 38-71-770

Employers affected: All employers that offer group health insurance.

Eligible employees: Employees continuously insured for previous 6 months.

Length of coverage for employee: 6 months (in addition to part of month remaining at termination).

Length of coverage for dependents: 6 months (in addition to part of month remaining at termination).

Qualifying event: Any reason employee or dependent becomes ineligible for coverage.

State Health Insurance Continuation Laws, continued

Time employer has to notify employee: At time of termination, employer must clearly and meaningfully advise employee of continuation rights.

South Dakota

S.D. Codified Laws Ann. §§ 58-18-7.5, 58-18-7.12; 58-18C-1

Employers affected: All employers that offer group health insurance.

Eligible employees: All covered employees.

Length of coverage for employee: 18 months; 29 months if disabled at termination or during first 60 days of continuation coverage.

Length of coverage for dependents: 18 months; 29 months if disabled at termination or during first 60 days of continuation coverage; 36 months upon death of employee, divorce or legal separation, loss of dependent status, employee's eligibility for Medicare.

Qualifying event: Termination of employment; death of employee; divorce or legal separation; loss of dependent status; employee's eligibility for Medicare.

Special situations: When employer goes out of business: 12 months' continuation coverage available to all employees. Employer must notify employees within 10 days of termination of benefits; employees must apply within 60 days of receipt of employer's notice or within 90 days of termination of benefits if no notice given.

Tennessee

Tenn. Code Ann. § 56-7-2312

Employers affected: All employers that offer group health insurance.

Eligible employees: Employees continuously insured for previous 3 months.

Length of coverage for employee: Three months (in addition to part of month remaining at termination).

Length of coverage for dependents: 3 months (in addition to part of month remaining at termination); 15 months upon death of employee or divorce (in addition to part of month remaining at termination).

Qualifying event: Termination of employment; death of employee; change in marital status.

Special situations: Employee or dependent who is pregnant at time of termination entitled to continuation benefits for 6 months following the end of pregnancy.

Texas

Tex. Ins. Code Ann. §§ 1251.252 to 1251.255; 1251.301 to 1251.310

Employers affected: All employers that offer group health insurance.

Eligible employees: Employees continuously insured for previous 3 months.

Length of coverage for employee: Nine months; for employees eligible for COBRA, 6 months after COBRA coverage ends.

Length of coverage for dependents: 9 months; for employees eligible for COBRA, 6 months after COBRA coverage ends. Three years for dependents with coverage due to the death or retirement of employee or severance of the family relationship.

Qualifying event: Termination of employment (except for cause); employee leaves for health reasons; severance of family relationship; retirement or death of employee.

Time employee has to apply: 60 days from termination of coverage or receiving notice of continuation rights from employer or insurer,

State Health Insurance Continuation Laws, continued

whichever is later. Must give notice within 15 days of severance of family relationship. Within 60 days of death or retirement of family member or severance of family relationship, dependent must give notice of intent to continue coverage.

Utah

Utah Code Ann. § 31A-22-722

Employers affected: All employers that offer group health insurance.

Eligible employees: Employees continuously insured for previous 3 months.

Length of coverage for employee: 12 months.

Length of coverage for dependents: 12 months.

Qualifying event: Termination of employment; retirement; death; divorce; reduction in hours; sabbatical; disability; loss of dependent status.

Time employer has to notify employee: In writing within 30 days of termination of coverage.

Time employee has to apply: Within 60 days of qualifying event.

Vermont

Vt. Stat. Ann. tit. 8, §§ 4090a to 4090c

Employers affected: All employers that offer group health insurance.

Eligible employees: All covered employees are eligible.

Length of coverage for employee: 18 months.

Length of coverage for dependents: 18 months.

Qualifying event: Termination of employment; reduction in hours; death of employee; change of marital status; loss of dependent status.

Time employer has to notify employee: Within 30 days of qualifying event.

Time employee has to apply: Within 60 days of receiving notice following the occurrence of a qualifying event.

Virginia

Va. Code Ann. §§ 38.2-3541 to 38.2-3452

Employers affected: All employers that offer group health insurance.

Eligible employees: Employees continuously insured for previous 3 months.

Length of coverage for employee: 12 months.

Length of coverage for dependents: 12 months.

Qualifying event: Any reason employee or dependent becomes ineligible for coverage.

Time employer has to notify employee: 14 days from termination of coverage.

Time employee has to apply: Within 31 days of receiving notice of eligibility, but no more than 60 days following termination.

Special situations: Employee may convert to an individual policy instead of applying for continuation coverage (must apply within 31 days of termination of coverage).

Washington

Wash. Rev. Code Ann. § 48.21.075

Employers affected: All employers that offer disability insurance.

Eligible employees: Insured employees on strike.

Length of coverage for employee: Six months if employee goes on strike.

Length of coverage for dependents: Six months if employee goes on strike.

Qualifying event: If employee goes on strike.

Special situations: All employers have option of offering continued group health benefits.

State Health Insurance Continuation Laws, continued

West Virginia

W.Va. Code §§ 33-16-2, 33-16-3(e); W. Va. Code St. R. 114-93-3

Employers affected: Employers providing insurance for between 2 and 20 employees.

Eligible employees: All employees are eligible.

Length of coverage for employee: 18 months in case of involuntary layoff.

Qualifying event: Involuntary layoff.

Time employer has to notify employee: Carrier must notify beneficiaries within 15 days of receiving notice from beneficiary of intent to apply.

Time employee has to apply: 20 days to send notice of intention to apply; 30 days to apply after receiving election and premium notice.

Wisconsin

Wis. Stat. Ann. § 632.897

Employers affected: All employers that offer group health insurance.

Eligible employees: Employees continuously insured for previous 3 months.

Length of coverage for employee: 18 months (or longer at insurer's option).

Length of coverage for dependents: 18 months (or longer at insurer's option).

Qualifying event: Any reason employee or dependent becomes ineligible for coverage (except employment termination due to misconduct).

Time employer has to notify employee: 5 days from termination of coverage.

Time employee has to apply: 30 days after receiving employer's notice.

Wyoming

Wyo. Stat. § 26-19-113

Employers affected: Employers not subject to federal COBRA laws.

Eligible employees: Employees continuously insured for previous 3 months.

Length of coverage for employee: 12 months.

Length of coverage for dependents: 12 months.

Time employee has to apply: 31 days from termination of coverage.

State Laws on Meal and Rest Breaks

Note: In many states, employees who qualify as professional, executive, or administrative workers are exempt from these meal and rest break requirements. Also, some states are not listed in this chart because they do not have general meal or rest break laws for employees in the private sector. However, some states have special break rules for specific occupations or industries, which are beyond the scope of this chart. For more information, contact your state labor department. (See the appendix for details.)

Alabama

Breast-feeding: No employment-specific laws. However, breast-feeding is allowed in any public or private location where the mother's presence is authorized.

Arkansas

Ark. Stat. Ann. § 11-5-116

Applies to: All employers.

Breast-feeding: Reasonable unpaid breaks to express breast milk; if possible, break time to run concurrently with other breaks.

California

Cal. Lab. Code §§ 512, 1030; Cal. Code Regs. tit. 8, §§ 11010–11170

Applies to: Employers in most industries.

Exceptions: Motion picture and other occupations. See wage orders, *Cal. Code Regs. tit. 8, §§ 11010 – 11160*, for additional exceptions.

Meal Break: 30 minutes, unpaid, after 5 hours, except employer and employee can agree to waive meal period if employee works 6 hours or less. Second 30-minute unpaid meal period when employee works more than 10 hours a day, except employer and employee can agree to waive the second meal period if the employee

works 12 hours or less and took the first meal period. On-duty paid meal period permitted when nature of work prevents relief from all duties and parties agree in writing.

Rest Break: Paid 10-minute rest period for each 4 hours worked or major fraction thereof; as practicable, in the middle of the work period; not required for employees whose total daily work time is less than 3½ hours.

Breast-feeding: Reasonable unpaid breaks to express breast milk; if possible, break time to run concurrently with other breaks.

Colorado

Colo. Code Regs. tit. 7 § 1103-1:7 and 1:8

Applies to: Retail and service, food and beverage, commercial support service, and health and medical industries.

Exceptions: Numerous exceptions are listed in the regulation.

Meal Break: 30 minutes, unpaid, after 5 hours of work; on-duty paid meal period permitted when nature of work prevents break from all duties.

Rest Break: Paid 10-minute rest period for each 4 hours or major fraction worked; if practical, in the middle of the work period.

Breast-feeding: Reasonable unpaid time to express breast milk for up to two years after child's birth.

Connecticut

Conn. Gen. Stat. Ann. §§ 31-51ii, 31-40w

Applies to: All employers, except as noted.

Exceptions: Employers who pay for rest breaks as described below, those with a written agreement providing other break rules, and those granted an exemption for reasons listed in statute.

State Laws on Meal and Rest Breaks, continued

Meal Break: 30 minutes, unpaid, after first 2 hours of work and before last 2 hours for employees who work 7½ or more consecutive hours.

Rest Break: As alternative to meal break, a total of 30 minutes paid in each 7½-hour work period.

Breast-feeding: Employee may use meal or rest breaks for breast-feeding or expressing breast milk.

Delaware

Del. Code Ann. tit. 19, § 707

Applies to: All employers, except as noted.

Exceptions: Employers with alternative written agreement and those granted exemptions specified in statute. Law does not apply to teachers.

Meal Break: 30 minutes, unpaid, after first 2 hours and before the last 2 hours, for employees who work 7½ consecutive hours or more.

Breast-feeding: Reasonable accommodations for limitations of a person related to pregnancy, childbirth, or a related condition may include break time and appropriate facilities for expressing breast milk.

District of Columbia

D.C. Code Ann. §§ 2-1402.82, 32–1231.01-32–1231.03

Applies to: All employers

Breast-feeding: Reasonable unpaid time to express breast milk; runs concurrently with other paid or unpaid breaks provided by employer. Employer must make reasonable efforts to provide a private, sanitary location (other than a toilet stall) for expressing breast milk. Employer must provide reasonable accommodations to nursing mothers, unless it would cause an undue hardship.

Florida

Breast-feeding: No employment-specific laws. However, breast-feeding is allowed in any public or private location where the mother's presence is authorized.

Georgia

Ga. Code Ann. § 34-1-6

Applies to: All employers.

Breast-feeding: At employer's discretion, reasonable unpaid break time to express breast milk. Breast-feeding is allowed in any public or private location where the mother's presence is authorized.

Hawaii

Haw. Rev. Stat. §§ 378-2, 378-91 to 93

Applies to: All employers.

Breast-feeding: Reasonable unpaid break time to express breast milk for one year after child's birth.

Illinois

820 Ill. Comp. Stat. §§ 140/3, 260/10

Applies to: All employers.

Exceptions: Employees whose meal periods are established by collective bargaining agreement.

Employees who monitor individuals with developmental disabilities or mental illness, or both, and who are required to be on call during an entire 8-hour work period; these employees must be allowed to eat a meal while working.

Meal Break: 20 minutes, no later than 5 hours after the beginning of the shift, for employees who work 7½ or more continuous hours. Hotel room attendants are entitled to a 30-minute meal break if they work at least 7 hours.

Rest Break: In addition to meal break, hotel room attendants must receive two paid 15-minute rest breaks, if they work at least 7 hours.

Breast-feeding: Reasonable unpaid break time to express breast milk.

State Laws on Meal and Rest Breaks, continued

Indiana

Ind. Code § 22-2-14

Applies to: Employers with 25 or more employees.

Breast-feeding: Employer must make reasonable efforts to provide a private space, other than a restroom, for an employee to express breast milk during nonworking hours.

Kansas

Kan. Admin. Reg. 49-30-3

Applies to: Employees not covered under FLSA.

Meal Break: Not required, but if less than 30 minutes is given, break must be paid.

Breast-feeding: No employment-specific laws. However, breast-feeding is allowed in any public or private location where the mother's presence is authorized.

Kentucky

Ky. Rev. Stat. Ann. §§ 337.355, 337.365; 803 KAR 1:065

Applies to: All employers, except as noted.

Exceptions: Written agreement providing different meal period; employers subject to Federal Railway Labor Act.

Meal Break: Reasonable off-duty period close to the middle of the shift; cannot be required to take it before the third or after the fifth hour of work. Coffee breaks and snack time do not count toward the meal break.

Rest Break: Paid 10-minute rest period for each 4-hour work period; rest period must be in addition to regularly scheduled meal period.

Breast-feeding: No employment-specific laws. However, breast-feeding is allowed in any public or private location where the mother's presence is authorized.

Maine

Me. Rev. Stat. Ann. tit. 26, § 601

Applies to: All employers, except those with fewer than 3 employees on duty who are able to take frequent breaks during the workday.

Exceptions: Collective bargaining or other written agreement between employer and employee may provide for different breaks.

Meal Break: 30 minutes after 6 consecutive hours of work, except in cases of emergency. Time may be unpaid if employee is completely relieved of duty.

Breast-feeding: Adequate unpaid time to express breast milk, or employee may use rest or meal time, for up to 3 years following childbirth.

Maryland

Md. Code Ann., Lab. & Empl. § 3-710

Applies to: Retail establishments with 50 or more retail employees.

Exceptions: Employees who work in an office or who work at a single location with 5 or fewer employees are not covered.

Meal Break: 30 minutes, unpaid, after 6 consecutive hours of work.

Rest Break: 15 minutes, unpaid, when working 4 to 6 consecutive hours. (This may be waived if the employee works less than 6 hours). Employees working 8 or more consecutive hours must receive a 15-minute unpaid break for every additional 4 consecutive hours after a meal break.

Breast-feeding: No employment-specific laws. However, breast-feeding is allowed in any public or private location where the mother's presence is authorized.

State Laws on Meal and Rest Breaks, continued

Massachusetts

Mass. Gen. Laws ch. 149, §§ 100, 101

Applies to: All employers, except as noted.

Exceptions: Excludes iron works, glass works, paper mills, letterpresses, print works, and bleaching or dyeing works. Attorney general may exempt businesses that require continuous operation if it won't affect worker safety. Collective bargaining agreement may also provide for different breaks.

Meal Break: 30 minutes, if work is for more than 6 hours.

Minnesota

Minn. Stat. Ann. §§ 177.253, 177.254, 181.939

Applies to: All employers.

Exceptions: Excludes certain agricultural and seasonal employees. A collective bargaining agreement may provide for different rest and meal breaks.

Meal Break: Sufficient unpaid time for employees who work 8 consecutive hours or more.

Rest Break: Paid adequate rest period within each 4 consecutive hours of work to utilize nearest convenient restroom.

Breast-feeding: Reasonable unpaid break time to express milk.

Mississippi

Miss. Ann. Code § 71-1-55

Breast-feeding: Employee may use meal or rest break for expressing breast milk.

Missouri

Breast-feeding: No employment-specific laws. However, breast-feeding is allowed in any public or private location where the mother's presence is authorized.

Montana

Breast-feeding: No employment-specific laws. However, breast-feeding is allowed in any public or private location where the mother's presence is authorized.

Nebraska

Neb. Rev. Stat. §§ 48-212, 48–1102

Applies to: Meal break provisions: assembly plant, workshop, or mechanical establishment. Breast-feeding provisions: employers with 15 or more employees.

Exceptions: Other written agreement between employer and employees.

Meal Break: 30 minutes off premises for each 8-hour shift.

Breast-feeding: Employers with 15 or more employees must provide reasonable accommodation to nursing mothers, unless it would cause an undue hardship. Accommodation may include breaks and an appropriate location for expressing breast milk.

Nevada

Nev. Rev. Stat. Ann. § 608.019, AB 113, § 5

Applies to: Employers with two or more employees.

Exceptions: Employees covered by collective bargaining agreement; exemptions for business necessity.

Meal Break: 30 minutes for 8 continuous hours of work.

Rest Break: Paid 10-minute rest period for each 4 hours or major fraction worked; as practicable, in middle of the work period; not required for employees whose total daily work time is less than 3½ hours.

Breast-feeding: Reasonable unpaid breaks to allow an employee to express breastmilk for

State Laws on Meal and Rest Breaks, continued

a child under one year of age. (Applies to: All employers. Exceptions: Employers with fewer than 50 employees, if complying would cause an undue hardship.)

New Hampshire

N.H. Rev. Stat. Ann. § 275:30-a

Applies to: All employers.

Meal Break: 30 minutes after 5 consecutive hours, unless the employer allows the employee to eat while working and it is feasible for the employee to do so.

New Mexico

N.M. Stat. Ann. § 28-20-2

Breast-feeding: Flexible unpaid breaks to use breast pump in the workplace.

New York

N.Y. Lab. Law §§ 162, 206-c

Applies to: Factories, workshops, manufacturing facilities, mercantile (retail and wholesale) establishments.

Meal Break: Factory employees, 60 minutes between 11 a.m. and 2 p.m.; mercantile employees, 30 minutes between 11 a.m. and 2 p.m. If a shift starts before 11 a.m. and ends after 7 p.m., every employee gets an additional 20 minutes between 5 p.m. and 7 p.m. If a shift starts between 1 p.m. and 6 a.m., a factory employee gets 60 minutes, and a mercantile employee gets 45 minutes, in the middle of the shift. Labor commissioner may permit a shorter meal break; the permit must be in writing and posted conspicuously in the main entrance of the workplace.

Breast-feeding: Reasonable unpaid break time to express breast milk for up to three years after child's birth.

North Carolina

Breast-feeding: No employment-specific laws. However, breast-feeding is allowed in any public or private location where the mother's presence is authorized.

North Dakota

N.D. Admin. Code § 46-02-07-02

Applies to: Applicable when two or more employees are on duty.

Exceptions: Waiver by employee or other provision in collective bargaining agreement.

Meal Break: 30 minutes for each shift over 5 hours; unpaid if employee is completely relieved of duties.

Breast-feeding: No employment-specific laws. However, breast-feeding is allowed in any public or private location where the mother's presence is authorized.

Oklahoma

Okla. Stat. Ann. tit. 40, § 435

Breast-feeding: Reasonable unpaid breaks to breast-feed or express breast milk.

Oregon

Ore. Rev. Stat. 653.077; Ore. Admin. R. §§ 839-020-0050, 839-020-0051

Applies to: All employers except as noted.

Exceptions: Agricultural workers and employees covered by a collective bargaining agreement.

Meal Break: 30 minutes for employees who work at least six hours, unpaid if relieved of all duties; paid time to eat if employee cannot be relieved of duty; a shorter paid break (but no less than 20 minutes), if employer can show that it is industry practice or custom. If shift of 7 hours or less, meal break must occur between hours 2 and 5; if shift longer than 7 hours, meal break must be between hours 3 and 6.

State Laws on Meal and Rest Breaks, continued

Rest Break: Paid 10-minute rest period for each 4 hours or major fraction worked; if practical, in the middle of the work period. Rest period must be in addition to usual meal break and taken separately; can't be added to meal period or deducted from beginning or end of shift to reduce length of total work period. Rest period is not required for certain solo adult employees serving the public, although they must be allowed to use restroom.

Breast-feeding: Employers with 25 or more employees must provide a 30-minute unpaid break for every 4 hours worked to express breast milk, for up to 18 months after child's birth.

Pennsylvania

43 P.S. § 1301.207

Applies to: Employers of seasonal farmworkers.

Meal Break: Seasonal farm workers are entitled to a 30-minute meal or rest break if they work at least 5 hours.

Breast-feeding: No employment-specific laws. However, breast-feeding is allowed in any public or private location where the mother's presence is authorized.

Rhode Island

R.I. Gen. Laws §§ 28-3-8, 28-3-14, 23-13.2-1, 28–5–7.4

Applies to: Meal break provisions: employers with 5 or more employees. Breast-feeding provisions: employers with 4 or more employees.

Exceptions: Employers of health care facility or employers with fewer than 3 employees on any shift.

Meal Break: 20 minutes, unpaid, within a 6-hour shift or 30 minutes, unpaid, within an 8-hour shift.

Breast-feeding: Reasonable unpaid break time to breast-feed infant or express breast milk. Employers with 4 or more employees must provide reasonable accommodations to nursing mothers, which may include break time and private space for expressing breast milk, other than a restroom.

South Carolina

Breast-feeding: No employment-specific laws. However, breast-feeding is allowed in any public or private location where the mother's presence is authorized.

South Dakota

Breast-feeding: No employment-specific laws. However, breast-feeding is allowed in any public or private location where the mother's presence is authorized if the mother is in compliance with all other laws.

Tennessee

Tenn. Code Ann. §§ 50-2-103(h), 50-1-305

Applies to: Employers with 5 or more employees.

Meal Break: 30 minutes unpaid for employees scheduled to work 6 consecutive hours or more, unless workplace environment provides ample opportunity for appropriate meal break. Tipped employees who work in food or beverage service may waive right to meal break if employee requests waiver, knowingly and voluntarily, in writing, and employer consents. Employer may not coerce employee into waiving right to meal break. Employer must post waiver policy that includes a form stating the employee's right to a break, how long the waiver will last, and how the employee or employer may rescind the waiver.

Breast-feeding: Reasonable unpaid break time to express breast milk.

State Laws on Meal and Rest Breaks, continued

Texas

Breast-feeding: No employment-specific laws. However, breast-feeding is allowed in any public or private location where the mother's presence is authorized.

Vermont

Vt. Stat. Ann. tit. 21, § 304

Applies to: All employers.

Meal Break: Employees must be given reasonable opportunities to eat and use toilet facilities during work periods.

Rest Break: Employees must be given reasonable opportunities to eat and use toilet facilities during work periods.

Breast-feeding: Reasonable time to express breast milk for up to three years after the child's birth. Breaks can be paid or unpaid. Employer not required to provide breaks if it would substantially disrupt its operations.

Virginia

Breast-feeding: No employment-specific laws. However, breast-feeding is allowed in any public or private location where the mother's presence is authorized.

Washington

Wash. Admin. Code §§ 296-126-092, 296-131-020

Applies to: All employers except as noted.

Exceptions: Newspaper vendor or carrier, domestic or casual labor around private residence, sheltered workshop; separate provisions for agricultural labor.

Meal Break: 30-minute break, if work period is more than 5 consecutive hours, not less than 2 hours nor more than 5 hours from beginning of shift. This time is paid if employee is on duty or is required to be at a site for employer's

benefit. Employees who work 3 or more hours longer than regular workday are entitled to an additional half hour, before or during overtime.

Agricultural employees: 30 minutes if working more than 5 hours; additional 30 minutes if working 11 or more hours in a day.

Rest Break: Paid 10-minute rest break for each 4-hour work period, scheduled as near as possible to midpoint of each work period. Employee cannot be required to work more than 3 hours without a rest break. Scheduled rest breaks not required where nature of work allows employee to take intermittent rest breaks equivalent to required standard.

West Virginia

W.Va. Code § 21-3-10a

Applies to: All employers.

Meal Break: At least 20-minute break for each 6 consecutive hours worked, unless employees are allowed to take breaks as needed or to eat lunch while working.

Rest Break: Rest breaks of 20 minutes or less must be counted as paid work time.

Wisconsin

Wis. Admin. Code § DWD 274.02; Wis. Stat. Ann. § 103.935.

Applies to: *Wis. Admin. Code § DWD 274.02 (all employers); Wis. Stat. Ann. § 103.935 (migrant workers)*

Meal Break: For most workers, 30-minute meal period is recommended but not required. Meal period should be close to usual meal time or near middle of shift. Shifts of more than 6 hours without a meal break should be avoided. If employee is not free to leave the workplace or relieved of all duties for at least 30 minutes, meal period is considered paid time. For migrant

State Laws on Meal and Rest Breaks, continued

workers employed exclusively in agricultural labor, 30-minute meal period required after 6 continuous hours of work, unless the shift can be completed in an additional hour.

Rest Break: For migrant workers not employed exclusively in agricultural labor, rest period of at least 10 minutes within each 5 hours of continuous employment.

Breast-feeding: No employment-specific laws. However, breast-feeding is allowed in any public or private location where the mother's presence is authorized.

State Laws on Family and Medical Leave

Arizona

A.R.S. § 23-371 and following

Employers Covered: All employers.

Eligible Employees: All employees.

Paid Sick Leave: Accrual rate depends on employer size. Employers with 15 or more employees: Employees accrue one hour paid sick time for every 30 hours worked, but cannot accrue or use more than 40 hours per year, unless the employer selects a higher limit.

Employees with fewer than 15 employees: Employees accrue one hour paid sick time for every 30 hours worked, but cannot accrue or use more than 24 hours per year, unless the employer selects a higher limit.

Employees may use sick time to deal with their own illness, to care for an ill family member, to deal with a public health emergency, to care for a child whose school or place of care has been closed due to a public health emergency, or to deal with the effects of domestic violence.

Arkansas

Ark. Code Ann. §§ 9-9-105, 11-3-205

Employers Covered: For adoption leave: employers that allow workers to take leave for the birth of a child; for leave to donate organs and bone marrow: all employers.

Eligible Employees: For adoption leave: all employees; for leave to donate organs or bone marrow: employees who are not eligible for FMLA leave.

Family Medical Leave: Employees must be given the same leave as allowed for childbirth to adopt a child no older than 18 (does not apply to stepparent or foster parent adoptions). Employees may take up to 90 days of unpaid leave to donate organs or bone marrow.

California

Cal. Govt. Code §§ 12945 and 12945.2; Cal. Lab. Code §§ 230 and following; Cal. Unemp. Ins. Code §§ 3300 and following; Cal. Lab. Code §§ 245.5, 246 and 246.5

Employers Covered: For pregnancy leave: employers with 5 or more employees; for domestic violence leave and school activity leave: employers with 25 or more employees; for family medical leave: employers with 50 or more employees; for paid family and disability leave: employers whose employees contribute to state temporary disability insurance ("SDI") fund; for paid sick leave: all employers.

Eligible Employees: For pregnancy, domestic violence, or school activity leave: all employees; for family medical leave: employee with more than 12 months of service with the employer, and who has at least 1,250 hours of service with the employer during the previous 12-month period; for paid family and disability leave benefits program: employees who contribute to SDI fund; for paid sick leave: employees who have worked at least 30 days within a year for the same employer.

Family Medical Leave: Up to 4 months for disability related to pregnancy (in addition to 12 weeks under state family leave law). Up to 12 weeks of leave per year to care for seriously ill family member, for employee's own serious illness, or to bond with new child. Employees who contribute to SDI fund may receive paid family leave benefits for up to 6 weeks of leave per year to care for a seriously ill family member (including a registered domestic partner) or bond with a new child; up to 52 weeks of leave paid by state fund for own short-term disability.

School Activities: 40 hours per year, but not more than 8 hours per calendar month, to enroll

State Laws on Family and Medical Leave, continued

a child in a school or with a licensed child care provider or to participate in activities related to the school or licensed child care provider.

Domestic Violence: Reasonable time for issues dealing with domestic violence, stalking, or sexual assault, including health, counseling, and safety measures. Family member or domestic partner of a victim of a felony may take leave to attend judicial proceedings related to the crime.

Paid Sick Leave: One hour of sick leave for every 30 hours worked; however, employers may cap use of sick leave at 24 hours per year. Employees may use sick leave for their own illnesses, to care for an ill family member, or to deal with the effects of domestic violence.

Colorado

Colo. Rev. Stat. §§ 19-5-211; 24-34-402.7

Employers Covered: For adoption leave: all employers who offer leave for birth of a child; for domestic violence leave and school activities leave: employers with 50 or more employees.

Eligible Employees: For adoption leave and school activities leave: all employees; for domestic violence leave: employees with one year of service.

Family Medical Leave: Employee must be given same leave for adoption as allowed for childbirth (doesn't apply to stepparent adoption).

School Activities: 18 hours per year, no more than 6 hours per month, to attend parent teacher conferences and meetings relating to special education, truancy, attendance, discipline, drop-out prevention, or response to intervention.

Domestic Violence: Up to 3 days in any 12-month period to seek restraining order, obtain medical care or counseling, relocate, or seek legal assistance for victim of domestic violence, sexual assault, or stalking.

Connecticut

Conn. Gen. Stat. Ann. §§ 31-51kk to 31-51qq; 46a-60

Employers Covered: For pregnancy leave: employers with 3 or more employees; for family medical or serious health leave: employers with 75 or more employees; for paid sick leave: service-industry employers with at least 50 employees.

Eligible Employees: For pregnancy leave and paid sick leave: all employees; for family medical or serious health condition leave: employees with one year and at least 1,000 hours of service in last 12 months.

Family Medical Leave: Reasonable amount of leave required for a pregnancy-related disability. 16 weeks per any 24-month period for childbirth, adoption, employee's serious health condition, care for family member with serious health condition, bone marrow or organ donation, or a qualifying exigency arising out of a family member's active duty in the military. 26 weeks per 12-month period for each family member who is also a current member of the armed forces and is undergoing medical treatment.

Paid Sick Leave: One hour of paid sick leave for every 40 hours worked, up to 40 hours accrued per year, for the employee's own medical needs or to care for an ill family member.

District of Columbia

D.C. Code Ann. §§ 32-501 and following; 32-1202, 32-131.01 and following

Employers Covered: Leave other than paid sick leave: employers with 20 or more employees; paid sick leave: all employers.

Eligible Employees: Leave other than paid sick leave: employees who have worked at company for at least one year and at least 1,000 hours during the previous 12 months; paid sick leave:

State Laws on Family and Medical Leave, continued

all employees accrue sick leave upon hire and may use sick leave after 90 days of employment.

Family Medical Leave: 16 weeks per any 24-month period for childbirth, adoption, foster care, placement of a child with the employee for whom the employee permanently assumes and discharges parental responsibility, or care for family member with serious health condition. Additional 16 weeks per any 24-month period for employee's serious health condition.

School Activities: Up to 24 hours of unpaid leave per year (all employees, all employers).

Domestic Violence: Leave described under "Paid Sick Leave" may also be used for employee or family member who is a victim of stalking, domestic violence, or abuse to get medical attention, get services, seek counseling, relocate, take legal action, or take steps to enhance health and safety.

Paid Sick Leave: Paid sick leave for the employee's own illness or to care for a family member. Amount of paid leave depends on employer size: employers with 100 or more employees must provide at least one hour of paid leave for every 37 hours worked, up to seven days of leave per year; employers with 25 to 99 employees must provide at least one hour of paid leave for every 43 hours worked, up to five days of leave per year; employers with fewer than 25 employees must provide at least one hour of paid leave for every 87 hours worked, up to three days of leave per year.

Florida
Fla. Stat. § 741.313

Employers Covered: Employers with at least 50 employees.

Eligible Employees: Employees with at least 3 months of employment.

Domestic Violence: Up to 3 working days in any 12-month period if employee or family/household member is victim of domestic violence, with or without pay at discretion of employer.

Georgia
Ga. Code § 34-1-10

Employers Covered: Employers with 25 or more employees.

Eligible Employees: Employees working at least 30 hours per week.

Family Medical Leave: No requirement to provide sick leave, but if employers do, they must allow employees to use up to five days of leave each year to care for a sick immediate family member.

Hawaii
Haw. Rev. Stat. §§ 398-1 to 398-11; 378-1, 378-71 to 378-74

Employers Covered: For childbirth, adoption, and serious health condition leave: employers with 100 or more employees; for pregnancy leave, temporary disability, and domestic violence leave: all employers; for bone marrow leave: employers with 50 or more employees.

Eligible Employees: For childbirth, adoption, and serious health condition leave: employees with 6 months of service; for pregnancy, domestic violence, and temporary disability leave: all employees.

Family Medical Leave: 4 weeks per calendar year for childbirth, adoption, or care for family member with serious health condition; "reasonable period" of pregnancy/maternity leave required by discrimination statute and case law; up to 7 days' unpaid leave for bone marrow donors and up to 30 days' unpaid leave for organ donors. Up to 26 weeks of temporary disability leave paid by state insurance program.

State Laws on Family and Medical Leave, continued

Domestic Violence: Employer with 50 or more employees must allow up to 30 days' unpaid leave per year for employee who is a victim of domestic or sexual violence or if employee's minor child is a victim. Employer with 49 or fewer employees must allow up to 5 days' leave.

Illinois

820 Ill. Comp. Stat. §§ 147/1 and following; 180/1 and following

Employers Covered: For school activities leave, employers with 50 or more employees. For domestic violence leave, all employers.

Eligible Employees: For school activities leave: employees who have worked at least half time for 6 months; for domestic violence leave: all employees.

School Activities: Eight hours per year (no more than 4 hours per day); required only if employee has no paid leave available.

Domestic Violence: If employer has at least 50 employees, up to 12 weeks' unpaid leave per 12-month period for employee who is a victim of domestic violence or sexual assault or for employee with a family or household member who is a victim. If employer has at least 15 but not more than 49 employees, up to 8 weeks' unpaid leave during any 12-month period. If employer has fourteen or fewer employees, up to 4 weeks' unpaid leave during any 12-month period.

Iowa

Iowa Code § 216.6

Employers Covered: Employers with 4 or more employees.

Eligible Employees: All employees.

Family Medical Leave: Up to 8 weeks for disability due to pregnancy, childbirth, or related conditions.

Kentucky

Ky. Rev. Stat. Ann. § 337.015

Employers Covered: All employers.

Eligible Employees: All employees.

Family Medical Leave: Up to 6 weeks for adoption of a child under 7 years old.

Louisiana

La. Rev. Stat. Ann. §§ 23:341 to 23:342; 23:1015 and following; 40:1299.124

Employers Covered: For pregnancy/maternity leave: employers with 25 or more employees; for leave to donate bone marrow: employers with 20 or more employees; for school activities leave: all employers.

Eligible Employees: For pregnancy/maternity or school activities leave: all employees; for leave to donate bone marrow: employees who work 20 or more hours per week.

Family Medical Leave: "Reasonable period of time" for pregnancy disability and childbirth, not to exceed 6 weeks for normal pregnancy and 4 months for more disabling pregnancies; up to 40 hours' paid leave per year to donate bone marrow.

School Activities: 16 hours per year.

Maine

Me. Rev. Stat. Ann. tit. 26, §§ 843 and following

Employers Covered: For domestic violence leave: all employers; for family medical leave: employers with 15 or more employees at one location.

Eligible Employees: All employees for domestic violence leave; employees with at least one year of service for family medical leave.

Family Medical Leave: 10 weeks in any two-year period for childbirth, adoption (for child 16 or younger), employee's serious health condition,

State Laws on Family and Medical Leave, continued

care for family member with serious health condition, or death or serious health condition of family member suffered while on active military duty.

Domestic Violence: "Reasonable and necessary" leave for employee who is victim of domestic violence, sexual assault, or stalking, or whose parent, spouse, or child is a victim, to prepare for and attend court, for medical treatment, and for other necessary services.

Maryland

Md. Code Ann., [Lab. & Empl.] §§ 3-801, 3-802, 3-803

Employers Covered: For adoption leave: employers with 15 or more employees; for military family leave: employers with at least 50 employees.

Eligible Employees: All employees for adoption leave; employees who have worked at least 12 months, and at least 1,250 hours in the last 12 months, for military family leave.

Family Medical Leave: Employee must be given same leave for adoption as allowed for childbirth. Employee must be allowed to take off the day immediate family member leaves for or returns from active military duty outside the United States.

Massachusetts

Mass. Gen. Laws ch. 149, §§ 52D, 105D, 148C; ch. 151B, § 1(5)

Employers Covered: For maternity and adoption leave: employers with 6 or more employees; for school activities leave: employers with 50 or more employees; for domestic violence leave: employers with 50 or more employees; for paid sick leave: all employers.

Eligible Employees: For maternity and adoption leave: employees who have completed the

employer's probationary period, or if there is no probationary period, employees who have completed 3 months of service as full-time employees; for paid sick leave: all employees accrue sick leave upon hire and may use sick leave after 90 days of employment; for all other leave: employees who are eligible under FMLA.

Family Medical Leave: Eight weeks total for childbirth/maternity or adoption of child younger than 18 (younger than 23 if disabled); additional 24 hours total per year (combined with school activities leave) to accompany minor child or relative age 60 or older to medical and dental appointments.

School Activities: 24 hours per year total (combined with family medical leave for medical and dental appointments).

Domestic violence: 15 days of unpaid leave in 12-month period if employee, or family member of employee, is a victim of abusive behavior, to seek medical attention or counseling, obtain a protective order from a court, attend child custody proceedings, and other related purposes. Employee may also use leave described under "Paid Sick Leave" for these purposes.

Paid Sick Leave: One hour of sick leave for every 30 hours worked, although employers may cap annual accrual at 40 hours per week. Employers with 11 or more employees must provide paid time off; employers with 10 or fewer employees may provide unpaid time off. Employees may use leave for their own illnesses or to care for an ill family member.

Minnesota

Minn. Stat. Ann. §§ 181.940 and following

Employers Covered: For childbirth/maternity and adoption leave: employers with 21 or more employees at one site; for bone marrow donation: employers with 20 or more

State Laws on Family and Medical Leave, continued

employees; for school activities: employers with 2 or more employees.

Eligible Employees: For maternity leave: employees who have worked at least half time for one year; for bone marrow donation: employees who work at least 20 hours per week; for school activities: employees who have worked at least one year.

Family Medical Leave: 12 weeks for childbirth/maternity or adoption; up to 40 hours paid leave per year to donate bone marrow; parent can use accrued sick leave to care for sick or injured child. Up to ten days if family member is killed or injured in active military service (all employers).

School Activities: 16 hours in 12-month period; includes activities related to child care, preschool, or special education.

Domestic violence: Employee may use sick leave for reasonable time off to receive assistance because of sexual assault, domestic violence, or stalking.

Montana
Mont. Code Ann. §§ 49-2-310, 49-2-311

Employers Covered: All employers.

Eligible Employees: All employees.

Family Medical Leave: Reasonable leave of absence for pregnancy disability and childbirth.

Nebraska
Neb. Rev. Stat. § 48-234

Employers Covered: Employers that allow workers to take leave for the birth of a child.

Eligible Employees: All employees.

Family Medical Leave: Employee must be given same leave as allowed for childbirth to adopt a child, unless child is over 8 (or over 18 for special needs child); does not apply to stepparent or foster parent adoptions.

Nevada
Nev. Rev. Stat. Ann. §§ 392.920, 613.335, 392.4577, 2017 Nevada Laws Ch. 496 (S.B. 361)

Employers Covered: All employers.

Eligible Employees: All employees. For domestic violence leave only: as of January 1, 2018, employees employed for at least 90 days and who are victims of domestic violence or whose family members are victims of domestic violence.

Family Medical Leave: Same sick or disability leave policies that apply to other medical conditions must be extended to pregnancy, miscarriage, childbirth and related medical conditions.

School Activities: Employers may not fire or threaten to fire a parent, guardian, or custodian for attending a school conference or responding to a child's emergency. Employers with 50 or more employees must provide parent with a child in public school 4 hours of leave per school year, which must be taken in increments of at least 1 hour, to attend parent-teacher conferences, attend school-related activities during regular school hours, attend school-sponsored events, or volunteer or be involved at the school.

Paid Sick Leave: Employee may take up to 160 hours of leave within one year of the incident(s) of domestic violence for the following purposes: to seek medical treatment, to obtain counseling, to participate in court proceedings, or to create a safety plan. Leave may be unpaid.

New Hampshire
N.H. Rev. Stat. Ann. § 354-A:7(VI)

Employers Covered: Employers with 6 or more employees.

Eligible Employees: All employees.

State Laws on Family and Medical Leave, continued

Family Medical Leave: Temporary disability leave for pregnancy/childbirth or related medical condition.

New Jersey

N.J. Stat. Ann. §§ 34:11B-1 and following; 34-11C and following; 43:21-1 and following

Employers Covered: Employers with 50 or more employees; for paid family and temporary disability leave, employers subject to the New Jersey Unemployment Compensation Law; for domestic violence leave, employers with 25 or more employees.

Eligible Employees: Employees who have worked for at least one year and at least 1,000 hours in previous 12 months; for paid family and temporary disability leave benefits program: employees who worked 20 calendar weeks in covered New Jersey employment; or earned at least 1,000 times New Jersey minimum wage during 52 weeks preceding leave.

Family Medical Leave: 12 weeks (or 24 weeks reduced leave schedule) in any 24-month period for pregnancy/maternity, childbirth, adoption, or care for family member with serious health condition. Employees may receive paid family leave benefits for up to 6 weeks of leave per year to care for a seriously ill family member (including a registered domestic partner) or bond with a new child. Employee may receive temporary disability benefits while the employee is unable to work, up to 26 weeks.

Domestic violence: 20 unpaid days in one 12-month period for employee who is (or whose family member is) a victim of domestic violence or a sexually violent offense.

New Mexico

N.M. Stat. Ann. §§ 50-4A-1 and following

Employers Covered: All employers.

Eligible Employees: All employees.

Domestic Violence: Employer must provide intermittent paid or unpaid leave time for up to fourteen days in any calendar year, taken by an employee for up to eight hours in one day, to obtain or attempt to obtain an order of protection or other judicial relief from domestic abuse or to meet with law enforcement officials, to consult with attorneys or district attorneys' victim advocates or to attend court proceedings related to the domestic abuse of an employee or an employee's family member.

New York

N.Y. Lab. Law §§ 201-c, 202-a. N.Y. Workers' Compensation Law § 200 and following.

Employers Covered: Employers that allow workers to take leave for the birth of a child must allow adoption leave; employers with 20 or more employees at one site must allow leave to donate bone marrow; employers with at least one employee for 30 days are covered by the state's temporary disability program 4 weeks later; for paid family leave, all employers.

Eligible Employees: All employees are eligible for adoption leave; employees who work at least 20 hours per week are eligible for leave to donate bone marrow; employees who have worked for a covered employer for at least 4 consecutive weeks are eligible for temporary disability benefits. For paid family leave, employees are eligible once they have worked for their employer for 26 weeks.

Family Medical Leave: Employees must be given same leave as allowed for childbirth to adopt a child of preschool age or younger, or no older than 18 if disabled; up to 24 hours' leave to donate bone marrow. Temporary disability insurance benefits available for up to 26 weeks while employee is unable to work. Beginning

State Laws on Family and Medical Leave, continued

in January of 2018, employee may take paid leave to care for a family member with a serious health condition, to bond with a new child, or for qualifying exigency arising out of a family member's call to active duty in the military. Employee can receive 50% of average wages for up to 8 weeks in 2018, which will gradually increase to 67% of average wages for up to 12 weeks by 2021. Leave is paid by the state, not the employer.

North Carolina

N.C. Gen. Stat. §§ 95-28.3, 50B-5.5

Employers Covered: All employers.

Eligible Employees: All employees.

School Activities: Parents and guardians of school-aged children must be given up to 4 hours of leave per year.

Domestic Violence: Reasonable time off from work to obtain or attempt to obtain relief from domestic violence and sexual assault.

Oregon

Ore. Rev. Stat. §§ 659A.029, 659A.150 and following, 659A.312, 659A.270 and following, 653.601 and following

Employers Covered: For childbirth, adoption, and serious health condition leave: employers with 25 or more employees; for domestic violence leave: employers with 6 or more employees; for leave to donate bone marrow: all employers; for paid sick leave: all employers.

Eligible Employees: For childbirth, adoption, or serious health condition: employees who have worked 25 or more hours per week for at least 180 days (except parental leave, which only requires that the employee has worked 180 days); for leave to donate bone marrow: employees who work an average of 20 or more hours per week; for domestic violence leave: all employees;

for paid sick leave: all employees accrue sick leave upon hire and may use leave after 90 days of employment.

Family Medical Leave: 12 weeks per year for pregnancy disability; additional 12 weeks per year for parental leave, serious health condition, care for family member with serious health condition, deal with the death of a family member, or care for child who has an illness, injury, or condition that requires home care; employee who takes 12 weeks of parental leave may take an additional 12 weeks to care for a sick child. Up to 40 hours or amount of accrued paid leave (whichever is less) to donate bone marrow.

Paid Sick Leave: Employees must accrue one hour of sick leave for every 30 hours worked, although employers may cap accrual and use at 40 hours per year. Up to 40 hours of accrued leave must carry over to the next year, but employers can cap total accrual to 80 hours. Employers with 10 or more employees must provide paid time off; employers with 9 or fewer employees may provide unpaid time off. Employees may use leave for their own illnesses, to care for an ill family member, to deal with domestic violence issues, or for any purpose described under the "Family Medical Leave" section. Different rules apply to Portland employers.

Domestic Violence: Reasonable leave for employee who is victim of domestic violence, harassment, sexual assault, or stalking, or whose minor child is a victim, to seek legal treatment, medical services, counseling, or to relocate/secure existing home.

Rhode Island

R.I. Gen. Laws §§ 28-48-1 and following; 28-41-34 through 28-41-42

Employers Covered: For family medical leave: employers with 50 or more employees.

State Laws on Family and Medical Leave, continued

Eligible Employees: For family medical leave: employees who have worked an average of 30 or more hours a week for at least 12 consecutive months; for school activities leave: all employees; for temporary disability and temporary caregiver leave: all employees who meet the earning requirements.

Family Medical Leave: 13 weeks in any two calendar years for childbirth, adoption of child up to 16 years old, employee's serious health condition, or care for family member with serious health condition. While temporarily unable to work due to disability (including pregnancy), employees can collect benefits from state insurance fund for up to 30 weeks. Four weeks of benefits are available as temporary caregiver insurance (to bond with a new child or care for a family member with a serious health condition); this time plus temporary disability time may not exceed 30 total weeks.

School Activities: Up to 10 hours a year.

South Carolina

S.C. Code Ann. § 44-43-80

Employers Covered: Employers with 20 or more workers at one site in South Carolina.

Eligible Employees: Employees who work an average of at least 20 hours per week.

Family Medical Leave: Employers may—but are not required to—allow employees to take up to 40 hours paid leave per year to donate bone marrow.

Tennessee

Tenn. Code Ann. § 4-21-408

Employers Covered: Employers with 100 or more employees.

Eligible Employees: Employees who have worked 12 consecutive months as full-time employees.

Family Medical Leave: Up to 4 months of unpaid leave for pregnancy, childbirth, nursing, and adoption; employee must give 3 months' notice unless a medical emergency requires the leave to begin sooner; these laws must be included in employee handbook.

Texas

Tex. Lab. Code Ann. § 21.0595

Employers Covered: Employers with 15 or more employees.

Family Medical Leave: No leave requirements, but employers that choose to provide leave to care for a sick child must allow leave to care for a foster child.

Vermont

Vt. Stat. Ann. tit. 21, §§ 471 and following

Employers Covered: For pregnancy/parental leave: employers with 10 or more employees; for family medical and school activities leave: employers with 15 or more employees; for paid sick leave: all employers.

Eligible Employees: For pregnancy/parental leave, family medical leave, and school activities leave, employees must have worked an average of 30 or more hours per week for at least one year. For paid sick leave, employees must have worked for a covered employer for an average of 18 hours per week for at least 20 weeks.

Family Medical Leave: 12 weeks per year for pregnancy, childbirth, adoption of child age 16 or younger, employee's serious health condition, or care for family member with serious health condition; combined with school activities leave, additional 4 hours of unpaid leave in a 30-day period (up to 24 hours per year) to take a family member to a medical, dental, or professional well-care appointment or respond to a family member's medical emergency.

State Laws on Family and Medical Leave, continued

School Activities: Combined with leave to take family members to appointments, 4 hours' total unpaid leave in a 30-day period (up to 24 hours per year) to participate in child's school activities.

Paid Sick Leave: Employee accrues one hour of paid sick leave for every 52 hours worked. For 2017 and 2018, employer may limit accrual to 24 hours of sick leave per year. For 2019, employer may limit accrual to 40 hours per year. Employers with 5 or fewer employees do not need to comply with the law until 2018.

Washington

Wash. Rev. Code Ann. §§ 49.78.010 and following, 49.12.265 and following, 49.12.350 and following, 49.76.010 and following, 49.86.005 and following

Employers Covered: All employers must provide domestic violence leave and paid sick leave; employers with 8 or more employees must provide pregnancy disability leave; employers with 50 or more employees must provide leave to care for newborn, adopted, or foster child, or family member with serious health condition.

Eligible Employees: For parental leave and leave to care for a family member with a serious health condition, employees must have worked at least 1,250 hours in the previous year to be eligible.

Family Medical Leave: Up to 12 weeks during any 12-month period for the birth or placement of a child, employee's serious health condition, or care for a family member with a serious health condition. In addition to any leave available under federal FMLA and state law,

employee may take leave for the period of time when she is temporarily disabled due to pregnancy or childbirth.

Domestic Violence: Reasonable leave from work, with or without pay, for employee who is victim of domestic violence, sexual assault, or stalking, or whose family member is a victim, to prepare for and attend court, for medical treatment, and for other necessary services.

Paid Sick Leave: Beginning January 1, 2018, all employees accrue at least one hour of paid sick leave for every 40 hours worked. No annual cap on accrual, but employees may only carry over 40 hours of accrued leave from year to year. Employees may use sick leave for their own illness, the illness of a family member, the closure of a child's school or day care due to a public health emergency, and to seek services relating to domestic violence.

Wisconsin

Wis. Stat. Ann. § 103.10

Employers Covered: Employers with 50 or more employees.

Eligible Employees: Employees who have worked for at least one year and have worked 1,000 hours in the preceding 12 months.

Family Medical Leave: 6 weeks per 12-month period for pregnancy/maternity, childbirth, or adoption; additional 2 weeks per 12-month period to care for family member (including domestic partner) with a serious health condition; additional 2 weeks per 12-month period to care for the employee's own serious health condition.

Index

On Nolo.com you'll also find:

Books & Software

Nolo publishes hundreds of great books and software programs for consumers and
business owners. Order a copy, or download an ebook version instantly, at Nolo.com.

Online Legal Documents

You can quickly and easily make a will or living trust, form an LLC or corporation, apply
for a trademark or provisional patent, or make hundreds of other forms—online.

Free Legal Information

Thousands of articles answer common questions about everyday legal issues
including wills, bankruptcy, small business formation, divorce, patents,
employment, and much more.

Plain-English Legal Dictionary

Stumped by jargon? Look it up in America's most up-to-date source for
definitions of legal terms, free at nolo.com.

Lawyer Directory

Nolo's consumer-friendly lawyer directory provides in-depth profiles of lawyers all
over America. You'll find all the information you need to choose the right lawyer.

SDHB2